CW00925745

A SOCIAL HISTORY OF THE NAVY
1793–1815

by the same author

ENGLAND'S SEA-OFFICERS

AFLOAT AND ASHORE

BRITISH SHIPS AND BRITISH SEAMEN

ARMADA GUNS

SHIPS AND SEAMEN OF BRITAIN

THE NAVY OF BRITAIN

SIR WILLIAM DILLON'S NARRATIVE (ED.)

HISTORY OF THE BRITISH NAVY

MICHAEL LEWIS
C.B.E., M.A., F.S.A., F.R.HIST.S.

A SOCIAL HISTORY OF THE NAVY 1793-1815

ILLUSTRATED

CHATHAM PUBLISHING
LONDON

STACKPOLE BOOKS
PENNSYLVANIA

This edition published in Great Britain in 2004 by
Chatham Publishing, Lionel Leventhal Ltd,
Park House, 1 Russell Gardens,
London NW11 9NN

And in North America by
Stackpole Books,
5067 Ritter Road, Mechanicsburg,
PA 17055

The Social History of the Navy was first published in 1960 by
George Allen & Unwin Ltd, London

British Library Cataloguing in Publication Data
Lewis, Michael, 1890–1970
The social history of the navy 1793–1815
1. Great Britain. Royal Navy – Military life – History – 19th century
2. Great Britain. Royal Navy – History – 18th century 3. Great Britain. Royal Navy – History – Anglo-French War, 1793–1802 4. Great Britain. Royal Navy – History – Napoleonic War, 1800–1815 5. Sailors – Great Britain – Social conditions – 19th century 6. Sailors – Great Britain – Social conditions – 18th century 7. Anglo-French war, 1793–1802 – Participation, British
8. Napoleonic wars, 1800–1815 – participation, British 9. Great Britain – History, naval – 19th century 10. Great Britain – History, Naval – 18th century
I. Title
359.1′0941

A Library of Congress Catalog Card No. is available on request

ISBN 1 86176 232 1

Printed and bound in Great Britain by CPD (Wales) Ebbw Vale

ACKNOWLEDGMENTS

MY thanks are due to the Director and Trustees of the National Maritime Museum for their kindness in allowing me to reproduce from their wonderful collection all those illustrations, individually acknowledged as they appear, belonging to the Museum; to the British Museum for its permission to use the water-colour heads of seamen by P. J. de Loutherbourg, and to the Royal College of Physicians for their leave to reproduce their portrait of Sir Gilbert Blane.

Next I would gratefully acknowledge the help and kindness that I have received from all the staff of the National Maritime Museum, especially Lieut-Commander George Naish and Miss K. A. Lindsay-MacDougall, both of whom have put me in the way of much valuable material.

For the rest, I have plagued many old friends with many problems and queries, cheerfully and expertly answered; and I have, I hope, made one or two new friends simply by plaguing them. In the first category I would mention Commander P. K. Kemp, Admiralty Archivist, and, in the second, Vice-Admiral N. A. Sulivan.

Above all, however, I must name two who belong emphatically to the first-named group. Professor Christopher Lloyd and Mr Richard Ollard, both of the Royal Naval College, Greenwich, consented to read the whole work in typescript, and discharged their undertaking with that sort of conscientiousness which everyone who knows them would expect. The result was that the typescript left their hands a much better and richer thing than it was when it reached them. Christopher Lloyd enriched it, mainly, on its historical side by bringing to my notice further important material. Richard Ollard's great contribution was on the literary side, giving me unstintingly the benefit of a discerning and scholarly mind. Only they can know how grateful I am; and both, I hope, do know.

CONTENTS

CONTENTS

ILLUSTRATIONS

LIST OF TABLES

MAP

GRAPH

FOREWORD

'THE GREAT WAR' AND THE NAVY

****

WHEN I and my contemporaries were schoolboys and undergraduates, our masters, tutors, and even textbooks told us of 'the Great War'. Make no mistake. They were not prophets. They knew no more about the Somme and the Battle of Britain than we did. They were only doing what their fathers and grandfathers had done before them. They were calling our last two French Wars 'the Great War'.

They were right, of course. Admittedly—now—if by the epithet 'great' we mean to measure wars in terms of world-upset, lives lost, wealth squandered, unmitigated misery to mankind, then the twentieth-century holocausts win every time, and are welcome to their horrid pre-eminence. Yet there is still something to be said for the old nomenclature. The 1914–18 War had been 'great' in men's vocabulary for a bare score of years before there came a second conflict which, at lowest estimate, was a serious competitor for the title—causing even (among its more trivial results) a certain embarrassment to historians and journalists, who had to think again. Now, perhaps, we are all a little chary of calling any war 'great', lest we have to change again in a hurry when faced with an even nastier affair.

My teachers at least had time on their side. Their Great War had a far longer innings: in fact it missed its century by only a single run. Three full generations of our countrymen lived their lives, placidly as it now seems, without any doubt about what the Great War was. There were not even any serious competitors: not, anyway, in these happy islands and in modern history. This, of course, was not through lack of wars: on the contrary, it was because of a glut of them, following so closely upon one another as to give no one of them time to earn the title. Thus an Englishman, aged 45 in 1793, had lived during four wars: and though *we* might call the second of them—the Seven Years' War—the 'greatest' of them, it is very doubtful whether he did. He would hardly have had the time before the next one arrived, apparently rubbing the greatness out of its predecessor. Again, he was only 67 when *his* Great War stopped: yet, in order to have had any temptation to revise his nomenclature, he would have had to live to the unlikely age of 166! Nor, really, was there any strong candidate from earlier days. To my knowledge, no other British conflict of modern times has been qualified by this particular adjective save only—by the Tories—'the Great Rebellion'. And perhaps there was some sense in this since—again in modern times—this affair did (thank God!) have the great merit of uniqueness.

Be this as it may, however, 'the Great War' which forms the background of this work is the one, lasting from 1793 to 1815, between Great Britain on the one hand and, on the other, the France of the Revolution and of Napoleon: the Great War of my boyhood. But it is only a general background. My particular object is to make a study of the officers and men of the Royal Navy who, in that war, helped England to 'save herself by her exertions, and Europe by her example'. But, having quoted—or, to be truthful, slightly misquoted—the great phrase of a great man, I must by no means slur over his context. William Pitt, in this his shortest, noblest and last public speech, was concerned to stress a fact which every thoughtful Briton must now know to be true—that wars are not won by individual efforts, but by whole communities pulling together as one man. Thus warned, therefore, I will not—I do not—assert that our sailors 'won the war'. But I do claim—and the overwhelming verdict of History supports me—that they played the major part in the victory. Here is no derogation of our Abercrombies, Moores, Wellingtons and their tough, much-enduring veterans, because the very pattern of the war was such that they could not possibly emulate the Navy's services. The conflict was essentially a clash between French land-power and British sea-power. Just as our victory on land was impossible until Napoleon was exhausted, so Napoleon's victory was impossible at any time unless or until he had won at sea. And both sides knew it before the end. We beat Napoleon at last on land, but only after—and because—he had failed to beat us afloat. So, too, we could afford to, and did, lose land-campaigns: but we could not afford to, and did not, lose campaigns at sea. Again, for more than half the years covered by hostilities, our troops, though busy enough upon the periphery, were off the main—the European—battlefield altogether: but not for a single hour were our ships off the seas, either the main or the subsidiary ones. And finally, it was not our Army which prevented France from playing the one card in her hand that we could not overtrump—seaborne invasion. It was 'those far-distant storm-beaten ships upon which the Grand Army never looked' which 'stood between it and the dominion of the world'.[1]

Like everything which is really British, the Royal Navy is the child of Evolution. The track of its progress is not a straight line, constantly rising. It is more like a spiral, and a meandering, bent-corkscrew spiral at that: with, sometimes, long declivities in its circumambient path. Yet, in the end, the acclivities have more than cancelled out the declivities: the general trend of the line has been upward. This peculiar mode of progress is not always easy to follow, and sometimes even harder to account for. Yet it has a long-term pattern, can we but find it. The declivities, on the whole, mark peace-periods: the acclivities occur in wartime; for then a kind of reluctant wisdom, born of self-preservation and fear of the consequences, has a way of penetrating into the minds of our people, government and governed alike, jerking them roughly into life. Moreover, the longer and sterner the war, the more pressing (and therefore the more obvious) becomes the need for progress. Hence the quicker and steadier the advance. For this reason alone the great length of our last French war—for the two are to all intents one—was of vital import to the naval profession. The Navy which began the struggle was a very different one from that which ended it. In 1793 it was essentially 'eighteenth century', with many clogging survivals from the seventeenth. By 1815, though much of the old dross remained, much also had been purged away, and what was left began, in many ways, to look like a modern navy. But it would be too much to expect such advance to continue when the spur was removed; and, sure enough, some of the old ups and downs returned with the peace, and new kinks developed. Yet much of the gain was not lost, and for this reason alone a study of the profession during the war is abundantly worth while. For many of the hardships and frustrations which it then endured were so obviously the growing-pains of the modern Navy.

Some of these devious paths of progress I have followed before, in my *Navy of Britain*; but not so carefully, and not nearly all of them, because, there, I was travelling faster and ranging over a much wider field. *The Navy of Britain* aspired to give a portrait of the whole Navy, through all

[1] Mahan, *Influence of Sea Power upon the French Revolution and Empire*, Vol. II, p.118.

its long history and in all—or most of—its many aspects. This book is, by comparison, a work of specialization. It is still a portrait of the Navy but only of the Navy during a particular 22 years of its long life, and only of one facet of it during that period—its people. Some reduplication, then, is there, but much more amplification. As when a fond mother has her young hopeful's face abstracted from his school-photograph, and enlarged—'blown up' is, I believe, the elegant modernism—to full cabinet size, so certain parts of *The Navy of Britain* have been taken from their wider setting and amplified into a full-scale volume. The result is, in effect, a fairly detailed Social History of the Navy between the years 1793 and 1815: a social history, moreover, of what is really a complete cross-section of contemporary British life. For that Navy, though itself a compact enough body, was assembled from all grades of British society and from all parts of the British Isles.

'Social' history concerns itself principally with 'people' rather than with 'things': so does this book. It seemed to me imperative, then, to treat my subjects biographically and, where possible, as individual human beings, for only so could their essential humanity be revealed. But this made my task no easier. Even the writer who successfully follows the fortunes of only, say, half-a-dozen heroes must have qualities in common with the juggler who keeps six balls in the air at once: and we admire the expertise of both. But what of half-a-million-odd heroes? Could any author compete with so many? Absolutely, of course, he could not. But what is his best hope of relative success? This, in effect, has been my problem, and the way in which I have tried to solve it is this. I have used the biographer's method of conducting my characters from the cradle to the grave; but I have subdivided them into a number of groups, each numerically very large. Next, I have picked out, where possible, such characteristics of each group as seemed common to most of its members. Then I have tried to establish the extremes of each group, and to delineate them: and, throughout, I have attempted to illustrate each hero (or group of heroes) by letting him (or a representative of his group) explain himself *verbatim*. This means, of course, that all the inset quotations in the book—and there are hundreds of them—are from contemporary writers. The List of Sources at the end shows who they are, though the 'chapter-and-verse' references of very nearly all of them are given in the textual notes. Of a good many of these authors there are no modern editions. But of others there are, and at this point I would take the opportunity of recording my vast and obvious debt to one particular body which exists for the sole purpose of providing rare and original naval material of this and similar kinds—that Society which figures much the most frequently in the List—the Navy Records Society (abbreviated in the text to 'N.R.S.'). But for its invaluable volumes I could hardly have proceeded upon this plan at all. Fortunately the Society is so very much alive—it has just produced its hundredth volume—that I can thank it 'in the flesh'. I cannot do this, however, to my three other most generous helpers, John Marshall, William James and William O'Byrne. For all are gone long since to a place where—can we doubt it?—faithful work done and infinite pains taken are allowed full value on the credit side of the Last Account.

PART ONE: ORIGINS
SOCIAL AND GEOGRAPHICAL

****

INTRODUCTORY

'QUARTER-DECK' AND 'LOWER DECK'

****

EVERY Fighting Service has, and must have, two main categories—'Officers' and 'Men'. The Royal Navy, in the late eighteenth and early nineteenth centuries, was no exception. The distinction existed: was indeed more than ordinarily marked. It was not only a naval distinction, but a sharp social one too. 'Officers', as contemporary society used that word, came from one walk of life, 'Men' from another: and, as it was not easy in Society to pass from a lower stratum to a higher, so, in the Navy, it was not easy for a 'Man' to become an officer. But it was possible.

In that day the phrase 'Officer and Gentleman' had real meaning, so real that any 'man' who rose to be an 'officer' might consider himself (were he not one before) to have risen also to be a 'gentleman': and his claim was often accepted by public opinion, and sometimes even by Society. But such a rise was rare. The great majority of officers were 'gentlemen born', or at least 'near-gentlemen-born', while the great majority of the men were not—not nearly gentlemen-born.

So far, however, the word 'officer' has been used here only in its social sense, as it was almost universally current throughout the country. But within the more closed community of the Navy itself it meant something rather different, because, here, there were three different kinds of officer—'Commissioned', 'Warrant' and 'Petty'—all entitled to the name, but differing greatly from one another in status. Later, we shall become more closely acquainted with these three grades. Here it need only be noted that, when Society labelled a person 'Officer and Gentleman', it really meant 'Commissioned Officer and Gentleman', and nothing else. For it was not 'being an officer' which conferred the social cachet of gentility. It was the holding of the King's Commission, and this alone, which did so.

The social élite of the Navy, then, was its commissioned officers—those whom the later nineteenth century called 'Executive Officers'. They even had a name for themselves. It was not 'Naval Officer'—which term had a much narrower connotation of its own[1]—but 'Sea-Officer'. And they were confined to four grades only, those of Flag-Officer, Captain, Commander and Lieutenant. To these must be added the officers of the sea-soldiers—before 1802 known as 'The Marines', after it as 'The Royal Marines'—who were, in exactly the same sense as the Sea-Officers, 'officers and gentlemen'. No one else in the Navy held the King's Commission; and so these, who did, reigned supreme, navally and socially.

Yet a Sea-Officer, like anyone else, will grow old: he will have to be replaced, and replaced by a much younger man who has been specially trained to succeed him. Hence the existence on board in Nelson's time of a very important class, known universally there as 'Young Gentlemen'. The phrase is beautifully simple, economical and descriptive. They were not Commissioned Officers: they were not Warrant Officers. Some, but not all, were technically Petty Officers—but 'Petty Officer' was, after all, only a local captain-conferred title. In the naval scene, therefore, they were of little apparent account. But socially, they were tremendously important—they were young *gentlemen*, the heirs to all that this magic word implied. They were, of course, the forbears of the Cadets, Midshipmen and Sub-lieutenants of our own day. They were not Sea-Officers—yet—but potential Sea-Officers, and in every social sense regarded as such.

Can we find some generic term which will cover all these privileged people, this élite of the ship-hierarchy? One privilege common to them all was the right to 'walk the quarter-deck'. Let us then confer upon them the epithet 'Quarter-deck', and, upon the rest who were not so privileged, the epithet 'Lower Deck'; for that was where most of them messed and slept: that was *their* deck. These terms, of course, describe, in the main, a social distinction, and, as such, cut at times across the naval lay-out; but not seriously because the Navy was too efficient an organization, even then, to allow class distinctions to impair its efficiency to any serious degree. But this distinction was such a very real one that, it is safe to say, everyone on board a ship of the period would know

[1] 'Naval Officer', officially and up to at least 1858, was the correct title of the Admiralty official in minor naval establishments and dockyards overseas. See the present author's *England's Sea-Officers*, London, 1948, p. 146.

instinctively not only to which category he himself belonged, but also where everybody else stood. Whatever his job might be, *everyone* knew whether he was 'Quarter-deck' or 'Lower Deck'. In all that follows, then, the terms 'Quarter-deck' and 'Lower Deck' are to be defined thus:—Every Commissioned Officer is 'Quarter-deck'; and every newcomer who enters the Service with the expectation, and the reasonable prospect, of 'walking the Quarter-deck' and, ultimately, of receiving the King's Commission, is 'Quarter-deck' too. He is a 'Young Gentleman'. But any man or boy who enters without such expectation and reasonable prospect, is not a 'Young Gentleman'; not 'Quarter-deck'. He is 'Lower Deck'. The impact of this distinction, so tangible as to be almost physical, is well expressed by that strange, forceful character Charles Reece Pemberton, actor, lecturer and author of the unique autobiography *Pel. Verjuice*. As a highly sensitive lad of 17 he was caught by a press-gang at Liverpool in 1806, and served afloat for six years.

'An English officer will respect his station though he be locked in a cupboard, six feet by four, for a month with a private. . . . He would be irremediably contaminated if he kneeled on the same hassock, at prayer, in a church, with a man in the ranks. Launch him in a jolly boat with a pair of mizentopmen, on the wide waste of the Atlantic, discipline, decorum and distance will be uppermost in his thoughts, the rules and guides of his steering and sail-trimming and biscuit-cracking.'[1]

Pemberton, it is true, was much given to hyperbole, and of course he was exaggerating here. But he reveals the essence of the matter. All this sounds, no doubt, the acme of snobbery to mid-twentieth-century ears. But this story is not laid in the twentieth century. It tells of what obtained 150 years ago, when 'class' loomed far higher than it does now, and when classes were incomparably more clear-cut.

Why, it may be asked, use the terms 'Quarter-deck' and 'Lower Deck' when there are ready to hand the modern words 'Officer' and 'Rating'? The answer is that neither is a substitute for the words chosen here. 'Quarter-deck' describes a social-naval attribute of the eighteenth century which has no counterpart in the twentieth-century navy, while 'Rating', though it did sometimes mean what we mean, unfortunately meant a number of other things too. It was an overworked, omnibus word, used in all sorts of different connections. Everything and everybody was 'rated'. Every ship had her 'rating'—First-rate, Second-rate,

[1] *Pel. Verjuice*, London, 1929, p. 151–2.

etc.—and, whenever a ship was put into commission, someone was 'rated' to every post on board, were it that of Captain, Boatswain, Cook or Swabber. These posts were all 'ratings': so were the people who filled them. Everyone was rated, and his rating instantly entered against his name in the official register—the Ship's Book. The word is one to use charily. If it cannot differentiate between the Captain and the Swabber it is not going to be of much use to us.

Later we shall see the whole ship-organization of that day, and we shall find that, there, this simple social division of everybody into 'Quarter-deck' and 'Lower Deck' will not altogether hold, or at least will stand in need of certain *naval* modifications. But it is so *socially* true that it is necessary to establish it as a prelude to our immediate aim—an inquiry into the family backgrounds and environments of officers; who they were and, still more, who their parents were.

CHAPTER I

PARENTAGE: SOCIAL BACKGROUND

A. OFFICERS

1. *O'Byrne and Marshall*

OUR basic material for this task comes, mostly, from two works which contain biographical details of several thousand sea-officers who served in our two wars. These biographies will be analysed along two different lines in order, first, to discover the social backgrounds of as many officers as possible, and second, to find their geographical distribution—what towns and counties they hailed from. This chapter is concerned with backgrounds.

The works in question are *Royal Naval Biography*, by Lieutenant John Marshall, published in London in 1825, and *A Naval Biographical Dictionary*, by William O'Byrne, published also in London in 1849.[1] Both are big, ambitious books, O'Byrne's running to 1,400 pages, each with two columns of small type, Marshall's (in its final form) to eleven substantial volumes, averaging some 450 pages each. The general object of both men is the same—to preserve a permanent record of their officers' professional services. For our immediate purpose both will be of immense use. But each has one considerable disadvantage. O'Byrne's weakness (to us) is that he includes only such men—all of them of Lieutenant's rank and upwards—as were living on 1st January, 1845 (with a very few exceptions to be mentioned later). Thus he omits all (or almost all) the officers who died during the wars or during the first thirty years of the subsequent peace. True, he records the many officers surviving in 1845 who joined after 1815: but these are no concern of

[1] A revised, second edition—not nearly so useful to us—began to appear in 1859, but petered out at the letter G, perhaps because his natural clients were fast dying off.

ours. Marshall also includes only the living—in his case those alive on 1st January, 1823. Thus he adds to our knowledge the biographies of many officers who died between 1823 and 1845—a large and important band. His weakness, however, is that he concerns himself only with those who reached, at lowest, the rank of Commander. The Lieutenants, much the most numerous group of all, are ignored.

In collecting material, both men pursued, roughly, the same tactics. They circularized their subjects, inviting their 'stories'. But O'Byrne went further than Marshall in one respect: he encouraged his correspondents, to all intents and purposes, to write their own notices. This had some advantages: it brought voluminous detail, and accuracy in simple facts which the writers would not, probably, falsify. But it also meant—such is human nature—that the subjects' interpretation of the facts might be a trifle—well—imaginative. For what these elderly gentlemen were being asked to do was to recapitulate events which occurred possibly fifty or sixty years ago, but certainly not less than thirty: highly colourful events too, and in striking contrast to the everyday occurrences which were now their lot. They had moreover—can we doubt it?—been swapping yarns about them with their cronies ever since, and retailing them to their children, and perhaps their grandchildren too. These are circumstances, admittedly, not altogether favourable to unbiased history. They seem to show an amber light which warns us, while accepting the main heads of information, to go slow over some of the details. Thus, to cite insignificant examples of what is probably rather common, a certain Captain Lovell claims somewhat loudly to have 'prevented a French foraging party 300 strong from levying contributions on the inhabitants of Altea'. Yet Sir William Dillon,[1] happening to touch at some length upon this very minor episode, squarely blames Lovell for not doing this very thing. Or again, we find G. A. Schultz, a Retired Commander in O'Byrne, but in 1797 a First Class Volunteer in the *Sandwich*, claiming that

'Immediately prior to Parker's execution, of which he was an eyewitness, his cot being directly over the one occupied by the latter, he had the opportunity of contemplating him while engaged nearly the whole night in writing. At about 11 p.m. the unhappy man gave him his prayerbook, with the words, "Here, Youngster, is a prayerbook for you".'

Well, it is possible—in those rough days they did odd things. But,

[1] *Narrative*, N.R.S., Vol. XCVII, p. 224.

even then, would a Young Gentleman, barely 12 years old, be slinging his cot above that of the most notorious of mutineers during the latter's last night on earth? Possibly, yes.... But who does not know how a good story sometimes grows into a better one through much telling? Is it not kinder to remember that, towards the close of a long life, fact and fantasy are apt to blur?

O'Byrne's work, then, may be generalized as a set of individual autobiographies and little else. There is but little 'chapter and verse' for any statement made. Marshall, however, is a good deal more objective. He issued questionnaires; he even invited personal interviews; but he did more 'editing'. He also included much really historical matter not derived solely from his correspondents—letters from other people, dispatches, extracts from courts-martial, etc.—material of which O'Byrne's pages are all but innocent. Clearly too he knew far more about the Navy and its ways: no wonder, for he was a veteran sailor who had served throughout both wars, only at their close to receive a Lieutenancy, as some sort of reward for those services 'in lieu of pension'. But O'Byrne was a civilian; a young one too, with no war-experience at all, having been born only in 1823.[1]

Many of the biographies are, of course, common to both writers, and in these O'Byrne borrows freely from Marshall. But each has his exclusive contribution for us—Marshall's such Commanders (and above) as were living in his day but dead in O'Byrne's; O'Byrne's all Lieutenants living in 1845. All told, the younger man has nearly 5,000 entries, of which we are directly interested in about 3,500, the rest being post-1815 entrants. Marshall has some 2,354 names, of which 206 are Flag Officers, 31 Superannuated Flag Officers, 1,103 Captains, 25 Retired Captains and 989 Commanders. Practically all concern us. Later, we shall use all O'Byrne's 3,500 for another purpose, but here, where our search is for social backgrounds only, barely half of them help us, along with a fraction only of Marshall's names. The reason is this. In the questionnaires sent out by both authors, all officers were invited not only to give the salient points of their service careers, but also to answer the questions 'Father's Name?' and 'Where born?' Unfortunately, however, a large number did not oblige: indeed, as far as 'Father's Name?' was concerned, only some 1,700 did so: and that figure is the aggregate from O'Byrne and Marshall combined. About 100 more are added here, culled from the *Naval Chronicle*, Burke's *Landed Gentry*, the *Dictionary*

[1] Marshall died in 1837, O'Byrne not till 1896.

of National Biography and other smaller sources, thus furnishing a total of 1,800 'family backgrounds'. These have been analysed in Table I. It is something: sufficient to illustrate certain wide trends, but not sufficient to enable us to regard the result as a cross-section of all contemporary officers. If we ask why so many refused, we plunge into the heart of the social question.

O'Byrne's invitation was issued in the 1840's, when Britain was still highly 'lordolatrous'; still highly conscious of the almost sacred prestige of 'Land'; still highly discriminating, perhaps contentious, over the use of the term 'gentleman'. Those therefore who could claim 'gentle blood' would, mostly, accept his invitation. Hence the 'Peerage', 'Baronetage' and 'Landed' categories are no doubt well-represented in our 1800: perhaps, even, the figures are not far off representing the full quota of the surviving officers who belonged to them. Most Naval Officers' sons, too, might well be proud of owning to their fathers' profession, if only because 'an officer was a gentleman'. The other professions are rather worse represented; but still not badly so, because the Church, the Law and even Medicine either had the 'gentility' label or aspired to it. That is, if a man were only the son of a poor country parson, doctor or solicitor with no particular pretensions to birth, he might well feel himself, as it were, socially upgraded by mentioning his father's profession, since many Churchmen, Law-men and Medical men *were* gentlemen. It is when the Business and Commerce section is reached that there is a sad falling off: for those who kept an unwearying eye open for such things might well suspect a 'gentleman engaged in commerce' of being a 'tradesman', or 'worthy merchant' of being mere camouflage for 'shopkeeper'. And Trade—especially Retail Trade—was *not* genteel in the 'forties. So but few of this group seem to have accepted O'Byrne's invitation, remaining content to supply 'professional' details while shying at 'family' ones. Indeed, such inside personal information as the author happens to possess all goes to show that, had every officer of 'business and commerce' affinities come out boldly with the information, that category would have been the largest of all. This conclusion is, admittedly, based upon a rather dangerous argument from the particular to the general. But there it is. I happen to know of perhaps a score of officers whose families were 'in business': and, in O'Byrne, not one of them supplies his 'family' details.

Marshall is a little, but not much, more helpful. He seems less class-conscious in minor ways. This is probably due to the nature of the man, for both his character as shown in his preface and his own naval background (which was not typical 'Quarter-deck') seem to reveal a person a good deal less 'lordolatrous' than O'Byrne. It may, however, have been a sign of the times. Perhaps the 'forties were more outrageously class-conscious than the 'twenties. Perhaps it is not altogether a coincidence that *A Naval Biographical Dictionary* and *The Book of Snobs* appeared within a year of one another.

TABLE I

SOCIAL STATUS OF R.N. OFFICERS' PARENTS, 1793–1815

Social Group or Occupation of Parents	Number in Group	Percentage out of 1800	Rank reached by 1849							
			Ad. of Fleet	Admiral	V-Admiral	R-Admiral	Captain	Commander	Retired Commander	Lieutenant
A. Titled People 1. Peers	131	7.3	2	18	15	24	57	12	0	3
A. Titled People 2. Baronets	85	4.7	0	18	4	7	36	14	1	5
B. Landed Gentry	494	27.4	1	24	29	49	142	102	24	123
C. Professional Men	899	50	5	62	49	81	305	189	36	172
D. Business and Commercial Men	71	3.9	0	3	6	4	20	16	2	20
E. Working Class	120	6.7	0	0	0	3	16	16	23	62
Total	**1800**	**100**	**8**	**125**	**103**	**168**	**576**	**349**	**86**	**385**

Significant, and sometimes amusing, are the differences of treatment when our two authorities are handling the same man. An adjective much favoured by Marshall is 'respectable'; a comfortable, defensive sort of word, used when a parent seems to stand in need of some bolstering. The kind of people who are 'respectable' in Marshall are Warrant Officers, R.N., Merchants and Attorneys (but not Barristers). Sometimes, even, a Surgeon is 'respectable'. But, in O'Byrne, such folk have mostly blossomed into Esquires: or, if not bolsterable enough, are simply omitted. Thus William Blight, who in Marshall is 'son of a respectable Warrant Officer in the Navy', has risen in O'Byrne to be 'son of an Officer in the Navy'. James Harris, in Marshall 'son of a respectable attorney', is, in O'Byrne, 'second son of Joseph Harris, Esquire, Solicitor of Leominster, co. Hereford'. On the other hand, Richard Douglas's parent—in Marshall 'Master Attendant at Sheerness Dockyard'—is quietly omitted by O'Byrne. The same fate overtakes Messrs. Turner and Matson, who (we know from Marshall) were wine-merchants, one from Portsmouth, the other from London. This snob-curtain, lowered so often by Marshall and so invariably by O'Byrne, is a source of regret, especially as the chinks in it through which Marshall occasionally lets us peep reveal tantalizing glimpses of a few whom he baldly calls 'tradesmen'—respectable ones, of course. But even some of the omissions are intriguing—particularly O'Byrne's. Some of them, we know from other sources, came from the higher strata of 'business'. Michael Turner, for instance (not in Marshall, being only a Lieutenant, and with no parentage in O'Byrne), belonged to a very wealthy London family which owned most of Putney and furnished several Masters of the Skinners' Livery Company. Nor does O'Byrne always mention really reputable parents. F. C. Annersley, fatherless in his *Dictionary*, was son of a Commander R.N. who was an 'Honourable'. Charles Rich's father was a full Admiral, J. A. Duntze's a Baronet: while Frederick Curzon was positively a near relative, if not actually the son, of a Peer. This last parent, however, probably got left out only because his son did not bother to give O'Byrne the information he sought. But the great bulk of the absentees, it seems certain, came from somewhere between the big City people, *via* somewhat less-monied families, down to those actually in retail trade: but not, probably, many of the last-named.

It is significant to notice, too, that the whole of our list of 1,800, drawn as it is from both our authors, contains only two 'farmers' (both in Marshall) and two 'agriculturalists'—one 'distinguished', one 'affluent'—in O'Byrne, naturally. Yet who can doubt that a good many more ought to figure in the lists, and would have done so, if only our authors (and perhaps the men concerned) could have risen above the snobbery of their day?

The last category—'Working Class'—is arrived at by quite different methods, to be explained later. The purpose of the later columns in Tables I and II will also be revealed shortly, when we have broken up our 1,800 known officers into their social groups.

2. *Social Groups*

A1. *The Peerage.* There are 131 scions of noble houses in Marshall and O'Byrne: all sons of peers, though many are not peers in their own right.

Those magnificent people had other work to do, in the House of Lords and on their great estates. Even such of them as were serving officers were apt to be frequent absentees—until Lord Barham, in the year of Trafalgar, largely put a stop to the practice. Most of the 131 were younger sons or, if elder sons, liable upon succession to their titles to give up the sea altogether. This is why, high as they tended to rise in the Service, they did not rise even higher. The whole subject of 'Interest' will concern us later. Here it need only be recorded that the ordinary peer, if he liked, had very nearly the whole British world at his feet, whatever profession he chose: but, oddly enough, not the naval world, for reasons most creditable to our commonsense. He could, almost with certainty, become a Captain: but after that, as we shall see, he had to take his place in the strictest and most inviolable of queues. How he did fare in the matter of naval promotion can be seen in the later columns of Table I, and in Table III, where the findings of the first Table are shown in percentages. Practically nine out of every ten peers' sons, we see there, became at least Post Captains, while not far short of half of them (45 per cent) went on to reach flag-rank.

The Aristocracy's contribution of 131 may not sound very large. But, relatively, it was. The whole Peerage was much smaller then than it is now; yet 131 is more than 7 per cent of all our 1,800 specimens. That compares well with the other groups. For instance, Army Officers' sons also show 7 per cent. Yet there were many more Army Officers than there were Peers. Certainly the Aristocracy was well represented in the naval Service.

A2. *The Baronetage.* This peculiarly British institution was richly represented too. Many of these sailor-sons of baronets had fathers who were first creations, for the honour was one which the governments of the day bestowed freely as a reward for fighting services of a not quite first-class order. Thus, where the really big figures like Jervis, Duncan, Keith, Nelson, Collingwood, Gardner, Pellew, Saumarez and Gambier received peerages, the next most deserving (or fortunate) sort like Curtis, Onslow, Orde, Duckworth, Calder, Strachan, Ball and Blackwood received baronetcies, as did the victors of outstanding small-ship engagements like Broke of the *Shannon* and Hoste of Lissa. So this long list of baronets' sons is not quite so indicative of blue blood and old families as it might appear, for many of them were the sons of first creations. Incidentally, 'first creations' themselves are not counted among the eighty-five unless they were also sons of baronets, because what concerns us here is not the men themselves but the stock from which they sprang. Had they been included, the average rank attained by the whole class (see Table III) would have been considerably higher: naturally, because they had all been honoured with baronetcies because they *had* done well, and were liable, therefore, to be flag-officers. Even as it is, however, their record, though a good deal below that of the peers, is a good way above that of any other group.

B. *Landed Gentry*. If we were to isolate all 'family details' in O'Byrne which relate to holders of land in these islands, the resultant volume would be very reminiscent of *Burke's Landed Gentry*. Yet, here too, we should walk warily. Neither Marshall nor O'Byrne was in any sense an expert in heraldry and pedigrees, nor particularly sensitive to the half-tones of English class-distinction. Rather, both—and especially O'Byrne—were amiable men who did not wish to give offence to anyone, least of all to potential subscribers. They would not, therefore, be over-critical of the 'social' material handed in to them, nor tempted to probe deeply into the intricacies of their clients' claims. Hence certain ugly little suspicions, especially of O'Byrne. If Marshall's plain 'farmer' can blossom, in O'Byrne, into an 'affluent agriculturalist', would our 'affluent agriculturalist' have any insuperable difficulty in turning up as 'U.V.W. Esq., of X Court, Y—shire'? I have even looked up some of O'Byrne's 'landed' folk in a near-contemporary Burke—itself an edition, by the way, sometimes suspected of over-leniency to 'landed' aspirants —and it must in honesty be reported that a good many of them are unaccountably absent from it. Still, this does not perhaps matter very much. Land is land; and there is no suggestion that the 'gentry' concerned possessed none of it. More likely, they had newly come by it; for Britain's commercial prosperity was by O'Byrne's time very much on the upgrade, and the successful merchant was busy digging his roots into the soil of Old England—Old Scotland and Old Ireland too. If we make a mental distinction between 'Landowners' and 'County Families', perhaps we shall satisfy everybody. Anyway, our tally from both authorities (but mostly O'Byrne) achieves a total of all but 500. At least it seems to show that British landowners (and particularly their younger sons) were playing a conspicuous part in the sea-defence of Britain.

Table III again shows how they fared for promotion; and that is comparatively badly. The eye has to travel quite a long way down the groups before discovering a worse. Perhaps this confirms the suspicion just ventilated. A real 'County' family was usually able to tap the flow of

Interest at a higher level altogether, if only because, at one point or another, it had often gloriously succeeded in catching for its son the daughter (usually the younger daughter) of a Viscount, or even a belted Earl. But such a coup was quite beyond the power of the parvenu who—and none knew it better than his Lordship—had once been an 'affluent agriculturalist': yes, and before that, perhaps, a 'respectable farmer'. Such people certainly brought the average down.

C. *The Professions*. Table I shows the 'professional class' as the largest single contributor to our 1,800 known parents. It provides, in fact, almost exactly as many as all the others put together. Now this does not mean that half the sum of all wartime naval officers came from professional homes. They certainly did not. It only means that half of this particular 1,800 did. And that is quite a different matter: for no claim is here made of having discovered the parentage of more than one in six of all wartime officers: perhaps only one in eight. *This* 1,800, it must be emphasized again, is not a cross-section of them all. It lists, proportionately, too many peers, baronets, landed folk and, probably, professional people. It omits far too many of the 'lower' social grades. Still, it is large enough to allow for worthwhile comparisons at the upper end. Thus, when it shows that there were more 'professional' sons than there were sons of the titled and landed people rolled together, we may safely accept the finding. Indeed there were probably very many more because, while suspecting that all, or almost all, the children of the first three grades acknowledged their parentage, we suspect that only a majority, and not all, of the professional sons did so. Be that as it may, however, the Professions were exceedingly well represented.

An even more valuable contribution to our social study, perhaps, is contained in Table II. Here the professional fathers of Table I are broken up into their respective professions. Nor, in this more limited field, is there any reason to suppose that the proportions are wrong, even when applied to all wartime officers. Thus if 44 per cent of our 899 professional sons were sailors' sons, we may assume that, roughly, 44 per cent of *all* professional sons were sailors' sons throughout the wars.

C.1. *The Navy*. We may now consider in greater detail the various 'professional' sub-groups. The first, both in size and interest, is the Navy.

There is nothing surprising in the size of the naval contingent. It is natural; and the same thing happens today, not only in the Navy, but in most walks of life, especially the professions. But if this be so, even now and in all professions, it was doubly, trebly so a century and a half ago and in the naval profession. For there every would-be officer had to find someone to take him to sea, or he would never get there. And who would do it more certainly than the boy's father? Or who, in nature, would look after him so well when he was there? And if, by lucky chance, that parent was highly placed in the Service, who could better look after his lad's career, obtain appointments for him, and promotion? Indeed, if an officer-aspirant were so unfortunate as to have neither naval father nor naval uncle or cousin, nor a close naval friend of his father or his mother, his outlook at the start was far from rosy, as we shall have many opportunities of seeing later on.

TABLE II

DETAILS OF PROFESSIONS IN GROUP C OF TABLE I

Break-Up of C (Table I) Professional Men	Number in Sub-Group	% of all Professionals	% of 1800	Ad. of Fleet	Admiral	V-Admiral	R-Admiral	Captain	Commander	Retired Commander	Lieutenant
1. Navy	434	48.2	24.1	2	28	22	41	130	90	20	101
2. Church	156	17.4	8.7	0	8	7	15	53	37	5	31
3. Army	132	14.6	7.3	1	14	8	11	53	27	3	15
4. Law	51	5.7	2.8	1	5	1	2	22	10	2	8
5. Civil Service	51	5.7	2.8	0	4	3	6	18	10	2	8
6. Medicine	50	5.6	2.8	0	3	6	1	19	9	4	8
7. Ministers, Governors, Diplomats, etc	18	2.0	1.0	1	0	1	2	9	5	0	0
8. The Arts	7	.8	.4	0	0	1	3	1	1	0	1
Total Professions	**899**	**100**	**50**	**5**	**62**	**49**	**81**	**305**	**189**	**36**	**172**

A naval father, then, was best: but a naval uncle was a good second-best, and if uncles had been counted as parents in my analysis the 'Naval' figure of 434 would have shot up sharply. The best-known naval uncle of those times was, of course, Nelson's mother's brother, Captain Maurice Suckling, and, later, we shall see him in action. But much humbler uncles could be very useful too. Even a Warrant Officer could, and sometimes did, prevail upon the Captain whom he served to undertake the 'protection' of a nephew. So 'nephew of a Purser (or even of a Carpenter or Boatswain) of the Royal Navy' is no rarity—in Marshall, of course—while 'son of a Warrant Officer' is fairly common.

Again we can see in the Tables how they fared in the Service. Their record is a shade better than that of the Landed Gentry, though not nearly so good as that of the titled folk.

C.2. *The Church.* The next largest 'professional' sub-group is the Clergy: with whom are grouped here the small 'Don' class from the Universities, all of whom were then in Holy Orders—many, indeed, incumbents of parishes too. The minds of many of us, perhaps, like to dwell lovingly upon those peaceful, rural parsonages, ruled by fine old Rector and busy wife, housing their generous quiverfuls of healthy, country-bred sons who go forth with their good parents' blessing to do battle for Old England. It is a pleasing picture, and it were shame to kill it. But was it true? Sometimes no doubt it was: but it must be owned, with regret, that an analysis of Marshall and O'Byrne does not altogether confirm it. The kind of parson who most commonly figures in their pages hardly seems to fit so idyllic a setting. Far too many of them —probably more than half—are quite exalted personages in the Church hierarchy—Canons, Deans, Bishops: even Archbishops. All too many of them seem to have aristocratic relations, and a surprising number of them are positively peers or baronets themselves. Far too many, also, have more livings than we should think proper today. In a word, a great majority of them are quite obviously not 'passing rich on forty pounds a year'. No aspersion is intended upon their goodness, but all the indications are that they were not particularly poor.

The best-remembered 'son of the parsonage' is, again, Horatio Nelson: and the Reverend Edmund, though certainly not a bad parson, and certainly not a rich one, was equally certainly worth a great deal more than forty pounds a year. Thirty acres of glebeland went with his parsonage and his three parishes. Moreover he, and still more his wife, were 'well-connected'. None the less, Nelson was a real son of the parsonage, and he was brought up as a child to a real country life on those 30 acres of glebe and garden. Moreover, he was a grandson of the parsonage too; doubly so, because both his grandfathers were clergymen. Perhaps our cherished mind-picture was really based, unconsciously, upon that old rectory of Burnham Thorpe in Norfolk, most English of counties. Must it be discarded? Perhaps—yet it may not be quite so fanciful as lord-loving O'Byrne would have us think. It is quite possible that his parson-parents are being somewhat 'written up' in the same way as some of the 'agriculturalists' were. Let us hope so, anyway.

In Table III the Church runs fairly level with the Navy and the Landed Gentry. Indeed, the kind of Interest at the Clergy's command was probably not dissimilar to that at the disposal of 'Land': for the social prestige of the sort of parson whose son entered the Navy corresponded pretty closely with that of the ordinary landowner. There are many 'county family' clergy in O'Byrne. Admittedly there are some who are more on the 'agriculturalist' level; yet even these could hardly be forty-pound-a-year men, if only because all Young Gentlemen afloat were compelled to live up to their gentlemanly claims. It was necessary for such lads to have an allowance of from £30 to £50 a year—in lieu of pay, of which, to start with anyway, they received none. Falconer[1] recommends £30 to £40: but some captains, anxious to keep up the 'style' of their ships, demanded more. Captain Andrew Douglas of the *Alcide*, for instance, expected young William Dillon's father to provide £50.[2] There were also messing expenses and, towards the end of the war, a compulsory fee for his Schoolmaster. Evidently no really poor country parson could face up to bills of this kind, unless he had an accommodating relative or two. Even the Rector of Burnham Thorpe, for all his 30 acres, had a family of eight when Horatio went to sea, and he could hardly have managed it without Uncle Maurice.

C.3. *The Army.* The Army, which comes next numerically, does not call for much comment. Men with commissions in the Army were normally, of course, 'Officers and Gentlemen' like their naval brethren: and Table III seems to show that, in this important matter of influence, the soldiers did not come off at all badly in comparison. In fact they lead all but the Peers and Baronets. Perhaps the Horse Guards, under the ever-watchful eye of the Duke of York, had little to learn about the workings of Interest. In his own day, and it was a long one, this same Royal Duke earned a reputation as a manipulator of patronage which was not wholely deserved, but which was as unenviable as his fame as a military leader.

C.4. *The Law.* Not much time need be spent upon the other professions, nor upon their showing in the Tables. Their numbers are rather small for useful percentage figures. The Law, in this respect like the Church, covers a very wide range of social gradations—from a Lord Chancellor, *via* a few judges, and rather more barristers, down to

[1] *Marine Dictionary*, 1815 (Burney's Edition), under 'Midshipman'.

[2] Dillon, op. cit., N.R.S., Vol. XCIII, p. 20.

genuine country solicitors. And its percentage results work out very much like those of the Church. Indeed the social gap between a Lord Chancellor and a country solicitor probably differed but little from that between an Archbishop and a humble country parson. The Law, however, does somewhat better in Post Captains.

C.5. *Civil Service.* Under this heading are included all who would now bear the name—that is, roughly, everyone holding an 'office of profit' under the Crown, but not belonging to a fighting service. These men also vary immensely in social status, the higher ones holding 'plums', sometimes virtual sinecures, through open patronage, the lower ones being hard-working officials with real jobs to do in government departments, stores or dockyards. They did rather well, especially in flag-officers. But then they would 'know the right people', being normally stationed at the heart of things.

C.6. *Medicine.* The comparatively good showing of the 'medical' sons is perhaps a little surprising, because the doctor-parents in Marshall and O'Byrne seem to have but few aristocratic connections. Medicine was not a profession which often took the fancy of the Peerage, so that even the most exalted medical fathers, though doubtless wealthy, are not, socially, very highly placed. About the best to which they can aspire is 'Physician to His Late Majesty', or 'Surgeon to H.R.H. the Duke of X'. They come out of it rather better than the Church and about level with the Law. In one respect these two are probably rather alike. Neither doctor-parent nor law-parent would feel the financial difficulties of, say, the church-parent, or even the less successful sort of naval-parent.

C. 7 and 8. *Ministers and the Arts.* Two other very small groups are kept separate. The first consists of Ministers of the Crown, Governors, etc. Among them there are even some Cabinet Ministers. We might expect such people to do better for their sons than apparently they did: but the numbers are too small to be of any great value. Yet one interesting thing is to be observed. They secured more Post Captaincies for them than any other group did. The reason for this will become apparent later. Here it need only be noticed that while a great man's Interest could readily secure a Captaincy for his protégé, and secure good posts for him after he was 'made post', no one, not even the Prime Minister, however prime a wangler he might be, could hurry his man up that overcrowded but strictly regulated post captains' ladder.

The 'Arts' group is weaker still in numbers, and is too small for percentage-figures to mean anything. Yet the group as it stands did well, with one Vice-Admiral, three Rear-Admirals and a Captain. The parents concerned were Dillon the author, Dr. Burney the musician and author, Cumberland the playwright, Beechey (with two sons) and Hoppner the portrait-painters, and Dodd the marine artist.

D. *Business and Commerce.* We can now return to the fourth of our main groups, these 'commercial' people—to whom we should add, could we but find them, a generous sprinkling of yeomen, and the bigger sort of tenant-farmers. In this group too there would certainly be a big social range, stretching, as we have seen, from people who were frankly 'tradesmen' up to really big business men in London and elsewhere. There are, for example, several scions of ship-building houses and ship-owning firms, both good money-makers. Indeed, the possession of some wealth was probably a factor common to all of this group.

All naval officers, we saw, claimed gentility, and not only intended to live like gentlemen but actually, within the limit prescribed by life afloat, contrived to do so. And all who aspired to join their number were expected to do the same: for which purpose, of course, they had to have the means. Nor did those means come from their wages, which were low. They came from their fathers' pockets. So, emphatically, money did come into the matter; and certainly money talked in the Britain of George III, if not quite so loudly as it does today. Even then it was not impossible to set a son up in a Service which was still highly exclusive, even when a man's own social pretensions were not great; but only if some degree of affluence could fill the social gap. In plain terms, it was always possible to *buy* one's protégé in, though not, perhaps, by any of the cruder forms of bribery; and not by the official means of 'Purchase'.

There was not, and never had been, such a thing as Purchase in the Navy; not, that is, in anything like the Army sense of the word. The Navy, though far from democratic, was not nearly so tightly aristocratic as the Army. Besides, the Navy's standard unit, the Ship, was quite unlike the Army's standard units—Troops, Companies and Regiments, which were pieces of private and negotiable property. The Ship was, and always had been, the property of the State, whether the State were represented by the Crown, by Parliament, or by both. So no 'R.N.' warship had ever belonged to a private individual, to be sold by him at will to any other private individual. And the same held—and holds—true of every bit of equipment on board which served to make the ship go or helped her to fight. All such things, without exception, were 'broad-arrow' goods, the State's property, not the individual's. There being nothing whatever to purchase, then, there was no System of Purchase. This is no case of higher standards in the Navy than in the Army. Purchase of the Army kind was just not 'on'. Any Captain who seriously offered to sell 'his' ship would no doubt have been packed off to the asylum at Hoxton used by the Navy. But in fact it never happened.

Bribery, however, was another matter. Who would dare to assert that favours, even hard cash, never changed hands in return for an appointment in a ship of war, or even for promotion to a senior rank? Indeed, some of the 'patronage' which we shall examine later, much of it almost openly practised, looks to modern eyes very much like lightly-camouflaged bribery. Even in the highest circles there was much of what is vulgarly known as 'You scratch me and I'll scratch you!', while, at a lower level, there are many cases of a Captain taking a youngster under his 'protection' to 'oblige' a man who has already 'obliged' him: and a few—not many—of captains doing this in return for the cancellation of actual debts. But instances of unadulterated bribery are very hard to find, and of successful ones even harder. The most barefaced attempt that has come to the author's knowledge was that perpetrated by a certain Lieutenant John Heally, an Irishman, who, in 1810, actually approached the Hon. Charles Yorke, then First Lord, and offered him £2,000 to make him a Commander. Yorke was not playing. The Lieutenant was summoned to the Admiralty, but evidently sensed danger before he arrived. Anyway, once there, he grovelled, expressing deep contrition for having made so monstrous a suggestion. His punishment perhaps gives us a clue as to how seriously the offence was regarded. He was ordered, curtly enough, to rejoin his ship and report to his C.-in-C., Sir Edward Pellew. What the Admiral said to him is not recorded, but Dillon, who tells the tale, states that Sir Edward 'did not mince the matter with him. He received a jobation that must have stung the coldest heart in existence.'[1] That was all, and Heally survived it, plodding on, a Lieutenant, for another 29 years until he was solaced with a promotion which was not really one at all—he was made a Retired Commander.

This was a crude case. His chances of success were extremely poor. It is not suggested that Charles Yorke would ever have sunk to taking a bribe like this: but, even were he tempted, the time chosen for the suggestion was ill-judged. Only the year before, Parliament had been investigating the big Army scandals associated with the notorious Mrs.

[1] N.R.S., Vol. XCVII, pp. 153–4.

Clarke. This woman had certainly been selling commissions under the very nose, though not probably with the connivance, of the Duke of York: who, in this case more foolish than criminal, had had to leave the Horse Guards. Thus everyone was on the look-out for just such a thing. So Heally failed. But what of less crude cases which—perhaps—did not fail? Here is our dilemma, common in all under-the-counter transactions. The guilty party tries his best to escape detection, and, if he succeeds, the crime remains undetected. But this in no way proves that the crime was not committed. Indeed, who, knowing the moral laxity of the day and the—to us—rank dishonesties almost openly condoned, can seriously doubt that it sometimes was?

Often, however, it was not a crime: at least, no one so regarded it. Lady Nelson, in what she clearly regards as a piece of tittle-tattle scarcely worth recording, mentions a case of what was probably going on all the time. A certain George Tobin was the son of a West Indian merchant, and he had—we are not told how—obtained his step to Lieutenant in 1790. There he looked like sticking, but not through want of help from the paternal purse:

> 'George Tobin still a Lieutenant. All Mr. Tobin's expensive presents to some Lords and Ladies and captains cannot get him made.'[1]

Mr. Tobin evidently had the will, and the money. His problem was to find the right palm to cross. He had failed to find it in 1797, but he seems to have had better luck soon afterwards, as George obtained his promotion in 1798, and the further step to Captain in 1802, so that he gets his flag at last. Some such secondhand bribery, indeed, was probably the normal way in which a man, not born into the 'right' set, got his son there by the judicious use of his strong suit—cash.

Be that as it may, however, one thing is sure. Somehow or other as the war grew older there appeared upon the quarter-decks of His Majesty's ships an appreciable group of men whose social qualifications were some way below those required in the earlier days, and far below those desired by the older sort of officer. The thing was something of a snowball. Once men who were 'not quite' began to command ships, they naturally began to surround themselves with other 'not quites' who, in due course, became qualified to admit more. Thus some ships came to be officered almost entirely by this new element. A man like Dillon, who to the twentieth century must appear to be the very quintessence of snobbery,

[1] Lady Nelson to her husband, 19.6.1797. N.R.S., Vol. C., p. 370.

often complains of this falling-off in gentility, both in individuals and in whole wardrooms: even in whole gunrooms, where the coming generation was maturing. It would perhaps be comforting to think that Dillon and his friends were on the way out, and that a more democratic officer-entry was on its way in. But History does not bear this out. There is abundant evidence that, when peace came, it was these—to Dillon—undesirables who, being given no appointments at all, and practically no promotion, were all frozen out of the Service. By the 1840's and '50's, when Dillon wrote, he informs us with no small glee that the Navy is nearly purged of them. By then, indeed, the Navy was, if anything, even more the preserve of the 'upper' and 'upper middle' classes than it was before the wars began. The really 'democratic' revolution in officering the fleet is largely a twentieth-century phenomenon.

Clearly this 'temporary democratization' accounts for quite a large number of the officers shorn of parents and backgrounds in O'Byrne. In his way, O'Byrne was as big a snob as Dillon: so were most of the officers in question if it comes to that. Thackeray makes it very clear in his brilliant essay that snobbery is not the monopoly of one class; it extends right through. So—here—these parvenus had reached their social bourne—the Quarter-deck. They were officers, and 'Everyone knows that Officers are Gentlemen'. Instinctively, then, they sought to forget, and let others forget, the stock from which they sprang.

The few collected here—a pitifully inadequate bag of seventy-one—do not emerge so badly from the ordeal of Table III, though their percentages are perceptibly worse than those of any other group yet discussed. But this comparative success is not altogether unexpected because, presumably, those who did declare themselves in O'Byrne would tend to belong to the most presentable—Dillon would say the least unpresentable—business and commercial families.

They are not, individually, a very distinguished lot. But two officer-sons of 'Business', neither included in O'Byrne, deserve mention. They were two of Nelson's own captains. One is in Marshall, the other is in neither. Thomas Troubridge, drowned in 1807, of course missed both. He was of Irish birth, but a Londoner born, son of a baker in the Strand. He is a shining example of an officer whose 'Interest' was of the slenderest but who rose through his own sterling worth. Yet even he could not have risen without a patron, and he was fortunate to find one while still young enough in that great judge of men Sir John Jervis, who, more than any man of his time, consistently put Service first and all other considerations a bad second. The other 'business' officer was Sir Edward Berry, son of a merchant (also of London) who died young and poor. Characteristically enough, Marshall does not furnish this information (though Berry, dying in 1831, appears in his pages). His entry is, 'Son of the late Edward Berry Esq, of London.' This officer's case, however, is a good deal more normal than that of Troubridge, because there was, this time, a convenient uncle—the Reverend Titus Berry who, as luck would have it, had been tutor to Lord Mulgrave, at the time a Lord of the Admiralty. This did the trick.

Both these great officers—even Troubridge, whose father was probably quite well-to-do—were 'Quarter-deck' people in the sense defined in our introduction. They had joined up with the legitimate hopes and prospects of 'walking the Quarter-deck' from the start, like all the other officers so far discussed.

Before leaving them, to look at 'Lower Deck' types, let us glance again at Table III. Were there really, it may be asked, so *many* who attained flag-rank? For the percentages are a great deal higher than those obtaining today. The answer is that the figures are much too high if we picture them all holding flag-*posts*—actually flying their flags, that is, at sea or ashore. They are also much too high if we picture them as being flag-officers during the wars. But most of them qualified on neither count. A big majority never flew flags at all, peace or war. If there had existed such a thing as 'Retirement' in any modern sense, most of them would have been 'officers on the Retired List', many of them 'Captain, R.N. (ret.)'. As it was, they had merely reached flag-rank by automatic promotion. Later on we shall meet these gallant old men, clinging on to life in the hope that the Flag would come before the funeral.

E. *Working Class*. The last category in the Tables is labelled 'Working Class'. The figure is 120, and it is reached by a method entirely different from that previously used: for, needless to relate, the necessary information seldom comes from O'Byrne, or even from Marshall. Yet—justice where it is due—18 of these 120 officers do actually proclaim that they were pressed into the Service in the first instance. This may spell a sturdy independence and honesty of outlook, or it may be an example of an attitude of mind not unknown today—'I'm a self-made man, I am. See from what humble origins I sprang!' But, whichever it is, it is fair to class them differently from all the groups already discussed. Most of them were in fact plain merchant seamen who, in any social census of the day, would appear among the 'working class'; the unprivileged, or, to use our naval-social phraseology, 'Lower Deck'. The other hundred-odd were not so easy to detect. A much more careful scrutiny of their records in Marshall and O'Byrne was necessary. Nor is it claimed here that they were all detected, or that the right ones were always discovered. Just how it was done will be told later, when the subject of 'Entry' is under consideration. Here we are still concerned with 'Pre-entry'—the social background of the entrants.

TABLE III

RANKS REACHED BY OFFICERS IN TABLE I, IN PERCENTAGES

Group or Occupation	Percentage Reached		
	Flag-Rank	Post-Rank	Below Post-Rank
A1. Peers	45	44	11
A2. Baronets	34	42	24
B. Landed Gentry	21	29	50
C. Professional Men (All)	22	34	44
1. Navy	22	30	48
2. Church	19	34	47
3. Army	26	40	34
4. Law	18	43	39
5. Civil Service	26	35	39
6. Medicine	20	38	42
7. Ministers (etc.)	22	50	28
8. The Arts	—	—	—
D. Business and Commerce	18	28	54
E. Working Class	2.5	13.5	84
Total	**22**	**32**	**46**

This 120, it must be remembered, is only the number given in our two authorities. There were certainly a good many more in the whole Navy—such of them, for instance, as had only reached the rank of Lieutenant when Marshall wrote, and who had not survived to qualify for O'Byrne. This would be a considerable number, since few of these men had gained their commissions when young, nor had they the influence to obtain much further promotion. An even larger class is missing also—those (of any rank) who were dead when Marshall wrote. Here the number of 'Lower Deck' officers would be particularly great, many of them having won their 'quarter-deck' status in the preceding War (of American Independence). Thus a man who had won his commission in, say, 1780, when already past his first youth, might well be dead by 1823.

Most of these Lower Deck promotions must have been real characters, eccentric often, but always magnificent seamen: and they had a real *raison d'être* in the Service. What this was may be described by that great seaman, Thomas Cochrane, Earl Dundonald. The year is 1793 and, on joining his first ship, the *Hind*, Captain John Cochrane (his uncle), he is introduced to her First Lieutenant.

'Jack Larmour—a specimen of the old British seaman little calculated to inspire exalted ideas of the gentility of the naval profession, though presenting at a glance the personification of its efficiency—Jack was in fact one of a not very numerous class whom, for their superior seamanship, the Admiralty was glad to promote from the forecastle to the quarter-deck, in order that they might mould into shipshape the questionable materials supplied by Parliamentary influence, even then paramount in the Navy to a degree which might otherwise have led to disaster. Lucky was the commander who could secure such an officer for his quarter-deck. On my introduction, Jack was dressed in the garb of a seaman, with marlin-spike slung round his neck and a lump of grease in his hand, and was busily engaged in setting up the rigging.'[1]

There is surely, here, something very typical of that blend of idiocy and commonsense so characteristic of the British Navy in the eighteenth century—if not indeed of the whole British people. Here is the Admiralty commissioning officers to train and discipline the men; and then, having commissioned the wrong people, from the wrong motives, it commissions men to train and discipline the officers: and, full and by, the fantastic system works. Dundonald gratefully acknowledges his debt to his 'sea-daddy', whose 'only ideas of relaxation were to throw off the lieutenant and resume the functions of Able Seaman'. This particular Jack became a Captain in the end (perhaps through the Cochrane Interest). But that was exceptional. Such men were seldom promoted: they were too valuable as Lieutenants.

James Anthony Gardner met with just such another in the *Edgar*. His name was John Yetts, and

'... when he commissioned the *Edgar* he had on a uniform coat made in days of yore, with sleeves that reached to his hips, a very low collar, huge white lapels and cuffs, the buttons behind at a good fighting distance, and the skirts and pockets of an enormous size. A red waistcoat, nankin breeches and black worsted stockings, with great yellow buckles

[1] *Autobiography of a Seaman*, p. 32.

on round-toed shoes, a hat that had been cocked, but cut round, with a very low crown so that he was obliged to keep his hand to his head to prevent its blowing off in the slightest breeze.'[1]

This costume, of course, was more than old-fashioned. It was not, and never had been, 'uniform'. Yetts was never promoted; but some of these 'tarpaulins', like Larmour, did go further. Gardner was shipmate with one in the *Barfleur*—clearly of another type altogether, and not a particularly pleasant one. His advancement, it would seem, brought out his failings. He was John Richards, made Post in 1809.

'This man belonged to the *Boreas* at the time my father was on board [circ. 1775–7]: he was then before the mast. When Captain Thompson was appointed to the *Alcide*, 74, he took Richards with him in a low capacity, and afterwards put him on the Quarter-deck [i.e. rated him Midshipman]: when his time was served he got made a Lieutenant. He was a good sailor, but proud, insolent, and vulgar in his language; full of strange sayings and low wit, and overbearing to those of inferior rank.'[2]

This was typical of the way in which the unusual step from Lower Deck to Quarter-deck was taken. The lucky man must catch somebody's eye, and that somebody must be a Captain at very lowest.

Dillon too had the experience of serving under a man who sounds like another Richards. He too hectored his underlings and made their lives unbearable. He was Henry Lidgbird Ball, a Lieutenant of 1778 and a Captain of 1795. But, while just as uncouth and churlish, he had a more distinguished career. He had been with Captain Arthur Philip at the first establishment of the convict station at Botany Bay, and at the founding of Sydney—a point on the north side of its harbour is still named after him. Later, he distinguished himself under Rainier in the Red Sea, and actually received his flag before the war ended, in June, 1814. He did not, however, fly it at sea.

It is hardly possible, now, to discover the numbers of these pre-Marshall Lower Deckers. But probably they equalled, at least, the 120 here analysed: and they too may fairly be described as 'Working Class'. But let us return to the contingent of Marshall and O'Byrne and see how they fared in comparison with their social superiors.

Their showing is not impressive. Only three of the 120 (or 2½ per cent)

[1] Recollections of J. A. Gardner, N.R.S., Vol. XXXI, p. 70.

[2] Op. cit., p. 115.

reached flag-rank, and not one flew his flag afloat. Only 16 (or 13.3 per cent) were 'made post', while 70 per cent had no real promotion after Lieutenant. This is only to be expected, because their Interest (apart from that of their original patron-captain) was usually non-existent. In fact, they went as far as they did only on their merits and, even so, aided by unusual good fortune. What those merits—and that good fortune—must have been may be better appreciated when it is recalled that the figure of 240—this 120, that is, *plus* the further 120 pre-Marshallites estimated in the preceding paragraph—really represents the sum-total, or something like it, of all the Lower Deck promotions throughout the wars. But as, serving first and last in the twenty-two years of hostilities, there were certainly not less than 600,000 seamen, and probably more, it would seem that, at best, only one in every 2,500 of them gained a commission at all. By a similar calculation we have six *very* lucky men who attained to flag-rank—three from Marshall and O'Byrne, and three pre-Marshallites. One out of every 100,000! And not one of them would have been an 'active-list' flag-officer today.

It may be mere coincidence that three of the sixteen Lower Deck Captains in Marshall and O'Byrne were closely associated with Nelson and Trafalgar, and that two of them were serving in the *Victory* on that great day. Moreover, one of them was actually her First Lieutenant—the officer whom we should now call her Commander. John Quilliam was not only 'Lower Deck': he was a pressed man. Not without cause does Marshall call him 'a favourite of fortune'. He was a Manxman (according to Marshall) or an Irishman (according to Beatson). How he came to be pressed or what Captain 'adopted' him neither of them states. He gained his Lieutenancy in October, 1798. This was fortune enough: but it was only the beginning of his. In 1805 he was sent to the *Victory* as Sixth Lieutenant. Yet Nelson appointed him First, the most responsible of all Lieutenants' posts. This was not, it seems, for the reason that would occur to one first—that the Admiral considered him superior to his fellows. It was, if we may believe Marshall, the outcome of a personal quirk of Nelson's. Lieutenants in flagships, always highly-placed for promotion, tended to come and go with bewildering frequency; and Nelson, it seems, thought that the constant shuffling of such a key-figure as First Lieutenant did not make for efficiency in his ship. So he deliberately appointed a junior one to the post. However that may be, Quilliam was the gainer. He not only served as First in the action: he also received the awards which traditionally went with that post. He skipped the rank of Commander altogether, and, on 24th December, was made a full Captain. Fortune's darlings are seldom very popular, and there was much discontent over this promotion, especially among the *Victory* lieutenants who were his seniors in ship-rank. Dillon, though not in the *Victory*, was one of the many who were thus overtaken by Quilliam. He ran across him in 1814, when the latter was commanding a crack frigate, and also comments, but not unkindly, on his luck, mentioning that Quilliam had been a seaman under him in 1795. He had the reputation of being a good one, but there are indications that he was tarred with the same brush as Richards and Ball. Indeed, it must have been tempting, in those days, for a 'Lower Deck' officer to take it out of a 'Quarter-deck' junior, particularly if, in his seaman days, he had come up against a martinet or two. There was nothing to prevent Quilliam from reaching flag-rank, save only the Common Enemy. He died in 1829, much too soon for it to come his way.

The best-known Lieutenant in the *Victory*, however, was not John Quilliam, but John Pasco; first in seniority but not in position, for he was Signal Lieutenant. He it was who had the hoisting of the Immortal Signal, and decided the final wording of it. Nelson told him to send 'England confides....' But, knowing that 'confides' was not in the Vocabulary signal-book then in use, he suggested substituting the word 'expects', which would not have to be spelt out: and Nelson agreed. The story that Nelson originally asked for 'Nelson confides . . .' is not nearly so well authenticated, though the historian William James mentions it. Pasco himself knew that his demotion to Signal Lieutenant might affect his career unfavourably, for, in the victory awards, the signal officer never did as well as the First Lieutenant: and, later, he told Nicolas how, just before the action, he went to state his case to Nelson. But, finding the little Admiral on his knees, he had not the heart to mention his private grievance. He even declared (in O'Byrne) that 'it was Nelson's *practice* to make the officer first on his list for promotion do the duty of Signal Officer, and the Junior that of First Lieutenant.' Whether he was right here or not, he certainly did suffer from the change-round. Had Nelson lived, he would no doubt have seen justice done, but as it was Pasco was only made Commander when Quilliam was made Post. Moreover, he had to wait five more years for the step which was so very important in the rather grisly 'survival stakes' of the day. Yet, though he lost the use of his right arm in the battle, he overhauled Quilliam by simply staying alive longer. He received his flag at last—in 1847—and enjoyed it for six years: but, again, never flew it.

There can be little doubt that Pasco was 'lower deck' too. Neither Marshall nor O'Byrne gives him away, nor does Sir John Laughton in the *Dictionary of National Biography*. Yet his Service record makes it look as though his origin was humble. His rating in his second ship, the *Pegasus*, is Gunner's Servant—not, as we shall see, a position holding much promise of advancement. That was in 1786, and as he had already been at sea for two years, he took eleven years to reach the Quarter-deck in 1795. It was an overlong apprenticeship for any Young Gentleman. That of itself, however, would not be conclusive proof. This is supplied by Byam Martin,[1] who records that

'he (Captain Pasco) was a Boy in the ship (*Pegasus*), Captain H.R.H. Prince William, and was the servant in the Midshipmen's berth in which I messed; he was afterwards by way of promotion handed over to John Baptiste, the Prince's steward, and now greatly to his credit he is high in rank, distinguished and respected. I never saw Captain Pasco from the time he was a servant until he came to wait upon me as a Commander when my flag was flying, and I was proud to have him at my table that day.'

What perhaps misled Laughton was the fact that O'Byrne showed him as entering his first ship as 'Captain's Servant', a rating which almost always spelt 'Young Gentleman'. But there always were a few of this rating who really were servants, and Pasco must have been one of them, for Byam Martin, who actually knew him as such, could not be wrong here.

So, after Vice-Admiral Lord Nelson and Captain Thomas Masterman Hardy, the two most important people in the *Victory* at Trafalgar were both 'lower deck'.

Another Tarpaulin who figured in the great battle was James Clephan, a merchant seaman from Fife impressed into the Navy in 1794. Greatly distinguishing himself in a desperate cutting-out foray near Brest in 1801, he was given a commission for it—quick going for a lower deck man. At Trafalgar he was in the *Spartiate*, and was promoted to her First Lieutenancy immediately after it. He rose in the end to be a Retired Captain.

All such people, it is well to remember, were the products of war, not

[1] Letters and Papers of Sir Thomas Byam Martin, N.R.S., Vol. XXIV., p. 28.

the results of any conscious design to admit the unprivileged into the pastures of the privileged. They were all, it is certain, men whose deeds were their recommendation, and their only one. War brought out their fighting qualities, and their Captains, seeing them at first hand, admired and rewarded them. After the war was over, few more, if any, reached the Quarter-deck for a long, long time to come. Like the small tradesmen and shopkeepers they were frozen out. That was easy enough, for the 'focs'le' man had not the wherewithal to buy himself there, as some of the former had. Not quite all of these Lower Deck officers, perhaps, were of so lowly a class. A very few—and they, very likely, failures ashore—may have drifted on to the Lower Deck and been promoted therefrom: men whose background and education warranted something better. But such were quite exceptional because, outside story-books, failures do not very often turn into successes. Still, such men, if socially 'quarter-deck' though navally 'lower deck', would stand a fair chance of taking the step, for the class instinct was very strong.

Normally, however, the gulf between the two decks was such a very real one that practically every lad who joined a ship of war knew very well what he might legitimately expect: and, if he did not before he arrived, he very soon found out. For, from the start, a 'lower deck boy' worked and messed with the Lower Deck, while the Young Gentleman was at once accepted in his appropriate mess in the Gunroom: and the treatment accorded him by the officers, from the Captain downwards, was entirely different from that given to the seaman-boy, even down to the dress he wore.

There were, however, occasional miscalculations beforehand, due as a rule to parental simplicity and ignorance which were exposed soon enough when the lad joined. One such case is worth recording at some length, because nothing could better illustrate the abysmal nature of the said gulf.[1] The late Mr. Leech had been valet to Lord William Fitzroy, son of the Duke of Grafton. His widow was lady's maid to Lady Spencer, Fitzroy's sister and wife of a First Lord of the Admiralty. The former Mrs. Leech, having married again, was living at Bladen near Woodstock, her new husband being a carpenter in the employ of the Duke of Marlborough. Her son Samuel, now 13, and employed as gardener's boy at Blenheim, had several cousins serving before the mast in the Navy, and conceived the ambition to do the same.

Then two exciting items of news reached the little home at Bladen.

[1] *A Voice from the Main Deck*, by Samuel Leech, London, 1844.

Lord William, a naval Captain, had been given a frigate, and he was coming to pay a visit at Blenheim. Rather unwillingly—for she had hitherto opposed the idea—the mother mentioned her boy's desire to her mistress who goodnaturedly passed it on to Fitzroy when he arrived. That nobleman, equally goodnatured, sent for little Samuel and asked him if he wanted to go to sea: to which the boy said, 'Yes, my Lord'. This, probably, was really all that happened. But, unfortunately, the incident sowed seeds of wishful thinking in several humble breasts:

'He [Lord William] was heard to say, before he left, that he would take me under his care, and see to my future advancement . . .' (who heard him, one asks). . . . 'These dazzling prospects not only wellnigh turned my brain, but decided my parents to send me to sea. To have their son an *officer* in the Navy was an unlooked-for honour, and they now entered into my plans and feelings with almost as much ardour as myself.'

Here indeed was Interest of the very highest order. Countess married to a First Lord! Patron actually in command of a frigate and a Duke's son! But—really, one would have expected the Duke's carpenter, the Countess's lady's-maid, even the Duke's gardener's boy, or at least one of them, to have known a little more about life as it was then lived. The very fact that Lord William knew the boy's background—and they knew he knew—should have warned them to stop daydreaming. Amid delicious bustle little Samuel was packed off to Gravesend, and, with a fluttering heart, yet intensely proud of his 'complete suit of sailor apparel—a tarpaulin hat, round blue jacket and wide pantaloons', he presented himself on board H.M. frigate *Macedonian*. . . .

Nobody had heard of him. His Lordship was not on board, but they let him stay. They put him in a mess of eight 'genuine weather-beaten old tars'. And there he remained.

'In performing the work assigned to me, which consisted in helping the seamen to take in provisions, powder and shot, I felt the insults and tyranny of the midshipmen. These little minions of power ordered and drove me round like a dog, nor did I and the other boys dare interpose a word. They were *officers*: their word was our law, and woe betide the presumptuous boy that dared refuse implicit obedience.'

So that was that. No one allowed *him* to have any doubt about whether he was 'quarter-deck' or 'lower deck'.

As it happened, he was not cut out for this sort of life. He hated every moment of it. He loathed the coarseness of the seamen's language, the brutality of the discipline. He had the sense to avoid trouble where possible by instant obedience to orders. He put the best face upon it that he could. But he got nowhere. After a while the *Macedonian* was engaged and captured by the U.S. heavy frigate *United States*. The prize was taken to New York, and Leech deserted, later—like many of his fellow-prisoners—joining the enemy's Navy. But his very first U.S. ship, the gun-brig *Syren*, met and surrendered to the British 74, *Medway*. Once again a prisoner, he was taken first to Cape Town and then to England. He was now in mortal danger. Were he recognized, he would certainly be hanged for desertion to the enemy. But now his luck was in. The war ended, prisoners were exchanged and, unrecognized, he was returned to New York. He continued for a time in the American service, but finding the discipline there nearly if not quite as brutal as in the Royal Navy, he left the sea for good and settled down as an American citizen. He was not a great man—though in his later years he was a very religious one—and he would never have made much of an officer. But the point is that he never had the remotest chance of becoming one. Late in the war (when he joined) there was no place at all on the Quarter-deck for the son of a valet and lady's-maid—unless, of course, he was also a tiger in a fight.

Yet earlier in the wars a young man with ambition could sometimes manage it, even without money. But he needed more worldly wisdom than the Leeches possessed, and he had to go the right way about it. Another young Samuel—Walters this time[1]—was the son of a carpenter practising in a small way in Ilfracombe: humble enough—in his way as humble as the Leeches. But, unlike them, he was not suddenly intoxicated by the prospect of becoming a gentleman. On the contrary, he decided that he would like to be one, and deliberately set about the task. To obtain a Lieutenant's commission seemed the surest and pleasantest way of doing it. So he started modestly. He was apprenticed as a Shipwright in a merchant ship and served out his time before the mast.

Among his fellow-townsmen was an up-and-coming family named Bowen. Their story in itself furnishes an interesting chapter in social history. There were five brothers, sons of an ex-merchant skipper. Richard, the third of them, was a very brilliant man. He had entered the Lower Deck young, and, by dint of real merit, had attracted the atten-

[1] *Samuel Walters, Lieutenant, R.N., His Memoirs*, edited by C. N. Parkinson, Liverpool, 1949.

tion of none other than Sir John Jervis, who thereafter 'protected' him, secured him a Lieutenancy, and saw to it that he was advanced successively to Commander and Captain. Jervis himself, a fine judge of men, predicted that he would go to the very top. So did Nelson. But it did not work out that way. He was killed, as Nelson so nearly was, in the abortive attack on Teneriffe in 1797. His younger brother George followed in his tracks and—having now a patron in the family—also rose to post-rank.

It was, then, to this family that young Walters attached himself: not to Richard or George, however, but to the second brother, John. This one, least successful of the five, was not even in the Navy, but a Captain in the East India Company. When he obtained command of a small Indiaman, Samuel joined up, still before the mast, as Shipwright's Mate. He made his voyage and two years later was home again, a sailor of some experience and no mean navigator, in which branch he had decided to specialize. His reason looks like deep calculation. Before he left the Indiaman he contrived to make a sufficient impression for Captain John to recommend him to the eldest of his brothers, James, who was just commissioning H.M.S. *Argo*.

But James Bowen must have a paragraph to himself. His was one of the success-stories of the war. He had begun, like his father, in the Merchant Service. Then, having learnt his navigation, he entered the Navy in that branch, and rose in due course to be a Master. As such he served for twelve years, and proved such a good and steady one that, on 1st June, 1794, he found himself Master of the *Queen Charlotte*, flagship of Admiral Lord Howe, and right under the great man's eye. The traditional story of what happened next is worth retelling. As the flagship neared the enemy line the Admiral cried, 'Starboard!' Bowen, plain, blunt and middle-aged, retorted, 'My Lord, you'll be foul of the French ship if you don't take care!' Howe, a saturnine-looking man—known indeed behind his back as 'Black Dick', though in fact he had a heart of gold—glared at him and snapped out, 'What's that to you, sir? Starboard!' At that Bowen gave the necessary order, adding in a loud whisper, 'Damned if I care, if you don't. I'll take you near enough to singe your black whiskers!' And he did. He brought the great three-decker so close under the Frenchman's stern that the tricolour at her ensign staff actually brushed the *Charlotte's* shrouds. 'Black Dick' was delighted, and, falling (metaphorically) upon Bowen's neck, promised him anything within reason that he liked to ask. Bowen suggested a commission, and the Admiral (who at that moment could do pretty nearly anything where Interest was concerned) not only procured it for him, but got him promoted to Commander in 1795 and to Captain two years later. Thereafter he never looked back. He was given jobs of the first importance and responsibility and later made a Commissioner of the Navy, a very lucrative post, becoming a Rear-Admiral in 1825. Here was indeed a unique career, for when he became a Lieutenant he was 43 years old, and in his wildest dreams could not have hoped to become a Captain at all, let alone a Flag-Officer. Nor apparently did his fortune spoil him, for Dillon, who served under him when he was a Captain, has nothing but good to say of him, his kindness and consideration for others.

But once more to Walters. See what this clever young man has done. He has found a patron: one, moreover, who has Interest out of all proportion to his social background: one ready to help a fellow-townsman, and especially one who was, like himself, a navigator. Help him he did. He had him on board as a First Class Volunteer—that is, in the true officer-succession (see p. 153): within six weeks Samuel was a Midshipman, and after seven years—only one more than the official minimum—he became a Lieutenant: officially, a Gentleman. He went no further; probably indeed did not deserve to, for his memoirs (parts of which are written in execrable verse) reveal a sensitive and artistic rather than a forceful personality.

Incidentally this story also illustrates the tendency, already mentioned, of the not-so-well-born Captain to introduce on to the Quarterdeck the not-so-well-born youngster. Though the Bowens were, socially, rather higher than the Walters, they were certainly not 'quarterdeck' in the then accepted sense.

A few more of these exceptional people are worth noticing. Alexander Wilson was one of the select band who ended with a Flag, though but a doubtful one. His career was not unlike James Bowen's. When first we hear of him he was Admiral's Coxswain to Sir Alexander Hood, later Lord Bridport. Now this rating was usually not only the man who steered the Admiral's barge: he was often his trusted body-servant as well, constantly about the Admiral's person. What Alexander did to induce his important namesake to 'adopt' him we are not told. All Marshall says—and O'Byrne copies him—is that his 'good conduct when Coxswain to the late Lord Bridport raised him to favour and promotion'. Anyway, his first commission is dated 1st June, 1794—the very day of the great battle in which he took part: and he was also in

Bridport's flagship a year later when that Admiral won his own battle off the Ile de Groix. For these, he was rewarded with two steps—to Commander and Captain—on the same days as Bowen. But thereafter he fell behind, because, in the last war-promotion, he was one of the few to be 'superannuated with the rank of Rear-Admiral': which was in fact the nearest thing then known to retirement.

James Hodgson had the experience of being pressed twice. This fate must have overtaken many lower deck men because, during the peace-interlude of Amiens, the Navy was largely demobilized (see graph, p. 119). He, however, came in earlier—in 1783, the last year of the American Independence War, when he was only 17. He was soon discharged, and returned, we presume, to his basic trade of merchant seaman. But he was only 27 when the Revolutionary War began in 1793, and therefore fair game for the very 'hot press' which then went into action. They got him again. This time he saw plenty of service, and made good, receiving his first commission after only four years—a remarkably short period of servitude for one in his position. But, though he continued to show his officer-like qualities on many occasions, he went no further, save that, forty years later, he was made a Retired Commander. This was indeed rather a typical 'lower-deck' officer's career. Exceptional merit could catch the eye of his Captain, who might get him on to the Quarter-deck: but thereafter, as we shall have occasion to see, he required an Interest altogether higher than a private captain's, or else the luck to be First Lieutenant in a general or single-ship action. Failing this, he would serve on as a working lieutenant—like Gardner's John Yetts—until (as happened to James Hodgson) he was rewarded with a snug billet ashore, at a Signal Station or in the Coast Guard.

We may conclude with the very curious case of David Ewen Bartholomew, an officer of whom it would be interesting to know more. Like Hodgson he was twice impressed, but the second occasion was altogether without precedent and caused considerable stir at the time. He came from Linlithgow, and he had already sailed before the mast in the Baltic and West Indies trades, and in the Greenland whale-fisheries. Then he was picked up by a gang in London in 1795. At that moment, it seems, he was just about to become a merchant-service officer, and he was no doubt disappointed. Yet he was a tough, able and persistent character, did well in various warships, and was warmly recommended to Sir Home Popham, of naval signals fame. This officer 'adopted' him, and made him Midshipman and Master's Mate in normal officer-sequence.

He also passed his Lieutenant's Examination, and was now fully qualified for his commission. But, before he obtained it, the Revolutionary War ended and he was discharged. Very soon, however, the Napoleonic War began.

He was under no obligation (save that of patriotism) to join up, and no press-gang found him. But, determined to become an officer in spite of his two disappointments, he wrote to the First Lord, fierce old St. Vincent, and asked for a commission which, he urged, not without reason, was his due. St. Vincent, who at the time was probably receiving hundreds of similar letters daily, replied very briefly with a refusal. Thereupon Bartholomew wrote again—and again. Ultimately, in fact, he wrote *eight* times. Then the First Lord lost patience. He sent for him, having first arranged with the officer of the local press-gang to be standing by in Whitehall. Bartholomew attended the summons, and was pressed then and there in the very hall of the Admiralty.

This caused a first-rate rumpus, which ended in the appointment of a Select Committee of the House of Commons. The thing was in fact partly political—St. Vincent had many enemies in Parliament. But there were legal objections too. There was no precedent for two features in the case. No First Lord, it appears, had ever before ordered the impressment of any individual by name: and it was exceedingly doubtful whether a man who had fulfilled all the qualifications essential for a commission was eligible for impressment at all. Obviously no officer could be impressed, as he was, *ipso facto*, a gentleman; and gentlemen were expressly exempted. The question was, was he near enough to being an officer to qualify for exemption as a gentleman?

The Select Committee sat, took evidence, and consulted five prominent naval officers. Three gave their opinion that the impressment was 'a violation of the ways of the Navy'; two thought not. The Committee accepted the majority opinion. Their report, printed by Marshall,[1] is a most interesting document, if only because the case seems to have turned on the *appearance* of the pressed man. Admiral Markham, the mouthpiece of the dissentients, based his justification of the impressment on the grounds that Bartholomew 'looked like a Boatswain'. But when everybody on the Committee had taken a good look at him, they decided that they 'cannot concur in describing his appearance to be at all like that of a Boatswain, or any such inferior officer', and accordingly pronounced in his favour.

[1] Under 'Post Captains of 1815'—Bartholomew, David.

But, as ever in this impressment business, 'possession was nine points of the law', and, long before the Parliamentary pundits had delivered their judgment, Bartholomew had been whisked off, passed through the Receiving Ship and safely drafted to sea. Nor, it would seem, was there anyone willing or influential enough to get him back. But Mr. Bartholomew did not mind; he was now patently on the road to success. His new Captain, from the first, gave him the duties, though he could not, of course, give him the commission, of Lieutenant. (St. Vincent left the Admiralty soon after, driven out by the politicians, though not as a direct result of the Bartholomew affair.) Then his old patron, Sir Home Popham, applied for him, and promotion was only a matter of time. It came in the form of the longed-for Lieutenancy in July, 1805. The sequel shows that it was well-deserved. He was evidently a most intrepid fellow: he performed all the dangerous tasks which came his way with marked success, and—even in the difficult later years of the war, when promotion was becoming harder to procure—he secured his second step to Commander in 1812. He was 'made post' in June, 1815. Both these last successes were won purely by merit. There is no evidence whatever of any particular backing. He was made a Companion of the Bath, also in 1815, and was employed even after the peace—a very rare achievement. But, sent to survey the Azores and the African coast, he succumbed to the climate and was buried at Porto Praya in 1821. David Bartholomew strikes one as a likely sort of man. It may not be discreet to pepper a First Lord with eight rounds of rapid pen-fire, especially when the target was so notorious a martinet as St. Vincent. But there is something refreshing about a man who knows so very exactly what he wants, and who gets it in the First Lord's teeth.

Indeed, all the members of the 'Working Class' officer-group were probably interesting people, whose stories would repay further study. That, however, is not easy because most of them reached the peak of their endeavours on the day they became 'officers and gentlemen'. Thereafter they were apt to descend again into the valley of obscurity.

B. MEN

If this be true of the few ultra-successful 'men' who became 'officers', it is evidently going to be a great deal truer of the infinitely larger numbers who did not. Indeed, we can go but little further than we have gone already, since no one ever did for the men what Marshall and

O'Byrne did for the officers. So it happens that the social backgrounds of very few individual men are known to us now, or even likely to be. Yet certain wide generalizations can be made, and they can hardly be wrong. For example, we shall discover later that something like three-quarters of the men comprising any ordinary Ship's Company were, by upbringing and training, seamen: and seafaring in this country was a markedly hereditary calling. To some considerable extent it still is, but it was more so 150 years ago. The sea-going community remained very much a race apart, of whom the ordinary landsman fought a little shy because they were so clannish and uncouth: in fact, so little like himself.

It is reasonable to suppose, then, that in a Table of Men's Parents compiled on lines like that of Officers' Parents, by far the largest group would be 'Seafaring Persons': and in all probability a Table of Grand-parents—and of Great-Grandparents too—would be just the same. Among the officers, we have seen, class-diffusion was wide, ranging from peers to humble craftsmen; and several of the groups and sub-groups run into hundreds each. Our hypothetical Table for the men, however, would not look like this at all. It would be a very top-heavy affair, with something like 75 per cent of them all grouped under the 'Sea-farer' heading. Only the last 25 per cent would be spread out—and spread, no doubt, over most of the trades and crafts then in existence. But though all but the 'Seafarer' group would be small, those many others would exist. 'The Boy who ran away to Sea', seeking adventure and dreaming of glory, is not entirely the product of the romantic novelist's imagination: nor is the slightly more orthodox youngster who badgered his parents into letting him go. Such might come from anywhere and from any home. Just such a one was poor little Leech from Oxfordshire. We are soon to meet, too, the famous—or infamous—Quota Men, many of whom were certainly not of sea-faring families, drawn as they were by law from every shire in the land. A few of such people are known to us, but not in large enough numbers to allow of any attempt at a satisfactory analysis. The fact is, we cannot delve into the men's parentage in detail. We must leave them 'in bulk'. It is a pity, but there it is.

CHAPTER II

HOMELAND: GEOGRAPHICAL DISTRIBUTION

A. OFFICERS

WE are now to use Marshall and O'Byrne again, for another purpose. They have helped us to collect, and analyse, the social backgrounds of 1,800 officers. They will also, with a little outside help, provide information on the home towns and counties of some 1,500. Many, indeed perhaps most, of this 1,500 are included in the 1,800, but not all. Those common to both lists are the officers who answered both the questions put to them by our authors—'Father's Name?' and 'Where born?' And most of the higher social-levels did so: or, even if they did not, their homes are not too difficult to discover from other sources. Peers and Baronets have well-known 'seats', while the usual formula for the 'landed' group is 'Son of A.B. Esq. of C.D., E-shire'. Among 'professional' sons, also, the representatives of Church, Law and Medicine are usually traceable to where their fathers ministered or practised. The other professions are not quite so simple, because the Navy, the Army and the Civil Service are all occupations which tend to take their practitioners away from the places of their origin.

On the other hand, there are several hundred names among the 1,500 which are not among the 1,800 at all. These were, mostly, men who, while shy of disclosing their birth, did not mind revealing their birthplace. The formula used by such folk is usually brief and to the point—'Z.Y. was born in Devon'; 'X.W. was born in Deal', or 'V.U. is a native of Fife'. Such people are useful, for, with them, we sense that we are breaking fresh ground *socially*. Perhaps half the 'working-class' sons that we have discovered (or think we have discovered) use one of these formulae—without mention of 'Father's Name'. The other half answers neither question. Yet it is this group which makes the 1,500, in its way, more representative than the 1,800, and therefore likely to provide a better cross-section of the whole geographical distribution than we could obtain from our social distribution. Thus, when we see in Table IV that the Devon quota of our 1,500 is easily the largest in England, we may take it as highly probable that Devon did actually produce more of the total number of English naval officers than did any other English county. For, with the 1,800, we had reason to suspect the upper social grades of being over-represented: but, here, there is not the same reason for suspecting any over-representation at all. So I have ventured, in Table IVA (Col. 4), to make an assessment of total numbers hailing from the leading counties. The figures are based upon the supposition that the home of one in every seven of our war-period officers has been discovered—that is, 1,500 out of 10,500: and all that has been done is to multiply the preceding column by seven. But evidently this very rough-and-ready estimate would become ever less and less accurate as the known numbers grew smaller. Thus, Devon's quota of 123, enlarged to 861 to represent the full quota of all officers, may not be wildly inaccurate: would be unlikely, for instance, to represent an error of more than 25 per cent. But if we do the same with Westmorland's solitary one-out-of-1,500, and assume seven-out-of-10,500, we might well be out by several hundred per cent. Quite arbitrarily, therefore, I have stopped the process when the enlarged total approximates to 100; that is, after the first twenty-three counties. The reader may easily pursue the policy to the end if it seems worthwhile. It must be emphasized, though, that all these 'estimated' figures are exceedingly tentative: indeed certain not to be *exactly* right: yet perhaps right enough to allow for the formation of a general picture.

From our Tables, too, we can assess the relative contributions of Britain's four components. The Census of 1801 gave England rather more than eight million inhabitants, and Scotland just over 1,600,000. England's population was just about five times that of Scotland. But as England's officer-contribution was also just about five times that of Scotland, their contributions *per capita* were almost exactly equal. Wales lagged behind. With about 560,000 people—rather more than a third of Scotland's total—she should have produced about seventy in order to keep on terms with her. But she supplied only forty-five. Ireland was even further behind. Her population in 1801 is not exactly known, but it must have been nearly three times that of Scotland: yet

TABLE IV
GEOGRAPHICAL DISTRIBUTION OF OFFICERS
1793–1815

A. ENGLAND

1	2	3	4	5	6
Order of Contribution	COUNTY	Contribution to Known 1,500	Estimated Total Contribution	Contribution per 10,000 of Population	Order per 10,000 of Population
1	Devonshire	123	861	3·62	2
2	Kent	106	742	3·44	3
3	Hampshire	89	623	4·06	1
4	London	61	427	·64	30
5	Cornwall	54	378	2·81	5
6	Somersetshire	47	329	1·72	10
7	Norfolk	40	280	1·47	12
8	Suffolk	38	266	1·81	7
9	Yorkshire	35	245	·41	36
10	Dorsetshire	29	203	2·51	6
11=	Northumberland	28	196	1·73	9
11=	Wiltshire	28	196	1·52	11
13	Staffordshire	27	189	1·11	18
14	Surrey	24	168	·89	20
15	Middlesex	23	161	3·22	4
16	Sussex	20	140	1·26	15
17=	Berkshire	16	112	1·45	13
17=	Herefordshire	16	112	1·80	8
17=	Northamptonshire	16	112	1·21	16
20=	Derbyshire	14	98	·86	21
20=	Essex	14	98	·61	31
20=	Gloucestershire	14	98	·56	32
20=	Leicestershire	14	98	1·08	19

she produced twenty-one *fewer* officers. In fine, per head of population, Wales was producing roughly twice as many as Ireland, while England and Scotland provided rather over three officers to Wales's two, and well over three to Ireland's one. These figures are recorded in no contentious spirit. Later we shall discover several reasons why the two more prosperous partners provided not only the greater actual numbers but also the higher proportions per head. More surprising to some, perhaps, will be the fine showing of Scotland. The profession of Sea-Officer in the eighteenth century has sometimes been regarded as some-

1 Order of Contribution	2 COUNTY OR ISLAND	3 Contribution to Known 1,500	5 Contribution per 10,000 of Population	6 Order per 10,000 of Population
24=	Hertfordshire	13	1·32	14
24=	Lancashire	13	·19	41
26=	Buckinghamshire	12	·65	29
26=	Durham	12	·81	22
28	Nottinghamshire	10	·71	26
29=	Cheshire	9	·46	34
29=	Warwickshire	9	·43	35
31	Cumberland	8	·68	27
32	Cambridgeshire	7	·79	25
33=	Oxfordshire	6	·55	33
33=	Lincolnshire	6	·29	38
35=	Bedfordshire	5	·79	24
35=	Shropshire	5	·30	37
37	Worcestershire	4	·27	39
38=	Huntingdonshire	3	·80	23
38=	Monmouthshire	3	·66	28
40	Rutland	2	1·20	17
41	Westmorland	1	·25	40
	TOTAL COUNTIES	1004	—	—
	Guernsey	11	—	—
	Man	5	—	—
	Jersey	2	—	—
	Alderney	2	—	—
	TOTAL, England	**1024**	**c. 1·20**	—

thing of a prerogative in southern hands: and this is true so far as England by itself is concerned, the English counties north of the Humber comparing but poorly with those south of it. But these tables show clearly enough that, further north still, in the Scottish Lowlands, the profession came into its own again, only to fade off once more as the Highlands were reached.

Let us now take the countries separately.

A. England

The first thing to notice is the predominance of the sea-shires. If for this purpose we count London as one, the first ten were all sea-counties.

The list is headed by three south-coast shires, well ahead of the rest—Devonshire, Kent and Hampshire. Their pre-eminence should cause no surprise. Devon has two waterfronts, each pierced with natural harbours well-suited for deep-water ports. Since the middle ages the sea has flowed freely in the veins of Devonians, both 'gentle' and otherwise. Kent has salt water on three sides. It has been consistently maritime ever since the Romans made Richborough their entry-port: and it contained four of the five original Cinque Ports. Hampshire has its deep sheltered Solent, its ideal anchorage at Spithead, its several inlets (including the commercial Southampton Water) where many of our early ships were built. Each contains, too, one of the traditional homes of the Navy—Plymouth, Chatham and, above all, Portsmouth, which became our main base not far off five centuries ago, and has usually remained so.

In these towns the naval element was—and is—both strong and static, and in the surrounding country naval families tended to settle in great numbers. They still do, especially round Portsmouth, though not quite so much now, perhaps, round the others.

London comes fourth, by virtue not only of its port but also of its teeming population: for though the 'Great Wen' was not nearly so monstrous as it is now, it still exceeded its nearest rivals in proportions very like the modern ones. But our figures may flatter London somewhat, because men 'born in London' were not necessarily Londoners. Cornwall comes fifth, easily the most sea-gripped county in England, with a hinterland not fertile enough to lure its people from the sea, and with its age-old tin-works beginning to give out. Its traditional preoccupations—some picturesquely exaggerated—were fishing, smuggling, wrecking and, in earlier days, piracy—all, reputable and disreputable alike, sea-occupations.

Somerset comes sixth: surprisingly, because her coastline is none too good for shipping. It is true that Bristol, then England's second port, lay only just across the Avon and spilt into Somerset: and a number of its forty-seven officers seem to have been nearly if not quite Bristolians. Yet probably it was not Bristol that brought Somerset to sixth place. Rather, it was Bath. So many 'gentry' came there for its waters, and often stayed for so long that, by the law of averages, an undue proportion of their ladies were brought to bed there. 'Born at Bath' is certainly a very common entry. This peculiarity has been allowed for where possible in making this analysis. Whenever the family of anyone 'born at Bath' was locatable elsewhere, that 'elsewhere' was chosen as his real home. But this was not always possible: and there were, naturally, a number of genuine residents—at least, their parents were such—'a respectable merchant of Bath' (Marshall) or 'an eminent physician of Bath' (O'Byrne). In spite of all precautions, however, Bath's famous waters have probably won for Somerset rather too high a place.

Two East Anglian counties, Norfolk and Suffolk, come seventh and eighth, but Essex—twentieth—lags far behind. It is indeed some of the lagging sea-shires that are most interesting. Yorkshire, far the biggest of all, does poorly. Though much of its huge acreage was then sparsely-populated moorland, and much of its coastline straight and uneventful, it still had (but for London) much the greatest number of inhabitants—nearly 860,000—and not inconsiderable shipping activities on the Humber in the south and on the Tees in the north. It comes ninth but, as we shall see, very much lower when its population is taken into account. Again, if Yorkshire fared no better, one might expect Northumberland to have fared a good deal worse. It does well, however, providing only seven fewer than Yorkshire. One reason for this may be that, like Cornwall, Northumberland held out few rival attractions by way of career for the landed gentleman, and especially his younger sons. Then there is Dorset—tenth—which does rather well, and Sussex—sixteenth—which one might expect to do better, for it had a long seaboard and was endowed with more than the average number of 'seats'. Of Durham—twenty-sixth—perhaps not much was to be expected, but what of Lancashire—twenty-fourth, and after Yorkshire the most populous county in England? There, perhaps, Trade proved too strong a rival attraction to War. Lastly, what of Lincolnshire—thirty-third? Here, probably, the historical social pattern of the county provides an explanation. Much of it, particularly its low-lying parts, has always been the home of the very small land-owner, of peasant stock, but not of landed gentry with 'Quarter-deck' pretensions.

Little need be said of the land-shires. All their figures are rather low. Wiltshire—eleventh—leads the field, the others following at short intervals until the tail is brought up by Rutland—two—and Westmorland—one. The former's smallness, in both area and population, and its very 'inland' position are quite sufficient to account for its lowly place, while Westmorland remained as wild and untamed as any part of the country.

Could it be contrived, though unfortunately it cannot, to insert upon our map of England one dot to indicate the actual home of each known

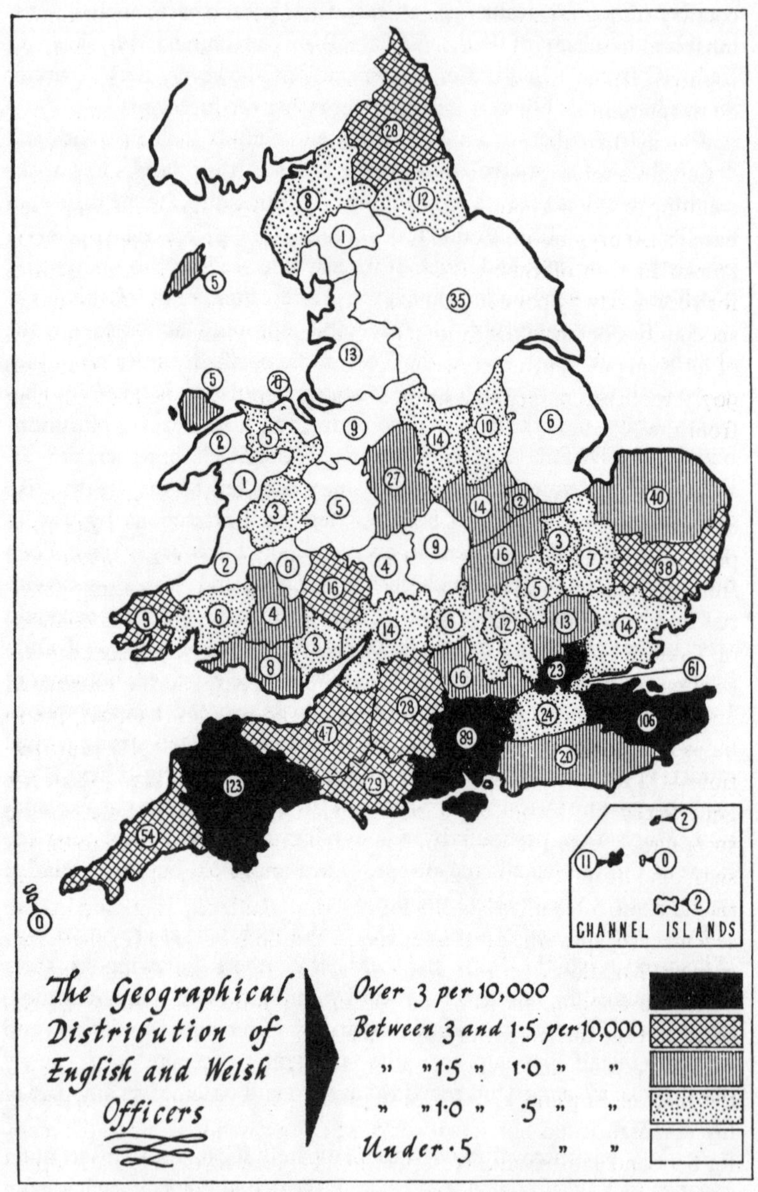
CHANNEL ISLANDS
The Geographical Distribution of English and Welsh Officers
Over 3 per 10,000
Between 3 and 1·5 per 10,000
" "1·5 " 1·0 " "
" "1·0 " ·5 " "
Under ·5 " "

officer, the pattern, probably, would spread fairly evenly over the whole country (though, naturally, the dots would be rarer in the more thinly-inhabited localities). These dots would represent, for the most part, the country seats of 'Land', Baronetcy and Peerage. The sea-shires would be so spotted too, but would show, in addition, larger concentrations of dots along their sea-coasts and even thicker clumps about their ports.

Certain simple comparisons emerge from all this. First—and again counting London as one—twenty English counties touch the sea, some barely: twenty-one do not. The former contributed 747 of the 1,004 known English officers: the latter, 257. The sea-shires, then, account for very nearly 75 per cent, the land-shires for 25 per cent. Second, the six counties north of the Humber, which comprise more than a quarter of all England, sent ninety-seven officers: those south of the Humber, 907. More than 90 per cent came from the South, less than 10 per cent from the North.

So far we have concerned ourselves only with the gross contributions of each county for this was our practical aim—to discover from what parts of England our officers came. Yet something else can be abstracted from the same figures—the relative contributions of the various counties in terms of their populations. These are shown in the last columns of Table IV, A. B. and C. (5 and 6), where the county-populations according to the 1801 Census are taken into account, and the number of known naval officers per each 10,000 of the population is shown. It will be seen that the three south-coast shires which led in total contributions still lead in contributions-per-head, though now Hampshire has gone ahead of Devon and Kent. London, Yorkshire and Lancashire sustain the greatest falls—from fourth to thirtieth, from ninth to thirty-sixth and from twenty-fourth to forty-first respectively. Middlesex, rising from fifteenth place to fourth, and Rutland, from fortieth to seventeenth, show the greatest advance. But both of these are somewhat suspect, Middlesex because some of its figures should almost certainly belong to London, and Rutland because the numbers involved are too small to bear the weight of any conclusion.

Both 'actual' and 'relative' county-contributions are indicated on the map of England and Wales opposite. With the small numbers at my disposal, it did not seem worth while to provide comparable maps for Scotland and Ireland. Nor, in either Table or map, have I attempted any 'Contribution per 10,000' for Ireland, because her population-figures for 1801 are much too uncertain to rely upon. But the Anglo-Welsh map shows two things—first, the actual number known to have come from each county, the figure being shown, in each case, within a small circle; and, second, the 'contribution per 10,000', indicated in five degrees of hatching.

There remain the islands. Wight was part of Hampshire, and under Hampshire her sons are included in the Table. Man, far off the track of the French Wars, produced five officers, not perhaps many for a population so largely maritime. The Channel Islands, however, right in the track of the wars, did better. Their contribution was fifteen officers. Of these, Guernsey is outstanding with eleven—a very remarkable record for an island with a population barely as large as Rutland's, and an acreage barely one-fifth of it. Moreover, among the eleven was one of the war's greatest sailors, James, Lord Saumarez. No Scillonian is mentioned, but one or two may have been entered as Cornishmen.

B. *Wales*

The Principality was not well represented in the Navy of the day. Much of it was still wild, backward country: the various parts of it were detached from each other: most of it was singularly remote from

TABLE IV

B. WALES

1 Order of Contribution	2 COUNTY	3 Contribution to known 1,500	5 Contribution per 10,000 of Population	6 Order per 10,000 of Population
1	Pembroke	9	1.61	1
2	Glamorgan	8	1·13	4
3	Carmarthen	6	·90	5
4=	Anglesey	5	1·48	2
4=	Denbigh	5	·83	6
6	Brecknock	4	1·24	3
7	Montgomery	3	·63	7
8=	Caernarvon	2	·48	8
8=	Cardigan	2	·46	9
10	Merioneth	1	·36	10
11=	Flint and Radnor	0	0	11=
	TOTAL, Wales	**45**	**c. ·60**	**—**

its bigger neighbour; and there was a language problem. As all but three of its counties have sea-coasts, no comparison between sea- and land-shires is profitable. But—as in England—the South did better than the North, its six counties giving twenty-nine officers to the North's sixteen. Another superficial resemblance is that its three south-facing sea-shires, Pembroke, Carmarthen and Glamorgan, furnished just over half the Principality's total. Pembroke—'Little England beyond Wales'—led the way. It had, even then, many close associations with the Royal Navy which had, in and after 1814, a permanent home at Pembroke Docks on the harbour of Milford Haven. Many of its people too were not only seafaring: they spoke English as their mother tongue. Glamorgan came next. It already had some commerce and a little industry, but the scale of it may be measured by the fact that, in 1790, Swansea was the proud possessor of two churches and 400 houses, while, in 1801, Cardiff boasted a population of 2,000! The little county of Flint, though a sea-shire, had no representative in Marshall or O'Byrne: nor had Radnor.

C. *Scotland*

Scotland, for our purposes here, may be likened to a sandwich. Its outer layers—pretty crusty ones too—were the Southern Highlands, and the inordinately thick northern slice consisting of the Grampians and the wild country beyond the Caledonian Canal. The comparatively slender slice of 'meat' in the middle was the Lowland Plain, with an extension east and north up the coastal plain to Aberdeen. This area contains the rivers and estuaries of Clyde, Forth and Tay; and the sixteen counties which compose it, or extend down into it, provided 154 of the known 197 officers: that is, over 78 per cent. But the Southern Highlands were not unrepresented. Thus the border—and landlocked—county of Roxburgh produced the surprisingly large number of ten, and, to the west, Dumfries, on Solway Firth, and sea-girt Wigtown contributed six and seven respectively. But once the real Lowlands were reached, the numbers rose considerably. Much the highest figures came from the Forth area. Midlothian (containing Leith and Edinburgh) brought in twenty-two, and, highest of all, Fife, on the north of the estuary, had twenty-nine. If we would bring these figures into line with those of the most prolific English counties, we should, as we saw (p. 61), multiply them by five. This would give us 145 for Fife, to set alongside Devon's 123, and 110 for Midlothian, which approximates

TABLE IV

C. SCOTLAND

1	2	3	5	6
Order of Contribution	COUNTY	Contribution to known 1500	Contribution per 10,000 of Population	Order per 10,000 of Population
1	Fife	29	3·09	3
2	Midlothian	22	1·80	6
3	Lanark	17	1·15	14=
4	Perth	15	1·19	12
5	Aberdeen	14	1·16	13
6	Roxburgh	10	2·97	5
7	Forfar (Angus)	8	·81	22
8=	Argyll	7	·86	20
8=	Ayr	7	·85	21
8=	Stirling	7	1·38	9
8=	Wigtown	7	3·06	4
12=	West Lothian	6	3·37	2
12=	Dumfries	6	1·10	17
14=	Berwickshire	5	1·66	7
14=	Renfrew	5	·64	25
16	Banff	4	1·08	18
17=	Caithness	3	1·33	10
17=	East Lothian	3	·66	24
17=	Inverness	3	·41	27
17=	Kincardine	3	1·14	16
17=	Orkney	3	1·23	11
17=	Selkirk	3	5·57	1
23=	Kirkcudbright	2	·68	23
23=	Ross and Cromarty	2	·36	28=
23=	Sutherland	2	·87	19
26=	Kinross	1	1·49	8
26=	Moray (Elgin)	1	·36	28=
26=	Peebles	1	1·15	14=
26=	Shetland	1	·45	26
30=	Bute	0	·00	30=
30=	Clackmannan	0	·00	30=
30=	Dumbarton	0	·00	30=
30=	Nairn	0	·00	30=
	TOTAL, Scotland	197	1·22	—

closely to Kent's 106. So, at the top as elsewhere, Scotland was doing just as well as England. Fife, like Kent, has salt-water on three sides of it, which no doubt helps to explain its lead among the Scottish counties. The third in the order was Lanark, with Glasgow and the upper Clyde. But the Firth itself is not so well represented, Renfrew on the south producing only five officers, and Dumbarton on the north, none. To the west of that, the plain is lost in the south-western spurs of the Grampians.

Proceeding north, now, from the Firth of Forth and Fifeshire, we reach the large (but only just maritime) shire of Perth. That comes fourth on the list, most of the officers which it provided coming from its south-eastern corner, where Perth itself stands upon the Tay. A good way down the Firth stands Dundee, in Angus, always a considerable port: and Angus stood seventh on the list. Now the plain narrows as we pass through Kincardine (with only three officers), and then we are at Aberdeen, also an old maritime and fishery centre. This county comes fifth, with a contribution of fourteen.

There remains the central massif of the Grampians, the rough country to the north and west of the Great Glen, and the yet more remote Western Isles, the Inner and Outer Hebrides. This, the true Highlands, was even then only beginning to play a conscious part in the corporate life of Great Britain. One full lifetime had not passed since Prestonpans and Culloden, and lowlanders had hardly forgotten the tartaned hordes with bared claymores and fiery crosses who brought death and ruin to their homes. To these warriors themselves, though much more civilized than of yore, it must have seemed a very far cry from the wild glens of the North to the trim, taut discipline of the Royal Navy. And very few had made the passage as yet. The four north and north-western shires (which include Skye and the Outer Hebrides) produced between them ten officers: and this area is rather more than one-third of Scotland.

Here, as in England, we should probably find an even, if dispersed, array of dots on the map could we but enter each man in his right place: but only, of course, in country where 'landed' folk had their estates. Again, too, we should find heavier concentrations along the lowland rivers and estuaries, and in towns along the coast. It is here indeed that we become aware of the frequency of the formulae 'born in Midlothian' and 'a native of Fife'—unaccompanied by 'Father's Name'. This awakens the suspicion that a goodly proportion of true lower-deck promotions came from these parts. And why not? They were tough, enterprising folk, rich in seafaring experience, in native shrewdness and, by comparison with most of England, in education. They were just the kind to catch the Captain's eye when hot work was afoot. Once on the Quarter-deck, they would make admirable Larmours and Yettses; and, though they might look a little out of place in the Captain's Cabin, they did not often rise to occupy it.

Yet good chances would come their way. The Scots were clannish people, and, once a Scot made good, becoming a Post Captain and commanding a ship, he would not hesitate to afford his 'protection' to the lads of his homeland. Just as the Gunrooms and Orlop-decks of titled Captains would teem with well-born youngsters, and those of Tarpaulin Captains with much humbler ones, so Geography often played a role similar to Class. When Lieutenant Dillon joined the *Glenmore*—a frigate, by the way, built of fir-trees from the Great Glen—he found that

'the officers appeared a nice set of gentlemen, but, the Captain being a Scot, they were all, nearly, from the same country, so that I found myself a sort of lonely person among them'.[1]

The Captain was George Duff, later to fall at Trafalgar while commanding the *Mars*. He certainly had some of the characteristics which unkind Sassenachs delight in attributing to the inhabitants of Aberdeen: to which county his wife, if not indeed himself, belonged.

'We were invited to dine in rotation with our Captain, at whose table the strictest frugality prevailed . . . The instant the quantity allowed was expended we rose, and the party broke up. It had more the bearing of a ceremonial meeting than a sociable one.'

This racial bar—for to such it almost amounted—led to certain minor unpleasantnesses, some of which had whimsical sequels. Dillon, young, pleasure-loving and liberal in his ways, found his companions a dour, economical lot.

'The next thing to annoy me was to observe that my messmates lived on the ship's provisions. Salt pork and beef would not renovate me after all my fatigues.'

He therefore laid in a private stock of fresh mutton for himself, and had it served to him by his servant at the common mess-table. In a

[1] *Narrative*, N.R.S., Vol. XCIII, p. 327.

strife of wills, and abetted by the savoury smell of roast mutton, Dillon prevailed.

'My messmates at first declined partaking of any. But it soon became evident that they were ashamed of not keeping a better table. They then agreed to purchase stock, helped themselves to my mutton, and offered to take the others off my hands.'

After this, things moved placidly enough until the *Glenmore* anchored in the Cove of Cork. Here the gay Dillon conceived the idea of a party on board to repay the hospitality of the local gentry. He was backed by the Scots Surgeon, but, of the other four in the mess, 'three would not join in anything leading to expense', and stood out. The Captain, when approached, allowed the ship to be used, but made an excuse to avoid attending. Undaunted by this lukewarmness, however, Dillon persisted, and the party was a huge success. National characteristics will out: and out they came here. After much thought Dillon had invited twenty-eight people, though he had the worldly wisdom to prepare for forty. One hundred and fifty arrived, and had a roaring time. After that, even Dillon was hardly able to keep pace with the invitations which showered upon him.

D. *Ireland*

There were ships as redolent of Ireland as the Scots ships were of Scotland: commanded by Irish captains, officered mainly by Irish officers, and largely manned by Irishmen. Ordinary day-to-day life aboard some of them must have been unusual, even exciting, because, beyond doubt, many of these 'Paddy Captains' did live up to what is expected of that volatile race. They got things done—they were fine natural leaders—but not usually in the sober way which obtained in English ships. One such Hibernian 'character' was Henry Darby, who commanded the *Bellerophon*, 74, at the Nile, and was wounded when his ship was dismasted in her desperately uneven fight with the enemy's three-decker flagship. Another was the Hon. Thomas Pakenham, son of Lord Longford, an eccentric and by no means mealy-mouthed officer who was the licensed wag of Howe's fleet in 1794.

Countless anecdotes about the Glorious First of June ran round the country, and several concerned this picturesque gentleman. Having fought a French ship to a standstill and completely silenced her, it was

TABLE IV

D. IRELAND

1 Order of Contribution	2 COUNTY	3 Contribution to known 1500
1	Cork	33
2	Dublin	22
3	Westmeath	13
4=	Wexford	11
4=	Tipperary	11
6	Waterford	10
7	Limerick	9
8=	Down	8
8=	Clare	8
10	Antrim	7
11	Queen's County	6
12=	Kildare	4
12=	Kerry	4
12=	Tyrone	4
15=	Meath	3
15=	Mayo	3
15=	Sligo	3
15=	Londonderry	3
19=	Louth	2
19=	Donegal	2
19=	Galway	2
22=	Roscommon	1
22=	Leitrim	1
22=	Wicklow	1
22=	Kilkenny	1
22=	Carlow	1
22=	Cavan	1
22=	Armagh	1
22=	Monaghan	1
30=	Fermanagh	0
30=	King's County	0
30=	Longford	0
	TOTAL, Ireland	**176**

said, Pakenham hailed her through a speaking trumpet with a string of oaths:—'—, —, you! Have you surrendered?' Back came a faint reply —'Non, Monsieur.' 'Then,' he thundered, aggrieved to the very soul, 'why the — don't you go on firing?' His most famous quip has often been retold in various forms. The battle was fought on a Sunday, and when it was over his ship chanced upon the mastless *Defence*, wallowing in the sea. This ship, commanded by the highly evangelical James Gambier, had covered herself with glory as the first to engage. As Pakenham came within hail, out came his trumpet, and he bawled across the waves, 'No time for prayers today, eh? But never mind, Jemmy. Whom the Lord loveth he chasteneth!' Dillon, who was an eyewitness, adds a lesser-known tail-piece. Gambier, after making a suitable answer, asked Pakenham if he had many men killed: to which the Irishman replied, 'Damme if *I* know. They won't tell me, for fear I should stop their grog!'[1]

[1] N.R.S., Vol. XCIII, p. 137.

Later he sent a boat to the *Defence*, to offer assistance. Like many captains, he was in the habit of dressing his men, and especially his boat's crew, all in the same rig, and that of his own designing. This was fair enough, since neither then nor for the next sixty years was there an official uniform for seamen. But Pakenham, it seems, went one better. When his emissary (whose name, M'Guire, betrays his origin) reached the gangway of the *Defence*, no one in that ship could make out what he was, he being 'dressed in a guernsey jacket with a welch wig' like the rest of the boat's crew. But 'when he reached the Quarter-deck we ascertained by the buttons on his smalls that he was a Lieutenant'. And not a very polished one either because, when Gambier addressed him, he replied with such a spate of oaths that the pious captain fairly ran away: and M'Guire, finding that everyone ignored him (for oaths cost a shilling each in the *Defence*[1]), soon took himself off, puzzled at his cool reception. Like master like man. Dillon, who was in many ways strait-laced himself and always ultra-conservative, did not approve of such aberrations in the Service. Yet he could not deny Pakenham's competence as an officer, though the 'discipline established on board the *Invincible*' was 'in direct opposition to the established rules of the Navy'. Incidentally, he is far more critical of Captain Duff's discipline in the all-Scots *Glenmore*, which he thought altogether too soft.

The Ireland of that day was very rich in lesser landed gentlemen but in little else: and their pedigrees were often longer than their purses. They formed a sort of closed aristocracy, the gulf between themselves and the true peasantry being quite unbridgeable. This probably helps to explain why Ireland's quota of officers was so much smaller than Scotland's. Whereas the 'lower deck' Scot always had a sporting chance of winning through to the Quarter-deck, his opposite

[1] The Regulations (1790) in force at the time laid down the following tariff for swearing, to be exacted by the Captain:

Commissioned Officers, for each offence, one shilling fine.

Warrant Officers, for each offence, sixpence fine.

Men, 'to punish them by causing them to wear a wooden Collar or some other shameful Badge of Distinction, for so long a time as he shall judge proper'.

Gambier enforced all these, including the collar (which he weighted with two 32-pound shots), making the culprit walk the Poop for several hours on end. But very few Captains paid any attention to the Order and, in 1806, it disappeared from the Regulations. See Dillon, op. cit., N.R.S., Vol. XCIII, pp. 97 and 104.

number in Ireland was too illiterate, poor and down-trodden to have any chance at all. And much the same holds on the commercial level. There were many industrious merchant and business families on the rise in Scotland, but in Ireland many fewer. So most of Ireland's 176 officers were sons of 'landed' folk, with a number of professional people and a few 'commercial' sons from Dublin. Few if any were 'lower deck'. Yet let no one think that any disparagement of the Irish as seamen is intended. Indeed no: as seamen-ratings their reputation stood very high, and they were much sought after by captains building up their complements. J. A. Gardner admirably sums up the Navy's attitude towards its 'Paddies':

'We had some from that land which produces the finest peasantry in the world on board . . . We had the O'Ryans, the O'Gallaghers, the Macartys, the O'Donovans, the Murphys, the O'Flahertys and the O'Flanagans; and great part of the Ship's Company were Irish, and very quiet when not disturbed.'[1]

But apparently, when disturbed, quite the other thing! Gardner goes on to tell of a

'tall, raw-boned Irishman, a Garry-owen boy that stood up manfully for the honour of his country . . . who did positively beat, at the back of the Point, Portsmouth, eleven men by cracking their heads at single-stick one after another'.

And he matches him with another who was seven feet high and was the terror of Devonport 'flourishing a shillelagh of enormous size, so that the constables when called out would fly like chaff at the very sight of him. He was, like the rest of his country, honest and brave, but woe betide those that insulted him.' When some facetious shipwrights called him a 'walking flagpole', he knocked several of them down, and challenged twelve more to fight him two at a time. They refused.

Such temperamental people were sometimes a nuisance, no doubt. Yet, when it came to the real test of battle and their blood was up, the Paddies were often irresistible, a mad humour blending with their devilry. A Cooper (or 'Bungs', as he was generically named) gives an unforgettable picture of one such occasion. The battle was at its height, when a wild Irish gun's-crew seized upon his 'study' (or cooper's

[1] N.R.S., Vol. XXXI, p. 51.

anvil) which he thought he had concealed, and, hooking it into their gun's mouth, fired it at point-blank range right through the enemy's side, causing a gaping hole and screaming like men possessed, 'Bungs for ever!'[1]

The geographical distribution of the Irish officers has some odd features. The numbers from the sea-board counties predominate, as expected. The proportion is 133 'sea' to forty-three 'inland' counties, three of the latter—Fermanagh, King's County and Longford—being unrepresented. But why should Wicklow, with its long coastline lying between Dublin (which boasted twenty-two) and Wexford (eleven), furnish only one? The outer pair, it is true, both contain considerable posts, while Wicklow, containing none, is largely mountainous. But there was surely some 'landed' element? Again, why does Westmeath, wholly landlocked, produce thirteen, enough to bring it up to third place in the whole country?

Classified by provinces, too, some of the figures are unexpected. Munster comes first with seventy-five, and Leinster next with sixty-four. This is not surprising. Munster contained the most maritime of the counties, led by Cork with thirty-three officers. This is almost phenomenal. Cork not only heads the Irish counties. It easily surpasses, in proportion, any county in the British Isles. Devon's contribution to the English total was just 8 per cent: Fife's share of the Scottish quota was barely 15 per cent. In Ireland, Cork's contribution was 19 per cent. Its many local land-owners bore close affinities to the British, while its admirable harbour, the Cove, was much used by the Royal Navy; its wartime base in Southern Ireland, and the assembly-point of trans-Atlantic convoys. Most of the other Munster counties supported it too. Tipperary came fourth in the list; Waterford sixth; Limerick seventh; Clare eighth; Kerry twelfth. As to Leinster, its nucleus was Dublin, second on the list with twenty-two officers; the long-established seat of government, the centre of officialdom, the home of such 'big business' as Ireland possessed. It also included Wexford, another port often used by the Navy, while the old 'Pale' country to the west of the capital was occupied by the most pro-English of the gentry.

The other two provinces show a remarkable falling-off. From Connaught, whose five counties between them supplied only ten officers, not much was to be expected, because it was still something of a 'wild west' comparable with the north-west of Scotland. But Ulster's weak-

[1] John Nicol, p. 58. See below, p. 91, note.

ness is less accountable. Only twenty-six officers came from the whole of it, and that the large old Ulster of nine counties, not the modern Northern Ireland of six—though this distinction made but little difference as Cavan, Donegal and Monaghan provided only four between them. County Down led with eight: Antrim (though it holds Belfast) had only seven, and the rest were nowhere. Can it be that Ulstermen were more chary than the others in answering Marshall's and O'Byrne's questions?

The distribution is certainly uneven, as a practical experiment will show. Follow up the Shannon from its mouth to Lough Ree, then cut across country to Dundalk in County Louth, thus dividing the island into two fairly equal parts. From the south-east half came 139 of our known officers; from the north-west half, thirty-seven: roughly 80 per cent from south-east, 20 per cent from north-west.

E. and F. Overseas

Of our 1,500, 1,442 are now traced to their homes. One more group, of fifty-eight, remains. It is wide-ranging, yet all in it have one thing in common—they were born overseas. Most of them—fifty—first drew breath in a British colony or possession. Let us take them first. All continents save Africa are represented.

TABLE IV

E. OVERSEAS (**British Empire**)				*F. OVERSEAS* (**Foreigners**)	
I	Europe		5	Hanover	4
II	Asia		3	France	2
III	Australia		1	Corsica	1
IV	America, Islands ...	21	41	Russia	1
	,, Mainland	20			
TOTAL, Overseas (British Empire)			50	**TOTAL, Overseas (Foreigners)**	8

Five came from Europe: three from Gibraltar and one each from Minorca and Malta. Four had British parents, the fifth was a native of Malta named Joseph Camillieri. His father, Gabriel, had been our staunch supporter during the long blockade which led to the island's capture in 1800, and had had most of his property confiscated by the French as a result. As some form of compensation to him, his son was taken into the Navy, given a commission and later made a Commander. He married a Kentish wife and settled down in England.

Next come three Asian representatives, though all of British birth:

sons of Anglo-Indians in official positions, and hailing, one each, from the dependencies of Bombay, Calcutta and Madras.

There was one representative from Australia. He described himself as of New South Wales, but that is all he has to say.

The contingent from the New World is much larger, and may be subdivided into men from the islands and men from the mainland.

There were twenty-one from the islands. One came from Newfoundland, two from Bermuda, and two from the Bahamas. One of the last-named rose to considerable naval eminence in his day. He was that same James Gambier whom we last saw running from the foul-mouthed M'Guire. His father was Lieutenant Governor of the Bahamas, and he was born at New Providence. Though he became a Peer and an Admiral of the Fleet, the impression he has left behind is not that of a great man, but rather of one particularly adept at playing his cards.[1]

The other sixteen Islanders all came from the West Indies. Of these, four belonged to Jamaica, one labelled himself vaguely as coming from 'the West Indies'. The other eleven all came from the Lesser Antilles. These islands, though small in size, had a wealth and importance far beyond their acreage because of the flourishing and remunerative sugar industry. They had their communities of prosperous estate-owners, and a close and constant connection with the Navy which, in wartime, invariably spent much of its time protecting them from their natural enemies in the French-held islands. Since 'Sugar' always commanded powerful parliamentary interest in England, a planter could usually find a suitable patron for son or nephew: and, had the will been as good as the opportunity, there might have been many more 'planter' officers. But in fact the movement was often the other way. There are a good many cases on record of naval officers on the West Indian Station marrying planters' daughters, leaving the Navy, and devoting themselves to the lucrative business of sugar-growing. The contributors to our officer-list were Antigua (three), Nevis (three), Barbados (two), and Dominica, Montserrat and St. Kitts (one each).

The other American contingent was the men from the mainland. There were twenty of them, and all but one (from British Guiana) were from North America. One was 'from Canada'; eight from Nova Scotia. Many British people lived and worked here, especially after the influx

[1] He enjoyed many important commands, but his actual sea-time when given his flag was only 5½ years. His aunt was married to Lord Barham, Comptroller of the Navy and First Lord of the Admiralty.

of Loyalists in (and after) 1783. Here were two British naval bases, St. John and Halifax, destined to become very active during the 1812–15 War. One of these Canadians was a distinguished officer—that same Admiral Sir Benjamin Hallowell (later Carew) who, as a Captain, after the Nile battle, sent Nelson the most original *memento mori* in the shape of a coffin fashioned from the timbers of the shattered *Orient*.

The remaining ten also came from the mainland of North America. Their birthplaces were: Massachusetts (two); New Jersey (one); New York (two); Rhode Island (two); Virginia (two), and 'America' (one). Why, then, do we call them British subjects? Because that is just what they were, both by birth and by choice. The oddity lies, not in the event itself, but in the timing of it. At the moment when these officers were born, and even, in most cases, when they joined the Service, Massachusetts, New York, etc. were not States of the U.S.A., but colonies of Great Britain: and the ten fathers concerned were ordinary British colonists of the pre-rebellion era who had every right to send their sons to serve in the Royal Navy, there to earn, if they could, the commission of their Sovereign, King George III. No American father (so far as is known to me) having become a citizen of the U.S.A. *then* sent his son into the Royal Navy: but not one of the ten sons, having secured a commission from King George, relinquished it to take up American citizenship.

The men in the last group of all, eight strong, were born on foreign soil. Yet even here four of them were subjects of George—not King George, but Elector George, for they were Hanoverians. So they too carried their Sovereign's commission. Of the rest, one came from Corsica, his naval link, no doubt, dating from the period (1793–5) when we were occupying the island. One came from Russia; not Russian by birth, however, but a member of the British colony of officers, technicians and commercial experts first invited into the country by Catherine the Great. The last two were Frenchmen—a circumstance not so odd when we recall that, throughout the wars, there were whole classes, even whole districts, which never took kindly to either the Republic or the Emperor.

B. MEN

Little more space will be accorded to the geographical distribution of the Lower Deck than was given to its social background. The reason, however, is quite different. It was lack of knowledge then. It is an overpowering surfeit of knowledge now; so overwhelming indeed that to analyse it in tabular form would be a matter, probably, of many years' labour. And it would not repay the doing. The necessary material, or most of it, is to be found in the muster-books of the ships. Every ship had one, written up every two months, and most of them survive. They carry a column headed 'Place and County where born'. So, theoretically, it could be done. But what an undertaking! We should certainly be dealing with many hundreds of thousands of individuals, and probably with several millions of entries, since most names would appear in several ships and in many muster-books of each. Moreover, the patient tabulator would have the fun of trying to follow all the John Smiths and the Tom Joneses through the whole length of their naval careers. But the strongest argument against attempting such a task is this. A comparatively cursory glance over a selection of the books leads to the conclusion, amounting to a virtual certainty, that the final answer can be deduced, accurately enough for all practical purposes, from other and much simpler sources. For instance, since we know that a very large number of them were the sons of seafaring persons, it is only reasonable to suppose that they hailed from the sea-shires, where almost all seafaring persons lived when ashore. And so it proves. In any muster-book taken at random an overwhelming proportion of the place-names and counties mentioned are by the sea. Further—and it must be admitted that, here, the count has been only cursory—there is little doubt that, should this hypothetical table be compiled, we should find the counties represented in much the same proportions as we found them in the corresponding officer-table. Devon, Kent and Hampshire in England, Fife and Midlothian in Scotland, and Cork and Dublin in Ireland would lead handsomely, and for the same sort of reasons. Indeed, in all probability, they would establish even bigger leads because, relatively, the contributions of the inland areas would be much smaller. In the officers' Table the heavy concentrations lay around ports and coastal areas, but, also, a lighter yet fairly even distribution lay over almost all inland areas too. These represented the contribution of the 'landed' classes and, to some extent, of the doctors, solicitors and parsons. But such folk would be making no appreciable contribution at all to the Lower Deck Table.

Not that the inland areas would be innocent of 'men'. They would not. People like our gardener's boy from Woodstock would be quite numerous; but as individuals, not as classes, and they would scarcely affect percentages at all. Indeed, the only source of 'inland' supply capable of doing that will be, as we are soon to see, the oft-maligned Quota-men (see p. 116)—and something like half, even of these, came from sea-shires. On the whole, it would be unwise to put the really 'inland' percentage of the men at higher than ten.

PART TWO: ENTRY

PROBLEMS OF RECRUITMENT

CHAPTER III

THE LOWER DECK: THE VOLUNTEER, THE PRESS AND THE QUOTA

HAVING examined in some detail the social and geographical origins of our Quarter-deck candidates and—a good deal more cavalierly—those of our Lower Deck people, let us now take our stand at the entry-port of a ship in the throes of commissioning, and, watching her new complement coming on board, enquire how they came to be there, and what happened to them next. But so differently had Quarter-deck and Lower Deck been recruited, so utterly differently were they now to be treated that, once more, their fortunes must be separately followed. This time the Lower Deck will take precedence.

The first thing that happened was that they were all 'rated'—and now we are using the word in its ordinary eighteenth-century sense. A small committee instantly met, representing all the ship's departmental heads. It consisted sometimes of the Captain, but always of the First Lieutenant, with the Master, Boatswain, Gunner, Carpenter and Purser; and every member of the new Company appeared before it. Most of them would slip into their accustomed places—the same rating as they held in their last ship. But it is those joining for the first time who concern us now. These would be examined briefly on their qualifications and be rated accordingly. If, for instance, a man had never been to sea before, and had no particular qualification in any handicraft, he would probably be rated 'Landman'—a new rating just introduced, and a very low form of marine life carrying a minimum of wages. If he had some sea-experience, he might be rated Ordinary Seaman, with more pay and more local prestige. If he had had a great deal of experience and was a handy, likely-looking fellow, the committee might be tempted to 'rate him able'—that is, Able Seaman, with more pay still and much more prestige. This was often against the rules: but that, as we shall soon see, would not greatly deter them. Again, though no seaman, the newcomer might have some knowledge of the carpentry trade, or perhaps know something about keeping books. Then he would find his way into the Carpenter's or the Purser's department. It was all quite sensible and business-like.

In the early years of the war everyone entering the ship was classifiable under one of two heads. He was a Volunteer, or he was a Conscript. But very soon—in 1795—there began to appear a third heading, which we will call for the present 'Quota-men'. These were a kind of cross between Volunteers and Conscripts—nearer to the latter. They will be discussed in their place.

A. VOLUNTEERS

The Volunteers themselves fall into two natural sub-categories—Boys, aged from 17 downwards, and Men, from 18 upwards.

1. *Boys*

A number of these would be 'quarter-deck' people—Young Gentlemen—but they are reserved for the next chapter. The rest would be bound for the Lower Deck. They would be too young for active work demanding a man's muscles: so, in this commonsense lay-out, they would not be put to men's work.

Whence did they come? Some would be boys like Sam Leech, who just appeared, without anyone pushing them, because they wanted to: because they were keen, or thought they were, on a sea life: because, perhaps, they dreamt dreams of excitement and adventure. Others came, no doubt, because they were unhappy at home, placed in a trade which they did not like or apprenticed to a master who bullied them. Fortunately, there survives the naval life-story of one of these, and a very valuable and interesting story it is.

In some ways, the career of Robert Hay[1] was like that of Samuel Leech. Both left happy non-naval homes to enter the Service as Boys: both were volunteers in the fullest sense. But there the likeness ends. Whereas Sam went with full parental consent, under the mistaken im-

[1] *Landsman Hay*, Ed. M. D. Hay, London, 1953.

pression that he was to become an officer, Hay ran away because he was bored with the trade to which he had been set; and he never had any illusions about the Quarter-deck. Again, while Leech was not cut out for the life, and soon discovered it, Robert was, though he did, rather unaccountably, desert three times—the last time successfully, after eight years at sea. He was, in fact, no more Quarter-deck in background than Leech, his father being a Paisley weaver. He gives a charming account of his 'Boy' days, when he soon found himself the servant of a kindly Lieutenant, and then had the good fortune to serve under Collingwood whom, with good reason, he idolized.

He sees life, therefore, through much more rose-tinted glasses than some of the others. This is a most natural phenomenon, of which we should not lose sight. Life—even pleasure—can be poisonous when one is unhappy: but even hardships are very easily borne, indeed scarcely noticed, when one is interested and prepared to be happy. This truth appears again and again in his narrative. Instead of a succession of brutal Boatswain's Mates and callous tyrannical officers such as fill Leech's or Pemberton's pages, we find a gallery of very human and, on the whole, kindly people of all ranks: from Collingwood and Pellew, for both of whom he is full of admiration, through good, fairminded Captains and friendly Lieutenants down to honest, competent and lovable seamen. Most of the officers, too, at one time or another and in different ways, take a real and intelligent interest not only in him, but in the other Boys, and in the other seamen. Truly the Navies of Hay and, say, Pemberton might be different navies altogether were not the narrated facts recognizably the same in each case. Hay's Service may not have been exactly Heaven, but it was very, very far from being Hell.

So much, then, for the real Volunteer Boys. But there were never enough Leeches and Hays: not nearly enough to satisfy the needs of the Navy at war. A much larger number were not quite such pure volunteers as this—lads perhaps unwanted at home, waifs and strays or (at worst) the Borstal Boys of their day. There were several quasi-philanthropic societies which concerned themselves with such people, and by far the most important of these was the Marine Society, founded in 1756 by the versatile Mr Jonas Hanway, pioneer of the umbrella in this country.

The full part played by this society in naval recruitment has yet to be told. In the two preceding wars its contribution had been considerable. In the wars here under consideration it was even greater. It handled three classes of potential recruit. One consisted of adults, and to these we shall return shortly. The other two classes were composed of boys whose normal ages would average 14 or 15, though some were as much as 17, some as little as 12. The surviving books of the Society seem to show that many were boys of the unwanted or waif class, or of those who had been in minor trouble. They came mostly from poor but respectable homes, some from the country, but more from the towns. The Society took them in, brushed them up, clothed and fed them. Most of them appear to have been in need of this last attention, for the records of the height of every one of them, meticulously entered in the books, show that, on the average, they were very small for their age. To some of them the Society gave an elementary grounding in seamanship and even a (very rudimentary) dose of the 'three R's', keeping them for as much as four months. But most of them it had for only a few days. It then disposed of them as they were applied for. In peace-time they went mostly into the Merchant Service, in wartime mostly into the Royal Navy; and they reached the warships under one of two names—'Apprentices' and 'Servants'. The details of each category are carefully kept, in separate books. The former were fully-articled and legally protected apprentices, with proper indentures covering, usually, a term of five years. The 'masters' in these contracts were mostly the Warrant Officers of the ships of war—the Gunners, Boatswains, Carpenters, etc.: but occasionally—and strangely—a Captain was a 'master'. Once on board, these lads were absorbed into the small 'families' or coteries of the various heads of departments. These were odd, tight, even jealous little corporations existing in every ship, made possible by the fact that these departmental heads were 'standing' officers, who were fixtures (like the 'standing rigging') each in his own ship for years on end, and not, like the commissioned officers and the ship's company, people who left when their ships paid off (see p. 261). The boys 'apprenticed' to them would, if lucky, rise slowly in their department, and might finally emerge as head of it, *via* the ratings of Gunner's (or Carpenter's) Mate or Purser's Clerk. The number of apprentices was quite large in peacetime, but much rarer in wartime.

The other group went on board as 'Servants', and without articles. They were usually dispatched in drafts, sometimes up to twenty strong, to the Captain of a ship about to commission, and were by him distributed to such of his officers as were entitled to personal servants—which they were and how many each was allowed we shall see later. The

Captain also kept a few for himself. These lads were real servants who waited literally upon their masters. This must be stressed because, as we shall see, most so-called 'servants' were not really menials, especially if they were 'Captain's Servants'. The number of these Marine Society boys joining as true servants was in the neighbourhood of 600 per annum at or near the beginning of the wars. Thus there were 582 in 1794 and 594 in 1795. Up to 1794 they appear, in the column of the Muster Book which records 'rating', as Servants, though, in another column which records whether they were 'volunteers' or not, they are labelled Volunteer. The common colloquial name for them was 'boys'. This was, in fact, just what they were. But, to avoid confusions, we should recall that this was not their official title. 'Boy', as an official name for a rating, came into existence only in 1794. Until that year, the lads' names appear in the main muster-lists immediately after their masters'. But after 1794 their names are removed from the main list and entered at the end, in a list of their own. And now they are no longer called 'Servant', but 'Boy', henceforward an official naval rating.

Thus the rating 'Servant' disappeared officially from the Navy. But since all those previously so called were still there, still doing substantially the same work as before, all that the Order of 1st April 1794 did was to change names, not facts. Still, the new ruling certainly clarified an obscure position. All ex-servants were now divided into three classes: in the actual words of the Order:[1]

Class I. 'To consist of Young Gentlemen intended for the Sea Service . . . : to be styled Volunteers and allowed wages at the rate of £6 per annum.

2nd. To consist of Boys between 15 and 17 years of age to be divided into watches with the seamen in order to make them such —at £5 per annum.

3rd. To consist of Boys between 13 and 15 years of age of whom Lieutenants and other officers who are now allowed servants might be permitted to recommend to the Captains, each of them one, to be the attendants upon such officers—at £4 per annum.'

The meaning is clear enough. Class I are the young 'Quarter-deck' Gentlemen (already there) whose fortunes we are to follow later. They

[1] Admiralty Order-in-Council, 9.7.1794.

are to be known in future as 'Volunteers' or (as usage crystallized the name) 'First Class Volunteers' or 'Volunteers of the First Class'. The second Class (already there) are the lads training to be seamen, and now to be known as 'Boys' or, more specifically, 'Boys, Second Class': while the third Class (also already there) are the lads who are still to be real servants of officers, but now to be known as 'Boys', or 'Boys, Third Class'. It is these last two whose fortunes we now follow.

Incidentally, though no one changed his job as a result of the Order, all were gainers in one rather unlooked-for way. For the first time they received wages: or, to be strictly accurate, they had the spending of wages which had hitherto been theirs only nominally. For their masters had pocketed them by right, in much the same way as, in the apprentice system, the master enjoyed his apprentices' labour for nothing, in return for teaching them his trade.[1] Now, however, the masters were to be recompensed by the State for this lost emolument, and the Boys were to receive at least a part of it. Even so it was not princely—£4 a year is 6/8 per calendar month. But it went up to £7 in 1806.

We rightly bring these lads under the head of 'Volunteer', though, sometimes, the strict voluntariness of their presence on board is arguable. It must often have been 'Hobson's choice', especially with many of the Marine Society boys. There was a tendency on everyone's part to bully these lads, yet they were really most important people—far more important to the well-being of the Service and its future than either they or their persecutors realized. Coming into the ship when still very young, and often having nowhere else to go, they tended to grow up in it and to stay there, becoming in time first-rate naval seamen in a Navy which was almost always short of that commodity.

2. *Men*

There were, of course, volunteers among the men too. Some, like Robert Hay, came solely because they wanted to, and without any outside pressure, because they had either patriotism or a liking for the life, or both. Two such happy warriors have left autobiographies, both of considerable interest and value. One was George Watson, son of a Newcastle merchant mariner, who, after six years at sea, volunteered in 1808

[1] C.f.—as late as 1792—in 32 Geo. III. cap. 33:—'Wages earned by an apprentice shall be paid to his master as usual . . . unless he shall be rated as a servant to an officer, in which case his wage shall be paid to such officer according to the usual practice of the Navy.'

at the age of 16. His immediate motive for so doing was unusual. Having a great friend serving in the *Fame*, he went on board that ship to visit him. No one sought to detain him, but

'I spent the evening with him very pleasantly, and the sailors of his mess, as their manner is in men of war, procured us plenty of wine, and everything that could be got to make a stranger comfortable; when morning came, and I should go ashore, I felt reluctant to part with my friend, and instead of doing so, I volunteered to serve his Majesty.'[1]

The other—an older man—also volunteered, but in the American Independence War and at the age of 21. He was John Nicol, son of a Scottish cooper, and born near Edinburgh; and he was as pure a volunteer as one can hope to find: for

'I had read Robinson Crusoe many times over and longed for the sea... Every moment I could spare was spent in boats or about the shore.'[2]

He had no opportunity to fulfil his ambition until he had completed his apprenticeship in his father's trade. Then he joined at once and, like Watson, never regretted it, though, when the Revolutionary War came, he did not volunteer again, having in the years between done quite well in the Merchant Service. He did not escape service, of course—he was impressed—but remained perfectly philosophic about it.

Both these attractive men belong to the same category as Robert Hay—save that they did not join as Boys. They were cheerful extroverts who did *not* find all their officers brutal and tyrannical, or their messmates the scum of humanity: especially Watson. All his Captains and most of his officers won his admiration and confidence in one way or another—even the Captain (Sir Charles Collier) who personally thrashed him with a heavy stick and then ordered him a dozen with the Cat at the gangway: even (stranger still) though he was quite positive that he did not deserve it. His attitude towards his brethren of the Lower Deck is almost as optimistic. There were clearly unpleasant characters there, and, reading between the lines, we can sense the roughness of the life—

[1] *Narrative of the Adventures of a Greenwich Pensioner*, by George Watson, Newcastle, 1827, pp. 64–5.

[2] *Life and Adventures of John Nicol, Mariner*, Edinburgh, 1822, p. 36. As the original edition is rather rare, the page references given here are taken from the more easily procurable modern edition of 1937 (Cassell). His portrait, facing p. 65 in this book, is taken from the first edition.

the language, the morals, the drunkenness, the frequent brawls. But he takes everything in his stride, and patently enjoys life.

Such men deserve all the respect and sympathy we can give them, for their patriotism and love of the Service must have been sorely tried before they were through with it—poor Nicol's in particular, callously left stranded as he was in his old age. Though he and Watson were much alike in their attitude to the Navy, their ultimate fates were very different. Watson, dangerously wounded in action and more or less crippled for life at the age of 20, received a Greenwich pension on which he was still living, in comfort if not affluence, when his book appeared fifteen years later. But Nicol, though he served right through two wars, was denied a pension and, writing as an old man, has lost some of his old optimism, though none of his happy memories—

'Then I must go to the poor's-house, which God in His mercy forbid. I can look to my death-bed with resignation: but to the poor's-house I cannot look with composure. I have been a wanderer and the child of chance all my days; and now only look for the time when I shall enter my last ship, and be anchored with the green turf upon my breast: and I care not how soon the command is given.'

Such single-minded men, however, were not the only volunteers. There were many others whose motives were not quite so pure. Every British seaman knew, from report if not from painful experience, what was in store for him when war broke out. He knew that the Government would begin by looking for volunteers—it was sensible enough to prefer them to conscripts—and that it would offer a sum of money known as a Bounty to anyone who 'entered volunteerly'. But he also knew that it would not find them—it never did—and that then it would resort to compulsion. Many a man, therefore, who felt himself liable to be conscripted must have argued thus: 'They will be after me anyway, and they will almost certainly get me. Better, surely, to volunteer now and earn the bounty rather than wait to be nabbed—perhaps painfully—and receive no bounty.' It is clearly impossible to gauge numbers here, but such a process of reasoning is so human and so natural as to make it a moral certainty that it was very common. Nevertheless, such reasoners are still entitled to the name of Volunteer.

The methods employed for voluntary recruitment were inadequate. Up to the outbreak of the Revolutionary War the men responsible for manning the ships were the Captains, each his own ship: and, on the word being given, they went into action, each in his own way. The most obvious way—that which hit the public eye—was the recruiting drive, organized in the places where seamen congregated: a matter of posters and improvised bands playing martial airs, and enthusiastic speech-makings crying up life afloat in wartime—the excitements, the glory, the food, the prize money, the rum—especially the rum. But these crude little demonstrations were never very successful, and the more intelligent captains had other resources. They would exploit their own personal and local connections. They would seek to enlist any men known to them—former shipmates, perhaps, or men from their own home-districts. But sometimes they went even further, with considerable success. Thus when Collingwood was raising his company for the *Mermaid* at the time of the Spanish Armament in 1790, we find him using a young man whom he was proposing to train for an officer. 'If he is a smart young man,' he writes, 'I think he might get fifteen or twenty volunteers (seamen) to come with him'[1]: and another young man was told that 'he must look out for volunteer seamen to bring with him'. What luck he had at that time he does not say; but, three years later, when the real war started, he had a great deal, though apparently it was the Service, not Collingwood, which benefited by it. Writing to the Secretary of the Admiralty, he tells him that

'. . . being particularly connected with Newcastle, I engaged my friends there to use their influence with the seamen, which they did so effectually that near fifty men entered . . .'[2]

But evidently someone was not playing the game because (he goes on) they

'. . . entered on the assurance given them by these gentlemen that they were to serve in the *Prince* (his ship). Only three of the number have joined the ship: some, I understand, have been drafted with other ships, several remain unappointed.'

The whole letter is indeed a protest against this breach of faith with the men. It is unlikely that he prevailed. What interested the authorities just then was bodies, in the gross: they were unlikely to let the wishes of any individual body incommode them. It was stupid, because it was

[1] Correspondence of Admiral Lord Collingwood. N.R.S., Vol. XCVIII, p. 27.
[2] Op. cit., p. 37.

bound to have the worst possible effect upon voluntary recruitment. But it was only too typical of Authority's attitude throughout.

Almost the only institution (other than a naval one) which concerned itself with adult recruitment was, again, the Marine Society, whose third activity (see p. 88) was the collection and fitting-out of grown-up volunteers. It did less for them than for the boys. It merely provided clothes for such as applied. These were called 'Landmen'—not a bad name since few, probably, were seamen by trade. Yet this word, like Boy, had its earlier unofficial and its later official meanings. Though the Marine Society's Landman had long been a familiar figure afloat, the Admiralty made 'Landman' an official rating only at about the time when our wars began. Then he took station after Ordinary Seaman, in pay and prestige alike.

The Marine Society's landman-scheme was important in two ways. It was popular with the men concerned, because a newcomer arriving in Marine Society clothes was well received on board and accorded rather more favourable treatment than most. It therefore helped voluntary recruitment. But it was also on no mean scale. The average number of landmen which it sent annually into the fleet as volunteers was almost exactly 1000—22,973 in twenty-two years.[1] They did not enter regularly, however. The first year saw 2,293 of them, and the numbers kept nearly as high for the next few years. They had fallen to 766, however, by 1799, but rose again for the last two years of the first war, reaching 1,811 in 1801. After the brief Peace of Amiens the annual figure never really recovered. There were 1,097 in 1804, and they topped the thousand for the last time in 1806. They then sank to their minimum—354 —in 1810, thereafter averaging about 700. Though the first war was a little shorter than the second, its landmen entries were more than double —15,919 to 7,054. Some of the reasons for this decline in numbers are clear enough. At the outset there would be more volunteers about—there always are, as witness the Kitchener armies of 1914–15. So the figures would in any case tend to fall away later. But there was also a special reason in this case. Many of the 'landmen volunteers' were of doubtful voluntariness. Some were indeed—like many of the Society's boys—sent in by the magistrates because they were not up to much good at home. Then, however, came the Quota Acts which, we shall find on examination, were tapping the same source of supply, and taking the sort of man who would, earlier, have been a Marine Society landman.

[1] National Maritime Museum, Marine Society Records, 57/031.

An incidental feature revealed in the Society's books is interesting from quite a different point of view. The exact height of every landman is entered. It is reasonably certain that the average stature of Englishmen has increased considerably during the last 160 years, and this is borne out by these figures. Of the 2,293 men handled in 1793, only seven are six-footers—the tallest six-foot-one. The range thereafter descends to five foot (with one solitary dwarf of four-foot-eight). But there are not many under five-foot-three, and the average would be around five-foot-five (or at most six). By 1813, however, there are no six-footers at all: none of five-foot-eleven either, only one of five-foot-ten and very few of five-foot-nine. The average would certainly not be more than five-foot-three, perhaps less. This confirms a fact known to us from other sources, and to be discussed later. Well before the end we were engaged upon the operation colloquially known as 'scraping the bottom of the barrel'. It was inevitable. The same thing happened in 1914–18 and, perhaps rather less so, in 1939–45.

The Marine Society was not in itself a recruiting body. Its clients, that is, came or were sent to it: it did not run after them. But all the above figures show that its place in the story of manning, as regards both men and boys, was very far from negligible.

Such then was the Volunteer element on the Lower Deck: not all, perhaps, equally entitled to the honoured name in its more altruistic sense—many of the Marine Society boys, for instance, and some of its men; and the bounty-hunters among the earlier volunteers. Yet all, officially, 'entered volunteerly', and all (except the boys) received the current volunteer bounty. Once on board, however, they were treated like everyone else, absorbed into the economy of the ship and rated according to their several capacities in the Ship's Book. But still their 'voluntariness' was recorded in that other column where the only alternative entry was—'Prest'.

B. PRESSED MEN

Prest! So we reach the sinister word, long before half of our Ship's Company has passed before our eyes. Hitherto the terms Conscription and Compulsion have been used here in describing wartime recruitment and its problems. But they were not the unpleasant words known to the British seaman-class of the day. Those were Impressment, and its instrument, the Press-gang.

Now in any discussion of these notorious and much-hated things, it is as well, at the outset, to differentiate between Impressment in the abstract—the principle of procuring men, if necessary by force, to serve in the Navy in wartime—and that concrete thing which actually procured them, 'the Press', operating through the press-gangs. The very words are conducive to muddled thinking because, etymologically, they are the wrong words. The correct root word, almost entirely discarded by the time of our wars, is 'Prest'. That (which was either noun or verb) meant 'enlistment money' or 'to engage for service by paying earnest money'. It was in the Navy, in fact, the equivalent of the 'King's Shilling' in the Army. Its derivation is the same as that of the French word *prêter*, to lend, and originally it carried no implication at all of 'pressing' (i.e. forcing). Yet, very early in our naval history, 'pressing' in its literal sense came to play a part, and an ever-growing part, because the prospects offered were in every way so poor and unattractive that only a few would accept them willingly. It was thus a kind of popular if macabre jest which converted 'prest' into 'press' and 'imprestment' into 'impressment'. For in fact the Prest had long been pressing men into the naval service by force, with a vigour and relentlessness which depended entirely upon the needs of the moment.

Indeed, 'Necessity knows no law'. The *principle* of Impressment was hardly to be disputed, and very seldom was, even by its victims. It was nothing more than one facet of that essential power which must reside in every sovereign state—the power to call upon its own people to defend it (and, by implication, themselves) in times of emergency and danger. Thus viewed, Impressment is not, as some imagine, a bad thing of the past. It was never abolished—no state could do that without abolishing itself. It is still with us: only now it passes under other and less hated names, like 'National Service' or 'Conscription'. The fact is, it was not the principle that was bad. What was wrong was its application.

Here we touch upon one of the most unyielding of all the problems which face sovereign states. It is by no means resolved to this day. It is quite certain that, in wartime, a nation will have to use as fighting men a much larger proportion of its total manpower than it will need in peacetime. Normally, too, it will need them quickly, certainly as soon as war breaks out and preferably well before that. What then shall the nation do? There are, broadly, two extremes. It can either maintain all the time, through peace and war alike, enough men for all its war-needs: or it can wait for war to come, pick up in a hurry the manpower it needs, and discard it again when the war is over. But these are extremes, and there are glaring disadvantages in both. Of the former—to apply our case to the Navy only—the expense is astronomical, the wastage of national manpower unthinkable, and the threat to morale inherent in giving too many men too little to do quite unacceptable. If the other extreme be accepted, the nation is bound to be caught quite unprepared when war starts; and—perhaps even worse—there will be no real navy in existence. For even if the ships which compose it have been built (perhaps for a previous war), they will be lying in port, unusable and unmanned. Nor, since man has long known that the handling and fighting of ships cannot be improvised or achieved without much practice, will any sort of effective fleet get to sea for years, even after the folk to man it have been procured. So, in effect, all nations with sea-interests have been compelled to compromise at a point somewhere between these two extremes: and, to this day, they still do so. What we have to see here, if we can, is the nature of the compromise in eighteenth-century Britain.

A compromise it was: as regards the ships and the officers, at a point about halfway between the extremes: as regards the men, much nearer to the 'no-navy' end. Between the wars a collection of ships was retained usually amounting to a substantial fleet. But most of them were, as the phrase went, 'in ordinary'—laid up at the naval ports with nothing but a skeleton complement of 'ship-keepers' aboard. Still, there they were: not enough for the new war yet enough to form the nucleus of a war-fleet. As for officers, they too existed in some numbers—a good many more of them than were needed in peacetime: most of them unemployed, and kicking their heels impatiently on half-pay: often, it is to be feared, longing for war to break out, since only so could they obtain employment. Again, as with the ships, there were seldom enough of them for war, but still a fairly well-trained nucleus.

The crews, however, were *not* there. In a normal peace-year a few ships were put into commission for a brief, and usually a 'summer' cruise. Enough men (for not many were needed) could be scraped together to take them out, and such men were all volunteers. It is tempting to see in such people the nucleus of a wholetime body of naval seamen. Most of them were probably Marine Society or ex-Marine Society products, or people similarly collected: men, that is, and boys, who had nowhere else to go when the cessation of war released their fellows from servitude in the fleets and sent them hurrying ashore, or back into the

Merchant Service. Having been drafted into the Navy, willy-nilly and often as mere children, they knew of no other way of life: so they just stayed on. And, in a way, they reaped their reward: for when war-expansion restarted, there they were on the spot, experienced men-o'-warsmen among a mixed bag of inexperienced and often unwilling shipmates. Inevitably it was they who were picked for posts of trust—topmen, captains of guns and even petty officers. They are worth remembering. They were a valuable hard core: but they were too few in number, and their presence was too uncertain, to make it either wise or realistic to regard them as the nucleus of a permanent naval-seaman corps.

The Impressment System had one all-important advantage in the eyes of all Governments. It was cheap. In peacetime the wage-bill was conveniently low. But, for this very reason, war when it came always caught us napping. Even if the ships were sea-worthy—and they seldom were—they still could not be mobilized until crews could be found for them. This fact alone will explain why 'press' affairs changed almost overnight from a state of semi-quiescence to one of hectic activity. From the moment when the Government decided to issue a general Press Warrant, things began to move at an ever-increasing tempo, until at last the main fleets were at sea. There was always, as we saw, a period of 'Bounties for Volunteers', but when the emergency was at all great it was reduced to all but nothing; or rather, Impressment at full blast started alongside it. A 'hot press' men called it. Thereafter, until peace came, that press continued, though not throughout at so high a temperature, since after a while it was only supplementing the Navy's strength and replacing its casualties, not trying to treble or quadruple it in a few weeks.[1]

The Government cannot be saddled with all the blame for the grossly unfair and perennially unpopular activities of the press-gangs. The country was not nearly wealthy enough to maintain, peace and war alike, a full and permanent body of seamen. It was therefore forced to rely, in 1793 as always hitherto, upon its one pool of suitable subjects, those who, peace and war, followed the sea for a livelihood—its merchant seamen and fishermen. And rely upon them it did, letting them man their merchant ships and fishing-boats undisturbed in peacetime, but when war came instantly conscripting for the Royal Navy as many of them as it required. In a word, the Merchant Seaman and what we

[1] See graph on p. 119.

now call the Naval Rating were, in the eighteenth century, one and the same person.

In the Navy this was perhaps inevitable, for here the problem differed widely from the Army's. For war-service in the Militia there was a ballot which, though sometimes rigged, still spread its net, officially, over all walks of life, and gave to each individual a chance of having to serve, but also a chance of escaping service. But in the Navy the incidence fell upon one class only—the seafaring community—so that the poor sailor, unlike, say, the ploughman, had practically no chance of escaping save by sheer personal evasion. Defenders of the Impressment System might argue, with Dr. Burney,[1] that the seaman had nothing to complain of, because he was exempt from the militia ballot. But this was a highly academic privilege, exchanging as it did a chance of escape for a virtual certainty of being caught. For not only was the seamen's pool regarded as the only source of naval supply: that pool itself was strictly limited in numbers. So, in the very nature of the case, the unfortunate seaman was bound to bear an unfair proportion of the burden.

In wartime, then, naval service for nearly all seafarers may have been inevitable. What was not inevitable was the Government's treatment of the men it took. It might at least have hammered out some scheme for selecting the ones it wanted: it might have put some term upon the length of time for which it took them. It could not promise them a very comfortable life in the Crown's service, since warships, which had to fight as well as to sail, were bound to be a great deal more overcrowded than merchantships which had only to sail. It could not guarantee them against danger, casualties and death in action, all of which were inherently more likely in warships in wartime than in merchant ships in peacetime. But it might have tried to compensate the seamen for the additional discomforts and risks which they were facing in its service. It might at least have been as careful as possible of their creature comforts—clothed them decently, fed them well, ensured that they were not cheated of their few rights by those whom it set in authority over them: and above all it might have paid them adequately—and adequately in this sense, must surely mean at least as much as when they were merchant seamen.

It did none of these things. Government succeeded government, but none of them ever devised a scheme for selection or length of service. All were content to send out their press-gangs to gather the men in

[1] Falconer's Marine Dictionary, 1815, under article PRESS.

promiscuously: if necessary, to knock them silly with a cudgel or the flat of a cutlass, and bundle them on board as mere prisoners: prisoners, moreover, without trial and with no time-limit set upon their sentence save only the duration of the war. Having collected them in the necessary numbers, Authority often found them surly and recalcitrant—and who can be surprised at that? Then it had to impose upon them a very strict and sometimes brutal discipline, suitable rather for the gaol-bird than for the free man. War-discipline admittedly was essential: so it flogged them for all sorts of offences serious and trivial alike, often indiscriminately and sometimes—but not so frequently as is sometimes supposed—with a brutality amounting to sadism. Then—just as bad, if not on the long view worse—it found itself compelled to curtail almost to nothing the men's shore-leave, alleging that, if granted it, the men would 'run' wholesale. As things stood, it was probably right. Where it was wrong was in landing itself and the men in the toils of such a very vicious circle. Once it had made life afloat tantamount to a term of imprisonment, it could hardly expect free men to volunteer for gaol.

Again, the men were consistently ill-fed—not in quantity but in quality. Adequate catering under eighteenth-century conditions was certainly no easy matter. But the food might have been a good deal better; and above all, the Government might have gone much further than it did in seeing that the men, in their defenceless position, were not habitually cheated by its own supply-officers, the Pursers. 'Pusser's tricks' were notorious, the most notorious, perhaps, being the 'Purser's Eights' (or '14 for 16'). This was a convention whereby that officer issued his stocks at the rate of 14 ounces to the pound, steering the value of the odd two into his own pocket. Yet even the pursers must not be condemned unheard. They too were victims of basic dishonesty in their employers, as we shall see later.

To crown all, successive governments consistently underpaid their naval seamen. They refused to play fair in the ordinary economic market. Relying upon their ultimate power of coercion, far from compensating the seaman for the additional discomforts and dangers which they demanded of him, they actually paid him a good deal less than he received from his merchant employers. Moreover—and, from the seaman's point of view, hardest to bear—they snatched him from his merchant ship just at the moment when his merchant-pay was about to increase, as it always did when war broke out. This was a matter of elementary economics too. At that moment the seaman was a commodity in heavy demand and short supply. Everyone wanted him: consequently his price rose. For instance, on the war-scare of 1791 known as the Russian Armament, the gangs came out, and merchant seamen's wages rose to £2 5*s*. a month: but those who were pressed got 19*s*. In the following year, however, the scare over, the gangs quiescent and the pressed men discharged, merchant-service wages fell to £1 10*s*.[1] Even in peacetime his wages had been rising gradually during the eighteenth century. Not so his naval pay, however. Here there was no rise at all between the time of Cromwell and 1797, when at last the long-suffering donkey showed uncomfortable signs of turning upon his master.

So much for the governments. Now what about the men? They were by nature and upbringing an unvocal company, and it is seldom easy to discover their thoughts. But when we do get a chance, we find them significant. Let there be no mistake: life in the eighteenth-century merchant service was no bed of roses either. The men lived just as rough, under conditions little if any better: the officers were little if any less tyrannous. If no press-gang knocked them over the head, the seaport crimps made them dead drunk and sold their inanimate bodies to the ship-masters. But they sometimes earned good money: they had at least the appearance of a free choice, and there was always a term set upon their bondage—the period of the individual voyage. In fact Hay, who ought to know because he sailed in both, declared that the wages, treatment and fare in a bad merchantman were all better than in a good warship.[2] In spite of all this, however, they seldom if ever cavilled at the underlying idea of Impressment. They knew that they must—that they ought to—serve against the foreigner. They were patriotic enough at heart, and they invariably showed themselves so when the true crux of action came. But a well-nigh impossible strain was constantly being put upon their patriotism; and, since they were not saints but particularly simple uncomplex men, they just did their best, most of them, to keep clear of the press-gangs.

The Impress Service

Throughout the whole of the Revolutionary and Napoleonic Wars Impressment was the main instrument of recruiting. Yet, in the course of them, there appeared certain changes in the system which, though few

[1] William Richardson, *A Mariner of England*, (London, 1908), p. 76.
[2] Hay, op. cit., p. 194.

realized it, marked the end of an epoch. Though the press-gang loomed larger in these wars than ever before, they were also, as it transpired, the last wars in which it operated at all.

From the very start the Revolutionary War bid fair to be on a larger scale than previous ones, demanding bigger fleets and therefore more seamen. It opened, as usual, with a 'hot press', but the authorities soon realized that it was not going to be—could not be—hot enough. Their first reaction, therefore, was to stoke it up by eliminating certain weaknesses and overlaps in the system as it stood. Hitherto, as we saw, the men primarily responsible for recruiting had been the captains of the various ships: and when their rather pathetic little recruiting-drives had failed (as they always did), they armed parties of their trustier men with sticks and cutlasses—but never firearms, for a recruit with a hole in him was obviously no good to them—and sent them out under a lieutenant to pick up what they could: if in harbour, in the streets and pothouses of naval and commercial ports; if at sea, in ship's boats and cutters to board homecoming merchantmen. The Law required a commissioned officer to be in charge. In earlier times there was a case of an irate merchant skipper attacking the uncommissioned leader of a gang, and (though he actually killed him) he escaped punishment: and, even in our wars, this rule was not always kept. In 1793, for instance, William Richardson[1] was actually pressed (for the second time in his career) by an Army Sergeant! But this was in Calcutta. Imagination usually fastens upon the town-cruising gangs, dragging the seamen from wives, children and sweethearts. But much the more prolific trips were those of the boat-borne gangs.

Here again the Law had something to say, ordaining that inward-bound ships only might be boarded, and that enough of the crew must be left to work the ship to its destination. But the press-officer was allowed to substitute men, from his own gang or elsewhere, to replace those taken. These were called 'ticket-men' and had, if members of the gang, to be very trustworthy, because they now had a heaven-sent opportunity to 'run' if they wished. In fact, these substitutes were always volunteers of sorts, and the 'ticket' was nothing but a protection, signed by their Captain, against the attentions of the Press when they made port. How necessary that ticket might be is shown by the following official letter, from Captain Peter Rainier, late of the *Astrea*:

[1] Richardson, op. cit., p. 96.

'Please to acquaint their Lordships that John Knight belongs to the *Astrea*. I have no reason to suppose he ever has had an inclination to desert: but by being sent away in a pressed man's room without a ticket in the hurry of service, has been prevented joining his ship through his simplicity in not being able to satisfy the officers on the impress service by whom he has been taken up. . . . I hope their Lordships will have the goodness to order him round to join the *Monarch* (Rainier's new ship) as soon as possible.'[1]

This almost plaintive appeal to the summit demonstrates at once the heat of the press and the ordinary captain's fear of losing a single good man. William Richardson, the Warrant Officer author of some very valuable reminiscences shows how indispensable these ticket-men were. At the time of the Russian Armament he was in the Merchant Service, Fourth Mate of a slaver called the *Spy*. Homeward-bound off Beachy Head, they were boarded by the *Nemesis* frigate which pressed the whole Ship's Company save only the Master, Richardson himself (who was acting as Chief Mate), the Pilot and four German sugar-bakers. Ticket-men then took over entirely and brought the *Spy* up the Thames.[2]

'Men in lieu' (as ticket-men were often called) were not always so trustworthy, however, as Rainier's John Knight, nor so valuable as to make an appeal to the Admiralty worth while. In fact, in the earlier war, there was a regular professional class of them which made this temporary substituting a full-time job. They were often, even, carried around in the press-tenders for the sole purpose of replacing pressed men. Needless to say, they were of very poor quality—indeed, so poor that the Impressment authorities had already discarded them as of no permanent use to the Navy. Later, as a class, they disappeared, but only because, as the supply ran out, no one was of too poor a quality to be swept into the net. But, before they disappeared, they had succeeded in bringing many a good merchant ship to an untimely end on the coasts of Britain.[3]

So long as the Captains had the main responsibility for catching their crews, there was always an element of inefficiency and wasted effort. To be successful Impressment had to command the advantage of surprise. The gangs must take their quarry unawares, or they would bolt like rabbits to their holes. Yet surprise was seldom achieved. The very machinery of getting out the press-warrants at the Admiralty, and

[1] Admiral James' Journal. N.R.S., Vol. VI, p. 225, note.
[2] Richardson, op. cit., pp. 65–6.
[3] *The Press Gang*, by J. R. Hutchinson, pp. 126–7.

sending them to the commanding officers at ports, could not be—or hitherto had not been—done quietly enough. The clerks who wrote out the warrants all too often let out the secret: 'which cannot be wondered at', wrote Sir Charles Middleton, the great Comptroller of the Navy in 1788,[1] 'when the advantages to be gained, by such information, in the Funds is considered.' He was right. The issue of general press-warrants almost always spelt imminent war, or at least the Government's anticipation of it, and such advance knowledge was worth a small fortune on 'Change. It was the proposals now made by this astute man which, being accepted, were responsible for a new and far more efficient organization —the Impress Service.

The new scheme was this. A very large supply of warrants was to be made out beforehand, with no date attached to them. Meanwhile, and also beforehand, branches of the new Service, with the requisite offices, rendezvous and tenders, and with special naval officers already appointed to them, were to be set up in all likely towns and ports, all ready (as the twentieth century would say) for Zero Hour. As far as recruitment ashore was concerned, the individual Captains were now relieved of the task: and high time too, their sudden and simultaneous irruption upon the streets, alleys and waterside taverns of the ports having hitherto been enough to scare the dead, let alone press-shy seafarers. Again, no longer now would be seen the unsavoury and rather silly spectacle of cut-throat competition between rival captains and rival gangs, all trying to do the same thing at the same time. Now the blow could fall silently, synchronized in every naval haunt. Now a big haul could be made at the best moment for making it—the first day. Thereafter, of course, the Impress Service would continue to function, rounding up recruits, though at a decreased tempo, throughout hostilities.

Under this new arrangement the port-tenders, when filled by the efforts of the local impress officers, conveyed the catch round to the nearest Receiving Ship. Both tenders and receiving ships were of very evil repute: the tenders small, old, dirty and grossly overcrowded, the receiving ships worn-out hulks, foul and decayed, lying in the bigger ports. Pemberton draws gruesome pictures of both. On reaching the tender, he is shown

'a hole . . . called the Steerage. . . . I looked down, and, as I did so, a hot and pestilential effluvia rose and enveloped me. I looked through a

[1] Letters of Lord Barham, N.R.S., Vol. XXXVIII, pp. 312–4.

heavy wooden grating, across which was a strong iron bar with a huge padlock attached to it; and I saw that which threw me back almost fainting with horror. . . . In that short glance I had seen a crowded mass of disgusting and fearful heads, with eyes all glaring upwards from that terrible den; and heaps of filthy limbs, trunks and heads, bundled and scattered, scrambling, laughing, cursing, screaming and fighting at one moment.'[1]

His charges against the hulk *Resolu* at Plymouth—'a human washing-tub on a grand scale where we were carried for the purpose of purification, fumigation, washing, scrubbing and scraping'—and the receiving ship *Salvador* which next imprisoned him, are of spiritual rather than material degradation. Here it is the cold savagery of the Boatswain's Mates, wantonly 'starting' the wretched prisoners with their knotted ropes, which is lashed by his bitter but powerful pen. Once drafted into a sea-going frigate, however, he is much happier, and in the end comes (if grudgingly) to love

'my roving dwellingplace, my wandering habitation, my beloved and beautiful home, the *A*[*lceste*], the happiest home I ever knew,'[2]

and her gallant, humane commander whom he almost worshipped, Captain Murray Maxwell.

Horrible as the conditions certainly were in the tenders and receiving ships of the Impress Service, the innovation had some good material results. It greatly increased the numbers taken, and eliminated the cut-throat competition of the captains. In the long run, however, there was one grave disadvantage. The insanitary conditions obtaining in the ships and tenders nourished the germs of Jail-fever, and many a man who, in the old days, might have escaped the Press now evaded his service in the Navy by being invalided out, if not actually 'D.D.'—'discharged dead'. We shall have to return later to this blight (p. 409).

From the start this Impress Service was a large organization. By 1797, for instance, it engaged the full time of one Admiral, forty-seven Captains and Commanders, and eighty Lieutenants, mostly, of course of the more elderly and less enterprising type now known as 'dug-outs'. Yet the life of an Impress officer was by no means devoid of excitement. His job must have been exceedingly distasteful, if only because prac-

[1] C. R. Pemberton, *Pel. Verjuice*, p. 101.
[2] Ibid., p. 244.

tically all the elements in the seaport were his natural enemies—the seamen, with their wives and families, for obvious reasons; the merchants, who in such places were often the municipal authority too, because they were equally anti-press on principle, wanting for themselves all the seamen they could get. Dillon, much to his disgust, found himself posted to Hull as a Lieutenant, and second-in-command, of the Impress Service there in March, 1803. This was the moment of the outbreak of the Napoleonic War, and though peace was only a matter of months old, the Navy had, as usual, been largely demobilized, so that all was to do again. He has left his impressions of the adventures and difficulties which confronted him.[1]

He had to walk warily, first, in order to keep within the law. For though the general statutes covering Impressment were somewhat hazy, the more detailed enactments were clearly laid down, especially as to who might be taken and who not. The accepted overriding principle, by 1800, was that Impressment referred only to one class of the community—those who made their living upon the water. 'Persons using the sea' was the original term, and all others were legally exempt, though whether they were actually so was another matter. That depended upon the immediate urgency of getting the ships to sea. But still there was room for debate about the exact interpretation of 'persons using the sea'. In Richard II's reign, when the earliest-known statute was passed (15 Ric. II, cap. 2), 'the sea' had been defined as covering 'the main streams of great rivers nigh the sea': but authority's tendency ever since had been to claim a wider and wider interpretation of the words, ever more favourable to the impresser. This was no hard task for the Crown lawyers, because words like 'main', 'great' and 'nigh' are after all relative terms: so much so, indeed, that, by the end of the eighteenth century, they had practically come to mean 'any salt water, and any stream of any river at any distance from it'. Moreover, when canals came in, the very words 'stream' and 'river' began to lose their pristine significance.

Yet, even with 'persons using the sea' there were exemptions which were by no means dead-letters. Merchant officers, for example—Masters, Chief Mates, Boatswains and Carpenters—could not be taken when at sea provided that their ships were of 50-tons burthen or over: nor could they be taken on land if, upon coming ashore, they hurried to a local Justice and swore to being what they professed. But they had to be spry. Mates other than Chief Mates were fair game in port, as poor

[1] Dillon, op. cit., N.R.S., Vol. XCVII, p. 9 *et seq.*

Richardson found to his cost as soon as the ticket-men had moored the *Spy* safely in Church Hole((see p. 103). The Captain went to Town, leaving him not only as Acting Mate, but as acting Captain too. Yet that did not stop a press-tender from coming alongside and carrying him off to the *Enterprise*, Receiving Ship off Tower Stairs. Nor did he have any remedy, for he had no 'protection'. That left the Pilot alone in his glory.[1] For Pilots were exempt too, that is, unless or until they ran a ship aground. There was surely some dry humour here, which must have made them extra careful in piloting Navy ships when the Press was out. Being by hypothesis on board at the moment of the accident, they had no chance whatever of escaping the penalty. Another important seafaring person who was exempt was one who could show that he had been using the sea for less than two years. This sensible exception had been made half a century before (13 Geo. II, cap. 17) in order to encourage men and boys to go to sea. In a nation already so dependent upon it, any discouragement here would have been fatal indeed. All these classes were exempt, always in law and usually in fact as well.

There were other vaguer and more temporary exemptions, such as men engaged in harvesting, or any 'gentleman'—though in practice he had to look like one (see p. 57). Nor could the Impress Officer afford to make a mistake with impunity, because the injured party could always take him to the courts. Here, so unpopular was the whole institution that the officer could expect no preferential, or even fair treatment: so much so that these cases seldom reached the courts, but were compounded in advance, the Impress officer, and even the Admiralty, almost always giving way. Sometimes, too, fishermen secured exemption. This was when the Press was not at its maximum heat, or when, from time to time, the Admiralty had qualms that it was overdoing its assault upon a basic food-supply. In this way, in November, 1810, the Jerseyman John Béchervaise[2] escaped impressment, though in fact he was not a fisherman, but a merchant seaman. The story reveals at once the difficulties confronting Impress officers and the subterfuges practised by the unholy alliance of shipping companies, ship's masters and merchant seamen. Knowing that he would have to go ashore in a press-infested district, Béchervaise secured from his company's Agent, and with his

[1] Richardson, op. cit., p. 67.

[2] Author of two charming but rare books of sea-reminiscences, *36 Years of Seafaring Life, by An Old Quartermaster*, Portsea, 1839, and *Farewell*, Portsea, 1847.

full connivance, a 'shipping-paper' (protection) as a fisherman. On landing, he was duly seized and hauled to the rendezvous, where he boldly flourished his bogus paper in the officer's face, and was grudgingly allowed to depart. The officer may well have suspected a fraud: but it would have been too risky for him to act upon his suspicions.

We have this case from the angle of a man who, though a good and honest one, is patently proud of his deception and its success. Let us return to the officer's side. Most of Dillon's troubles are implicit in his job. On his arrival in Hull, the first man he met was an ex-shipmate, a sailmaker, who had liked and respected him when he had served with him in the first war. The man greeted him cheerfully, but 'when he heard the reason for my presence in that town, he took to his heels and was out of sight in no time.' Wise man! He was one of the choicer morsels that Dillon was after, and knew it.

The elderly officer in command was content to take his station at the Impress office, and to leave the dirty work to his Lieutenant who, contrary to the general rule, was still young and very active. Dillon soon discovered how dirty the work was. The tricks and subterfuges were endless. Some were of the crudest, like throwing bricks at him, firing shots through his window, and attempting to rescue pressed men by force. Against these he could obtain the constables' protection. Others were rather more sophisticated. Once the clerk of a big firm of merchants called on him and actually offered him £300 if he would liberate a single individual whom he had secured. This was an interesting fellow, a carpenter by trade and a fine upstanding man. Dillon, probably, had no right to touch him, for he could not take a merchant service carpenter, while if he was not a seaman at all he also had no right to him. He was almost certainly the latter, but Dillon took him and hauled him off to the rendezvous. On the way, however, the gang chanced to pass down the street where he lived. His wife saw what was happening, and her screams collected a crowd which attempted a rescue but was beaten off. So Dillon got him in safely, and it was then that the merchant's clerk tried bribery, and also failed. Let Dillon himself tell the sequel:

'When the Surgeon came for the usual examination the room was full, as several seamen had been taken that night. Just at this moment the carpenter's wife was heard in the street calling her husband. My attention being taken up with my official duties, I did not hear them: but I noticed this powerful fellow drawing towards the window. I instantly changed my position and got near to him. However, the Surgeon putting some question to me relating to the person then before him, I naturally in replying closed towards him. The instant my eyes were turned to another object, the carpenter . . . with an exertion beyond all description, threw open the window and leapt out. He fell upon all fours, then, taking off his shoes, ran off, effecting his escape. His hat and shoes were brought to me, these articles being all we had of the carpenter.'[1]

No doubt the Navy lost a good man: yet perhaps our sympathies, like the crowd's, lie with the carpenter.

Dillon's 'natural enemies', however, were sometimes even sharper than this. Another trick, which he discovered only after being once or twice deceived, was for people to write to him saying that they were seamen, and that they would 'enter volunteerly' if he would appear at a named place and time. He attended several such rendezvous and hung about for a long time. But never a man appeared. They had given themselves a few restful hours!

More subtle still were the wiles of some of the merchants, wealthy residents of Hull. At first he fell into the net they spread. They soon discovered that our young Lieutenant—he was only 23—was something of a *bon-vivant*, averse to neither good wine nor pretty faces. So they invited him to their dinners and dances: even, perhaps, arranged banquets and balls expressly for him. He relates with honest pride what happened one night at the house of 'one of the leading merchants'. There was 'a princely table', and 'a vast quantity of choice wine' was circulated. His host cunningly persuaded him to do justice to them by judicious flattery, declaring that he, and he alone among the guests, had shown the superiority of his palate by choosing the best vintage: and he caused fresh bottles of it to be opened just for their two superior selves. When pleasantly mellow—he had much too good a head to go further than that—he was taken to the 'Grand Ball'. Once there, that artful merchant said:

'"If you want a pretty girl for a partner, let me know. I'll take care to provide you with one." I opened the Ball with the Lady Mayoress, a regular beauty. But after I had taken her to her seat, I could not persuade any of the other young ladies to dance with me. Therefore for some time I remained an idle spectator.'

[1] N.R.S., Vol. XCVII, pp. 10, 11.

Here, it would seem, was faulty staff-work, Clearly those young ladies had not been properly briefed, and, seeing in the stranger nothing but the unpopular Impress Officer, determined to snub him. But that was not the role for which they had been cast. The host was at hand, watching: and, muttering no doubt 'This will never do!' approached Dillon and

'enquired why I was not dancing. I told him the reason. Then, taking me by the arm, he led me round the room, and, stopping opposite to five or six beautiful girls, "Did you ask her?" he demanded. "Yes," said I. "I have asked the whole of them, but they are engaged." "Now then," said he, "decide which you prefer." I pointed her out. "Very well," he replied. "Leave me for a moment." I followed his instructions. In a few seconds he rejoined me. "Now go," said he, "to the fair one. You will not be refused." I did so accordingly, and the young lady gave me her arm. So much, I thought, for being a judge of good burgundy!'

His last remark reveals, perhaps, how neatly he had been deceived. Is it hard to guess what the wily merchant whispered to the fair one? Anyway —*the Press-gang was not out that night.*

Yet Dillon was no fool. He learnt as he went along, retaliating in kind and contriving to strike a balance between duty and pleasure. He continued to

'attend these pleasant dinners in uniform, my host placing me between two amiable young ladies, supposing that their attractions would ensure my company for the remainder of the evening. However, on those occasions I directed the leading man of my gang to call at the house where I dined at about eight o'clock, and to send a note up to me. He also brought with him a bag containing a change of dress. Then I hastened away, in spite of all the entreaties of the fair ones. Below, the contents of the bag were turned to account, and in the course of a couple of hours I had probably secured seven or eight fine seamen.'

Elsewhere, he says that he made a habit of constantly changing his dress: which, with the above evidence, seems to prove that he did not always hunt in uniform. This, as we saw, was illegal; but no doubt he thought that all is fair in love—the ladies liked a man in uniform—and in war—he could get nearer to his quarry in plain clothes. According to his own account (but he was a rather self-satisfied young gentleman, not apt to minimize his own exploits) he discharged his distasteful job with considerable success, securing 150 prime seamen in six weeks.

This was not bad, but it was nothing like a record. The following feat was performed at much the same time as Dillon's effort at Hull.

'Whilst off Gravesend on his way to the Nore, Captain Thomas Manby received an express from Town, directing him to commence an impress at midnight: this order was promptly obeyed, and before sunrise on the following morning, 394 prime seamen were secured.'[1]

There was evidently a right and a wrong way to go a-pressing. How important was the element of surprise another illustration will show. Once more the period was the same—the outbreak of the Napoleonic War.

Captain George Wolfe, appointed to the *Aigle* frigate, was ordered to Portland to enlist volunteers (if he could) and to impress seamen. On arrival he reported to the Mayor of Weymouth, who promised to help by sending constables to keep order. Already Wolfe had made a fatal mistake, as the sequel shows. The news of his errand was out: the local seamen fled in a body to the Bill, where they got into touch with the quarrymen, as tough a crowd as any in England. A press-gang landed, but it was attacked and beaten back to its boat. Wolfe, relying on the Mayor's promises, now landed in person with fifty seamen and marines: but they were instantly fired on. They seized two men, but the rest, clearly a mere advance-guard, at once fell back to the Bill, where was stationed a force of 300 strong, armed with muskets, pistols and cutlasses plundered from a troopship lately wrecked in the neighbourhood. Their leaders it seems—or at any rate their instigators—were two of the Mayor's constables! This formidable army did not wait to be attacked, but threw itself upon Wolfe and his party, wounding sixteen or seventeen of them. The Captain himself, according to his own account,[2] was seized and 'cruelly treated'. At this, losing patience, he ordered his marines to open fire, and four of the 'enemy' were killed. The rest fled so fast that only three could be taken. In this fracas nine of the *Aigle's* men were so badly hurt that they had to be discharged from the Service. Result, five up, sixteen down and four dead!

This was not the end, however. Wolfe immediately sent off two officers to report to the Admiralty. As they landed they were recognized

[1] Marshall, II, 208.
[2] Marshall, II, 317.

by the mob, seized, and committed to Dorchester gaol by the Mayor, perhaps under duress. An inquest on the bodies followed, and the Coroner returned a verdict of Wilful Murder against not only the two prisoners but also the Captain, his First Lieutenant and the Lieutenant of Marines. The officers surrendered themselves and were tried at the Summer Assizes. But now someone was playing a part whose outlook was less parochial—the Judge—and in the end they were all acquitted, on the ground that they had acted in self-defence. But Wolfe did not escape censure. The Court informed him that, when acting under an order from the King-in-Council, he should not have got into touch with the Mayor or anybody else. He should have gone in, by night, without a word to anyone. Then his score, instead of being 'minus eleven' might have been more like Manby's 'plus 394'.

Pressing at sea was another matter. Here there were no impress officers and establishments, and captains still had to obtain their men by the old method of direct seizure. In a frigate acting as escort to a convoy the thing was easy. 'As we had so far brought them [the convoyed ships] into safety,' wrote Dillon, of the year 1801, 'we pressed a few seamen out of them.'[1] This is not mildly facetious. It reflects a serious and rather important fact which, incidentally, goes far towards explaining why our frigates had as a rule such good, smart crews. The escorting Captain was not allowed to reduce the complements of outgoing merchantmen. However much he might covet their best men, he was responsible, first and foremost, for the safe delivery of the convoy, and would interfere with its sailing efficiency at his peril. But once there, or almost there, that was quite another matter. He took his pick—before entering the outward-bound port, where other British ships would want to share with him. Indeed the poor merchant seaman was never safe. Even the letters of marque of Privateersmen gave no cover.

'An English privateersman occasionally crossed our path, and we generally helped ourselves to one or two good seamen, just as the case would allow.'[2]

And once, out of the same ship, it was '13 stout fellows'. As for poor Bartholomew James, arriving in the Downs in 1793 in a privateer of his own, he had every single member of his crew incontinently pressed.[3]

Another class of seafarers which provided first-class material was the

[1] N.R.S., Vol. XCIII, p. 368.
[2] Op. cit. 380.
[3] Journal, op. cit., p. 225.

smuggling fraternity. They were usually very fit men, notoriously bold and dexterous in their seamanship, especially in small craft: most attractive press-fodder in that they were not 'protected', and so unlikely to start unpleasant repercussions if pressed wholesale. But to off-set these two advantages (from the Impress officer's point of view) there were two distinct drawbacks. First, they were apt to resist desperately when tackled, and, second, once taken they were so bold and active that they were not very easily kept. Thus Captain Robinson of the *Proteus* once secured a fine batch of them after a furious fight, and was so pleased with their seamanlike looks and performances that he manned his barge with them. When, however, he sailed soon afterwards to the West Indies and landed at St. Kitts, all but one of them deserted and were not retaken.[1]

Dillon once had an exciting experience with another type of sea-user —a British Slaver from Guinea. Her skipper was crude but crafty. When Dillon boarded him he was all smiles and apologies. 'I'm so sorry,' he said in effect, 'but it's after eight o'clock. That is closing time in a Slaver, as you doubtless know. I'm bound by Act of Parliament to lock up the slave-room at that hour, and by Act of Parliament may not unlock it before tomorrow morning. Unfortunately, most of my crew are locked in there too!' This was ingenious, because he was right about the Act, though it was unusual to put the crew in with the slaves. Still, he might have done so—when he saw a man-of-war approaching. And if that man-of-war had been in a hurry, the trick might have succeeded. But Dillon was in no hurry. His riposte was, 'All right. I'll stay here till morning': which he did, having sent to warn his Captain to stand by. He passed his time in searching the Guineaman outside the slave-room, unearthed four men and sent them off to his frigate. But now the skipper of the slaver, outwitted in sharpness, began to turn nasty. He started edging away from the frigate and, when Dillon ordered him to wear ship and bring her back, he refused outright. Thereupon the Lieutenant, a small man and almost alone on board, but never lacking in courage and energy, seized the wheel himself and began to put the helm over: at which the Master, now beside himself with fury, rushed at him and spun the wheel violently back. One of the spokes caught the surprised Dillon on the mouth, and he fell, bleeding profusely from lips and gums. This scared the Master, for so to handle a commissioned officer of His Majesty's Navy might well bring him to the gallows. He gave up

[1] Nicol, op. cit., pp. 40–1.

his attempt at escape and tried to staunch the blood. Meanwhile Dillon's Captain, noticing that something was amiss, sent a boat with an armed guard. Dillon had won the second round too. In the morning, when the slave-room was unlocked, eleven of the Guineamen followed him to his frigate.

Hitherto, our witnesses have been mostly officers of the Royal Navy. There was, of course, a reverse to the medal. The skipper of the Guineaman was only doing what every victim of the Impressment System did—which was everything possible to evade it. Hence a perennial tussle of wits—no holds barred—between trapper and trapped. Robert Hay, who, between his last two desertions, made a voyage in a merchantman to the West Indies, relates how, as a matter of course, his skipper had 'stow-holds' carefully built in among the cargo: and one of these Hay used himself on the homeward trip. He gives a most exciting account of how the press-gang searched the hold where he lay concealed between the second and third layers of sugar-hogsheads. Plunging his cutlass between two casks, 'I see you, old genius,' one cried. 'And I see you, young fellow', said another. 'You may as well come out quietly . . .' This, however, was too stereotyped a trick to be dangerous. Robert lay doggo. 'Happily I was more than a cutlass length down.'[1]

In this instance the evader escaped. Here is an example of one who did not, ingenious as he was. Captain John Harvey Boteler—midshipman at the time (early in 1814)—tells the story.

'I was here told off to attend a press-gang: we had intimation of a lot of seamen hid in a small public house in the cove, and after a scrimmage secured very prime hands. Such a scene: a wake was got up, women howling over a coffin where a corpse was said to be. But our Lieutenant would not believe them, and sure enough out popped a seaman who laughed himself when all was over.'[2]

This episode could hardly take place other than where it did—in Ireland! But, all over the world, the catcher had to be spry and, as in this case, he often had the last word, though he did not always deserve it. There were certain pieces of evidence which were always regarded as sure signs of a man's maritime occupation. Thus in 1799 a certain John Teed, when pressed because he was 'in appearance very much like a sailor', vigorously denied the fact.

[1] Hay, op. cit., p. 208.
[2] *Recollections*, N.R.S., Vol. LXXXII, p. 44.

'"Strip him," said the officer ... In a twinkling Teed's shirt was over his head . . . Devices emblematic of love and the sea covered both arms from shoulder to waist. "You and I will lovers die, eh?" said the officer with a twinkle.'[1]

Other 'identifications' were widely regarded as almost equally infallible, though with much less justice. Thus to be guilty of having bandy legs in a seaport town when the Press was out was highly dangerous, and many a little tailor who had never set foot in a boat paid the penalty.[1]

Another ingenious technique was developed by Dillon when he himself became a frigate captain escorting a convoy. Whenever one of his charges behaved badly or refused to obey orders—and this happened fairly frequently—he went on board, pressed two or three of his best seamen and gave in exchange some of his own 'hard cases'. He thereby killed some four birds with one stone. He kept within the law (which allowed an exchange, though not a diminution); he punished the erring ship-master for his lapse, and made him more amenable in the future; he rid himself of his own trouble-makers, and he improved the efficiency of his own people.

Anyone who reads Dillon, or any other officer, discoursing upon Impressment as he saw it in real life, cannot but be struck by the remarkable callousness of it all. When he 'presses five stout seamen', he does so in precisely the same tone, and with exactly the same nonchalance, as when he 'takes on board half a dozen bullocks'. But so it always is and must be. Familiarity breeds callousness no less than contempt. It was the thing to do, the thing that he had always seen done. Dillon, it is true, was not particularly humane, or even imaginative. But that made no difference. Kindlier men than he could not avoid the infernal cruelty of it as seen from the victim's angle. Here is one typical example—one of untold thousands. It is narrated, not by an officer, who would probably be case-hardened, but by one who had himself been pressed. Robert Wilson was in 1807 a seaman, signalman in the frigate *Unité*, Captain Patrick Campbell.

'15th Jan. One William Skill, seaman, being in the prize in tow of us, fell overboard and was drowned . . . We had pressed him out of the India fleet, just on his return from a three-year voyage, pleasing himself with the idea of beholding those he held most dear (a mother and sister) for whom he had brought presents many a long mile: and although in his

[1] Hutchinson, op. cit., p. 244.

time aboard us he had made away with most of his apparel for grog, which he was fond of, yet the presents remained untouched, hoping one day to take them home himself.'[1]

Yet Captain Campbell, whose praises Wilson is for ever singing, was a just, humane and enlightened officer. But what could he do? His ship had to be manned, and he knew no other way. And indeed there was none; and would not be until the Olympians, who sat enthroned miles above the Campbells and the Dillons, condescended, themselves, to take the matter in hand. But this did not happen at all during our wars.

C. THE QUOTA

The Impress Service was an innovation which improved the machinery of Impressment, for so long the main form of rating-entry into the wartime Navy. In itself, however, it created no new form of entry, for it touched none but pressed, or pressable, men. But very soon after the war began there appeared a new sort altogether which was not quite either of the then existing forms: neither volunteering nor pressing. Like most new things in this country, it was forced upon the authorities because the existing forms were not adequate: they did not provide enough recruits. We can see clearly enough now what was happening. The one and only pool from which, hitherto, all naval ratings were being drawn was beginning to run dry, because it was no longer large enough for the greatly enlarged supply now required. That pool had hitherto been, of course, the whole seafaring (or, if one prefers it, the waterfaring) population of these islands: and, up to now, it had been capable, but sometimes only just capable, of supplying in wartime a sufficiency of both merchant and naval seamen.

Now, however, it was being forced upon the notice of those responsible for conducting the war that there were not enough seafaring persons to go round. There were still enough to fill the strictly naval requirements, no doubt; and these might be redirected into the Navy by more and ever-fiercer pressing. But this could only be done at the expense of the other partner, the Merchant Service; and no intelligent man could fail to realize that the overdraining of that service was no remedy at all. For trade was at once the true source of British prosperity and the provider of almost all her sinews of war.

Let us see what the problem looked like in figures. The graph on

[1] *Five Naval Journals*, N.R.S., Vol. XCI, p. 159.

page 119 shows the establishment of seamen and marines voted by Parliament every year, from January, 1793, when we were still at peace (though the commotions across the Channel might have warned us how unstable that peace was), down to January, 1817, by which time the demobilization of the fleets after Napoleon's final fall was complete. In some years, we note, there were supplementary estimates—indeed, in 1802, two. Here we see the sudden and vast demand for naval man-power during the first few years of the Revolutionary War, and the reason why the drain on the Seaman Pool, already felt in previous wars, now became too much for it. In January, 1793, the demand stood at 25,000, a figure a little but not much above average peacetime levels. It could be, and was, met. A hasty supplementary vote raised the total to 45,000; and this too was met by ordinary press-gang methods reinforced by the improved machinery of the Impress Service. The demand for 1794 was 85,000, and this too was met, but with considerable difficulty —enough difficulty to warn the Government of trouble ahead. For William Pitt the Younger, then Prime Minister, knew that our naval effort would have to be a great deal bigger yet. So, in 1795, 100,000 were voted.

How were they to be found? The press was at white heat already and, in pressing, there was obviously a Law of Diminishing Returns. Pitt, therefore, was forced to do something about it: and he did—something which was, in principle, not only quite new, but also quite right. If the Seaman Pool was really failing, then some other pool must be tapped. In a word, if there were not enough seamen, non-seamen must be introduced. This is what, in effect, he did—or tried to do—in his two Quota Acts of March and April, 1795. But again, as so often in our history, how to do it was a matter of trial and error and, unfortunately, the error predominated. As in the case of Impressment itself, the principle was sound enough: it was the machinery which was defective.

What happened was that ordinary Impressment went on, but the Acts allocated to the various geographical divisions of Britain, its counties, cities and towns, the responsibility of finding an additional *quota* for the fleet. It was done on roughly numerical lines. Thus Yorkshire was called upon for 1,081; Rutland, 23; London 5,704; Radnor, 26, and so on. The men picked, it is true, went through the motions of volunteering, and actually drew the very considerable bounties that went with the scheme. But, since the various geographical quotas *had* to be found, here was no true volunteering. What was really being introduced was the principle of Conscription. Yet they were not at all like the pressed men of the old sort, who were supposed to be—and who mostly were—seafarers. These quota-men, though some of them might be seafarers, were none of them supposed or required to be so. What the scheme was in fact, if we would tie a modern label on it, was 'Selective National Service'. And it failed—for fail it did—because those important people, the Selectors, being the wrong selectors, selected the wrong people.

It was perhaps inevitable. These selectors, in practice the town and county authorities, were being asked to perform a perfectly new kind of duty, and were not qualified to do it. They were not very politically educated, their attitude was likely to be over-parochial, and too narrow to grasp the wider issue of what was best for the whole country. Yet they saw readily enough where their own local interests lay and, though there were exceptions, these inexperienced and far-from-impartial people ran true to form. The scheme soon degenerated into a sort of minor gaol-delivery. The counties tended to select their 'bad boys', their vagrants, tramps and idlers. It suited the Justices of the Peace to conclude that the local poacher would be as destructive to French sailors as he was to English birds—and possibly they were right, though there was no shred of evidence to prove it. The town and city authorities sent worse types still—their undesirables; beggars; minor thieves and pickpockets, or people who looked as though they might pick pockets. They even, sometimes, gave the delinquents who appeared before them the alternatives of Quota or Quod. Another provision of the Act, which certainly did not improve quality, was that a quota-man, once picked, might find a substitute if he could. This, if anything, merely served to lower the general standard, because, if a man had the wherewithal to buy himself out, he must have been a person of at least some substance: which, by hypothesis, the substitute was not. Parliament, however, could hardly withhold this right since, by law, anyone in the Service could buy himself out—if he could afford it. But the price was stiff: in 1811, for instance, a discharge cost £80, and examples of its being bought are rare.[1]

On a sheer count of heads, probably, the Acts may be accounted a success. There is reason to suppose that the trickle of true volunteers, the press-gangs and the quotas between them did secure the volume required, until at any rate the last few years of the war. The Census of 1801—the earliest—whose returns were based on parishes, shows such

[1] See p. 328.

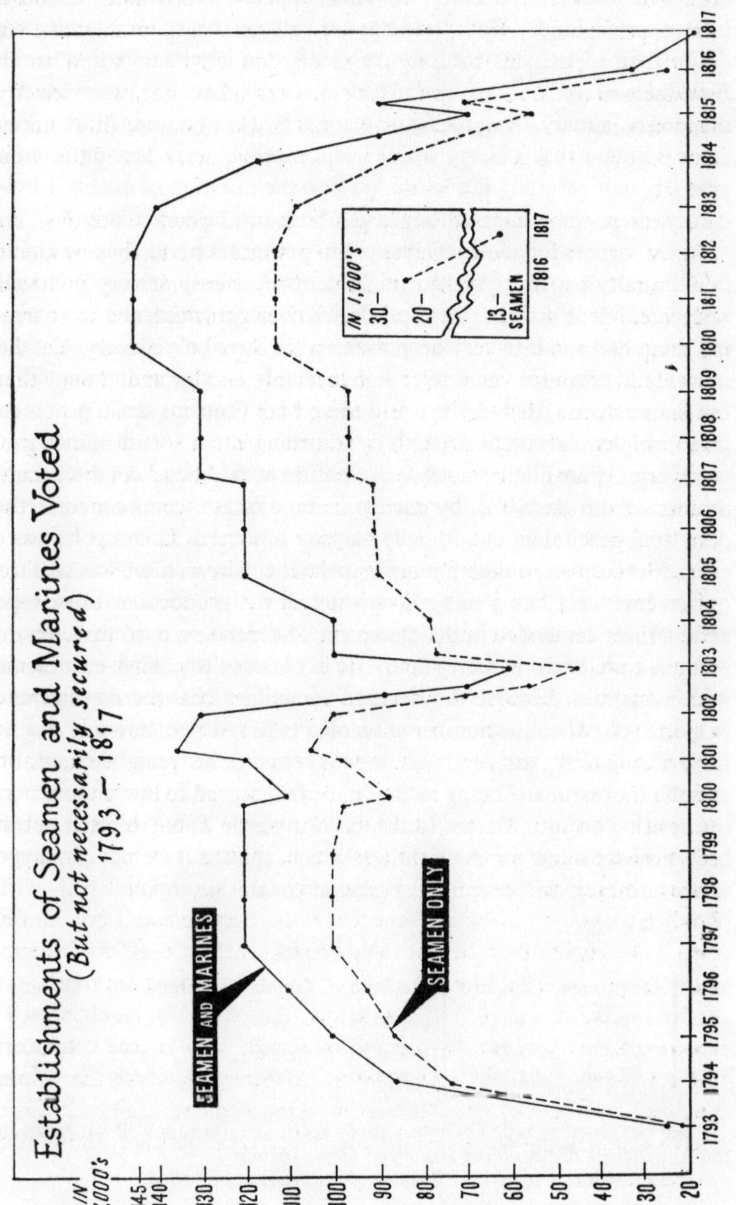
Establishments of Seamen and Marines Voted
(But not necessarily secured)
1793 – 1817
SEAMEN AND MARINES
SEAMEN ONLY
IN 1,000's
145
140
130
120
110
100
90
80
70
60
50
40
30
20
1793
1794
1795
1796
1797
1798
1799
1800
1801
1802
1803
1804
1805
1806
1807
1808
1809
1810
1811
1812
1813
1814
1815
1816
1817
IN 1,000's
30 —
20 —
13 —
SEAMEN
1816
1817

people as were not normally resident in parishes under separate headings. One such is 'The Navy, including Marines': another is 'Seamen, in Registered Ships'. Both headings are valuable to us, though we may doubt their meticulous accuracy, especially the latter's. We find in the *Establishment of Seamen and Marines Voted*[1] that 120,000 were demanded in January, 1801, the figure being raised to 135,000 in March. The Census shows that 126,279 seamen and marines were serving in that year (though naturally it does not go into the question of quality). Evidently, then, the numerical target had been hit, or very nearly.

Again, figures for a few separate years—1794, 1800 and 1804—survive in Admiralty papers.[2] Parliament, it seems, had been asking for actual numbers; but it is clear that the Admiralty clerks concerned in obtaining them had run into very deep waters, and were only able to supply a monthly average for each year; and that only an approximation. Who can blame them? All over the world there were Captains striving to keep their complements up to strength by securing men in a score of different ways, some quite illicit: but also, all over the world, men were disappearing daily from on board, by enemy action, disease, common accident, desertion, invaliding, etc. in daily varying numbers. This report, however, does furnish enough figures to make it appear that total annual requirements were being met, though not in the proportions of seamen and marines demanded in the estimates. The marines, in all three years, seem to have been in short supply. It is not easy to compare demands with actualities, because the demand sometimes changed in mid-year (e.g. in 1800, when the number of seamen required went down in March from 97,304 to 87,304), and—as in 1804—where the 'years' do not tally exactly, the 'estimate' being made on 1st January while the 'actuality' is the position on 16th March. In the following little Table an attempt has been made to allow for these things: which, though it cannot claim absolute accuracy, still permits the general conclusion to hold.

	SEAMEN		*MARINES*		*TOTAL*	
Year	Demanded	Obtained	Demanded	Obtained	Demanded	Obtained
1794	72,885	73,835	12,115	7,908	85,000	81,743
1800	92,304	93,813	22,696	19,398	115,000	113,211
1804	78,000	84,168	22,000	15,663	100,000	99,831

[1] See Graph on p. 119. The yearly totals voted are given by William James in the Appendices of his *Naval History of Great Britain.*

[2] P.R.O. Adm. 7/567 Misc. *Progress of the Navy*, 1756–1806.

I have nowhere seen this shortage of marines noticed; nor, therefore, any reason given for it. Yet surely one is to hand. Not all marines were picked men, of course; as we shall see, there was sometimes a strong 'foreign' contingent among them. But they were seldom real scum. Among their leading functions were the guarding of officers and the prevention of mutiny, and it would have been folly to put small-arms into the hands of notoriously unstable and untrustworthy people. Hence the very lowest levels—quota-men and the like: and it was only that category, we must remember, which enabled required numbers to be obtained—were rated Landmen, and given the duties of 'waisters' or of 'idlers' (see p. 273), where they could do essential if unspectacular work as tailors or hairdressers, or in keeping the 'heads' clean, without endangering the safety of anyone. They were not allowed in as Marines, who therefore remained under complement.

The other valuable figure to be gleaned from the Census is the total number of merchant seamen, or rather, such of them as were in registered ships. This figure is 144,558. The sum of these two categories—'the Navy' and 'the Seamen'—should, at first sight, yield the total size of the whole Seaman Pool. It is 270,837. But both figures need adjusting. By 1801 the quota-men had been coming in for some years, and many of them were certainly not seamen at all. So the true 'seaman' part of the Navy total must have been less than 126,279. On the other hand, the figure 144,558 represents only the merchant seamen in registered ships. So there must have been more than this all told. The surplus in the latter case—the seamen in unregistered ships, many fishermen and some watermen—is probably greater than the deficit in the former—the landlubbers in the Navy, so that the real Seaman Pool was probably rather greater than 270,837—say 300,000. Further—and especially towards the end of the war, when the 'numbers voted' rose to 145,000—another sort of 'seaman', not counted in the Census figure at all, ought to be added—that is, the foreigners serving in the fleet, of whom we shall shortly hear more. These might bring the full number of seamen available to Britain (though not all British), either for the Navy or for the Merchant Service, to about one-third of a million.

It is very regrettable that the Navy's first attempt at National Service, a thing so admirable in itself, should have foundered simply because of faulty selection. For so it was. Sufficient bodies were forthcoming but, full and by, they were the wrong bodies. Their arrival on shipboard, also, caused much ill-feeling among the better men already there. The

Quota bounties were higher, usually much higher, than those originally offered to the genuine early volunteers. Hence, naturally, there was legitimate grumbling among the latter. They were as a whole worthier, steadier and more experienced men and they could not help knowing it. Why, they could hardly fail to ask bitterly, why pay four times as much for a miserable specimen who is patently not worth a quarter of ourselves? Indeed, they might have said *fourteen* times, as witness the oft-quoted passage from Edward Brenton, himself a contemporary historian and an active sea-officer:

'The quota-bounty given in 1795, 1796 and 1797 we conceive to have been the most ill-advised and fatal measure ever adopted by the Government for manning the fleet. The seamen who voluntarily enlisted in 1793, and fought some of the most glorious of our battles, received the comparatively small bounty of £5. These brave fellows saw men, totally ignorant of the profession, the very refuse and outcasts of Society, fleeing from justice and the vengeance of the Law, come on board with bounty to the amount of £70. One of these objects, on coming on board a ship of war with £70 bounty, was seized by a boatswain's mate who, holding him up with one hand by the waistband of his trousers, humourously exclaimed, "here's a fellow that cost a guinea a pound!"'

Many serious results stemmed from this indiscriminate importation of poor material. One was that it cast a slur upon the very large seaman-element in the Navy. Indeed, even to this day there are those who are deceived into thinking that the whole Service was corrupted and ruined by the influx: who, because some—even many—of the quota-men were bad, would write off the whole seamanhood of Britain as worthless scum who could only be brought to a semblance of discipline, and induced to do their duty, by the constant and savage application of the lash. Nothing could be further from the truth. It is a monstrous calumny. But it is also an absurd one. In real life things do not work out like that. It simply is not possible for officers, however talented, however bold and however brutal, to whip real courage, cheerfulness and endurance into a crew mainly composed of gaolbirds, ne'er-do-wells and puny starvelings: and every contemporary history, biography and autobiography, dozens of which survive, gives the straight lie to any such caricature of the British Seaman of Nelson's day.

A sense of proportion is particularly important here, and there is to hand an unexceptionable person to supply it. The Reverend Edward

Mangin, a writer of no mean ability and repute, and in no sense a seafaring man, once tried the experiment of a cruise as Chaplain in a man-of-war in wartime. He has left a most revealing account of his—to him—novel experiences. He is patently unbiased, and his view of all the strange things he saw and the strange people he met is informed with good, plain commonsense, of which quality he evidently possessed great store. This is what he says of the Ship's Company which had just joined the *Gloucester*, Captain Robert Williams:

'*Sunday, June 14th.* I read prayers and preached to the now entire Ship's Company. The newcomers . . . were drafts from the *Namur* and *Dreadnought* [Receiving Ships]: many of them thoroughbred seamen, and the whole was as fine an assemblage of men as could be seen. I stood on the Poop, and viewed them as they passed muster on the Quarter-deck to be entered on the ship's books . . . Of these, nearly 400 were men above the ordinary size and in the prime of life.'[1]

The date is important. It was not in the earlier 1790's, when the Quota 'infection' was unknown: not in the late 1790's, nor even in the 1800's, when, according to the pessimists, the venom was slowly but surely working through the veins of the Old Navy with such devastating effect. It was in 1812, when the war was nearing its end; when the poison must have done its foul work—if it ever did it. But is *this* the description which an intelligent and very observant man would give of a cowed, broken community, lashed to despair, seething with discontent, interlarded with vice, crime and ill-health? Indeed it is not, for such a community never existed.

Yet we must not go too far the other way. There *was* a pernicious leaven working, or striving to work, in the healthy lump: and it did not work entirely in vain. Thus, no doubt, it brought with it the necessity for more, and harsher, punishments: and the punishments, as ever, were brutal. The Cat fell, more often and more harshly, upon the backs of the men as a whole; but not more heavily upon those of the real volunteers and the old pressed men. Indeed, it is significant to find that both these older classes seldom if ever complained of the institution of flogging: on the contrary, they almost always approved it, in principle at least, as some sort of safeguard, not only to the efficiency of the ships they served in and were proud of, but also to themselves. We have read the Officers' view. Let us read the Rating's—the steady old-fashioned

[1] *Five Naval Journals*, N.R.S., Vol. XCI, p. 19.

seaman's. He knew his quota-men at first hand—he had to live with them!

'Them was the chaps as played hell with the fleet! Every grass-combing beggar as chose to bear up for the bounty had nothing to do but dock the tails of his togs and take to the tender. They used to ship in shoals: they were drafted by forties and fifties to each ship in the fleet. They were hardly up the side, hardly mustered abaft before there was "Send for the barber", "shave their pates", and send them forward to the head to be scrubbed and sluished from clue to earing afore ye could venture to berth with them below. Then stand clear of their shore-going rigs! Every finger was fairly a fish-hook: neither chest nor bed nor blanket nor bag escaped their sleight-of-hand thievery. They pluck you —aye, as clean as a poulterer, and bone your very eyebrows whilst staring you full in the face.'[1]

The *real* British seaman was usually a simple soul, obstinately conservative, ill-educated and, as we have much cause to lament, unvocal. In just one respect it is possible to argue, then, that the quota-men performed a useful service. Among the newcomers there were individuals who had had a better education, and who certainly knew much more about the world outside the Navy. Some of them were even relatively well-educated men, though they seldom made good use of that advantage. Still, the *savoir faire* was there, and unquestionably they contrived to impart a fraction of it to the true seamen. They certainly implanted in them, for instance, some realization of how grossly they were being exploited. This, without bringing the seamen down to anything like their own level, yet led to a much greater incidence of unruliness, insubordination, 'shot-rolling'[2] and even mutiny. All the contemporary writers, without exception, note—and deplore—a very marked falling-off of discipline throughout the Navy, beginning in 1795, culminating in 1797, the 'year of mutinies', but continuing, more or less sporadically, for years afterwards.

The men behind the famous Spithead affair of 1797 have never really been identified. This alone argues some considerable cleverness in

[1] Quoted by Commander C. N. Robinson in *The British Fleet*, p. 438.

[2] i.e. rolling 32-lb. shots along the deck at unsuspecting officers, from a distance and on dark nights. Similar activities symptomatic of the unrest then prevailing were the dropping of objects (e.g. marlinspikes) 'accidentally' from aloft, and leaving buckets etc. in dangerous and ill-lighted spots between-decks: not quite 'mutiny', and very difficult to bring home to the culprit.

them, for ringleadership in mutiny was highly dangerous. They were, however, almost certainly not of the old seaman stock. They showed themselves too subtle and sophisticated for that. The historian's favourite candidate for leadership was one Valentine Joyce, a Quartermaster's Mate of apparently good character, certainly a strong man, and, in his way, a wise one; probably, also, *affairé* and too well educated to have been a professional seaman. He is said to have been assisted by a lawyer named Evans, serving in the fleet under an assumed name; and certainly someone among the delegates seems to have possessed real legal knowledge. All is shadowy: but a trained lawyer on the Lower Deck in 1797 can hardly have been other than a quota-man. Indeed, one of the few items on the credit side of the Quota's account was that it induced the real seamen to assert their rights when they did. Unquestionably, that self-assertion led in the end to a better, happier and more efficient Navy. Not that the Spithead leaders were bad men themselves. Clearly they were not. Their remarkable talents of organization were balanced by a surprising display of moderation and good sense: which in its turn merely goes to show that not all quota-men were bad men, and that the Spithead fleet was very fortunate in its leaders.

The Nore fleet was a great deal less lucky. Here the leader, Richard Parker, was certainly a quota-man, and an educated one. He was the son of a 'respectable' Exeter baker (just about in Marshall's sense), and his mother is said to have been of gentle birth. Indeed, he himself seems to have been sufficiently 'gentle' to have entered the Navy as a prospective officer, and to have been rated Midshipman. He is even said to have gone one step further and become, for a short while, an Acting Lieutenant—all but a commissioned officer. Further stories (of which, after he reached notoriety, there was a large crop, not all to be credited) represent him as earning considerable prize-money in the American War, and leaving the Navy in order to spend it in riotous living—a doubtful story, as Captain Brenton, who knew him, says that he was only thirty at the time of his execution in 1797.[1] Another story, more probable from what we know of his medical history, is that, taking a poor view of his Captain, he had the temerity to call him out and, as a result, was thrown out himself. All such stories, however, true or otherwise, show us a man well educated, but hasty, unbalanced and a bit of a waster. Thereafter he became something of a nomad, and we lose sight of him. But later he turned up in Scotland, now married and trying to eke out a living as a

[1] Brenton's *Naval History of Great Britain*, I, 296.

maker of golf-balls and a schoolmaster. At the outbreak of war he re-entered the Navy and became a Midshipman for the second time. History, however, repeated itself. He was in trouble again, court-martialled and disrated for disobedience, finding himself once more 'on the beach', invalided for rheumatism. He fell into debt, and was imprisoned in Edinburgh with no hope of release. Here is no bad illustration of how the Quota worked, and why its recruits were hardly of the best. With no other prospects whatever he accepted the bounty, some say of £20, some of £30, and so made his third bow to the Navy in the *Sandwich* at the Nore. Here the officers saw only a likely-looking fellow—Brenton says that he possessed a good and even handsome presence—and, discovering that he evidently knew the ways of the sea, rated him Able Seaman then and there. It was doubtless these qualities of education, natural expertise and presence which made the mutineers pick him as leader, though experience was soon to show that he had few of a leader's assets.

In truth Parker was what modern medicine would probably class as a neurotic rather than an indictable criminal. Indeed Brenton, who had watched him at close quarters, actually says as much, though no one else does—'I have no doubt that he was at times deranged'—and also that he had suicidal tendencies[1]. This is interesting: for here is the man who is so often held up as an outstanding example of the criminal types which the Quota-system let into the Service. I believe, myself, that 'criminal' is not the right word with which to describe most of the 'bad boys' of the Quota. It is misleading because, when we of the twentieth century hear the term, we read into it something considerably different from what the eighteenth century meant by it. We should remember that quite a big proportion of the unfortunates who got to know the insides of eighteenth century prison-ships, prisons and even convict-ships would, today, go no further downhill than to the local neurotic hospital: or perhaps not so far even as that; perhaps only into the hands of a kindly Probation Officer. No: among the quota-men there were no doubt a few major criminals, but very few. Rather more were neurotics, even psychopaths, like Parker: but, much more numerous than both these two put together were the social misfits and outcasts of the countryside and the riff-raff of the new town-slums, the latter physically insignificant like the 70-pound man; victims of under-nourishment and stupid, heartless legislation: the dirty, mean products of economic

[1] Op. cit., II, 297.

squalor, the jetsam of the Industrial Revolution, the new submerged poor.

A pretty crew they were to be pitchforked into our first line of national defence, our main spearhead of attack. Yet so it was; and that is the measure of the failure of our first groping experiment in National Service, our first enforced departure from our traditional source of naval supply—the Seaman Pool. As it happened, we had no further occasion to experiment for a century. Still, it looks as though our errors were not quite in vain. At any rate, when we tried National Service again, first in 1916, then in 1939, we certainly made an infinitely better job of it.

D. FOREIGNERS

One more category of rating in H.M. Ships calls for consideration—the Foreigner. It seems strange at first sight that the Royal Navy in its prime admitted men of alien race in quite considerable quantities. But what has gone before in these pages will surely give the reason. It was the compelling demand for sheer numbers, and, in addition, the need constantly experienced by captains on foreign stations to make up day-to-day and month-to-month wastage in their crews. At home the necessary figure could usually be reached (though at the expense of quality), at any rate until the final boosting up of our man-power in 1811 to 145,000 per annum. But, abroad, things might be much harder if there happened to be no available British merchant ships from which to press men. In such circumstances, the captains would often take the easy option, and pick up foreigners. An easy option it was because, in almost all ports, British or foreign, commercial or naval, there were many individuals from other seafaring nations who were stranded, permanently or, more often, temporarily: just hanging about waiting for another merchantman in which to sign on, and therefore ideal press-gang fodder: seamen, often good ones too: men, moreover, unlikely to be able to 'state a case' and make trouble for the pressing officer: men who probably had no friends at all in the ports in which they were stranded, which were often foreign to them too.[1] Sometimes, indeed, they did not have to be pres-

[1] For instance, on the demobilization following the 'Spanish Armament' of 1790, there was a glut of British seamen in British ports, and American merchant skippers found that they could secure good British labour at about half the price they were paying to their own crews. Thereupon many of them callously abandoned their American seamen, leaving them stranded in British ports. (J. F. Zimmerman, *Impressment of American Seamen*, New York, 1925, p. 32.)

sed. Being 'on their beam-ends' as the phrase goes—and went—they gladly volunteered. They were in larger numbers than is sometimes supposed because, then, as in most other periods, the merchant marines of the various sea-using nations, our own included, were a very cosmopolitan lot. The races were apt to become so inextricably mixed that, at several moments in our history, our own governments had been frightened by the phenomenon and had sought, not very successfully, to limit the numbers of foreigners in ships of British register. Of course, they had little success: for the influx was, indirectly, their own doing. It was an integral part of the whole manning-problem. While volunteer-bounties, the press-gangs and the Impress Service were busy draining British seamen from merchant ships, the merchants themselves, in self-defence, could do nothing but sign on foreigners to replace them.

But things would not, and could not, stop there. Captains, at their wits' end for naval seamen, would be sure, sooner or later, to press the foreigners as well as the Britons out of the merchantmen which they boarded. It was, in fact, an everyday occurrence. Samuel Leech, for instance, remarks, quite *en passant*, how his frigate, the *Macedonian*, entering Lisbon, 'had resort to the press-gang which was made up of our most loyal men armed to the teeth: by their aid we obtained our full numbers'.[1] The recruits would be a mixed bag—some British deserters from R.N. ships who had taken advantage of Sunday shore-leave often granted in foreign ports: some seamen from British merchantmen in port, who might be British-born, but again might not; and frankly foreign seamen from any foreign ship that might be in, or from foreign ships recently taken by us as Prize. Actually, Leech names only one category, but that an interesting one.

'Among them were a few Americans. They were taken without respect to their protections which were often taken from them and destroyed. Some were released through the influence of the American consul: others, less fortunate, were carried to sea to their no small chagrin. To prevent recovery of these men by their consul, the press-gang usually went ashore in the night previous to our going to sea so that, before they were missed, they were beyond his protection.'

It was the allegation of such high-handed acts as these, it will be recalled, which was the main cause of the Anglo-American War of 1812:[2]

[1] Leech, op. cit., p. 28.

[2] See Appendix, p. 434.

but it is only fair to add that we denied having perpetrated such practices, and that Leech's evidence is not quite so damnatory as it may sound because, when he wrote it, he had been for many years an American citizen. Elsewhere, and still quite casually, he mentions many other aliens by name—another American who fell overboard and was lost, a Swede who fell overboard and was saved; a Portuguese Boy, a Malay serving as a steward, 'Black Tom', a Negro, and some Frenchmen; Italians and Spaniards who (though excused from fighting and flogging) were taken on as a musical band, and all 'rated'.

The story is the same in any ship that we care to investigate. In May, 1808, for instance, the *Implacable*'s Ship's Books give this picture. It is worth giving in detail as a specimen of what (her own Captain says) 'may be considered applicable to every British ship, with the exception that [his italics] *very* few of them have so *many native subjects*'.[1]

BRITISH (White Men)		OTHERS			
England	285	Jamaica	1	Corsica	1
Ireland	130	Trinidad	1	Portugal	5
Wales	25	St. Domingo	2	Sicily	1
Isle of Man	6	St. Kitts	1	Minorca	1
Scotland	29	Martinique	1	Ragusa	1
Shetland	3	Santa Cruz	1	Brazil	1
Orkneys	2	Bermuda	1	Spain	2
Guernsey	2	Sweden	8	Madeira	1
Canada	1	Denmark	7	U.S.A.	28
Total	**483**	Prussia	8	West Indies	2
		Holland	1	Bengal	2
		Germany	3	**Total**	**80**

Total Complement 563

Percentages

British	86%
Others	14%

Even in the *Victory* at Trafalgar—surely the one ship and occasion above all others where one might expect an all-true-blue British crew—there were seventy-one foreigners, drawn from twelve nationalities, one of which was French. Surprising? Perhaps. None the less it is a *small* figure—8 per cent only, as compared with the 'below-average' *Implacable*'s 14 per cent. And what whim of fortune set Frenchmen in such a place at such a moment? Dillon perhaps gives us the clue. After the

[1] Sir T. Byam Martin, Journals and Letters, N.R.S., Vol. XII, p. 10.

First of June action in 1794, his ship, the *Defence*, received on board fifty-six Frenchmen, prisoners from the captured enemy ship *Northumberland*.

'Some of them, very fine, powerful men, tried hard to be received as volunteers on board the *Defence*. There was no end to their praises of our conduct and of our victory. But their offers were not accepted.'[1]

Most of the best French seamen came from Brittany and Normandy, two French districts but little in sympathy with the Revolution as it developed in Paris. Even then several parts of North-west France were in open revolt against the Republic, so that many of these men may have regarded themselves as patriots; in some ways not unlike the Free French of World War II.[2] Dillon gives our reason for not accepting them:

'Strange to say, all the foreigners we had on board had deserted their guns, except one. As this fact had been ascertained, there was no desire to add to their number by allowing the Frenchmen to form part of our crew. This conduct of the foreigners made a lasting impression on my mind, never to employ them in any ship I might command. Consequently, when I rose in the Service, my first object . . . was to get rid of all of them.'

No doubt they were palmed off on recalcitrant merchant-masters in exchange for prime British seamen!

He gives details of the bad conduct of two of the *Defence*'s foreigners. One was first captain[3] of one of the guns in Dillon's charge. He deserted his post during the action and went below. There he showed the Surgeon a wound on his neck which in fact he had sustained from the blow of a handspike, delivered by the gun's second captain[3] as he sneaked off. The other was a marine—'one of the finest-limbed men I ever beheld', who, when all was over, was dragged feet first from under the hen-coops on the Poop, where he had cowered throughout the action.

This, however, was in 1794, before the old recruiting channels had run dry. Eighteen years later things looked different. Those fifty-six stout Frenchmen would hardly have been refused then. Almost exactly

[1] N.R.S., Vol. XCIII, p. 142.

[2] We had valuable help from some of them, especially such as were pilots, who, throughout the wars, aided our navigation off the French coasts. (Richardson, op. cit., p. 324.)

[3] See p. 278.

twice as many men were wanted, and all known supplies had been tapped and tapped until they were all but dry. We have seen the position in the *Implacable* in 1808. In the *Warspite* in 1812 they were worse.[1] There were ninety-seven foreigners on board—eighty-three seamen and fourteen marines—in a complement about the same size as the *Implacable*'s. The marines were mostly Germans. The seamen may be divided into two groups—fifty who are classified simply as 'Foreigners' and thirty-three who are 'volunteers from prison-ships'. These latter, to judge by their names, were mostly Scandinavians and Baltic Germans—no Frenchmen. They were probably merchant seamen taken in enemy-controlled ships, or neutral ships which had failed to pass our scrutiny and been condemned as Prize. All of them had volunteered but recently, and were very likely pro-British at heart because Napoleon's Continental System had made France most unpopular in those countries which lay under her heel, especially the maritime ones. They would also, almost certainly, be real seamen. The other group, fifty strong, were mostly old-stagers (thirty pressed and twenty volunteers)—some of them very old stagers, led by a pressed Minorcan and a Norwegian volunteer, both with twenty years' service. The largest single contingent came from America, but it was only ten, and included two long-term volunteers of nineteen and eight years respectively. The remainder were mostly North Europeans, Sweden leading with six (all pressed): and, this time, there was a Frenchman, a volunteer from Orleans, and two French colonials, both pressed. Here the proportion of foreigners is rather over 17 per cent, and it is evidently considered rather too high to be safe, as the correspondence in which the list appears shows concern over the number.[2]

In this ship the aliens look a reasonable lot, especially the old-stagers. But that this was not always so the episode of the *Albanaise* shows.[3] This was a small bomb-ketch recently taken from the French, and employed, late in 1800, in the western Mediterranean for carrying messages, escort duties and the like. Her officers, apart from her Captain, Commander Newcombe, were of distinctly poor stuff, her complement small and of bad material. Many of them were Portuguese, Spaniards and Italians, picked up locally as shortages occurred. There were also

[1] Keith Papers, N.R.S., Vol. XCVI, p. 321.

[2] National Maritime Museum, MS.9281. Keith Papers, Admiralty Letter 19.1.1813.

[3] *Mariner's Mirror*, Vol. XLIII, p. 194.

on board a number of Spanish prisoners taken from prizes—dangerous passengers, especially when they had compatriots among the crew. The result was mutiny. The officers were overpowered at night and the ship was carried into Malaga and surrendered. The ringleader seems to have been of British extraction, but several of his foremost abettors were Portuguese and Italians; and the very high foreign percentage undoubtedly had much to do with the affair. Such conduct in aliens is hardly surprising. There was no particular reason for expecting any great degree of loyalty among such people. What is more surprising—and highly creditable—is that the British elements almost always behaved themselves so well, since they can have had little but patriotism to set against the hardships they were expected to endure. Without loyalty to Britain (which presumably most foreigners did not possess) what indeed *did* they owe the Royal Navy?

So far we seem to have saddled the Captains with the blame—if such it can be called—for recruiting foreigners. Yet, often, they had nothing to do with it. The aliens were sometimes sent to them, wholesale, by the Admiralty. In 1799, for instance, the *Canada* received, in a single batch, a draft of sixty Spaniards straight from prison-ships;[1] while after Trafalgar the Captain of the *Conqueror*, ordered to give up one-quarter of his carefully-trained crew to man one of the prizes, received, among the riff-raff he got in exchange, thirty-six Spanish prisoners just caught. He protested, but was not allowed to refuse them. However, he was a man of resource. As soon as his ship returned to her station off Vigo, he 'gave them leave to go on shore, and they never returned'.[2]

Sir Charles Ekins himself points out some of the disadvantages in using enemy prisoners. Here is one. In one of his ships was a volunteer Marine who had entered with a bounty. Having attacked a messmate with a knife, he was had aft for punishment at the gangway. But before it could be inflicted he protested officially to the Captain, denying the latter's right to touch his person. He was, he said, the subject of another power and a prisoner of war, and demanded to return, unpunished, to his prison-ship. He was right, apparently, both in fact and in law. He was a Frenchman, and after the Admiralty had considered his case he was sent back, unpunished and still in possession of his £6 bounty.[3]

Here, as ever, our concern is primarily with the British Navy. But

[1] Sir Charles Ekins, *Naval Battles*, 1824, p. 172, note.
[2] Ibid., p. 171.
[3] Ibid., p. 173.

that this foreigner-problem was not confined to one side only let one example show. Just now we wondered, mildly, at finding a Frenchman in the British flagship at Trafalgar. But, if Ekins is to be believed, in the French flagship on that occasion there were eighteen Britons.[1] They were all deserters, he tells us, and nearly all of them were killed in the action: which perhaps was lucky for them.

E. DESERTERS

The presence of these Britons in an enemy ship leads to another aspect of this manning question, hitherto mentioned only in passing. In describing the struggles of our authorities to secure enough seamen, we have so far considered mainly the factor of Recruitment. There was, however, another factor altogether, working in a diametrically opposite direction—Desertion. In spite of all that those responsible could do, in spite of wholesale restriction of shore-leave, drastic punishments inflicted upon those caught, and forfeiture of all back-pay, allowances and privileges, men deserted in a steady stream. The most cursory glance at any original Ship's Book will reveal a monotonous repetition of the letter 'R', signifying that the man against whose name it was placed had 'run'. Our sea-journalists also produce constant instances of it. Men might, and did, desert anywhere, even when there was but little chance of getting clear. Their favourite moment, naturally, was when their ships were in home ports: but then that was among the harder moments, because the authorities were at their most vigilant. None the less, Robert Hay brought it off—twice. The first time was under quite exceptional circumstances. His frigate, the *Amethyst*, was wrecked close to Plymouth in February, 1811, and when, half-drowned, he reached the shore, he simply walked off.[2] He got clear away, and even made a voyage to the West Indies in a merchantman before being pressed anew, this time in London. He was sent to the *Ceres*, guardship at the Nore, and from here he escaped again. This affair was a more calculated one, and he had to swim six miles to the Isle of Grain. He had taken the precaution, though, to provide himself with five bladders, and made the shore with a companion and without grave danger, getting clean away, this time for good.[3] Such fortune, however, did not come the way of a ship-

[1] Sir Charles Ekins, op. cit., p. 278.
[2] Hay, op. cit., p. 187.
[3] Ibid., p. 227.

mate of Pemberton's, who was drowned in Milford Haven on a swim not half so long.[1] For, once determined to run, a man would often do so, on the most unlikely occasions, braving even shark-infested tropical waters or taking the risk of being marooned on uninhabited islands. Many, too, deserted at foreign ports of call. Here, as we have seen, they could be fairly confident of finding employment, sooner or later, in merchant ships whose Masters, so short of hands themselves, were not apt to ask awkward questions. Many—probably many thousands—joined the merchant ships, and even the warships, of the U.S.A. (see p. 434). But a 'run' man's life was miserable. He was a hunted fugitive, in constant fear of recognition and of being hauled back to condign punishment, sometimes even to a 'flogging round the fleet'. In practice, however, unless actually taken in arms against us, he was seldom executed, or even maimed beyond recovery: and with good reason. Deserter or not, he was still a 'hand' and, as such, a commodity more valuable alive than dead.

Desertion was not the only 'minus' factor in the manning problem. There was a perennial and by no means negligible drain from 'invaliding' too. But desertion was the larger, and it was large indeed. The size of these wastages is well revealed in a pamphlet entitled *Strictures on Naval Discipline.*[2] 'When the mode for supplying the British Navy with seamen is taken into consideration,' the author remarks drily in his introduction, 'it will not be a matter for surprise to find they desert.' He goes on to give figures for one period between May, 1803, and June, 1805. Here they are:

Invalided by Surveys of Captains and Surgeons	3017
Able Seamen deserted	5662
Ordinary Seamen deserted	3903
Landsmen deserted	2737
Total number lost to Service in 25 months	15,319

What an indictment of the System these figures reveal! See how they rise as the men become more senior and therefore, one might suppose, more trustworthy. But it is not altogether surprising. The 'Ables' and the 'Ordinaries' had had, on the whole, more time to decide how uncomfortable and ill-used they were: they had also, the more trusted they

[1] *Pel. Verjuice*, pp. 127–31.

[2] By Ad. Philip Patton (Murray & Cochrane, Edinburgh). No date, but contemporary.

were, the better opportunities for running; and the better seamen they were, the more they realized how much better paid and more comfortable they would be (or thought they would be) in other jobs, in the Merchant Service, ashore or under other countries' flags. That they were often wrong in their conjectures is neither here nor there. They were mostly simple souls—the better the seaman, as a rule, the simpler the man. The whole of this Table bears tragic witness to, perhaps, folly on the one side, but certainly to heartless stupidity on the other.

F. COMPOSITION OF A TYPICAL SHIP'S COMPANY, CIRC. 1812

Here, in conclusion, is an attempt to allocate percentages to the various types described above. As they would not be the same throughout the wars, a date must be decided upon: and this is 1812, when recruitment problems were at their most unrelenting stage.

First come the Boys who, if we allow the doubtful cases of some of the Marine Society lads, were all volunteers. Even in the most desperate manning crises, the Navy never sank so low as to impress children. These Boys would average about 8 per cent of a typical crew.

Next come the men-volunteers—those, that is, entering of their own accord on the small initial bounties, either direct or through the Marine Society; and that larger company who volunteered to avoid impressment. Both these groups counted as volunteers and received the volunteer-bounty: and they normally constituted the cream of the Ship's Company. Here numbers would vary considerably between ship and ship. Much depended upon the reputation of the Captain. If he had a name for ferocity; if he had an 'ill-luck' reputation in the matter of prize-money, or even if his ship was known to be posted to an unhealthy station, or one far from the usual haunts of prizes, then he secured very few. If on the other hand he was noted for moderation and fairness (even though strict); if he had acquired a 'lucky' name, and was known for a bold man who would not let chances slip, or if he was appointed to a good prize-making station like the Indies (East or West) or the Mediterranean, then he would do relatively well. But, even at best, it was never a large percentage. Nelson, always a popular man to serve with—not for his prize-luck, which was inconsiderable, but because the men admired him and knew that he would look after them—had 22 per cent of his *Victory* crew entered volunteerly at Trafalgar. Frigate captains with fabulous prize-reputations like Cochrane sometimes did better still, but for a sober line-of-battle ship 22 per cent was much above the average. An unfavoured captain would be lucky with 8 per cent, and 15 would be perhaps a fair average. If we add to this 15 a few of the foreigners who might be volunteers—say 2 per cent of the whole Ship's Company—and, of course, the 8 per cent contingent of Boys, we reach a figure of 25 per cent. And this is about all the 'volunteer' contribution—just about one quarter of the whole. These were mostly, but not all, seamen by trade, and might hail from any part of the British Isles.

There were certainly family traditions in this matter of volunteering for the Service. Leech, for instance, wanted to take the plunge because he heard so much about the life from his cousins, the Turners of Wanstead. This must have been a splendid family. There were twenty-two brothers and sisters in that one generation, at least six of whom, and almost certainly more, were naval seamen, almost certainly volunteers: so was one of their uncles, and their grandfather. Further, they seem to have been devoted to the life, open-hearted and open-handed young fellows who could not sing its praises loudly enough: which was all the more odd seeing that three of the family had died at sea and two more were drowned in the *Blenheim* when she was lost without trace. Possibly young Leech exaggerates their merit somewhat, for they were his boyhood's heroes: yet what would not one give for the chance of an evening with the Turner family, sitting round the paternal hearth at Wanstead and swapping yarns? As we left them, what should we think of the exponents of the all-scum theory? And who can study, dispassionately, the pages of Hay, Watson and Nicol; of Wilson, of Richardson, and even—sometimes—of the sensitive Verjuice and the disillusioned Leech, and continue to hold that jaundiced view?

The third, and much the largest, group was that of the Pressed Men, perhaps 50 per cent of an average Ship's Company. These should by right (and by law) have been seamen—or at least water-men—every one. But probably, in fact, as many as 5 per cent were not—men like Pemberton and his drowned shipmate. Still, most of the 45 per cent, let us make no mistake, were good, sound stuff too. The sea in the days of sail was no place for the weakling, and these were Britain's old seamen stock. Even the 5 per cent, wrongly hauled in, were unlikely to be weaklings, for the press-gangs' temptations to exceed their rights would be the stronger if the quarry were an upstanding fellow, the weaker if he were a weed. The athletic Hull carpenter who eluded Dillon is probably a case in point. So we have accounted for some three-quarters of our Ship's Company without any serious falling-off of quality.

It may be urged that fifty is too high a percentage for impressed men: and certainly, in most muster-books that we examine, we do not find two 'Imps' for every 'Vol'. But we must not forget a practice which consistently overweighted the 'Vol' entries. In most, if not all, rendezvous to which, in the first instance, a man captured on land was taken, the officer in charge gave the victim the option to volunteer, offering him the current bounty and even urging him to take it.[1] Naturally, the man often succumbed. After all, he was well and truly caught and, unless he could show a valid 'protection', or prove that he was not eligible press-gang fodder, he was most unlikely to escape anyway. If he agreed, he was labelled 'Volunteer'; but it would entirely falsify our present purpose if we labelled him other than 'imprest'. Moreover, we have Nicol's word for it that the real hundred-per-cent volunteer was not very common:

> 'I was surprised to see so few others who, like myself, had chosen it [a naval career] for the love of that kind of life. Some had been forced into it by their own irregular conduct, but the greater number were impressed men.'[2]

The fourth class are the Foreigners. They would vary a great deal, but most of them would certainly be seamen, handy about the ship if sometimes suspect in fighting her. As there were many less than usual in the *Victory* (8 per cent), rather less than usual (14 per cent) in the *Implacable*—if we may trust Byam Martin—and rather more than usual (a good 17 per cent) in the *Warspite*, it would be reasonable, and not too high, to put the average at 15 per cent. As we have seen, a few of these—say 2 per cent—would be, and have been counted as, volunteers. So we have now accounted for 88 per cent, and all of them had their strengths, some in personal qualities, some in seamanship, some in both. Anyway, they were by no means 'riff-raff'.

There remains only the fifth group. These were, for the most part, the quota-men and odd debtors, 'My Lord Mayor's men' and petty miscreants, sometimes actually from the gaols and 'given the option':

[1] Cf. Hay, op. cit., p. 219. Though given the choice, he refused it. Being a 'run' man, he would have seriously aggravated his already serious offence if proved, when caught, to have taken any bounty at all.

[2] Nicol, op. cit., p. 36.

admittedly, as a class, of poor material: some of them the 'fish-hook' folk, and many, no doubt, gentry who 'left their country for their country's good':[1] a few of them seamen, or ex-seamen like Parker, but mostly not; and very few of them (save perhaps some of the country types—poachers and the like) of sufficient stamina, either moral or physical, to make useful ratings.

It would be a mistake to suppose, however, that even in this lowest group *all* were 'pound-per-pound' men. Some—notably the small subcategory of 'Lord Mayor's men' just mentioned—were very likely well-fed enough, if not in the past too well-fed. The Reverend Edward Mangin's quick eye soon spotted some of them in the *Gloucester*,

'. . . men with a claim to the title of gentlemen . . . There were in the different crews many such, under fictitious names, acting as common men: thoughtless or profligate young fellows who could no longer subsist on shore—and indeed not the most hopeful of my flock.'[2]

—young blades, in fact, who for various reasons had fallen foul of My Lord Mayor and his constables, or, feeling that they were about to do so, had chosen this means of making themselves scarce for a while. It would be pleasant to think that serving their King and Country afloat at last made good men of them. Perhaps it did, sometimes. But no case is known to me.

The total strength of this unsatisfactory group is hard to assess. The Ships' Books seldom help us to distinguish them. What we do know is that there were none at the start, but that they grew gradually in numbers. These numbers, certainly, have often been exaggerated, and, in this author's view, it is doubtful whether they ever exceeded 15 per cent even in the worst-manned of ships. The 12 per cent allowed here—for 1812—is certainly high enough. They did much harm, of which the most lasting, perhaps, has been to give the whole Navy a much worse name than it deserved.

In the figures given below for an average 1812 crew, no meticulous accuracy is claimed: for, obviously, ship would differ markedly from ship. Yet certain features strike the eye boldly. First, only about one

[1] The author of this famous line, George Barrington, pickpocket and writer, might have been, but actually was not, one of them. He was once in a prison-hulk, but did not 'volunteer' for the fleet. Instead, he was transported to Botany Bay where he made good.

[2] Mangin, op. cit., p. 21.

quarter came willingly: but, second—and herein lies the secret of their inherent efficiency—only about one quarter were really new to the job. Three out of every four were conscripts, but three out of four (not the same three) were seamen born.

MODES OF ENTRY
in an average ship of 1812

Groups	*Per Cent*	*Voluntary*	*Compulsory*	*Seamen*	*Non-Seamen*
Volunteers (Boys)	8%	8%	0%	8%	0%
Volunteers (Men)	15%	15%	0%	10%	5%
Pressed Men (British)	50%	0%	50%	45%	5%
Foreigners	15%	2%	13%	12%	3%
Quota-men, etc.	12%	0%	12%	0%	12%
Totals	**100%**	**25%**	**75%**	**75%**	**25%**

G. WIDOWS' MEN

No account of the eighteenth-century Navy can afford to ignore its notorious ghost-ratings that flit, disembodied, through its annals. But they must come last, after all real men have had their turn. They were very easily recruited, never in short supply. Their quality never varied because they were all made of paper—names only in the Ships' Books. But they drew the wages of Able Seamen and, since for obvious reasons they had no appetites, were allowed the value of the rations they did not eat. They existed at the rate of one per hundred of every Ship's Company so long as the total complement of the Navy was under 20,000: but at the rate of two per hundred when it exceeded that figure. For long, fictitious names had been given to them, and so the order still stood, even in the Regulations of 1808: but by the time of our wars they were usually entered simply as 'Widows' Men'. It was a realistic name because that was their sole *raison d'être*—to finance a fund for 'the relief of poor widows of Commission and Warrant Officers of the Royal Navy', to quote the words of the 1808 Admiralty Regulations: and until 1814 this was the sole source of relief available for such people. It was a beneficent idea, but its implementation was, to say the least, rash, especially in an environment where peculations large and small were in any case everyday occurrences. Why the authorities allowed so clumsy an expedient to continue for so long it is hard to say, seeing that, for many years now, they had known the approximate total of the whole seaman-complement, and could therefore, by the simple process of dividing that total by 100 (or by fifty if the total were over 20,000), have discovered what sum was due to the widows, and so abolished the whole ghost-tribe. They would thereby have removed from those concerned with the Ships' Books a source of grave and perennial temptation.

CHAPTER IV

THE QUARTER-DECK: OLD AND NEW ENTRIES

SO MUCH, then, for the people whom we of the twentieth century call 'the ratings'—the Lower Deck. But we saw that, in Nelson's day, *all* who joined a ship of war were rated upon entry, and, though naturally they changed their ratings, remained 'rated' throughout their careers. It is with those not yet discussed—those not 'Lower Deck'—that this chapter deals: the 'Quarter-deck' or 'Commissioned Officer' type. How did they secure their places on board? In what ratings were they entered, and what work was expected of them therein? Such are the questions which must now be answered.

First let us note the limitations of those apparently impeccable pieces of evidence, the Ship's Books, which purport to inform us precisely the rating of everyone on board and, by implication, exactly what his work was, the date of his rating and his age. It is all circumstantial enough, but how misleading let one entry show:

H.M.S. Seahorse

Date	*Rating*	*Name*	*Age*
5th April, 1774	Able Seaman	Horatio Nelson	18
	" "	Thomas Troubridge	18

The last column records a falsehood, for reasons which will become apparent later. But the first three record true—though to us misleading—facts. On the day named these two incomparable officers were so rated in the named ship. But did they perform the duties of Able Seamen? Clearly not: at that moment both of them were 15 years old. Then were they like Sam Leech, when his name appeared in the books of *H.M.S.*

Macedonian as 'Boy'? Or like tens of thousands of Smiths, Browns and Joneses who appear as 'A.B.'s' in hundreds of other books? Again no. Between Sam and Horatio there was a great gulf fixed, recognized by everybody on board (including, of course, Sam and Horatio). The difference was that Sam was 'lower deck' and Horatio 'quarter-deck', with all the consequences which that distinction implied. Put brutally, there were kicks going: Sam was at the receiving-end of the boot, Horatio at the delivery-end. This is not to accuse Nelson of brutality which was quite foreign to his nature. It is merely to point out that Nelson was of the class 'Young Gentleman', which could dispense kicks, while Leech was of the class 'Boy' and had to receive them. Actually, Nelson was not rated Midshipman at the moment, though he had already been one and was soon to be one again. But, then as ever, he 'walked the Quarter-deck' which Sam never visited save perhaps as a defaulter. We have already examined the social cause for this—Nelson's father was a clergyman and a gentleman, wielding considerable 'quarter-deck interest': Leech's father was a gentleman's valet, wielding none at all. We must now examine the curious mechanism which brought not only Nelson but also all the other Young Gentlemen, his contemporaries, into the ship and directed their steps Quarter-deckwards.

The story of Officer-entry is long and complex: long because by our period it was already two centuries old: complex because it was so typically English, and therefore a dilatory process of trial and error, a phenomenon not of revolution but of evolution. To trace that story in detail would require a book all to itself.[1] All that is possible here is to summarize the progress made by the end of the eighteenth century when our officers were themselves entering. By then, the ways in which 'Young Gentlemen' might join were, basically, restricted to two: two ways, enormously unequal in numbers of entrants. Let us call them 'the New Way' and 'the Old Way', and, contrary to custom, begin with the New.

THE NEW ENTRY

This new way was the modern way, but in embryo. When young men want to become officers nowadays, they (or their parents) apply to the Admiralty and, after they have been tested and examined in various

[1] A book which in fact the present author has written called *England's Sea-Officers*.

ways *by* the Admiralty, are, if successful, accepted by it: wholly taken over by it and by it trained to become Naval Officers. Once it considers them to be sufficiently trained, it gives them commissions as officers.

Like all highly-developed processes, this one had to have a historical beginning and, in a country like ours, we may be sure that it will be quite a modest, unspectacular beginning. So it was. In 1676 little Mr. Pepys, that tremendous naval organizer, invented a person called a 'Volunteer-per-Order'; a young gentleman to whom he gave what was in effect—though the term is an anachronism—an 'Admiralty Nomination'. This took the form of a letter from the Crown which the youthful aspirant took on board with him and handed to the captain of the ship. This letter being a 'King's Letter', the Captain had to accept and act upon it. He had to take the lad, and train him in his profession according to the accepted standards of training then in vogue. He did not like it as a rule: the young gentleman filled up one of the fixed number of 'ratings' on board which, otherwise, he could have filled with candidates of his own. But there it was. The little nuisance—'King's Letter Boy' he somewhat contemptuously called him—had arrived and could not be dismissed. For Mr. Pepys—and, after him, his successors at the Admiralty—had an uncomfortable way of keeping an eye upon one who was after all their own protégé, and (when they remembered, which was not always) of seeing that their youngster had a fair deal. In due course, for instance, he had to be made a 'Midshipman-per-Order' and, ultimately, given a commission. After that he fell into the ordinary run of commissioned officers.

This was the beginning: and it was a very small one. It is not easy to discover either the names or the numbers of these early King's Letter Boys because, once in, they tended to be secretive about their unusual and unpopular mode of entry. But the figure was very small—5 per cent would probably be too large, 10 per cent certainly so.

During the eighteenth century this 'Admiralty-Entry' developed, though it did not grow numerically. The principal change began in 1729 when the Volunteer-per-Order ceased to go straight to sea, letter in hand, but was instead received into a new establishment, opened in 1733 on purpose to cater for him. This was in Portsmouth dockyard, and was known for the first forty years of its life as the Naval Academy. It would be quite wrong to think of it as a democratic institution, founded to open a career to the talents. On the contrary, its forty pupils were to be 'the sons of the Nobility and Gentry'. Even so, it sounds somehow mildly progressive, as though the Navy thought it would be a good thing to introduce initial training, and even initial education, into its ranks. But an examination of motives, again not easy, seems to reveal that there was little of this idea either. Rather, probably, the Admiralty's argument would have sounded something like this: 'These scions of the Nobility and Gentry have such a very large pull anyway in the matter of Interest that they are bound, whatever we do, to rule the naval roost when they grow up. So it might be prudent to try and see that they are a little better trained to our ways than are their lowlier brethren.'

The Academy flagged, however. For one thing, it inherited much of the King's Letter Boy's unpopularity, because captains still had to receive, willy-nilly, these 'College Volunteers' when their school-days were over, just as they had had to accept the Volunteers-per-Order. Besides, it is clear that the 'Academites' themselves disliked it; and perhaps no wonder, since, after all, it was 'school', and the life there was not nearly so free as that which they—the privileged—could lead on ship-board. Also, many of the senior officers, not having had the advantage themselves of much theoretical schooling, tended (being human like other people) to ask, 'What's the use of book-learning to sea-officers anyway?' So even the limited numbers necessary to fill the Academy were seldom if ever forthcoming, though the Admiralty did all it could to popularize it. In 1748, for instance, when the commissioned officers went into uniform, 'a new suit of blue cloaths against His Majesty's birthday' was granted annually to every student, to show the world that their Lordships considered the Young Gentlemen to be of officer-status. But still the Academy flagged. By 1773 it contained a mere fifteen sons of Nobility and Gentry, and the Admiralty lowered its sights a little, ordaining that fifteen of its places should in future be filled by 'sons of officers'; who also were to be excused the payment of bills. In that same year too they dressed King George in his best and sent him down, as we might say, 'with good press-coverage' to inspect the establishment. He came, gave his blessing to all he was shown and departed, having added the epithet 'Royal' to its name.

But still the Volunteers (or their parents) fought shy—especially the noble and gentle ones—and even the *Royal* Naval Academy never filled. Here is small wonder, perhaps, when we hear of the very highest admirals of the day sniping at it. Rodney did in his time and, at the turn of the century, St. Vincent himself was asking a prospective parent the terse question 'are you so partial to that seminary as to hazard a son there?' Again, in 1801, he dismissed it curtly as 'a sink of vice and abomination'.[1] Evidently there was something behind this very outspoken assault, especially during the '70's and early '80's when perhaps he knew it at first hand. Its reputation was very bad, the principal charge against it being that the young gentlemen did no work at all, and that no one tried to make them. Indeed, if we are to believe the slightly priggish young Trevenen who was there in the mid-'seventies, this was not the worst of it. Some were confirmed drunkards, some practised blasphemers, and some both.[2] Not bad for young gentlemen of from 11 to 17 years old.

But still it survived; indeed improved somewhat, and, at last, when the wars were 13 years old and the demand for officer-recruits was at its peak, it suddenly began to increase, first to 80, then to 100. It was also modernized and otherwise brushed up. Its buildings were enlarged in 1806; it received a completely new syllabus and—more important—a first-class new headmaster, or Professor as they called him. This was James Inman, author (among other works) of Inman's Tables, and a leading expert in ship-construction, gunnery and mathematics. At the same time the name of the establishment was changed to the Royal Naval College, still of Portsmouth.

To the last it is not always easy to discover which officers graduated at the College, and for the same reasons as before. Yet certainly a few eminent ones did come in that way. Nor is their success altogether surprising. For the education which the place purveyed, though it may have been far from good by modern standards, can hardly have been worse than that accorded to the ordinary run of officer, which was often *nil*. Oddly enough, Rodney himself was all but a student, and would have been had they not taken so long to build the Academy in 1733. As it was, he was the last King's Letter Boy. Other famous ones, of our period, were Philip Vere Broke, hero of the *Chesapeake* and *Shannon* duel, a highly intelligent man and a great gunnery-expert: and Thomas Byam Martin, one of the great frigate captains who ended his career as Admiral of the Fleet and left behind invaluable memoirs. He allows us a glimpse of the Academy as it was in 1785–6 when he was there. It was no longer a 'sink', apparently, but he is critical. He praises the individual masters, including Mr. Bailey, then headmaster. But he declares that it 'was not well-conducted' and that 'there was a screw loose somewhere'

[1] N.R.S., Vol. XCII, p. 472.

[2] MS. Memoirs of James Trevenen, by C. V. Penrose.

TABLE V. OFFICER-ENTRY

METHODS OF ENTRY	HIGHEST RANK REACHED, 1848									AVERAGE		SOCIAL TYPES			
	I	II	III	IV	V	VI	VII	VIII	IX	X	XI	XII	XIII	XIV	
	No.	Admiral of the Fleet	Admiral	Vice-Admiral	Rear-Admiral	Captain	Commander	Retired Commander	Lieutenant	"Mark"	Rank Reached	"Officer"	"Lower Deck"	Unknown	No.
A. 'Rating' entries															
a. 'servants'															
1. Admiral's	7	0	0	0	3	1	0	2	1	2·6	Nearer Capt. than Cdr.	5	1	1	7
2. Captain's	144	1	16	25	30	19	17	25	11	3·1	Just above Capt.	124	7	13	144
3. Lieutenant's	13	0	1	0	0	3	5	3	1	2·2	Rather above Cdr.	7	3	3	13
4. Other Officers'*	17	0	0	1	0	1	6	5	4	2·1	Just above Cdr.	9	3	5	17
Total 'Servants'	**181**	**1**	**17**	**26**	**33**	**24**	**28**	**35**	**17**	2·92	Just below Capt.	145	14	22	181
b. other ratings															
5. Master's Branch†	16	0	0	0	1	2	1	5	7	1·6	Halfway between Cdr. and Ret. Cdr.	8	1	7	16
6. Midshipman	366	0	6	6	21	66	84	46	137	1·9	Nearly Cdr.	365	1	0	366
7. Petty Officer‡	14	0	0	0	0	1	0	0	13	1·1	Barely above Lieut.	9	2	3	14
8. Able Seaman	305	0	3	5	14	33	55	71	124	1·7	Much below Cdr.	217	51	37	305
9. Ordinary Seaman	80	0	0	1	3	7	12	13	44	1·5	Nearer Ret. Cdr. than Cdr.	54	5	21	80
10. Landman	58	0	0	0	0	2	7	10	39	1·2	Ret. Cdr. exactly	42	4	12	58
11. Boy, 1st Class	15	0	0	0	1	2	3	3	6	1·7	Much below Cdr.	9	0	6	15
12. Boy, 2nd Class	32	0	0	0	0	5	6	2	19	1·5	Nearer Ret. Cdr. than Cdr.	23	3	6	32
13. Boy, 3rd Class	35	0	0	0	0	5	4	4	22	1·3	Just above Ret. Cdr.	20	4	11	35
14. 'Boy'	41	0	2	0	3	11	8	7	10	2·2	Rather above Cdr.	33	4	4	41
Total 'Other Ratings'	**962**	**0**	**11**	**12**	**43**	**134**	**180**	**161**	**421**	1·73	Much below Cdr.	780	75	107	962
c. 15. Unspecified (Pre-1794)§	60	1	9	7	7	9	13	11	3	3·0	Capt. exactly	41	3	16	60
Total 'Rating' Entries	**1203**	**2**	**37**	**45**	**83**	**167**	**221**	**207**	**441**	1·97	All but Cdr.	966	92	145	1203

B. 'VOLUNTEER' ENTRIES															
16. R.N. College, Portsmouth**	97	0	2	4	9	30	21	5	26	2·3	Nearer Cdr. than Capt.	97	0	0	97
17. 1st Class Volunteer	1581	0	4	7	49	325	270	107	819	1·7	Much below Cdr.	1581	0	0	1581
18. 2nd Class Volunteer	63	0	0	0	0	6	14	3	40	1·4	A little above Ret. Cdr.	35	0	28	63
19. 3rd Class Volunteer	35	0	0	0	1	3	5	2	24	1·6	Halfway between Cdr. and Ret. Cdr.	25	3	7	35
20. 'Volunteer'	143	0	2	2	7	37	31	12	52	2·0	Cdr. exactly	102	2	39	143
21. Unspecified (Post-1794)††	311	0	0	0	0	28	47	3	233	1·3	A shade above Ret. Cdr.	194	6	111	311
Total 'Volunteer' Entries	**2230**	**0**	**8**	**13**	**66**	**429**	**388**	**132**	**1194**	1·70	Much below Cdr.	2034	11	185	2230
C. 22. SUPERNUMERARIES	34	0	0	0	0	1	9	7	17	1·4	A little above Ret. Cdr.	28	0	6	34
SUMMARY															
A. 'RATING' ENTRIES	1203	2	37	45	83	167	221	207	441	1·97	All but Cdr.	966	92	145	1203
B. 'VOLUNTEER' ENTRIES	2230	0	8	13	66	429	388	132	1194	1·70	Much below Cdr.	2034	11	185	2230
C. SUPERNUMERARIES	34	0	0	0	0	1	9	7	17	1·4	A little above Ret. Cdr.	28	0	6	34
Total	**3467**	**2**	**45**	**58**	**149**	**597**	**618**	**346**	**1652**	1·80	A good way below Cdr.	3028	103	336	3467
D. 23. UNSPECIFIED (dead before 1845)‡‡	104	2	34	26	15	20	6	1	0	4·16	A little above Rear-Ad.	97	1	6	104
GRAND TOTAL	**3571**	**4**	**79**	**84**	**164**	**617**	**624**	**347**	**1652**	—	—	3125	104	342	3571

* Consisting of: Master's, 4: Gunner's, 3: Purser's, 2: Surgeon's, 1; and 'Servants' (unqualified), 7.

† Consisting of: Master's Mate, 13: 2nd Master's Mate, 1. The other two are clearly special cases—'Acting Master' and '2nd Master and Pilot'.

‡ Consisting of: Clerk, 9: Schoolmaster, 3: Yeoman of the Powder Room, 1: Purser's Steward, 1.

§ All, or almost all, belong to 'Servants' or 'Other rating' Entries. It is not possible to differentiate between them.

** Admiralty-appointed—the only entry that was.

†† All, or almost all, belong to 'Volunteer' Entries, mainly 1st Class Volunteer.

‡‡ Appearing in O'Byrne's foot-notes. Not reckoned in calculation of 'Average Rank reached'.

(though he does not say where). It had improved greatly under Inman, he said; yet he finally threw in his weight with St. Vincent, concluding that 'a well-regulated man of war and a really good schoolmaster, and where the Captain really takes an interest about his boys, is a preferable course of education'.[1] But we should remember that the conditions which he postulates for a good ship-education were far from normal then. In his young days captains who took that kind of interest in their boys were the exceptions, while a 'really good schoolmaster' was a greater rarity still.

However, for good or ill, there they were when the wars started, this small band of college-trained young gentlemen. And they were, though they could not know it, the guinea-pigs of the New System. If we would obtain some idea of their numbers in the Navy, we may press O'Byrne once more into service. This time it will be O'Byrne alone, for he consistently includes one valuable item of information which Marshall almost always omits. He records, much more often than not, his officers' first rating on entering the Service. So, with no difficulty other than that inherent in analysing a large number of names, we can discover the initial ratings of nearly all the officers who, having fought in the Great Wars, survived till 1845. This has been done, and the result is to be found in Table V. There are, it will be observed, 3,467 officers whose initial rating we know.[2] This figure, it will also be noticed, is much larger than those assembled either for 'Social Background' or for 'Geographical Distribution'—indeed, more than the sum of them: and, in this case, we shall be much more justified in considering our 3,467 as a fair cross-section of *all* initial entry ratings. It is in fact about one-third of them all.

Now let us look at B.16 in Table V, labelled 'R.N. College, Portsmouth'. Of our known 3,467 only ninety-seven were College boys: that is, a mere 2.7 per cent. This may seem unduly small, but in fact it is unduly high: for closer examination of O'Byrne reveals that (as we might expect) the majority of this ninety-seven entered late in the wars,

[1] Martin, op. cit., N.R.S., Vol. XXIV, pp. 23–4.

[2] Not 3,571, the 'Grand Total' figure given in the Table, because the last entries of all (at D.23) are labelled 'Unspecified', and O'Byrne does not tell us their initial ratings. These are the 'Distinguished dead' officers described at p. 171 below. On the other hand, the numbers shown at A.c.15 and at B.21, though also labelled 'Unspecified', may be included here because, though we do not know exactly what the initial rating was, we know that it was *not* College Volunteer.

and into the enlarged College of 1806. These 'Collegers' were by hypothesis younger than the (fewer) 'Academites' who had entered before the enlargement: they were therefore, by the laws of nature, more likely to survive up to 1845 than their older predecessors. The whole wartime percentage of College Volunteers, then, will be lower than 2.7: perhaps considerably lower, but let us be content to reduce it only to 2½ per cent.

These College Volunteers were the only Admiralty-appointed entrants in the Royal Navy throughout the wars: the only representatives of the New Entry which now provides 100 per cent. All the rest—the whole 97½ per cent of them—entered by methods in which the Admiralty had no hand whatever. They constituted the 'Old Entry'.

THE OLD ENTRY

A.a. Servants

That some thirty-nine out of every forty naval officers entered the Service without any Admiralty sanction, or even 'vetting', sounds almost incredible. Yet so it was; and the system has been called, not altogether unjustly, the 'pitchfork' system. But this name is misleading because it seems to imply that there was no order at all in the process, and that anybody could decide who were to be the future officers. This was not so. There was one person—or rather one very well-defined class of persons—who held the key in hand. That person was the Captain. He could take into his ship when he commissioned her anyone he liked; and the only posts he could not fill with his own untrammelled choices were those of the officers, commissioned and warrant. These, then as now, were appointed to the ship by the Admiralty. Hence another name has been bestowed upon this mode of officer-entry—the 'Captain's Servant' entry. There is much truth in this title too; but a glance at our Table will show that we can probably find a better. We notice that the actual phrase 'Captain's Servant' appears there (A.a.2) as one subdivision of 'Servants' Entry' (A.a), itself a sub-division of 'Rating Entries' (A); and that the actual number of 'Captain's Servant' entrants is a mere 144—only 4 per cent of the whole. If then we give to the whole a name proper to only 4 per cent of it, we may cause confusion. We cannot change the name of the four-per-cent, because this was their official name, as recorded in the Ship's Books. We must therefore find a new name for the whole: and 'Captain's Protégé' would fill the bill. For all were that, Captain's Servants and the rest alike.

Clearly this brings the Captain into the forefront of naval life. And indeed in many respects, of which this is but one, the Captain of a warship was a sort of king-pin without which the ship, and the whole Navy, would have disintegrated. Early in this twentieth century it became the fashion to allude facetiously to the Captain as 'the Owner'; and though by then he had lost some of his omnipotence, it yet enshrined an essential truth, greater a century and a half ago than it is now. Indeed, if we are content to regard 'the Owner' as 'the Leaseholder', and not 'the Freeholder'—for his control lasted only during his tenancy—the title is admirably descriptive of an eighteenth- and early nineteenth-century naval captain.

Here, however, we are concerned with only one of his extraordinary powers—that of officer-selection. It was vast enough. He could not, of course, give commissions—that is, make Lieutenants. This was, and always had been, a royal prerogative: for it was a King's Commission, and none but the Crown, on the recommendation of its accredited representative, the Admiralty, could confer it. But he could select, appoint, and present to the Admiralty for commissions practically all the available candidates, so that the Admiralty, and therefore the Crown, could not do other than commission his nominees. True, the Admiralty could select as between the Captains' candidates, taking, say, A and C while rejecting B and D. But that was all, since A, B, C and D were, all alike, Captains' nominees. The sole exceptions were the College Volunteers; that is, 2½ per cent of the numbers wanted. And they, clearly, would go nowhere towards officering the whole fleet.

The origins of the system lay far back in time, in the days when there was no organized corps of officers at all, nor indeed any organized Navy: and the system itself was in many ways analogous to the Apprentice System in wider walks of life, and as sometimes practised *in* the Navy by the Warrant Officers (see p. 88). It was even very like it in its economic aspect. Just as 'the master' in commerce and the mechanical trades took apprentices in order to initiate them into his craft, ultimately to set them up on their own, the while lodging and feeding them, and receiving some payment from the learners' parents, so the Captain took on such protégés as he cared to select, on the understanding that he would teach them *his* craft and—tacitly—do his best when the time came to launch them out as officers like himself: at the same time seeing that they were boarded and fed, and even being paid for his pains. But there were two differences. A Captain's Servant, unlike a true Apprentice, did not have proper legal articles, because captains could seldom think in terms of five years, the normal apprenticeship period. Long before that, probably, they would have relinquished their command and, very possibly, not received another. In such circumstances they would have nowhere to put an apprentice-officer, and could do nothing for him. Secondly, as the State was a party to the transaction, and was obtaining its future officers from it, the 'keep' came out of the State's pocket, and so, indirectly, did the Captain's remuneration, which was the wages which the State paid to its 'ratings'. For, naturally, every post on board carried certain wages with it, and everyone on board had a post. But, like the real servant-boy, the protégé did not receive those wages. His 'master', the Captain, did. In the early days there had been much to be said for this near-apprentice scheme: and if we would cavil at it, our criticism should be directed not to the scheme itself, which had after all produced almost all our eighteenth-century officers, but to its overlong survival.

It must be owned that, by the last decade of the century, it had become something of an anachronism to retain in the hands of individuals powers which should, in any organized public service, have reverted to the State. It had always been open to certain abuses because, on earth as opposed to heaven, private individuals often have private views to forward, and these do not necessarily correspond with public views. Thus the Captains had always, in some degree, used this great source of 'naval interest' to further their own ends. The good ones, no doubt, saw to it that such ends were not too flagrantly antagonistic to the Country's good. But they were not all good ones. Anyway, it was only in human nature for them, when making their choice, to favour their own sons and nephews, those of their friends, and those of persons whom it was their clear interest to 'oblige'. Imagine, for example, an important public figure who has it in his power to dispose of the command of good ships or profitable stations. Suppose he wants to send a son to sea. Will he have to look far for a Captain who will consider it a privilege to look after his young hopeful? This indeed was one of the least bad results of the system, for the worst it did, probably, was to make the whole profession something of a tight social club, whose members tended to come from one distinct, if fairly wide, social class. We have already seen how this same law operated once a breach in the exclusive wall was effected, even to the length of making whole wardrooms 'aristocratic' or 'tarpaulin', 'Scottish' or 'Irish'.

Up to 1794 the commonest post to which a Captain's Protégé was rated was that of Captain's Servant. Commanding officers had always been allotted a generous bevy of servants—more than any but the most aristocratical could ever find a use for. Indeed, if we go back to Elizabeth I's day, we find something almost unbelievably spacious in the ideas current on the subject. An ordinary captain was entitled to four servants for every hundred of his Ship's Company while, if perchance he was a knight, he could have eight. So, from the very start, he began to fill up his surplus servant-ratings with his own protégés. Most of the other officers were entitled to servants too, but on a far less lavish scale. Still, as Table V shows, even here a few servant-posts were redundant, and they could be used for the same purpose. We find, on examining O'Byrne, that most of these 'Lieutenant's Servant' or 'Master's Servant' posts were filled with relatives, a Lieutenant's son, for example, or a Master's nephew. At first sight, then, it may look as though these lesser officers had some minor share in the Captain's officer-selecting monopoly. But this was not so. The Captain, not the Lieutenant, was 'the Owner', though he would sometimes oblige his underling by letting him take his son to sea with him as Lieutenant's Servant. The Admiral's Servants were rather, but not basically, different. The Flag-Officer was allowed an enormous 'retinue', but, for one thing, he needed more real servants; and, for another, he did not have to worry unduly about finding a place for this own protégés. As we have seen, there was sure to be a long queue of enthusiastic captains volunteering to oblige him.

B. *Volunteer Entries*

There, then, is what is described in Table V as 'A.a. Servants' entry: and it is only 181 strong. Was it then so important after all? The answer is, Yes—because of what happened in 1794. We saw how the Order-in-Council of 16.4.1794 affected the Lower Deck Boys. Now we must see how it touched the Quarter-deck lads. Since Elizabeth's time the knightly captain had lost his privilege of 'eight per hundred' but, up to this year, the 'four per hundred' still obtained for all. It had even come to be acknowledged for what it really was—an extra source of income, supplementing a captain's basic pay.

By this Order-in-Council all Officers' Servants as such (including the Captain's Servants) were abolished and 'in lieu of servants a compensation . . . [was to be] . . . made to the Captains, Lieutenants and Warrant Officers of H.M. ships equal to the net wages of the number of servants to which they were respectively entitled'. This sounds like a stupendous revolution, but it was really nothing of the kind. It merely acknowledged a *fait accompli*. Yet it had the effect of changing a good deal of the old nomenclature; for the Order proceeds:

'And no Boys should be allowed to be borne on the books of H.M. ships in future under the denomination of Servants to the Captain, Lieutenants and Warrant Officers: but instead thereof a certain number to be borne on separate lists after the Ship's Company, in classes of the following descriptions:—'

There follows the break-up of the old rating of 'Servant' into three clear sub-divisions, now to be known officially, not as 'Servants' but as 'Boys' or 'Volunteers'.

This Order, as it concerned Classes II and III, was quoted and fully discussed in the last chapter (p. 89). Here our concern is solely with Class I:

'*Class I.* To consist of young gentlemen intended for the sea-service . . . to be styled Volunteers, and allowed wages of £6 per annum.'

Thus was born the name which figures more largely than any other in our Table—Volunteer of the First Class or, by inevitable abbreviation, First Class Volunteer. In the Table (at B.17) there are no less than 1,581 of them. Who are they? Well: what's in a name? They are the younger brothers of our old friends the Captain's Servants (*plus* a few Lieutenant's and other officer's Servants): all those ex-Servants, that is, who were not, and never had been, menials at all, but had always been budding officers: those who, in 1843, came to be called, as they are still called, 'Naval Cadets'. This change of name instantly explains why the 'Servant' entry in general and the 'Captain's Servant' entry in particular are so small. No recruit joined it—by that name—after 1794. Yet, since the old 'Servants' (most of them) and the New 'First Class Volunteers' are only different generations of the same people—that is, youths bound for the Quarter-deck—we must add the two figures together if we would discover the true dimensions of the old 'Servant' (mainly Captain's Servant) entry. We should also, for accuracy's sake, add in the small group (A.b.11) of 'Boys, 1st Class'. They must be the same class of person, using, however, the correct though less usual alternate name of Boy (see above). If then we anticipate history by nearly fifty years, we may call them all 'Naval Cadets'. So far as our Table is concerned, all that has happened is this: of these 1,777 'cadets', 181 of them (having entered before 1794) are called 'servants'—144 of them 'Captain's', thirty-seven of them other officers'—and fifteen of them are called 'First Class Boys', while the remaining 1,581 (who entered after 1794) are called 'First Class Volunteers'. But it must be stressed again that every one of them, whether Servant or Volunteer, is a Captain's Protégé.

The Second and Third Class Volunteers of the Table (B.18 and 19) were mostly pre-1794 entrants who, had they joined after that year, would have been Second and Third Class Boys. Most of them might have described themselves to O'Byrne as 'Servants' (Captain's or otherwise) but perhaps they thought that 'volunteer' sounded better. Nor were they exactly wrong because, as we have seen, all these youngsters were officially Volunteers. The fact that they started in an apparently 'lower deck' rating, however, does not mean that they were necessarily lower deck types. Most of them, probably, were lads bound for the Quarter-deck but fitted, *pro tempore*, and for the Captain's immediate convenience, into an ordinary rating. Later, but after our period—in 1824—the title Second Class Volunteer was bestowed upon a different person altogether—an aspirant for the Navigation Branch, who was to a Master what a First Class Volunteer was to a Commissioned Officer. Those labelled plain 'Volunteer' in the Table (B.20) are mostly First Class Volunteers too. And again, in so calling themselves they are being strictly accurate according to the 1794 Order which (see above) actually ordains that they are 'to be styled Volunteers'.

The last group of Volunteer-entrants is the large one labelled in the Table 'Unspecified (post-1794)'—B.21. Here O'Byrne has failed us: mainly, one suspects, because his correspondents failed him. Perhaps O'Byrne himself was not very interested in them, and we need not be either. They were all late entrants: so late that, though they entered before 1815, they had not received commissions by that date. They must be included, however, because they fought in the wars, though not as commissioned officers. As a rule they have little to say for themselves. Many omit not only their first rating but almost all other information. Very likely, indeed, they had but little to record. Their war records were hardly likely to be impressive, through no fault of their own: and even employment, let alone adventurous employment, became quite rare as the Navy entered its weary post-war slump. They did very badly in their subsequent promotions, but this is hardly surprising either, because they had few chances of distinguishing themselves, and promotion was becoming ever slower and more uncertain. Moreover, many of them, being very young in 1815, had not risen, even by 1848, as high as they were destined to go. O'Byrne's unfinished 1859 edition gives them rather better figures.

A.b. Other Ratings

So much for the various categories of 'Servants' and—much the same people, though named differently after 1794—the 'Volunteers'. There remain the officers tabulated in the sub-section A.b. who joined as 'Other Ratings'. Again everyone in this section too, though neither Captain's Servant nor 'Volunteer', is a Captain's Protégé. After all, Captain's Servant was only one of many ratings. There were scores more, and each one was in the gift of 'the Owner'. Naturally he had to fill most of them with real solid men who could do the hard work involved. But there was nothing to prevent him, should he think fit, from filling a few of them with his protégés. How often he did so is clearly revealed by the great number—962—of 'other ratings' shown in the Table, and the large number of different posts which they filled—there are sixteen different ones. But this great variety of names must not allow the fact to be concealed that they were his protégés, all of them.

IRREGULARITIES

We have now reached the point where we have to deal with the extraordinary crop of irregularities which flourished throughout the Service: products, mostly, of that basic anomaly already noticed—the Captain's anachronistic powers of officer-selection. Again the story must be divided into 'pre-1794' and 'post-1794'. Before that date—and very strictly speaking—a Captain was *supposed* to keep the number of his protégés down to the number of servant-posts in his gift. But there is little evidence that he ever troubled to do so, unless indeed he happened to have run out of protégés. And no one in authority seemed to be put out by it. So the pre-1794 appointment of protégés to these 'other ratings' was—if the paradox may be forgiven—normal though irregular. In 1794, however, the Admiralty was obviously trying to reduce such appointments, with the ultimate intention, probably, of eliminating them. This holds too for all the other irregularities and anomalies still to be recorded. Authority was trying to put its house in order all round. But it was an uphill task. It was an Augean Stable very difficult to cleanse, piled high as it was with the accretions of centuries. We are face to face, in fact, with a very old and very powerful Vested Interest whose holders, unfortunately for the reformers, were all (or almost all) the higher officers of the Navy—its Captains directly, and, indirectly, even its Admirals. For all stood to gain by retaining, and to lose by abolishing, their vested interest. Further, the body which had to cleanse the stable was the Admiralty, itself largely composed of the very men who stood to gain by its corruption. No wonder the process was slow and uncertain: in fact the greater wonder is that it started at all, and that is succeeded in the end. That it did so is due, of course, to the ultimate pressure of outside public opinion, exerted gradually through Parliament and the politicians.

This, however, is a much later phase of the story, which lies well outside our period. So let us return to 1794. In that year it was laid down, not for the first time, but now with more insistence and rather more effect, that the total number of a Captain's protégés must not exceed the quota of First Class Volunteers allowed in each ship. This figure, being still four-per-hundred of the total crew, was in every ship a fixed and known number. Thus the issue was at least being simplified. The Government was saying in effect to the Captains, 'We are proposing to abolish all these odd ways of officer-entry, leaving only one way, that of First Class Volunteer. But we accept the existence of your vested interest: we recognize that, in scrapping all "Servants", we shall be depriving you of an established monetary perquisite—viz. the value of their wages—and we will pay you the equivalent ourselves. But we expect you to play fair. You, in your turn, must give up entering Young Gentlemen in other ratings.' So any Captain who after 1794 appointed protégés to ratings other than First Class Volunteer was being guilty of both an irregularity and an illegality.

But he was also, alas, engaged upon a pastime very dear to frail humanity—the game known as 'eating one's cake and having it too'. He was drawing both his grant-in-lieu-of-servants and the wages of his irregularly-rated protégés. Unfortunately many—perhaps most—Captains did not see it like that. They clung, as folk will, to a vested interest which they regarded as an inalienable right: and, as a rule, they pocketed the proceeds with impunity, for two simple reasons. The first was a very human one: most of the potential policemen who should have caught hem, and most of the potential judges who should have convicted them, sympathized with them, and did not try very hard to catch them.

The second reason was a much more practical one. Such irregularities were very hard to detect; often all but impossible. The Captain was so complete an 'owner' in his own stronghold that he normally ran no risk of detection at all. To illustrate this, let us take once more the case of Nelson and the *Seahorse*. It is pre-1794, it is true, but it illustrates a captain's immunity as well as any. We noted that the Ship's Book was correct in all details but one. Only the entrant's age was wrongly stated. Nelson was not 18, but 15. It is quite a well-known fact—now—that he was born in 1758, and therefore only 15 in 1773. But who in authority knew or worried about it then? Several months, or years, after the entry was made, some minor Admiralty clerk might run a perfunctory eye down the relevant page of the muster-book. But how could he know, when he reached the entry 'A.B. Horatio Nelson', that the person in question was not a perfectly ordinary A.B. like the man who appeared next above him? No sort of general register of seamen existed at that time, so that he had no book of reference to consult. So how was he to spot that there had been an irregularity at all? Indeed it was too easy: and of course the captains knew it. Fundamental dishonesty? Certainly, but perhaps thoughtless dishonesty, because the heinousness of all such 'practices' cannot usefully be divorced from the general morality of the society which condones them. What, we may ask ourselves, is our attitude in this mid-20th century towards our business neighbour whom we suspect of entering on his 'expense-sheet' items which may well make the Recording Angel blush as he reads them? Do we drop a line about him to Inland Revenue? Do we cut him at cocktail parties? No? Then why not? Possibly because some of us may remember having read somewhere a text which begins 'Let him who is without sin . . .'

This particular regulation-dodging device whereby a captain contrived to take to sea more than his permitted ration of protégés was, however, only one of several irregularities: many of them, by comparison, much harder to justify: some, in fact, very heinous indeed. Yet there is this common to very nearly all of them—they were things that were 'done', usually done with impunity and seldom raising any protest on the score of morality.

We have used an Able Seaman entry as an example. Such entries, the Table shows, were very numerous; indeed the most numerous save only for the Midshipman entry. That was a rather special case, involving an irregularity of quite a different kind which will call for attention later.

Meanwhile, it is clear that, of all 'other ratings', that of A.B. was the most fancied by captains for their protégés. The true A.B. was of course the most skilled seaman on board, and his rating was in the straight line of seaman-promotion to Petty Officer and even Warrant Officer. Rules governed him, and always had. He must have served afloat in subordinate capacities for not less than three years, and must be not less than 18 years old. Nor were seamen often given the rating when so young as that, unless they were exceptionally skilful and steady men. Incidentally, the existence of such rules shows why the man responsible for the *Seahorse*'s books in 1773 had to record his lie about Nelson's age if he wanted to escape detection. For our hypothetical clerk, who did not know Nelson's real age and therefore never detected any irregularity at all, would instantly have spotted one had he read 'A.B. Horatio Nelson, aged 15'.

It will be seen in the Table (Columns II to XI) that a start as A.B. got a lad as far along the road to ultimate promotion as most 'other rating' starts. But that was not very far, at least compared with any of the old 'Servants'. And another thing may be noticed. Column XIII shows that no less than fifty-one men—and those not 'quarter-deck types' but real 'lower deck'—started as A.B.'s and finally reached the Quarter-deck. If we are suspicious, as we have every cause to be, we might scent another irregularity here. For if 'none are to be rated Able but such as have been three years at sea' how could anyone *start* as A.B.? But for once our suspicions are not confirmed, because years in the Merchant Service counted as 'years at sea': and in fact many, perhaps most, of the best naval seamen had acquired their proficiency in the other Service—George Watson, for instance, who was 'rated Able' upon joining: rightly in that he had six years' experience in the other service, though irregularly in that he was only 16.[1] Such men, on entering the Navy, were usually in competition with material of a much lower quality. Lastly, the Table shows that these fine seamen who started as A.B.s furnished almost exactly half of all the Lower Deck people who ultimately reached the Quarter-deck. It need not surprise us. Here, obviously, was the pick of the Lower Deck.

Before turning to the other irregularities and abuses, let us carry the story of the Captain's officer-selection to the end of our period, and rather beyond it. The Order of 1794, it will be noted, had done nothing at all to break that privilege. Authority had changed the names of can-

[1] Watson, op. cit., p. 67.

didates for commissions: it had limited their numbers within certain bounds—or had tried to. But it had done nothing to take from the captains their monopoly of choosing the candidates. Nor did it do so while the wars lasted. Immediately after their conclusion, however, it moved at last. In July, 1815, it ordained that no Midshipman should be received on board and entered in the Ship's Books unless or until he had received Admiralty sanction. This was an immense advance, and it went far, ultimately, towards destroying the Captain's selection-monopoly; for, though he could still produce the material, he now had to submit it to Admiralty approval, with the corollary implicit in that—that the Admiralty might refuse to approve. But few seem to have noticed the implication, and those who did put a wrong interpretation upon it. The highly class-conscious Dillon, for instance,[1] though himself a Captain, entirely failed to perceive in the order an assault upon the cherished privileges of his naval class. He only saw in it a buttress to his social class, an attack upon the breed of 'not quite' officers who had recently been worming their way on to his beloved Quarter-deck: and he actually gave it his blessing. Indeed he may well have interpreted the Admiralty's motives rightly. This may well have been one of them. But there was probably another. With the war just over, the responsible people at the top could hardly fail to view with disquiet the dangerous accumulation of wartime officers. They must have seen that it ought somehow to be reduced to peacetime levels, and they may have thought it only prudent to try to prevent an unrestricted flood of new recruits. That, probably, was all. They were out to control numbers, and perhaps to 'improve' social quality, not to claim the right of selection. They probably did not realize the much wider implications of their action, which was nothing less than a first nibble at the Captains' age-old vested interest. For such without doubt it was. It was this Order of 1815 which was, ultimately, to drive the Captains right out of business as officer-selectors, and to give the Admiralty control of its own house. It was a lengthy process, however. The vested interest died hard: indeed, the very last nail was driven into its coffin only in 1914.

More Irregularities

The way is now cleared for the consideration of further irregularities. Before breaches of rules are exposed, however, it is wise to discover what the rules themselves were. Their details had several times been

[1] N.R.S., Vol. XCVII, p. 339.

changed, but their main features were quite old, originally stemming, as most of our naval organization did, from the busy brain of Mr. Pepys. He it was who first made rules as to who might be appointed Lieutenants and who not. His candidates had to have reached the age of 20; and to have had at least three years of sea-service, one of which must be spent as Midshipman. Then, armed with his carefully written-up journals, and certificates of sobriety, diligence and ability signed by his previous commanding officer, the candidate had to make his appearance at the Navy Office. There he was put through his dreaded ordeal—an oral examination in seamanship, navigation and a number of other cognate subjects. If he satisfied his examiners, he became eligible for a Lieutenant's commission, though it did not follow that he received it.

These remained the basis of all subsequent rules, though there had been minor changes. Thus, when our wars began, the minimum length of servitude before securing a commission was six years, two of which had to be spent as Midshipman or as Master's Mate. This latter, who was once only what his name implied—the Mate, or assistant, of the Master—was now approximating to what he was destined to become—a Sub-Lieutenant.[1] He became even more like one just before the wars ended, when a would-be Lieutenant was required to show two years' service as Midshipman *and* two as Master's Mate. A minimum age of 20 was still in force.[2] He still had to produce his journals and certificates of officer-like qualities which now, in addition, had to vouch for six full years' servitude, all signed by his various captains. The Lieutenant's exam. was still there too; but, if abroad, the officer might now come before a board of three senior Captains instead of having to wait until he returned to London.

Here we leave the Lieutenant, to return to him later. Indeed, his minimum qualifications have been summarized here only in order to reveal the various ways in which they were circumvented. The only other fact that need be remembered now—and we must for the present take it for granted—was that it was vital to every ambitious young officer to acquire his first commission at the earliest possible age.

[1] But see p. 198.

[2] And remained so, it seems, until 1806, when it was changed to 19. Both Collingwood (N.R.S., Vol. XCVIII, p. 155) and Dillon (N.R.S., Vol. XCIII, p. 267) refer to a minimum of 21. But no documentary evidence of such change can be found. If it ever took place, it must have been after 1803, when an O.-in-C. (19.1.1803) mentions 20, and before 1806, when the new Instructions definitely make it 19.

We step down, then, to Midshipman. He, in his modern role of potential officer, was slightly pre-Pepysian. It was the Cromwellians who originally had the idea of making his rating a stepping-stone to the Quarter-deck. They were using a rating already there; a responsible and relatively well-paid rating too, filled by a good man—not boy. For this reason there still survived, at least up to Nelson's time, a number of this older midshipman-type; good solid 'lower deck', who might be of any age from, say, 20 to 50. But for many years the ordinary run of midshipmen had been, as they are now, the commission-aspiring 'young gentlemen'. Two rules, both dating from Pepys's time, governed the rating at the outbreak of our wars. First, no one could receive it until he had been at sea for two years; and, second, he was not allowed to begin his two-year qualifying period—not allowed at sea at all—until he was 13 years old, or, if a naval officer's son, 11 years old. The explanation of this 'social' differentiation is nowhere forthcoming. Perhaps it arose from the fact that an officer's son would almost certainly start his naval life under the eye of father or uncle who, if anyone could, would do his best to look after the child.

So much for rules. But—our Table shows some 366 officers who allege that it was as midshipmen that they *first* went to sea. How can that have been? A few, a very few—probably less than a dozen of them—may have been the old sort of midshipman: and we shall meet one or two later. But what of the rest? Unquestionably they were telling the truth. What they were doing was regulation-dodging; and solely with a view to becoming Lieutenants as early as possible.

Strangely enough, some of the rules were kept, especially those dealing with the Lieutenants: or rather, perhaps one should say, the fiction of keeping them was rigidly maintained. Foremost among these was the six-year rule. The Admiralty invariably insisted upon having six years'-worth of seagoing certificates under their noses before they would issue a commission. There was a gentle irony in this. It was like one lone platoon gallantly standing its ground in the midst of a crumbling line with the infiltrating enemy on either flank, riding over them and tunnelling beneath them. Infiltration was all too easy, so long as no one was attempting to defend all the other breaches and gaps. The Admiralty wanted its six years' service? All right. It should have it.

a. *Early Entry*

There were several ways of setting to work, two very common indeed.

First, one could break the entry-age regulation, and send a lad to sea before he was 13 (or 11, if a naval officer's son). We have seen how simple and undetectable it was to give a false age in the days before the compulsory registration of births. To quote but three examples, all from the very top flight of officers, Nelson went to sea at 12, Collingwood and Cornwallis at 11: and their fathers were none of them naval officers. But these boys were grown men compared with others. Edward Hamilton's father took him to sea with him when he was just seven, and, at eight, the child 'fought' in a full-scale action. This early initiation into the grimmer aspects of life apparently did no harm to little Edward, who lived to become a knight and a full Admiral: yet the thing was no less ridiculous for that. Stranger still was the early career of one Daniel Woodriff. This warrior went afloat as Lieutenant's Servant to his father when under three years old and, at that age, was wrecked in the West Indies. At five, he accompanied his father round the world.

Such extremely early ages are of course exceptional, but entry at round about nine was not at all unusual, and it sometimes led to absurd situations. Young Hood Christian, for instance, went to sea with his father, then a senior Captain, when just under eight. So, when Dillon became shipmate with him in 1796, he was a seasoned campaigner of 11, with a good three years of 'time' to his credit, and a Midshipman withal. One day his father, now Rear-Admiral commanding the squadron, took him out on duty in his boat. The lad became obstreperous, as 11-year-olds will, whereupon the Admiral incontinently spanked him in front of the whole boat's crew: of which little Hood, more hurt, one imagines, in his dignity than elsewhere, complained bitterly to Dillon afterwards.[1] Then there was little Charles Boys, Midshipman in the *Thetis* in 1793, to whom everyone was devoted for all that he had one habit uncommon in Midshipmen—he sucked his thumb.[2] Poor child! He lost a leg at the First of June next year and, though he lived to become a Captain, died of Walcheren fever in 1809. Dillon's own youthful experiences are not lacking in pathos either. When he joined the *Saturn* he was nine, and very small for his age. One might have expected the rough seamen to snigger at him (up their sleeves, of course) as he strutted about in his tiny blue coat, white breeches and silk stockings. But no—

'What was still more strange, one or two of the seamen devoted them-

[1] Dillon, op. cit., N.R.S., Vol. XCIII, p. 237.
[2] Op. cit., p. 84.

selves to me, and would often carry me in their arms to explain several parts of the ship in answer to my inquiries.'[1]

Was it so strange? Those seamen, surely, were sober, elderly ones, married perhaps and with little boys of their own whom they seldom if ever saw. And here was just such another, a bright-eyed friendly child asking eager questions. After all, they were men; and who shall blame them if they sometimes lavished upon him a little of their starved affection, forgetting that he was 'quarter-deck', and that so much as to touch an officer was Mutiny, punishable with Death? As we are not informed to the contrary, we can thankfully suppose that any officer who witnessed one of these acts of mutiny found something more profitable to look at in the opposite direction. After all, officers were men too.

The gain accruing to these young regulation-breakers was obvious. If they joined at nine, they could be Midshipmen at eleven, and have their six years' servitude behind them by the time they were fifteen. But, it may be asked, how did that help them? Surely they would have to wait four years (at least) before they could become Lieutenants? That is so—officially. But no rule was more universally dodged than this one of a Lieutenant's minimum age. True, a birth certificate was demanded. But this was a mere bagatelle. About the turn of the century, Admiral Sir George Elliot tells us, a crown-piece handed to the porter at the Navy Office as one went in to be examined produced a certificate showing one to be any age one liked to mention. This perhaps helps to explain the formula commonly used by Lieutenants' Examining Boards. They seldom wrote 'The candidate is' (mentioning his age). They put 'The candidate appears to be': which at once covered themselves to some extent and shows us how difficult the regulation was to enforce.

But if—like William Dillon's father, Sir John—a man chanced to be fastidious, even conscientious according to his (to us) peculiar lights, he might object to anything quite so crude. In that case there were other ways. Hearing from his son in the West Indies that the time had come to produce a suitable certificate, this worthy and intelligent man—an author of no mean repute—instantly put himself into a coach. There he fell into conversation with a naval officer, and to him revealed the object of his journey—a visit to Birmingham where William had been baptized, to see if he could persuade the parson there how important it was for

[1] Op. cit., p. 15.

William to appear somewhat older than he was. Actually, says the younger Dillon naïvely, and one would have thought superfluously, 'my Father was fully aware that I had not acquired the age . . . [but] thought that a pecuniary consideration to the Parish Clerk would remove all difficulties'. At this the knowing naval officer laughed heartily, and offered to furnish the necessary certificate at the next stage-halt. But Sir John demurred. That smacked too much of the Porter and his five shillings. So the good man continued his journey to Birmingham. Unfortunately, however, the clergyman was away from home, and Sir John had to apply directly to the Clerk. 'But,' adds young Dillon quite unblushingly, 'that individual proved to be a strictly honourable person, and refused all my Father's offers to change the date.'

So Sir John had to be content with an utterly useless piece of paper which positively told the truth—that William was only just 16!

So far candour has been the order of the day. But now a discreet curtain is lowered, hiding heaven knows what. Only two more facts are on record.

(1) The genuine certificate was not sent in: the original remained among William's papers, and is now in the author's possession.

(2) Young Dillon's commission to Lieutenant is dated 29th April, 1797. He was still 16!

What happened? There are all sorts of intriguing possibilities. Did the honourable knight find a somewhat less honourable Clerk to seduce, or did he have another go at the parson, and seduce him? Did he make contact again with his knowing coach-friend, or did he just swallow his scruples and pay his crown-piece at the porter's lodge? Nor can the possibility be quite overlooked that he chose the cheapest and most obvious course of all—and forged the thing himself.

The clue to this odd story is plain enough. It is the whole body of late eighteenth century public morality. In all ages 'dishonour' is what men consider dishonourable. 'Everyone does it!' If the highest court in the land, the High Court of Parliament, is filled quite openly by every form of bribery: if all—or most—of the Civil Service posts are sold, exchanged, inherited or otherwise wangled: if Army and other contractors are scarcely bothering to conceal how they have come by their war-profits—if such things are 'done', was good Sir John so very dishonest? And was it not almost reasonable for him to suppose that a provincial parish clerk would not turn up his nose at a pecuniary inducement?

1. Nelson and his father (I) Horatio, aged 18. (His Captain's uniform was added later.) *From an oil painting by J. F. Rigard in the National Maritime Museum*

(II) The Rev Edmund, aged 78. *From an oil painting by Sir W. Beechey in the National Maritime Museum*

2. Parsonage House, Burnham Thorpe. Nelson's birthplace. *From an oil painting, artist unknown, in the National Maritime Museum*

3. 'England': James Bowen. 'A Success Story.' *From an oil painting, artist unknown, in the National Maritime Museum*

4. (I) 'Scotland': Admiral Lord Duncan. *From a mezzotint*

(II) 'Channel Islands': Admiral Lord Saumarez. *From a*

5. (I) 'Ireland': Captain Sir Henry Darby. *From a mezzotint by R. Erlom after Sir W. Beechey in the National Maritime Museum*

(II) 'Colonial': Sir Benjamin Hallowell (later Carew). *From an oil painting, artist unknown, in the National Maritime Museum*

6. John Nicol, seaman. *From the line-engraving frontispiece to his 'Life and Adventures'*

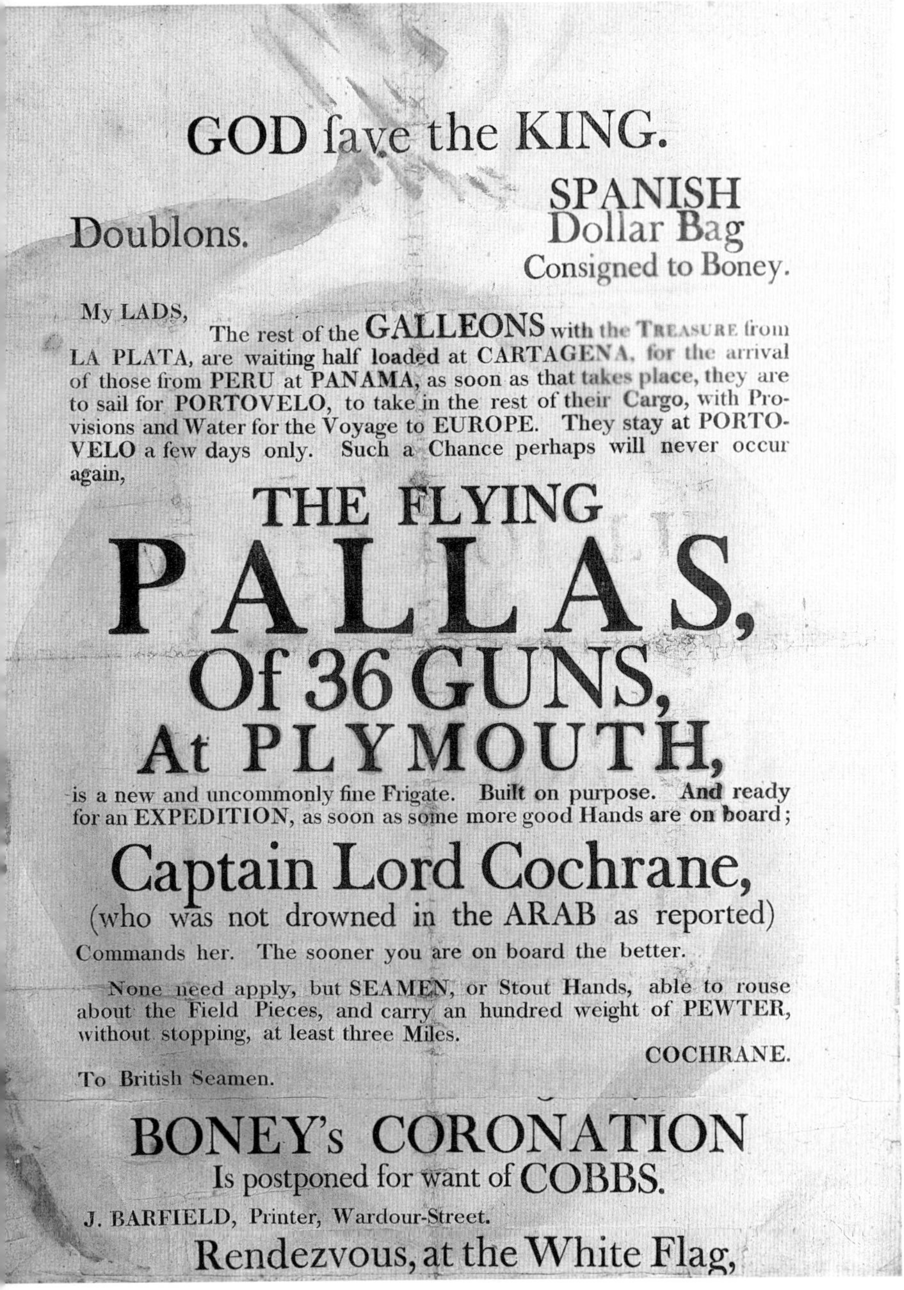

GOD save the KING.

Doublons.

SPANISH
Dollar Bag
Consigned to Boney.

My LADS,

The rest of the GALLEONS with the TREASURE from LA PLATA, are waiting half loaded at CARTAGENA, for the arrival of those from PERU at PANAMA, as soon as that takes place, they are to sail for PORTOVELO, to take in the rest of their Cargo, with Provisions and Water for the Voyage to EUROPE. They stay at PORTOVELO a few days only. Such a Chance perhaps will never occur again,

THE FLYING
PALLAS,
Of 36 GUNS,
At PLYMOUTH,

is a new and uncommonly fine Frigate. Built on purpose. And ready for an EXPEDITION, as soon as some more good Hands are on board;

Captain Lord Cochrane,
(who was not drowned in the ARAB as reported)

Commands her. The sooner you are on board the better.

None need apply, but SEAMEN, or Stout Hands, able to rouse about the Field Pieces, and carry an hundred weight of PEWTER, without stopping, at least three Miles.

COCHRANE.

To British Seamen.

BONEY's CORONATION
Is postponed for want of COBBS.

J. BARFIELD, Printer, Wardour-Street.

Rendezvous, at the White Flag,

7. A recruiting poster. *From the original in the National Maritime Museum*

8. The Press:
'Jack in the Bilboes'.
From a mezzotint by Ward after Morland in the National Maritime Museum

9. Two seamen. (I) *Left:* Thomas Ramsay, who boarded the *San Josef* with Nelson at Cape St Vincent. (II) *Right:* Name unknown. *Both from water-colour drawings by P. J. de Loutherbourg in the British Museum*

10. Richard Parker, mutineer. *From a stipple by Bailey after Sansom in the National Maritime Museum*

11. (I) Tom Allen, Nelson's coxswain. *From an oil painting by J. Burnet in the National Maritime Museum*

(II) Joe Miller, Greenwich pensioner. *From an oil painting by J. Burnet in the National Maritime Museum*

12. Sir Thomas Byam Martin (centre aet. 12) with his mother and elder brother. (His name has been 'on the books' for five years.) *From a plate in his 'Letters, vol. I', published by the Navy Records Society*

13. Sir William Dillon (aet. 70). *From a lithograph by C. Baugniet*

These are to certify the Principal Officers & Commissi-
ners of His Majestys Navy that Mr William Dillon
served as Boatswains Servant onboard of His Majestys
Ship Hermione under my Command from the
16th of August 1783 to the 15th October following then
as Captains Servant to the date hereof during which
time he discharged his duty with Sobriety, care &
diligence & was always obedient to command —

Given under my hand onboard
His Majestys Ship Hermione at
Chatham 5th October 1785.

John Stone

Recommended by William Westly Poole Esqr Brother
to Lord Mornington —.

14. The 'wrong William' certificate. *From the original in the author's possession*
(See page 169)

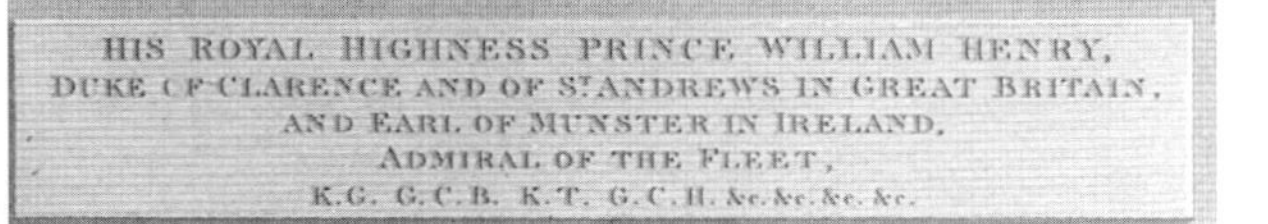

15. Nineteenth-century Admirals of the Fleet. (I) The youngest: Prince William Henry (aet. 46). *From a line engraving by William Skelton in the National Maritime Museum*

(II) The oldest: Provo Wallis (aet. 100). *From a photograph in the National Maritime Museum*

16. (I) 'Jobber': Admiral of the Fleet Sir Peter Parker. *From an oil painting by L. F. Abbott in the National Maritime Museum*

(II) 'Anti-jobber': Admiral of the Fleet John Jervis, Earl St Vincent. *From a mezzotint by J. R. Smith after Stuart in the*

b. *Book-Entry*

But no doubt some fathers with a high sense of parental duty and, still more, some mothers with loving hearts might hesitate to pitch their little ones so young into such a very rough school as a man-of-war. Very naturally—so naturally that such good folk had long since been accommodated. 'You do not want to enter him on the Ship's Books and send him to sea so young? Very reasonable. Then *don't send him to sea*! His name on the books will do just as well, since every month when it is there will count towards his six years.' There was, however, one theoretical disadvantage to this scheme. It involved regulation-breaking of a kind which, apparently, everyone was prepared to take in his stride. But it also involved something of a much less venal sort—*law*-breaking. And the law to be broken—'Thou shalt not steal!'—was not only a moral law: it was a statute law also, and a criminal offence. It is true that stealing was not the primary object of these 'book-entry' people. Yet it had to be a feature of this particular racket because every name on the books meant wages for somebody, and somebody had to draw them. So long as that name represented a real person, even a real protégé so long as he was there in person, the Captain was entitled by the rules of contemporary morality, and even by law, to draw the wages, even though the person concerned, being an infant, could not earn his pay. But as soon as a Captain drew wages for a name unaccompanied by a body, he was guilty of obtaining money under false pretences.

Yet—so much for public morality—the 'name-on-books' trick was very widespread, commoner if possible even than 'early-entry'. Nor, it would seem, did any moral obliquity attach to it. Naturally, while it was actually being done one did not shout about it, especially in the Waiting Room of the Admiralty, though of course one knew that their Lordships upstairs—their Naval Lordships anyway—knew all about it: were indeed probably doing it themselves 'on the side'. But, once it was done, reticence appears to have been quite unnecessary. Anyway, in O'Byrne, there are literally hundreds of entries like this, taken at random

'*George Vernon Jackson*, born 13th July, 1787. . . . This officer (whose name had been borne since 5 May, 1795 [aged eight] on the books of the *Trident*, *Minerva*, *Princess Augusta* and *Maidstone*) first embarked, in 1801, [aged 14] as Midshipman on board the *Trent*. . . .'

There is here no attempt at concealment, and presumably no consciousness of guilt, for *Captain* Jackson did not have to tell the world about it half a century later. Indeed, all who mention their 'book-time' seem rather proud of it than otherwise. During the years 1795–1801, no doubt, Master Jackson was quietly receiving his education at home or at school like any other civilian boy. In 1801, however, he went to sea with the most important lieutenant-qualification in his pocket—certificates adding up to six years' service in H.M. ships.

Yet this example—with some 300 others—illustrates something else—that the people concerned in a transaction which, to us, is at best shady were not complete fools. Clearly too they had much of the Navy's real interests at heart. For no one thought of actually making Jackson a Lieutenant in 1801. His parents would not expect it: no Captain would consent to play on such terms, and the Admiralty would certainly not have permitted it. Young Jackson's knowledge of the naval profession being, presumably, non-existent, no one wanted, or would allow, such vitally important people as Lieutenants to have no experience. In this particular case, our officer had to wait eight more years for his first commission: but the reason for this was probably lack of the right 'interest' for that stage of his career—a matter which we shall have to discuss later. We can, however, glean one thing more from this record. It explains how it came about that some 366 lads contrived to break the 'two-years-at-sea-before-Midshipman' rule. The Captain of the *Trent*, seeing six years of pre-Midshipman time vouched for upon his certificates, would make no bones about rating him Midshipman at once. And most of the other 365 boys would have similar papers to show.

A few more examples will illustrate various other facets of the 'entry-book' game.

Alfred Luckcraft juggled successfully with two regulations—'book-entry' and 'early-entry'—and broke both. From the ages of 7 to 9 his name was on the books of the *Monarch*: then, at 9, he embarked in her as First Class Volunteer.

Richard Sainthill's father, a Master, R.N., evidently knew the ropes. He got his boy's name on the books of the *Speedwell* when the child was 2, though he only had him on board when he was 13.

David Gilmour could hardly complain of a humdrum youth. He was 'on the books' at 4: but when, at 10, he went to sea, he shipped for some unstated reason in a merchantman. From this ship he fell into a shark-infested sea whence he was extracted with difficulty. Only then, with six years' sea-time at his disposal, he joined H.M.S. *Guardian*, instantly to be involved in one of the most terrible shipwrecks of the period, when the whole ship's company were saved after incredible hardships only by the superb pluck and skill of their commander, Nelson's 'gallant good Riou'. Not bad for a 14-year-old Midshipman!

William Hotham (afterwards Admiral Sir William, G.C.B.) coolly took the best of *three* possible worlds. He was 'on the books' at seven: he next went to Westminster School till he was 13, then went to sea for a few months; then joined the Royal Naval Academy for a spell before finally joining a ship. Within four years of this he was a Lieutenant.

Our last example is also the best-known—and perhaps the most flagrant. It concerns that great man, Thomas Cochrane, Earl Dundonald. Let him outline the story himself;

'My father turned his attention to myself. My destination was originally the Army. . . . Unfortunately my *penchant* was for the sea: any hint, however, to this effect was peremptorily silenced. . . . My uncle, the Hon. Captain, afterwards Admiral Sir Alexander Cochrane, had the sagacity to perceive that [my] passive obedience on this point might one day come to an end. . . . Unknown to my father, he had entered my name in the books of various vessels under his command, so that, nominally, I had formed part of the complement of the *Vesuvius*, *Carolina*, *La Sophie* and *Hind*: the object—common in those days—to give me a few years' standing in the Service, should it become my profession in reality. Having, however, a relative in the Army who possessed influence at the Horse Guards, a military commission was also procured for me, so that I had simultaneously the honour of being an officer in His Majesty's 104th Regiment and a nominal seaman on board my uncle's ship.'[1]

His book-time began when he was five and a half: he went to sea at 18. Is it fair to enquire what Captain Cochrane of the 104th, alias Tommy Cochrane, Rating R.N., was really doing during these twelve and a half years? He was at various schools, and finally at work rounding off his education in Monsieur Chauvet's academy in Kensington. Not for nothing were the Cochranes famed as inventive geniuses.

Yet this book-business was illegal too. It was 'false muster' and, very occasionally, but more frequently as the wars grew older, Nemesis caught up with its practitioners. But to do so she had to run very fast, and even when she had her hand on the victim he sometimes wriggled free. As early as 1788 Captain Isaac Coffin was accused by the Master of his own ship of 'knowingly signing a false register'. Here is a well-known

[1] *Autobiography of a Seaman*, p. 28.

danger to all transgressors—that some vindictive underling may 'split'. He had—there could be no denying it—signed the book for four Captain's Servants who—well: wherever they were there was no trace of them on board. The plain duty of the Court Martial which sat upon him was to cashier him. But the members of that court were all naval officers, and all, almost certainly, guilty at some time or another of that very crime. It is evident that they were acutely embarrassed because, quite arbitrarily, they softened the sentence to one of dismissal from his ship. But the First Lord, no less a person than the great Admiral Howe, and therefore well acquainted with the regulations, ignored the Court's finding and struck his name off the list. Coffin appealed, on the ground that the Admiralty had no power to overrule the verdict of a Court Martial, a court of justice. The case was therefore submitted to His Majesty's judges who, never very kindly disposed to the Admiralty's juridical claims, declared Lord Howe's action illegal. So Coffin, though he lost his ship, was reinstated and died a full Admiral.

But just now and again—and at diminishing intervals—Nemesis won. When she did, it was usually because the delinquent had no 'interest', and had gone just a shade too far, shocking the morality of even that easy-going age. This is what Lieutenant William Walker did in 1801. He had entered his own son, aged *one*, as an A.B., and—the humorist—he had drawn £5 bounty-money for him. He was only a Lieutenant, and he seems to have had no influential friends. So he was convicted and dismissed the Service. Yet even in this extreme case, it is clear, it was not the ship's-book offence which roused the Court's indignation. It was that £5 which they could not quite swallow. They thought—and who will contradict them?—that this looked rather too much like rank theft.

The Walker case was naturally much discussed and, after it, officers were at least more circumspect. There was never quite the old security again. Captains now came to insist more and more upon the occasional presence on board of their 'book-entries'; and from time to time paid dearly for neglecting to do so. In 1805, for instance, J. A. Norway, a Commander captaining the *Tromp*, fell foul of his spiteful old Carpenter who brought him to a Court Martial for having *one* book-entry who never put in an appearance: and, though the Court probably knew that it was primarily a case of spite, the offence was proved as 'false muster' and Norway was dismissed the Service. After that Captains sinned at their peril. But they went on sinning.[1]

[1] Richardson, op. cit., p. 206.

c. *An Uncommon Irregularity*

Only one more way of attaining the same agreeable ends will be mentioned here, and that, by its very nature, was uncommon. Sir John Dillon is again the hero and, this time, he appears in a much less equivocal light. Just as he was considering sending young William to sea, he received a surprise visit from a distant relative, older than himself, whose name was also Sir John Dillon: and who, by a strange coincidence, also had a son called William, older than our William. As soon as the elder Sir John heard that the younger William was to go to sea, he remarked, in effect, 'Now isn't that lucky! A few years ago that is what I intended for *my* William. We have changed our minds now, but I still have a perfectly good certificate for my William's service—nearly three years'-worth. Your lad shall have it. I'll send it along.'

He sent it along. But, strange as it may seem, the younger Sir John would not use it: not, it would seem, on account of the inherent dishonesty of the transaction, but because (says young William) 'he was determined that I should take my chance and rise by merit'. And to that determination they clung, father and son. As we have seen, William was a regulation-dodger in 'age-of-entry'; but all his certificates of service, which survive, represent in-the-flesh presence on board the named ships. He was never a 'book-entry'. This particular certificate is reproduced opposite page 193. Had our Dillons accepted it, they might well have been guilty of a double deception. It is not possible now to tell whether it originally represented a mere 'book-entry', or whether the elder William had actually served the alleged time in the *Hermione*. Be that as it may, however, they would certainly have been guilty of deliberately false impersonation, and it was probably this which struck the younger Sir John as a thing 'not done'. Later, as it happened, there came an occasion when it would have been very useful to our William and, momentarily, he may have regretted that his father had not used it. His ship, the *Prince George*, had participated in Lord Bridport's action off the Ile de Groix in June, 1795, and, in reward, one of her Midshipmen was to be promoted Lieutenant. Dillon was senior Midshipman, and his Captain went so far as to congratulate him publicly upon his advancement. Unfortunately, however, he could muster only 5½ years'-worth of certificates and so lost the prize, though this one would have given him nearly eight. But we need not sympathize with him unduly. He was quite philosophic about it himself, seeing that he was still under 15! Besides, his Captain consoled him by rating him Master's Mate.

None the less, we may perhaps compliment Sir John on an exhibition of morality well in advance of eighteenth-century standards. It is a pity that he suffered a relapse with the Parish Clerk two years later.

In the new 1808[1] issue of the Regulations, several of those dealing with the entry of officers were tightened up, and safeguards were inserted. It was now laid down, for instance, that the muster-books containing the details of all the Ship's Company should be signed, every time they were sent in—at two-monthly periods—by both Captain and Lieutenants personally 'that their signatures may be compared with any certificates said to be given by them'. This must have made offenders feel uncomfortable. False entries were evidently becoming more risky. Yet there can be no doubt that many irregularities remained to the last. Thus, in theory, after 1794 there should have been no 'other rating' entries at all, since all Young Gentlemen were expected to enter as First Class Volunteers. Yet they still entered a-plenty. There is a lad entering as Midshipman in August, 1814, which can only mean that 'book-time' was flourishing then. There is also a Third Class Boy in 1814. He should have been (after the Order of 1794) a real servant. But most certainly he was not, being in fact the son of Admiral Sir Henry Blackwood, Nelson's frigate captain at Trafalgar. There are 'A.B.'s' entering up to 1807 at least—officer-types too. On the other hand, there are First Class Volunteers joining at 10 or younger—for example, Richard Lewis, who entered as one in 1806, aged under 7. His is an odd case for, though the son of a naval officer and a protégé of the Duke of Kent, he took thirty-two years to become a Lieutenant.

The later columns of the Table show that some entry-ratings carried better chances than others of going high in the Service. Columns X and XI represent an effort to assess the 'average expectation' of men entering under the various ratings. The process must be somewhat arbitrary and approximate. Each candidate has been 'marked' according to the highest rank he attained, in a way shown in greater detail at page 199 below, where the whole question of promotion within the Service is discussed. Column X shows this average mark, and Column XI explains it in terms of 'average expectation' rank. In these columns we see that all 'Servant' entries promised well, compared with either 'Other Ratings' or 'Volunteers'. The average rank-expectation of a 'Servant' was nearly a Captain, while those of both the other two were a long way below

[1] The enlarged edition of *Regulations and Instructions* was issued in 1808, but many of the individual regulations included in it date from 1806, or even earlier.

Commander. Of the 'Servants', the average 'Captain's Servant' did best of all. He might expect to become a Post Captain, with a little to spare. The success of the 'Servants' is not surprising. Since they were all in by April, 1794, they were almost all 'pre-war'. They were therefore in the better position to profit by war-promotion, which, for obvious reasons, is always easier than peacetime promotion; partly because of the greater number of posts going, but mainly because they tended to get the better ones, being already trained men when the newcomers were learners. The ratings with the worst chance of promotion were the Petty Officers, most of whom were Clerks, or Pursers' assistants, and not normally 'combatant' at all. Though not really 'lower deck', they were very doubtful 'officer-types'. The same applies to the Schoolmasters. But such officers are few and far between anyway. The worst-off rating which reaches any size is that of 'Landman'. But then, what influential Captain, obliging a rich, gentle or influential parent, or 'protecting' a bright boy, would rate him among the lowest and most despised grade on board? On the whole, the figures come out as we should expect.

The 'Supernumeraries' (C.22) need not detain us. They were a job lot, and mostly self-condemned 'irregularities', mainly of early date. The Admiralty Regulations are constantly dinning into the Captains that Supernumeraries—that is, men carried additional to the allowed number of ratings in each category—were to be cut to a minimum and, where possible, eradicated.

The extraordinarily high figures in the Table at D. 23 (Unspecified, Dead before 1845) are *hors concours* in this calculation. Their high 'rank reached', it will be observed, is not allowed to affect the rest, and their very presence in O'Byrne needs a word of explanation. There are only about 100 of them and, unlike all the officers dealt with in his main text (whose common factor was that they were alive), these were all dead, and relegated to footnotes. The material used by O'Byrne, therefore, is inevitably secondhand, and not nearly so detailed as the rest, seldom giving information on either their social backgrounds or their method of entry. They were all the fathers, uncles or even grandfathers of the living, serving officers of 1848, and are included only because, in their day, they had been important naval people. For this reason they are by no means a cross-section even of their own day, let alone of O'Byrne's: and it would be unrealistic to let their high average of rank-achievement (which is above Rear-Admiral) affect the main body of O'Byrne's contemporaries. They are interesting chiefly as a posthumous gallery of 'distinguished dead'.

To conclude this necessarily cavalier treatment of thousands of individuals, we will examine a few unusual or exceptional cases. First, some of the few out-of-the-ordinary Midshipmen. Jeremiah Coghlan had been for three years a boy in the Merchant Service when, in 1796, he displayed outstanding gallantry and initiative in rescuing fifty men from a wrecked East Indiaman. This came to the ears of Sir Edward Pellew, that great fighter, then in command of the *Indefatigable*, and he was so favourably impressed that, then and there, he 'offered him his patronage if he would consent to enter the Navy'. Rarely indeed were Merchant Service boys—no high form of marine life—thus approached, hat in hand as it were, by distinguished Post Captains. Naturally, he leapt at the chance, joined the *Indefatigable* and was rated Midshipman at once. Thereafter he never looked back. He was a man after Pellew's heart, was given his Lieutenant's commission after four and a half years, rose to be a Post Captain and, had he but lived a little longer, would have won his flag. This gallant sailor cannot be classed 'lower deck' according to the definition used here, because he must have entered the *Indefatigable* with high hopes—and prospects—of a commission, protected as he was in such a quarter. In that respect, therefore, he was 'quarter-deck' like any other Midshipman. What was unusual about the case was that Pellew was acting quite regularly in rating him Midshipman: not a 'quarter-deck' Midshipman, but one of the old sort who, as we saw, was a perfectly ordinary rating. For that post Coghlan had the necessary qualification—sea-experience.

But an even clearer example of the old sort can be found. Richard Greening had spent five years in the Merchant Service when, at the age of 20, he was pressed into the Navy on the outbreak of the Napoleonic War. His Captain, Gardner, seeing that an experienced seaman had fallen into his net, promptly rated him Midshipman: perfectly legally too, and, this time, considering him to be one of the old type and not a protégé. So he was: unlike Coghlan, he was the true 'lower deck' of our definition, who had not wanted to enter the Navy at all and therefore entertained no hopes of a commission therein. He received one ultimately, however, though only in 1816, as a concession 'in lieu of pension' —like Marshall's Lieutenancy (see p. 29). His case is a very rare one, for here is a true lower-deck, 'non-officer type' starting his naval life as a Midshipman: a real survivor of the pre-Cromwellian Midshipman.

There is probably another such among O'Byrne's 366 Midshipman Entry, though O'Byrne does not reveal the fact. Samuel Jackson was a fellow-apprentice with young William Richardson in a North Sea coaster, like him designing to become a Merchant Service officer. However, for some reason not divulged, he joined the Navy as a Midshipman, thereafter rising steadily and ending as a Rear-Admiral with a fine record. He may well have been pressed, though O'Byrne does not say so: nor—true to form—does he mention his comparatively lowly background. He was certainly not 'officer-type' in a social sense, and probably not 'quarter-deck' in our naval sense. In fact he was probably another Midshipman of the old sort like Greening, rated as such by his first naval Captain because he had the required seatime and experience.[1]

Here are a few more oddities.

Henry Nazer received on entering the unusual rating of Second Master and Pilot. His Captain and patron was unusual too—his brother William, a Lieutenant-in-command. Whether William was acting regularly depends upon Henry's previous qualifications which are not known. But it worked all right—for Henry. He rose to be a Commander, though William, who died soon afterwards, did not.

Hamilton Davies came in with an even humbler patron and an even odder rating. The former was a Midshipman commanding a fire-brig. The latter was Yeoman of the Powder Room—usually, and for obvious reasons, a post of immense responsibility given to a particularly trustworthy and usually elderly seaman. Davies may or may not have been trustworthy. But nobody could accuse him of being elderly. He was 10.

Now for two unusual volunteers, original people swimming against the contemporary current. During our wars there were many who deserted the Navy, to find jobs ashore or in the Merchant Service, and there must have been many thousands more who would have done so had they dared. These two did just the reverse. They deserted their other jobs and ran away to the Navy. They were in fact examples of that 100-per-cent volunteer boy (see p. 86) who chose the Navy for love, and in spite of opposition. John Hickman, 'having cut and run from the Merchant Service after three years of wearisome employment in it, entered on board the Deptford tender:'[2]—which, of course, was the

[1] Richardson, op. cit., p. 6.
[2] O'Byrne, under Hickman.

Impress tender! What must the Gang have thought when he climbed over the side and explained his business? He was promoted to Lieutenant. We may hope his waiting-period was not equally wearisome; but not too confidently, as it was twenty-five years.

During the wars, again, the Marine Society handled thousands of little waifs and strays, and most of them, as we saw, must have been but half-hearted volunteers. John Smith (B), however, was definitely not half-hearted. Left destitute by a mad father, he 'was bound apprentice to a mechanical trade'[1] by his relatives, but ran away and applied to the Marine Society, who equipped him and sent him to sea. Such enterprise had its reward. Twenty-four years later he was a Post Captain: indeed, Marshall says that he was the only Marine Society boy ever to become one. But then Smith, though fully 'lower-deck' in our naval sense, was socially of 'officer-class', being of quite good birth and education.

There is, lastly, William Elliott, an officer of unusual candour for his times:

'He entered the naval service, 21st February, 1795, with no better prospect than that of ultimately becoming a Purser: his only professional friend being Mr. P. Ellery, Captain's Clerk of the *Irresistible*, 74, commanded by the late Admiral John Leigh Douglas, who allowed him to join the ship as an assistant to his amanuensis.'[2]

Could anything be more depressing? An assistant clerk to a Clerk, the latter, of no quarter-deck pretensions whatever, his only fount of Interest. But the young man was eminently persistent, able, brave and it must be admitted, lucky. He fought at the Ile de Groix, at Camperdown, at Copenhagen, at the taking of Monte Video and in a host of small-ship actions. Indeed, his rise was very rapid—as rapid as that of the average officer-type. He was made Lieutenant in 1802, Commander in 1809, Captain in 1810—Post Captain at 28 with no aid whatever from a Patron. It is a refreshing record, for it shows that, in spite of the dead hand of Interest, real merit could be rewarded even then. It was further recognized too, for when he died, still in full employment, in 1838, his style was Captain Sir William Elliott, R.N., Knight, C.B., K.C.H., K.T.S.

[1] Marshall, XI, p. 407.
[2] Ibid., IX, p. 197.

SOCIAL TYPES AGAIN

In conclusion, the final columns in Table V (XII, XIII and XIV) require some explanation. The earlier columns, as we have seen, record the actual entry-rating of 3,467 officers. They are shown as entering under some thirty different rating-names: and some of these, as starting-points, were a good deal more promising than others. But what the Table has not shown, so far, is which officers were 'quarter-deck' and which 'lower deck', for here the entry-ratings are valueless—an 'A.B.', for instance, might be either. In most cases, however, we can discover which is which, and must do so if only to explain how, in Chapter I, we reached our figure of officers of 'working-class' origin (p. 44). The attempt is made in the last three columns of the Table, first for each rating separately, and finally for the whole lot. This assessment appears in the last row but two under Columns XII, XIII and XIV. The figures there given read:

SOCIAL TYPES

'OFFICER'	'LOWER DECK'	UNKNOWN	TOTAL
3,028	103	336	3,467

An apparent discrepancy instantly appears. Table I in Chapter I showed 120 officers of probable 'Working Class' extraction. This shows only 103. But these are taken from O'Byrne only, for reasons given at page 148. On the other hand, the 120 come from O'Byrne and Marshall combined, most of them common to both. But, naturally, some of Marshall's officers had died before 1845—to be exact, seventeen—and these do not appear in an analysis abstracted wholly from O'Byrne.

Perhaps it may appear presumptuous to give these figures. The sceptic may ask, 'How do you come to know the ambitions and prospects of so many officers? You claim to know them in 3,131 cases out of 3,467—roughly 90 per cent.' The answer is that 'know' is rather too positive a word to use in connection with my claim. Rather, I infer—but with fair grounds for the inferences. Indeed, there are almost certainly errors, in all categories. But such guesswork as there is, is strictly confined in extent, first because of the introduction of my 'unknown' column, and second because O'Byrne himself gives so many clues, while many others are present in the entry-ratings themselves. Thus the largest entry of all—'First Class Volunteer'—is composed entirely of 'quarter-deck' people: for when the Admiralty invented that grade in 1794 it actually defined it as 'young gentlemen intended for the sea-service'. The same is true of all the College Volunteers, who were 'sons of the Nobility and Gentry' or, at lowest, of Naval Officers. Again, an overwhelming number of those with the entry-rating of Midshipman may be safely regarded as 'quarter-deck', though, in this case not quite all. So already we have accounted for well over 2,000 of our officers who are all 'quarter-deck'.

There are further generic clues. 'Captain's Servants', in overwhelming proportions (though again not quite exclusively), are 'quarter-deck'. So are those—or almost all those—whose family details are given in O'Byrne. Parents in this group would not dream of sending their boys to sea unless they were sure that they would 'walk the Quarter-deck' when they got there.

So much for the relegation of whole entries and classes to the 'Officer' column. But plenty more clues are to be found in the texts of the individual biographies. Thus whenever we find a boy entering as A.B. at the age of 13, we know he was 'quarter-deck', for a 13-year-old 'lower deck' entrant could not be rated A.B.: there would be no point in it, as he could not possibly do the work. Or again—'William Johnson entered the Navy, July, 1803, as Supernumerary . . . transferred as Midshipman, August, 1804, to the . . . promoted to the rank of Lieutenant, October, 1809.' We see Mr. Johnson's advantages at once—one instead of two years as Midshipman: his Lieutenancy punctually after his six years. No lower-deck lad could expect such luck. Again, most of the (many score of) cases where the Captain and the youngster bear the same surname. Again, every lad who enters really young—he must be 'quarter-deck': there was no place on the Lower Deck for passengers, especially baby ones. And so must every 'book-entrant' be—his name was only on the books in order that he might acquire subsequent 'quarter-deck' benefits. And so on, until nothing but a minority is left.

Then, however, we must begin looking more carefully at each case on its merits. We are approaching the genuine 'lower-deck promotion'. Thus, if we meet a man who entered the Navy on board H.M.S. *A*, Captain Z, and then served in several other ships with several other Captains, and with no mention of his ratings in them, we begin to grow inquisitive. Then if, after several more years—perhaps many more—our man emerges at length as Midshipman or—even more suspicious—Master's Mate; and perhaps, after yet more years, becomes 'Acting

Lieutenant' and, ultimately, confirmed Lieutenant, then it begins to become clear that he enjoys none of the ordinary forms of Interest at all, and we may infer that he never had any: that is, that he was 'lower deck' according to our definition—one who entered the Service without the hope or reasonable prospect of becoming a commissioned officer. Striking cases of this sort have here been labelled 'Lower Deck': less striking ones, or cases where uncertainty exists, have been labelled 'Unknown'.

There, then, for what they are worth, are the findings. The percentages derivable from them are sufficiently remarkable, and accurate enough to be worth recording.

Of the 3,467 officers considered, 87⅓ per cent were of 'Officer-Class' origin, 3 per cent of 'Lower Deck', and 9⅔ per cent uncertain. Most of the 'uncertains' should probably be added to the 'Officers'.

PART THREE: THE PROFESSION

PROSPECTS, CONDITIONS OF SERVICE AND REWARDS

CHAPTER V

THE NAVAL HIERARCHY: RANK, PROMOTION, AND APPOINTMENTS

OUR officers and men are now entered and safely aboard. The next step will be to give some account of their professional careers: to what commands they were appointed, to what ranks they rose by promotion, and how they could best achieve that promotion. This will lead to that difficult but fascinating something known to most of them as 'Interest'—the working of the influence of other people, whether naval or civilian, upon their careers. To such aspects, dealt with in this and the following chapter, we may give the title of 'The Naval Hierarchy'. But this Part, concerned as it is with our subjects' professional life, must go further, and include some account of their daily lives afloat, and how each fitted into the social hierarchy of his ship. And, in the last two chapters of this Part comes an examination of the more mundane economic side: what rewards came the way of naval men—indeed, one might almost say, what inducements took them to sea and kept them there. Pay was one inducement but not, as we shall see, the only or even the main one.

In this chapter, then, we deal with the Naval Hierarchy, with the ranks within it and the machinery of promotion. But since in the Navy of the time promotion was still so closely bound up with appointments, we must, concurrently, study these too.

Once more we shall use O'Byrne who, again, has done much of our work for us. Against the name of every officer he set the rank or grade he held in 1848—or, if he had died after 1845, his rank at the moment of death.

He shows no less than sixteen different grades: Admiral of the Fleet, Admirals of the Red, of the White and of the Blue: three Vice-Admirals with these colour-qualifications: three Rear-Admirals with the same: three sorts of Captain, one printed in ordinary capitals, another in heavy gothic lettering, the third with the word 'Retired' in front of 'Captain': Commander, Retired Commander, and Lieutenant. The analysis undertaken here, fortunately, does not need so large a number. It has been reduced by exactly half and, in Table V (pp. 146–7), the eight that remain head the columns numbered from II to IX. Column I is reserved for the numbers in each category. These ranks have a distinctly modern look: indeed, were we to substitute 'Lieutenant-Commander' for 'Retired Commander', and add 'Sub-Lieutenant' at the end, our columns would include all the Flag- and Commissioned-Officers of today. But things are not quite so simple as that. What we are about to do, in fact, is to assist at the creation of the modern ranking system—the disappearance of the old 'colour' flags, and the reduction of all Captains from three sorts to one sort. But we shall not complete the process, because the creation of the Lieutenant-Commander and the Sub-Lieutenant, as substantive ranks, is entirely outside our period:[1] and 'Retired Commander' has nothing to do with 'Lieutenant-Commander'.

Admiral of the Fleet (Column II)

This rank—the first of O'Byrne's sixteen—must be retained. These great ones were rare in our wars—a good deal rarer than they are today—because only one of them was in existence at a time: and between 1815 and 1848 there were never more than two; not always that. Once created, the Admiral of the Fleet remained upon his lonely pinnacle until he died. But he seldom lasted for very long because he was bound to be old before he reached it.

The reason why there came to be two is interesting. Though the office no longer conferred upon the holder the right to command important fleets, as once it did, it still had immense prestige. Its holder was still titular 'Commander-in-Chief', and on show occasions—reviews and the like—still automatically took command, his Union Flag flying proudly at the main. Senior officers, therefore, coveted the post not a little. Imagine then their feelings when in 1811, upon the death of the then holder—Sir Peter Parker—at the age of 90, there was appointed in his room Prince William Henry, Duke of Clarence and later King William IV. In his earlier days he had been a serving officer, but he had never flown his flag at sea in any real command, and his various promo-

[1] But see p. 198.

tions had been far swifter than normal. Worse still, it was a life-appointment, and he was only 46: which meant that he would almost certainly outlive all the distinguished veterans of his day. Since then, of course, many Princes of the Blood have been Admirals of the Fleet, with results that have done nothing but good to the Navy and the nation. But then the prince's tenure does not deprive any professional officer of the honour since, the one-at-a-time rule being broken, there is no reason why there should not be an extra one. As it was, the Duke (or 'the Sailor Prince') reigned afloat—though practically always ashore—for ten years. But then, in 1821, the new King, George IV, listened to the Navy's grievance and, without demoting his brother, allowed a second officer to come up beside him. Thus the last year of a great sailor's long life was somewhat cheered. Admiral Earl St. Vincent, more than anyone else the architect of Britain's naval victory and now in his 87th year, at last became Admiral of the Fleet, the King having the grace to send him personally the heavy gold-mounted baton of office.

O'Byrne has two Admirals of the Fleet, Sir James Whitshed, then 86 years old, who had entered the Service before the American Independence war began and had so far won the 'survival-stakes' as to reach the top in 1844, though he died in the following year. The other, Sir George Martin, some two years Whitshed's junior in both age and service, had reached the rank in 1846 and died after only nine months in it. The careers of two others, however, are briefly recorded among O'Byrne's 'distinguished dead'—Sir Peter Parker (1799–1811) and the pious Lord Gambier (1830–33).

There are among the biographies, of course, several future Admirals of the Fleet, waiting in the hope of outlasting their seniors; Sir Thomas Byam Martin, for instance, and that amazing survival, Provo Wallis, the uniqueness of whose record must be our excuse for leaving our period rather far behind. He appears in O'Byrne as a mere Captain of twenty-nine years' standing. He was born in 1791 and had, according to O'-Byrne's main text, entered the Service, and actually served, as an Able Seaman on 1st May, 1795—aged 4 years and 18 days. In the appendix, however, he himself seems to have corrected O'Byrne, affirming that he did not actually go to sea till 1800. This, as we have seen, was nothing out of the ordinary. But the rest of his career certainly was. In 1813 he was Second-Lieutenant of the *Shannon* when that frigate fought her never-to-be-forgotten action with the American *Chesapeake*. The First-Lieutenant was killed and Captain Broke dangerously wounded, so that young Wallis found himself in temporary command, and brought the prize safe to Halifax. For this he was promoted Commander, and his future was assured. The great naval slump following the war caught him, but he survived it, being made Post in 1819; and thereafter he had but to remain alive and wait his turn. It was a long wait, but he could well afford it. In 1851 he became a Rear-Admiral, and now promotion came more rapidly—his rivals were dying off fast. He was a Vice-Admiral by 1857 and a full Admiral in 1863. He then enjoyed a stroke of luck. A proper system of retirement was just coming in, and as, by this time, he was in his '70's, he could scarcely hope to avoid the 'shelf'. But in 1870 a special clause in the relevant act ordained that any veteran officer who had commanded a ship during the French Wars should not have to retire: and Wallis qualified, by virtue of his few days' command of the *Shannon*. Doubtless the Government felt fairly safe. There were very few survivors who could benefit, and the chances were that they would not enjoy the privilege for long. But Provo Wallis was one too many for them. In 1877 his turn came, and he was Admiral of the Fleet. He was now rising 87 and, though naturally he was no longer employed, was in excellent health. He survived the 1870's: he survived the 1880's. On his hundredth birthday in 1891 he could still read and write without difficulty, and enjoy the congratulations showered upon him from all over the English-speaking world. He was indeed a unique survivor of a world gone for ever. Queen Victoria had had her golden jubilee: the Victorian Age itself was drawing to a close: the 'naughty nineties' had come, and here was Provo Wallis to be seen any day in his home near Chichester—Wallis of the *Shannon* who had been fleet-mates with Nelson, with St. Vincent, with Howe. But even Wallis was not so immortal as he must have seemed. He died in February, 1892, in the 101st year of his remarkable life.

Here then is a strange reflection. Wallis, as Admiral of the Fleet, never retired. So not a few hardy veterans of World War II—let us specifically mention Sir Roger Keyes, also Admiral of the Fleet—served in the Navy with Wallis. And Wallis had served in the Navy with Sir Peter Parker, born in 1721. More, if we stretch a point and allow Wallis's book-time to count, we can go even further back. He was 'entered', we saw, in 1795—incidentally figuring on the Admiralty's pay-roll for a little matter of 97 years. In 1796 died one John Forbes, also Admiral of the Fleet, whose eyes first beheld the light a fortnight before it was extinguished in Queen Anne's. He went to sea in 1726: Keyes died in

1945. So three officers had served in the Active List of the Navy, without a gap and not even 'retired', for a matter of 219 years.

Admirals (Columns III, IV and V)

O'Byrne's next nine grades of Flag-Officer can be telescoped into three. The 'squadronal colours' had long since lost their original significance, which was to differentiate the three squadrons of the huge fleets which fought against the Dutch in the seventeenth century. So large were they indeed that the squadrons themselves had to be divided into three, and each of these 'divisions' was big enough to require a 'Flag-man' to control it. Hence three Admirals, one to each of the Red, White and Blue Squadrons; three Vice-Admirals, one to command each of the van divisions of the three squadrons, and three Rear-Admirals to command the rear divisions. Hence too the sequence of titles from Admiral of the Fleet, the man in command of the whole array, down to the Rear-Admiral of the Blue, the comparatively humble 'flag-officer' who controlled the rear division of the rear (or blue) squadron. But in those vast fleets the man commanding the whole was inevitably also the Admiral of the Red; for the logical position of both of them in that most symmetrical system was the same. Both must be at dead centre of the line, the one to command the whole line, the other to command the red (and central) squadron in it: and there could be no point, indeed no sense, in having two such important people so close together in the line, let alone in one ship. So in fact, and for so long as this big-fleet system lasted, there were only nine, not ten, Flag-Officers: that is, no separate Admiral of the Red.

This arrangement faded out very early in the eighteenth century. Our Dutch War strategy had demanded one major fleet, but our French War strategy required several smaller ones. So the system died: yet, by that well-known quirk in the British character, the nomenclature seemed to have no difficulty in surviving the dead system. All the names remained though their original functions were gone, and the titles, which once described positions in the line, came to describe something quite different—their ranking positions vis-à-vis each other. They must even have been a sore trial to the ambitious flag-officer on his upward course: for, having at last attained the honour of a 'flag', he must climb wearily through nine grades or ranks in order to emerge at the top. Then, early in the next century, in 1805, when logic would seem to point to a reduction of numbers, they were actually increased. The grade of Admiral of the Red was inserted between Admiral of the Fleet and Admiral of the White. There were now *ten* steps on the flag-officer's ladder.

How dead these titles had become by the nineteenth century is shown by the fact that the Royal Navy, all of it, was coming more and more to use the 'white' flag with its red St. George cross and the union in the top canton—the familiar White Ensign. Yet the long innings of the 'colours' persisted right through our period, right on to O'Byrne's day and for sixteen years beyond. Only in 1864 was the White Ensign officially adopted for the Royal Navy, the Blue going to the Reserves and the Red to the Merchant Service. At the same time the colours at last went out of the flag-officers' titles too, and the number of their grades was reduced to the present four. All that we have done here, therefore, is to anticipate officialdom by sixteen years; and, in the Table, Columns III, IV, and V read respectively 'Admiral', 'Vice-Admiral' and 'Rear-Admiral'. There is no column for Commodores. This word never did, and does not, signify a definitive rank; and no such heading ever did, or does, appear in the Navy List. Then as now a Commodore was a Captain temporarily in charge of a small squadron or a shore-post of outstanding importance. He is—and was—a Commodore because of the post he holds, not because of the rank he has reached. When he gives up his post he will be once more—and will once more dress like—an ordinary Captain.

Throughout our wars everyone 'on the Flag List' held his place strictly by his seniority thereon. He could neither pass nor be passed by his neighbours.

Captain (Column VI)

Where O'Byrne shows three sorts of Captain, Table V shows but one. Two of his groups are amalgamated, the third being relegated to the lower grade of Commander which occupies Column VII. This needs explanation.

O'Byrne's 'CAPTAIN', printed in ordinary small capitals, is exactly what we now call a Captain. So too his own contemporaries named him, though they often added the word 'Post', making 'Post Captain': and called the process of being made one 'being made post'. Indeed it was this 'being made post' which was the really crucial point in the naval officer's career. It was naturally very important to be made a Lieutenant because only so did he become a commissioned officer at all: only then could he start his journey up the naval hierarchy. As we shall see, it was not necessarily easy to make this start, but anyone who failed to do so was of no interest to O'Byrne: nor, at this stage of our story, to us. So let us assume that our naval man has, somehow or other, got himself made a Lieutenant. Again, he will not necessarily obtain his next step, to Commander. Then he will remain a Lieutenant and, incidentally, never get into Marshall at all, though O'Byrne will notice him. But again let us suppose him lucky. Another promotion-step is negotiated, and he is a Commander. Now at least, as the name implies, he will have a 'command' of his own: he will have the sole ordering of a ship, though it will be but a small one.

On the face of it, the jump from commanding a small ship to commanding a big one does not sound very great. Surely, one might suppose, it should only be a question of time before he is given a larger ship—a Captain's command; a Post Captain's command, or, as they said then, a 'Post Ship' of Sixth-rate or upwards. But no: it did not follow at all. Here was at once the hardest and the most vital step in his professional career. Here 'Interest' was more essential perhaps than at any other stage. Let us make no mistake. Talent, professional skill, officer-like qualities were always of prime importance; and such qualities in abundance would usually, in the long run, enable their possessor to reach the bottom rung of the Captain's ladder. That was because, by and large, so many of the people who had the wielding of Interest also had at heart the good of the Service and the State, and would often exercise their great powers in the right direction. But, it is much to be feared, the opposite was even truer. A man not markedly endowed with such qualities, but blessed with powerful Interest, would certainly attain the goal—and often, indeed usually, before the better man. It is here that the great importance of the step must be emphasized. It was not only that the naval captain was, as we have seen, such a very key person in the Navy of his day. It was also because advance to future naval heights became more or less certain from the day that he was made post. For there was one all-important difference between this step and all preceding ones. Becoming a Lieutenant did not necessarily mean becoming a Commander, nor did a Commander necessarily become a Captain. But a Captain, once made, was certain, subject to two provisos—one a pretty considerable one—of becoming an Admiral of the Fleet.

The provisos were these. First, he must not allow too huge and obvious a blot to soil his naval escutcheon. If he did, he ran the risk of being 'broken'—dismissed the Service. But this was rare, and there was, during our wars, a way of avoiding it: not one that would appeal to ambitious and patriotic men, but still open to him. He could avoid employment. This would, of course, make a difference to his professional career, but none to his ranking progress. Once on the bottom rung of that 'post' ladder, he would go on mounting it as long as he lived, whether he were employed or not. And, like the Admirals, he would retain his exact place on it. Here is one rather extreme example of the way in which things might work. A certain Edward Ratsey was 'made post' into the *Sir Edward Hughes*, 38—a frigate and therefore a 'post ship'. This was in 1806. He brought her home safely (without any bad blot) just one year later. Thereafter he ran no further risk of blots because he went, and remained, on half-pay. He never went to sea again. In fairness be it said, there is no evidence that he refused any ship: much more likely, the Admiralty never asked him. But such are the facts. By O'Byrne's time he was Rear-Admiral of the Red—the senior sort of Rear-Admiral. But this was not the end of him—O'Byrne, we must recall, only records the facts as they stood in 1848. By 1868, when over 90, Ratsey found himself the Senior Admiral. He was by then, it is true, what they called 'on reserved half-pay', but at that age he could hardly be otherwise. Yet there he was—right at the top, though, after one year as Captain, he had not been at sea for sixty-one years!

This leads to our second proviso—a more serious one. Our junior Captain, en route for his Admiralship of the Red, or of the Fleet, had naturally to take the precaution of remaining alive. If he failed there, he would get nowhere—navally speaking. So it cut both ways. Ratsey rose so high simply because he lived so long. On the other hand, two of the most brilliant young officers of the whole war-period were Sir Philip Broke, captor of the *Chesapeake*, and Sir William Hoste, victor of Lissa, the most striking frigate-action of the war. Broke died, not indeed young, but far from old, when he was a mere Rear-Admiral. Hoste, dying younger, was still a Captain. And the greatest of them all provides an admirable example of the 'ranking' advantage of staying alive. Nelson himself, though favoured in his younger days with all the three elements which really counted—plenty of Interest, plenty of opportunities for action and a naval talent which has not been exceeded, or exaggerated—Nelson himself was never an Admiral. The highest he could reach was Vice-Admiral of the White—exactly halfway up the long Flag-Officers' ladder. It is quite easy to calculate when, had he lived, he would have reached the top to become Admiral of the Fleet. It would have been in 1844: thirty-nine years after Trafalgar and in the 87th year of his life.

From all this, then, we see the great importance not only of being 'made post', but also of being made post young—as young as possible. For rising through the Captains' list was a long business at the best of times; and there were no short-cuts. The same held for rich and poor alike. Ratsey was a man of comparatively humble origin, but no one could pass him. On the other hand Algernon, fourth Duke of Northumberland, though 'made post' in 1815 and incidentally (like Ratsey) never to go to sea again, did not become a Rear-Admiral till 1850. Nor could genius help. Nelson, a Lieutenant at 18½, a Commander at 20 and a Captain at under 21, served brilliantly through two wars in which, for obvious reasons, promotion was more rapid than in times of peace; and before he was through the Captains' list he was a Knight of the Bath and a figure with a worldwide reputation. But that made no difference: it could not shorten his eighteen years' service as Captain. This, be it observed, was rapid progress. The rate of climbing from bottom to top of the list slackened after his time; and the unfortunates caught by the war's end had to wait more than twice as long. Dillon, for instance, waited thirty-eight and a half years.

The men, then, marked 'CAPTAIN' in O'Byrne were all full-blown Post Captains: all—in theory though, alas, not always in practice—'active' in the sense that, if only they could live long enough, promotion was certain to come to them.

O'Byrne's next category is that in which the word **Captain** is printed beside the names in heavy gothic type. There is something almost funereal about this solemn lettering. Possibly O'Byrne thought so when he used it. For these were the exceptional few who had given up the promotion-race without resigning life itself, where the many had determined only to give up both at once. These were the Post Captains, of various seniority, who had 'accepted the retirement' of 1846. That word 'accepted' tells the whole story. Even in 1846 the Admiralty could not order its officers to retire. It could only bribe them to do so: and it was high time it tried. With a Captains' list dangerously overweighted with ever-ageing men, some such step was being forced upon it. There was no war on, but Britain still had fleets, and fleets still required admirals. And still there existed no machinery for passing the younger and more vigorous officers through the impenetrable block of seniors clinging to the upper rungs. All the important posts, therefore, went to men who in nature had seen their best days. In 1845 Admiral Sir David Milne, then 82 years old, died in full active employment as Commander-in-Chief, Plymouth. Ten years later the same key command was held by Sir John Ommaney, of just the same age. But this was the worse case because we were now at war. Indeed it is said that the anxiety of having to fit out the Baltic Fleet for the Russian War was a contributory cause of his death: and that may well be. Even under the hard conditions of life afloat, septuagenarians were common. Sir Robert Stopford was still holding the important Mediterranean Command in 1841 when he was 73, and, in 1851, Lord Dundonald hauled down his flag for the last time, as Commander-in-Chief, West Indies, when he was 76.

At last, however, in 1846, the Admiralty's reluctant hand was forced, and it instituted what was in effect Retirement. It offered its older post captains a substantial rise in half-pay, raising the figure, in fact, to what they would get if they waited for their hypothetical flags: but, in return, they were to relinquish their places on the Captains' seniority list. Their response was curious and rather pathetic. Even if they stayed on to receive their flags, they could not possibly hope to be allowed to fly them at sea—doubtless the ambition of them all—because they would still have to outlive all who were already flag-officers. Yet few if any of the older captains (who, having waited the longest, were now coming within sight of the prize) 'accepted the retirement'. The only ones who did were some of the comparatively junior ones: those, presumably, who reckoned that, in this macabre gamble, the odds were all on Death. Sadly, then, they relinquished their ambitions for ever: and these are the men recorded in gothic capitals.

O'Byrne's third category consists of men labelled 'Retired Captain' in ordinary small capitals. For the purposes of our Table, the gothic-lettered group are classed as Captains: for such they were, all having been 'made post' in younger, happier days. All had fought in the Great Wars too, some even as Captains. But O'Byrne's third group cannot be so classed because, when they 'accepted the retirement of 1840'—and one or two other smaller ones—they were not, and never had been, 'made post'. They were in fact plain Commanders whom the Admiralty induced to 'make way for younger men': and for reasons precisely similar to those which were to make them approach the Captains in 1846. This 'retirement' must have been a comparatively easy choice for these elderly Commanders. They had almost everything to gain. They too would realize that, even if promoted, they would be most unlikely ever to be given actual command of a post-ship: far too many real captains were in the queue for the few ships in commission. But they had two immediate consolations—they received a rise in half-pay, and they did become 'Captain'—a title they were not at all assured of otherwise. Moreover their friends could, and doubtless did, conveniently forget the word 'retired'. Some of them too had been waiting a very long time. The senior Retired Captain, for instance, was Thomas Dalby who had been a Commander for forty-six years and had held the King's commission for sixty-two. But there was also Commander Charles Robinson who seems to have refused the offer, though he was six months senior in the rank to Dalby, and could hardly keep anybody waiting much longer seeing that he had already spent seventy-three years in the Service. Yet he is still going strong in O'Byrne, still (theoretically) 'active' though he had now been in the Navy for eighty-two years, and was actually at safe moorings in Greenwich Hospital. Doubtless his bones are mingled with the many thousands who rest in the old naval cemetery there.

Commander (Column VII)

This column contains the Retired Captains just discussed and also the true Commanders—that list which, in 1848, is still headed by old Robinson. During our wars these latter were not, as they are now, the executive seconds-in-command to post captains. They were still what their name implies—commanders of ships in their own right, though the ships which they governed were small—the below-sixth-rate 'non-post' ships. So they were Captains in the original sense of that word, and would always be referred to as such in their own ships—'Captain', that is, *of* that ship, though only Commanders by rank and in the Navy List. Precisely the same thing happens today, when many a ship goes to sea with a Commander as her Captain: and he is still, usually and very rightly, referred to aboard as 'the Captain'. Moreover, in smaller craft still, a Lieutenant-Commander—even a Lieutenant—may be 'the Captain'. This is good sense. The man in charge is—and for many centuries has been—'the Captain'. There is an anomaly in this rank, but it does not lie there. It lies in the name now given to the Second-in-command of a bigger ship, whom we call 'Commander', though Nelson knew him only as 'First Lieutenant'. It is hardly a logical name because, though he runs the ship, he certainly does not command it. The Captain does that. This again is rather typical of the British nation. We make changes in our own time and in our own way, but we hate changing names which are familiar. It is only when the history behind the story is unravelled that we see how the apparent anomaly came about of having two entirely different names for two classes of officer who were doing essentially the same thing—viz. commanding ships; and how we now have only one name for two men who are doing quite different things—commanding small ships, and being seconds-in-command in big ones. The French, more etymologically exact, have always avoided the first of these anomalies. To this day they call both these officers 'Capitaines', but they have two grades—'Capitaine de Vaisseau' and 'Capitaine de Frégate'—which names describe exactly the distinction between our Nelsonic Post Captains and Commanders.

Again 'Post' is the operative word. It is a strange story. Very soon after we began fighting at sea we discovered that there were two posts on board that must be filled by competent persons—that of Master, the expert in navigation, and that of Captain, who from the first had directed the fighting but soon came to direct the whole: for we also quickly discovered the elementary truth that a divided command is fatal. So the Captain became, and remained, more important than the Master. Yet the Master remained essential too, since the ship lost all value if cast away. So every ship of any size had to have both posts filled, the Captain's and—now under him but still as essential as ever—the Master's. Such ships were 'Post Ships', and their captains were 'Post Captains'. Though in our wars with Holland we required many large ships, we needed many small ones too. But, England being still a relatively small and poor country, economy was a prime consideration. So the Government had to economize, in small ships, by making do with only one head man and dispensing with the other. It would be folly to dispense with the Master, and yet someone must command the whole concern. To the problem thus posed there was only one answer. The Master must command, Authority having first seen to it that the Master selected was capable of taking command. Or, put the other way about, the man who was to be Commander must also be a trained navigator or Master.

Hence there emerged upon the naval scene two kinds of ship—'post' and 'non-post'—and two kinds of team to sail and fight them. The team allocated to the post-ship was a team of two—a Post Captain to fight the ship and command the whole, and a fully-qualified Master, under him in all save navigation. The team allocated to the non-post ship was a team of one, who was to be Master and Commander combined—or, if one preferred it the other way about, Commander and Master. Here is the cradle of the naval Commander. For a while both terms were current: but gradually 'Master and Commander' gained ground and 'Commander and Master' lost it until, by the opening of the eighteenth century, lo and behold, there was a naval personage with the now well-established title of 'Master and Commander'. This described him exactly. He was supposed to be capable, were his ship small and manageable enough, both to navigate her safely and to fight her effectively. But evidently he was a good step lower in status than his opposite 'big-ship' number, the lordly Post Captain who could concentrate upon his command and his fighting, and leave the navigation to a subordinate carried for no other purpose.

It was not very long, however, before Authority began to find that this scheme, pretty and economical as it sounded, was not always very efficient. Mishaps began to occur in non-post ships. Sometimes the Master-half of the dual personality turned out to be an indifferent executive officer: perhaps he could not handle men well: perhaps he quarrelled with his junior officers. More often, probably, the Commander-half proved to be rather an amateur navigator, and the price in wrecked ships and drowned men had to be paid. So at length, in 1746, there was introduced into the non-post ships a hitherto nebulous figure called a 'Second Master', to whom was assigned the task of undertaking the commanding officer's navigational duties. This was really the turning-point in the story because, with his arrival, the whole meaning was knocked out of the title 'Master and Commander'. For now the non-post ship had lost its dual-personality team of one and, in common with the post-ship, had its team of two, with exactly the same duties. Yet, both in 'command' and in 'navigation', the post-ship and its team were still comfortably ahead in prestige. On the executive side one was only 'Commander' while the other was 'Post Captain': on the navigational side one was only 'Second Master' while the other was full 'Master'.

At this point, of course, had our processes of thought been logical, we should have dropped the now redundant 'Master and' part of the title. But this was happening in England, where people dislike altering names. So no changes of title occurred in either big or little ships: and the dual-personality officer, who was now a pure-and-simple 'Commander', went on being dubbed 'Master and Commander'.

But that is a cumbrous title and, though officialdom did not budge, naval usage gradually stepped in and abbreviated it: and only one abbreviation was feasible, because the first half was already bespoken. The title 'Master' was hallowed by extreme age—save for 'Boatswain' it was the oldest on shipboard. So the popular abbreviation had to be 'Commander', which became more and more universal as the eighteenth century proceeded. Yet still the Admiralty made no move. In 1793, when our wars began, the Navy List still showed 'Master and Commander' in full. But war is a notorious iconoclast and, in 1794, the 'Master and' was, as it were, officially torn off and jettisoned. There remained 'the Commander'—an executive commissioned officer whose sole function was to command a small, under-sixth-rate ship. In fact, when the Admiralty wished to create a new Commander, what they had to do was to appoint him to a non-post ship. He was then automatically 'a Commander'. If by any chance their Lordships' clerk ever got confused and appointed him to sixth-rate-or-higher by mistake, they had 'made him post', and he was a Post Captain. But such a thing is not recorded.

The change which converted this officer into the modern Commander took place during and after our wars. This arose through the promotion to Commander's rank of First Lieutenants engaged in hard and successful fights, both single-ship actions and fleet-actions, the commanding officer himself being promoted from Commander to Captain. These advancements let us call for convenience 'hero-promotions'. The Admiralty's original intention, no doubt, was merely to reward and encourage meritorious officers. But in practice it soon led to something much more than this. In one important respect it signalized a complete departure from former practice. Hitherto every 'promotion' had been bound tight to a definitive 'appointment'. No officer had been 'promoted commander' —i.e. given Commander's rank as such. He had always been 'appointed Commander of' a named ship, the operative document being a 'commission to act as Commander of'. In a word, the term 'Commander' signified a *post*: it was not a *rank*. The same had applied to Commanders being appointed Captains, and to hitherto uncommissioned men being appointed Lieutenants. In this latter case, indeed, the 'post' aspect of the proceeding had been still more heavily underlined, for such an officer was, up to May 1795, commissioned to be 'Third Lieutenant (or Second or First as the case might be) of' the named ship. Having secured such postings, however, their recipients had in effect secured an advance in rank—a promotion—and figured thereafter in the Navy Lists under their new grades and titles. This old procedure must always have posed difficult problems for the Admiralty but, until now, it had been able to preserve the old way because it did not have to promote an officer until it had a suitable appointment to post him into. But now the problems became much more difficult; indeed ultimately insoluble. For having once established the precedent of promoting an officer 'on the spot', as it were, for services already rendered, and not because it had a suitable post ready for him, the Admiralty could hardly draw back, and refuse to future heroes what it had given to earlier ones. That would only convert encouragement, which was the object of the whole thing, into discontent. But so would its failure to find its hero a new ship. It would be a distinctly back-hand reward for valour to promote the deserving officer and instantly to put him on half-pay because it had no post to put him into. The same dilemma covered Captains and Lieutenants too, though our concern is here with the Commander.

This was what was happening with ever-increasing frequency. Even before the wars ended there were too many of this new class of commandless commanders: too many men, that is, with the *rank* of Commander and too few *posts* that Commanders could fill. And after 1815 things became far worse because hundreds of small non-post ships were laid up or sold out of the Service, thus reducing chances of employment still further. From this dilemma the Admiralty at last extricated itself, to some extent, by the device of promoting deserving First Lieutenants in bigger ships to Commander's rank, without removing them from their posts: or, if they were already of Commander's rank but unemployed, putting them into other big ships to do First Lieutenants' work, at the same time letting them keep their Commander's rank. The result of this was that, after a short time, the posts of First Lieutenant in all big ships came to be filled by officers of Commander's rank. So it came about that, without any definitive order being made, Commanders, in addition to their older duty of commanding small ships, found an entirely new field of duties open to them as Second-in-command of big ships. This remains the position to this day. The Commanders were actually luckier than both their seniors and their juniors. There grew up an equally formidable list of redundant Captains; who, however, were given no comparable chance of employment, though occasionally they might receive a non-post command as a sop. But it was the poor Lieutenants who suffered most, because they lost for good a naval post which in the past had always been regarded as not only a Lieutenant's perquisite but also his best perquisite—that of First Lieutenant.

Retired Commander and Lieutenant (Columns VIII and IX)

These two—O'Byrne's lowest categories—may engage our attention together because they were essentially the same person. They were the officers who failed ever to command any but those tiniest ships which alone were 'Lieutenants' commands'. For a Retired Commander was not a Commander who had retired, but a Lieutenant who was granted, upon retiring, a purely paper-promotion (with an augmentation of pension). Indeed 'Retired Commander' is hardly a phenomenon of the wars at all. When all effective fighting had stopped, in December, 1814, there appears in the Navy List a small category called 'Lieutenants Superannuated with the rank of Commander', but this is not quite the same thing. It is just a matter of 'anno domini'. The Senior here is John Cowe, who had been made a Lieutenant sixty-seven years before. (Incidentally, the Lieutenant who heads the main list—one hesitates to say 'active' list—and therefore not 'superannuated': not lucky enough to have caught the selector's eye—is George Spearing, of the same seniority, and probably of much the same age, as Cowe. We are also informed that he is 'unfit to serve at sea,' which seems a little gratuitous seeing that he could not possibly be under 85 and was probably well over 90.)

If, then, O'Byrne's Retired Commanders were all Lieutenants when the wars ended, why, it may be asked, should they not be grouped with them here, just as the Retired Captains were grouped with the Commanders? This might have been done without much loss of accuracy. But they are kept separate because an investigation of them individually reveals a good many representatives of that interesting class, the 'Lower Deck' men who achieved commissioned rank. But the number of O'Byrne's Retired Commanders is quite considerable—346—and a final modest promotion to this grade may be regarded as the height of legitimate aspiration not only to Lower Deck people but also to quite a large class of other commissioned officers—those who unfortunately enjoyed little or no worthwhile Interest. The Authorities began in a small way to face the problem of their many redundant Lieutenants in 1816, by inviting a few to step out as 'Retired Commander': and they repeated the exercise, on a somewhat larger scale, in 1839. These moves, however, merely nibbled at the surface of the problem. Another nibble came in 1857, but it was only in 1864, years after O'Byrne's time, that they made a clean sweep by transferring to the Retired Commanders' list, in a single day, several thousand redundant Lieutenants. So at last the survivors—and many of them had fought in the wars, though mostly not as commissioned officers—received recognition long overdue, and could at least call themselves Commanders.

The people hoping for Lieutenancies came off badly too, both during the later years of the war and after it was over. There were a good many 'hero-promotions' at this level, but far more commissions were still being secured by Interest in one or other of its many forms. There were not, however, nearly enough Lieutenants' posts to go round, since no one had attempted to regulate the number of aspirants for them: and they could by no means keep pace with the push of Midshipmen and Master's Mates awaiting their turn. For such people, though they could without undue difficulty collect all the qualifications for a Lieutenancy, even to passing the Lieutenant's Examination, were finding it ever harder to obtain the commission itself: so much so that, towards the close of the war, there all but appeared a new grade altogether known as 'Passed Midshipmen'. Some of these, in despair, even gave up their expectations of obtaining commissions and became Master's Mates of the old sort, whose goal was to become a Master and not a Lieutenant at all. In the early years of the new century, Earl St. Vincent, when First Lord, tried to ease the situation by creating posts known as Sub-Lieutenancies. To these we shall return shortly, when we shall see that they did not mean the creation of a new rank.

By 1815, then, there were many hundreds—probably thousands—of men whose desire for, and original expectation of, a commission remained unsatisfied. Nor did the Admiralty altogether neglect them. Such as were 'young gentlemen' of the ordinary sort mostly achieved their Lieutenancies in the end, though often after a weary wait. Others, in quite large numbers, received commissions at the very end of the war, perhaps unexpectedly and for another reason altogether. Worthy people of long service who would now be turned off would, in fairness, have to be compensated somehow, if only with a pension. But this meant new legislation, for the number of people legally eligible for pensions was limited to Warrant Officers and but few others. It was then, it seems, that the Admiralty hit upon the idea of awarding Lieutenancies to such people 'in lieu of pension'. One such recipient whom we have met was our stand-by, John Marshall, and another was Richard Greening (see p. 172). There was still, of course, no such thing as 'retirement' in our modern sense.

These 'lieutenancies-in-lieu-of-pension' go far towards explaining a phenomenon which would otherwise have amounted to gross lack of foresight on the Admiralty's part. This was the lavish handing out of lieutenants' commissions early in 1815, just at the moment when Authority must have realized that there were already far too many for post-war requirements, and that every genuine new one would merely make the promotion and appointment blocks more intractable. The figures are instructive. During 1813, the last full war-year, 218 lieutenants' commissions were given—a monthly average of eighteen. In 1814—which was mostly a peace-year since Paris fell in March—the annual number was 319 and the monthly average twenty-six. January 1815 was a very quiet month with only seven commissions given. But February 1815 alone shows 558 and March, 275. These were not promotions arising from the renewed threat of war, because Napoleon only reappeared in France at the beginning of March and the promotions during the remaining Hundred Days average only sixteen a month. They clearly represent deliberate policy, and are excusable only when it is realized that they were almost all 'lieutenancies-in-lieu-of-pension'. As such they did not block promotions, or even appointments. They were dead-ends so far as the recipients were concerned. In fact, though the Admiralty did not use the unpopular phrase, these men were really 'retired lieutenants', drawing lieutenants' half-pay in lieu of other awards.

Sub-Lieutenant (No Column)

We saw (p. 182) that the creation of the *rank* of Sub-Lieutenant lies outside our period. But the creation of a *post* of Sub-Lieutenant lies within it. In 1804 an Order-in-Council established

'an additional officer, under the style of Sub-Lieutenant . . . in all brigs . . . commanded by Lieutenants, the said Sub-Lieutenants to be taken from the list of young men who have passed an examination and are qualified to serve as Lieutenants,'[1]

and a few months later they were ordered to be appointed to sloops, bombs and fireships.[2] The reason given is that there was a serious shortage of 'fit persons to serve as Second Masters', and that 'there should be a trustworthy second officer in them upon whom the command may devolve in the absence of the Lieutenant'. But there was another reason. There were far too many young men, of long Midship-

[1] Adm. O.-in-C. of 5.12.1804.
[2] Adm. O.-in-C. of 15.8.1805.

man and Master's Mate standing, who had passed the statutory Lieutenant's exam and were waiting for a place on the Lieutenants' overloaded list. Too long a wait, the Admiralty realized, was too fierce a discouragement, and here it saw a chance of giving such people, while they waited, the sop of doing Lieutenants' work. But this was all. It is clear that the *rank* of Lieutenant was not to be theirs, for the Order goes on to say that 'they should not be placed upon the general list of the Lieutenants in Your Majesty's Fleet'. They were—but only while holding their posts as Sub-Lieutenants—to draw Lieutenants' pay, but not their 'allowance for compensation' (see p. 305 *et seq.*), nor their much larger share of prize-money (see p. 318); and, above all, not to receive the coveted commission.

The 1804 Sub-Lieutenant, then, was the temporary holder of a post, not the permanent holder of a rank; and he disappeared at the end of the war when his temporary post was no longer necessary. His title, it is true, was revived in 1861: but it then designated something quite different. In the meantime, in 1840, a whole new class—the former Master's Mates of the officer-succession—were given commissions, and so elevated into a substantive rank intermediate between Midshipman and Lieutenant: and, twenty-one years later, the title of this class was changed to Sub-Lieutenant. The true analogy to the Sub-Lieutenant of the 1804–15 period, then, is not the Sub-Lieutenant of 1861, but the Commodore of all periods: for, just as there has never been a section in the Navy List headed 'Commodore', so there was not, in 1804–15, a section labelled 'Sub-Lieutenant'. Therefore, in the general naval hierarchy now under discussion, he has no place at all, though of course he did have a place, and an important one, in the hierarchy of any little ship to which he had been appointed.

Rank Reached (Columns X and XI)

The significance of Columns X and XI was explained on page 170. All O'Byrne's officers, we saw, have been 'marked' with the intention of striking an average in each entry-category and so gauging the promotion-chances of each sort. There, however, the marking system was not explained. That must come now, when we can gauge the relative values of the ranks. The man who had by O'Byrne's time attained only to a Lieutenancy received one mark: if he had become a Commander he was awarded two: if a Captain, three: if a Rear-Admiral, four. With the Retired Commander a compromise was necessary. He must not have two marks since, for all his enhanced title, he never did the work of anyone higher than a Lieutenant. So his mark must be a good deal nearer to a Lieutenant's than to a Commander's: yet not quite so low as the former's since he had certainly gained a little on him. He has therefore been awarded an arbitrary 1¼. As to the higher Flag-Officers, it would be equally unrealistic to raise each grade by one because, here, the gamble with Death was such an obvious factor; and that had but little to do with either professional efficiency or even professional success. So, again arbitrarily, a Vice-Admiral was allotted the rise of a half-mark over a Rear-Admiral, and an Admiral a like advance over a Vice-Admiral. Thus the Admiral stands at five. That rare specimen the Admiral of the Fleet was allowed a full extra mark, on the principle that 'unto him that hath shall be given'.

Column X, then, shows the 'average mark' in each category: Column XI has merely translated the figures in terms of rank. It represents the average expectation of each entry-category.

One last general summary, not shown in Table V, may be made. It is possible to show what percentage of O'Byrne's 3,467 officers reached each of the various ranks. The result is as follows:

Of the officers in O'Byrne who served during the wars, received commissions (either during or after them), and survived till 1845,

0.06	per cent reached the rank of	Admiral of the Fleet
1.30	,, ,, ,, ,, ,, ,,	Admiral
1.67	,, ,, ,, ,, ,, ,,	Vice-Admiral
4.29	,, ,, ,, ,, ,, ,,	Rear-Admiral
17.22	,, ,, ,, ,, ,, ,,	Post Captain
17.82	,, ,, ,, ,, ,, ,,	Commander
9.99	,, ,, ,, ,, ,, ,,	Retired Commander
47.65	,, ,, ,, ,, ,, ,,	Lieutenant

Simplifying still further by uniting all Flag-Officers at one end and, at the other, relegating the Retired Commanders to their real place among the Lieutenants, we reach these results: to which are added three other sets of percentages—those of the best form of entry, the Captain's Servants, those of the worst (strictly, the worst of the bigger categories), and those of the outstanding 'distinguished dead' of O'Byrne's footnotes.

Rank Attained	O'Byrne's 3,467	Entered as Captain's Servants	Entered as Landmen	'Distinguished Dead'
Flag-Rank	7⅓%	50%	0%	74%
Post-Rank	17¼%	13¼%	3½%	19%
Commander	17¾%	11¾%	12%	6%
Lieutenant	57⅔%	25%	84½%	1%

It needs no close scrutiny of these figures to perceive that it behoved any young man of ambition to enter as a Captain's Servant and not as a Landman—if he could. And he could, for certain, did he but possess just one thing—*Interest*.

CHAPTER VI

THE NAVAL HIERARCHY: 'INTEREST'

SO far, the word 'Interest' has intruded upon these pages with the insistence of a bell: a merry carillon for those who command it, a mournful toll for those who do not, beckoning on or repelling every Naval Officer of our period. It deserves a chapter to itself, showing in what it consisted, who wielded it and how it worked in the Navy of the day. In short, this chapter is an analysis, hitherto (to the author's knowledge) unattempted, of Naval Interest.

It is divisible first under two main headings—Service Interest and Non-Service Interest. In the first the wielder of it is a naval man or body of men. In the second he stands right outside the Navy. Each main heading may be sub-divided, the first into four sub-headings, the second into three. The four wielders in the first group may be defined as (A) Captains, (B) Admirals ('on the spot'), (C) The Admiralty and (D) Admirals ('remote'); in the second, (A) Important Personages (not M.P.s), (B) Royalty, and (C) 'Parliamentary'.

A. 'SERVICE'

(a) *The Captains*

At the start of a would-be officer's career this brand of Interest was essential, as we have had occasion to see. Without it he could not even get on board as a prospective officer. Thereafter it continued to be our young man's mainstay until he received his first commission. It was the Captain alone who arranged for his admission as a Young Gentleman—unless he were one of the few College products. The Captain alone rated him Midshipman, alone rated him Master's Mate: and the Captain could, if he liked, appoint him, locally in the ship, an Acting Lieutenant. He could go no further himself, for the granting of a commission was quite outside his powers. But he could—and, if he wanted his young friend to succeed, had to—recommend him for a commission to the Admiral under whom both were serving. Thereafter his active importance waned, though, as we shall see, it did not vanish. The process just described, it should be noted, was the normal one. The other forms of Interest yet to be discussed could no doubt sometimes override a Captain who was unwilling to advance an underling. But that did not often happen.

(b) *The Admiral-on-the-spot*

This officer now assumed the leading role. He could confirm a Captain's local appointment of Acting Lieutenant, and he was the man who recommended the Admiralty to turn the acting post into a full one—i.e. to give the aspirant a Lieutenant's commission. It does not follow that he always did so: very likely he had candidates of his own. In that case he would say in effect to the Captain, 'I'm sorry, but I'm putting my man, not yours, into your Lieutenant's post, and shall of course recommend the Admiralty to confirm him. Your man must wait.' And wait he did because, where Interest was concerned, an Admiral's guns were of a much heavier calibre than a Captain's. Still, normally, the Admiral would attend to the representations of his captains sooner or later, though it might be later.

Important as the Admiral's benevolence was at the first commission-stage, it grew to something like paramountcy at the next. Here he was usually the principal actor, the Captain's help being now limited to strong recommendations. At this stage the normal move was for the local Commander-in-Chief to collect into his flagship the officers whose promotion he wished to procure. This was why a flagship-lieutenancy was so much sought after: it was what a later age called a 'promotion-billet'. But now the Admiral was not having things all his own way. If a non-post command fell vacant, he could put in his first choice and ask the Admiralty for confirmation. He was more likely to succeed if he was C.-in-C. of a foreign station than if he commanded a home one, for the former could give the commission, though it lasted only 'until the pleasure of the Admiralty shall be known', while the latter could only fill the post, and not give the commission until he had Admiralty approval. This did not make much difference in practice, however, since in neither case was confirmation automatic. The Admiralty might well have other ideas. So we must ascend to

(c) *The Admiralty*

This meant 'Their Lordships', the collective Board of Admiralty. As this body directed the whole Service, 'Admiralty Interest' was in theory —and in the long run actually—the best to have behind one. Yet, in two respects, it did not operate quite so successfully and inevitably as might be expected. First, in any tussle of wills between Admiralty and Admiral-on-the-spot the latter had the considerable short-term advantage of having actually put his candidate into the post. Indeed, especially on a distant station far from Whitehall, he could always hedge and buy time, even ignoring for quite considerable periods their Lordships' order to 'promote so-and-so into a sloop', defending his failure to take action, for instance, by averring that no suitable command was vacant. He would have to give way in the end, of course, if the Admiralty insisted: but as often as not, by the time several letters had passed back and forth, another command had fallen vacant and he was able to satisfy both the Admiralty and himself.

The other factor which sometimes weakened Admiralty Interest was that the Board itself might be divided. Not all its members counted equally in this matter: as a rule, in fact, only two counted at all—the First Lord himself and his principal naval adviser whom nowadays we call 'First Sea Lord'. In any clash on this level the First Lord held most of the trumps because on all promotions and all permanent appointments the last word was his. Much turned on the character of the individuals concerned. If the Naval Lord was a forceful man and the First Lord less so, the former could do a great deal. But, more often, the First Lord kept a tight hand upon the very useful patronage which promotions and appointments conferred upon him. This was perhaps a pity because, during our period, the First Lord was usually a civilian and politician, and he was apt to let politics into an affair where it were better left out. He was apt, too, to find himself subject to a number of outside pressures, mostly civilian.

(d) *The Admirals* (*'remote'*)

One of these pressures, not civilian, was that exerted by other big naval figures, not the immediate Commander-in-Chief of the Officer concerned. Indeed, were their name big enough, they might not even be employed at all. People like Howe or Bridport, even when at home, in Town or at Bath, could do a great deal. Their influence all over the Service was naturally very great. They knew everyone who mattered—had very likely earned the gratitude of many of them by helping on their earlier careers by use of Interest—and they had the entrée everywhere. It is not always easy to see this kind of Interest in action because, from the nature of it, it was somewhat back-stair. Matters would be quietly arranged during a friendly call, with no witnesses present, or in some apparently chance meeting at the Club. It was all the more potent because of the strong class-ties which bound most of the Navy's 'upper ten'. These, among other things, tended to produce the reaction, 'Old So-and-so helped me when I was a youngster. I can't do less now than help a youngster of his!' Later we shall see some remarkable manifestations of this form of 'loyalty'. Certainly the young officer who had the Interest of one of these great ones behind him was very fortunate indeed.

B. 'NON-SERVICE'

(a) *Important Personages* (not M.P.s)

These might well be peers of the realm, but also any member of that considerable band which mid-twentieth-century slang has labelled 'V.I.P.' but not members of parliament who deserve a separate heading of their own. The 'V.I.P.' impact in some ways resembled that of our 'Admiral (remote)'. It was exerted, usually, upon the Admiralty, though often also upon the Admiral-on-the-spot and it worked, mostly, at private-interview and 'club' level. The potency of such Interest is at times hardly credible, and its net spread wide. Of the commonest sort—where the protégé was a relative of the Important Personage—endless cases could be cited: indeed, as has been shown, the son, say, of a Duke was most unlucky, or peculiarly incompetent, if he failed to reach post-rank. But here are two examples wherein the V.I.P. was unrelated to the beneficiary.

George Langford was, in 1808, a Commander by rank but Captain of the *Sappho*, a non-post brig of 18 guns. He captured a Danish privateer of superior force to his own after a stiff fight. He thus became a candidate for a 'hero-promotion' to Captain. But the Admiralty decided against it on the grounds that the captive was a 'private' and not a 'public' ship of war. So nothing was done about it; nor, clearly, was anything going to be done when (to quote Langford's own words)—

'... my friend the Hon. Henry Pierrepont who had been our Minister in Sweden . . . hastened to the Admiralty . . . [and] said he:—"You must promote my friend Captain L!"'[1]

Authority demurred, gave its reasons and tried to argue the case. But no—'My friend Mr. P would not quit the Admiralty until he had obtained my advancement.' Whether the prospect of sharing his room in perpetuity with the importunate Mr. P, or whether—which is much more likely—Mr. P had some *quid pro quo* to offer, the gallant Captain does not say. But Mr. P not only prevailed: he even got his man's post-commission ante-dated to its proper place on the all-important Captains' Seniority-list. Need it be added that the Honourable Mr. Pierrepont was not only a Personage in his own right? He was exceedingly well connected—with the family of Earl Manvers, with the extinct dukedom of Kingston and even—a naval link—with the family of Admiral Boscawen.

Our other example concerns Dillon himself. His father—not himself quite a Personage, yet one who consorted with many of that eminence—numbered among his acquaintances Martin, Lord Hawke: not, notice, the great Admiral Edward himself, now no more, but his son and heir, the second baron, who was not in the Navy at all. One day in 1794 when young Dillon, not yet 14, went to see him, Lord Hawke took him aside and spoke as follows:

'Let me explain my intentions towards you. When there is a general naval promotion, I am always allowed to provide for one friend, to get him made either a Lieutenant, a Commander or a Post Captain. Therefore, when your time is up, let me know, and you shall be my Lieutenant. In short, you are as sure of the commission as if you had it in your pocket.'[2]

Here is a very curious case. It was partly 'V.I.P.' Interest: but it was also 'Admiral (remote)'—indeed very remote: almost 'Admiral-inherited'.

In the event Dillon did not avail himself of this promise. He obtained his first step without it, to the intense delight of his father who reckoned that the promise still stood, and could be played, joker-wise, on the next trick—promotion to Commander. But before this happened Lord

[1] Dillon, op. cit., Vol. XCVII, p. 357.
[2] Dillon, op. cit., N.R.S., Vol. XCIII, p. 157.

Hawke became involved in a serious row with the First Lord and, before he recovered his influence, died.

Not every would-be wielder of influence, of course, was so successful as Pierrepont or Hawke. That was impossible, for far too many people were playing the game. Imagination boggles at the thought of all the missives which must have been flying round the world, all and sundry busily recommending all and sundry to everyone who mattered. There is an element of real humour in one remark of Dillon's, though it was quite unconscious. In 1800, when he was barely 20, he and his father were happily engaged in collecting Interest for his promotion to Commander. Evidently, careful siege was being laid to his Admiral-on-the-spot, Lord Hugh Seymour. He thought he was doing pretty well, and that he was a special favourite of the noble Commander-in-Chief: and his reason for this belief is singularly illuminating:

'That feeling was verified by my Captain's bringing me a message some time afterwards from Lord H. Seymour, desiring me to write to my father not to send any more letters of recommendation in my behalf, as he had already received quite enough—about forty, he said.'[1]

Dillon's attitude is one of unalloyed satisfaction. It does not occur to him that such a torrent might do more harm than good. Clearly he feels that this formidable concentration of Interest can only impress Lord Hugh into favouring him. Perhaps, even, he was right: but that we shall never know, for the sequel was a tragedy. Soon afterwards the Admiral died very suddenly. Dillon thought this hard, and said so; especially when Seymour's successor showed in no uncertain way that he had 'made other arrangements'. Dillon had to wait. Nor was it only the great who were thus shamelessly canvassed. Their wives were too. No sooner was the news of the Nile known in England than Lady Nelson has to complain of

'the very extraordinary applications I have had made me—"If I would only ask Lord Spencer [First Lord], it would be complied with immediately." '[2]

But the quiet little woman wisely refused to play—except on behalf of one or two of her own relatives.

[1] Dillon, op. cit., N.R.S., Vol. XCIII, p. 402, note.
[2] N.R.S., Vol. C, p. 459.

(b) *Royalty*

It would not be surprising to find that Royal Interest was both extensive and effective. Yet there is little evidence either for or against it. That, however, may be because, if or when exerted, it would most likely be worked privately. The King himself, a good, simple man, probably interfered but little in such matters, though obviously, when he did, his wishes went a long way. Byam Martin gives one instance[1] which is perhaps typical, at once benign and innocuous. His Majesty had been enjoying himself, cruising in the Channel in a frigate. Soon after he left her, an accident befell one of her Lieutenants, a certain John Servante. This officer, no longer young, was (according to Martin) 'fit for anything rather than a sea-life', and was well aware of the fact. When appointed to the frigate he was, of all unlikely things, the Mayor of Barnstaple, from whose chain of office he had no desire whatever to be parted. As a result of a lubberly act, he broke both legs in several places. His Majesty, hearing of it, sent him his personal condolences, with the assurance that 'he should be provided for'. Servante, 'a man of no ambition and of a mean mind', replied that 'the command of a Packet would compass his highest ambition', and instantly obtained it, with a pension of £80 per annum from funds controlled by the King. This involved no promotion, and the job was a very secondary one where an indifferent officer would do a minimum amount of harm. So George III gratified his own kindly nature without unduly harming the Service. Would that all patronage had followed such lines!

The Prince of Wales, it seems, was not fond of the Navy at all.[2] He had one favourite officer, however, John Willett Payne, who was for a time his secretary. No doubt he saw to it that Payne had good appointments, including the Treasurership of Greenwich Hospital. But he could not have helped his promotion, as Payne was already 'on the Ladder' when they first met, and not even the Heir to the Throne could hurry him up it. The Interest of the Duke of Clarence was no doubt considerable in his 'active' days as Captain: and when at length he was made Lord High Admiral in 1827, he became for the short time in which he held the post the very fount of promotion. But this was by virtue of his unique office rather than of his royalty. Between these two periods, though (or perhaps because) he was Admiral of the Fleet, he was usually far from *persona grata* at the Admiralty, and his support

[1] N.R.S., Vol. XXIV, p. 171.

[2] Dillon, op. cit., N.R.S., Vol. XCVII, p. 433.

might even tell against a protégé. In the post-war years, we know, he did exert himself on Dillon's behalf—not to obtain promotion for him as he was already a Captain, but to secure him an appointment, a thing requiring just the same sort of influence. He failed egregiously—if he really tried. Dillon thought he did, but it may be doubted because, even when Lord High Admiral, he got nothing for him; and, even when King, did nothing for the first five years of his short reign. Yet, being intensely wrapped up in the Service, he certainly had the reputation of faithfully supporting former shipmates, and certainly tried to procure commissions and appointments for them, even if he did not often succeed.

Of the other royal brothers, the Dukes of York, Kent and Sussex all tried to help Dillon—or said they did. But all their efforts came to nought. The genuineness of York's attempt may be doubted too, as he had at one time a grudge against him, even getting him deprived of a command: and it seems strange that a man who for so long had something of a monopoly of Army patronage at the Horse Guards could not do better with his neighbours at the Admiralty. As for the eccentric Sussex, whose equerry Dillon was for many years, he certainly tried, and tried hard. But equally certainly he cut no ice at all: indeed, Dillon suspected that his efforts were actually injuring his cause. Perhaps he was right. As a body, the Princes were far from popular: further—and more important—they probably had not much to offer the Admiralty in exchange for its favours.

(c) *Parliamentary*

For there lay the crux of the whole system, certainly where the higher promotions and appointments were concerned. Reduced to its meanest terms it was just the old political game of give and take—'you oblige me, I oblige you'. So the man who had his views attended to by the Admiralty was usually the man who had some tangible return to offer. For 'the Admiralty' in this connection really meant 'the First Lord', a member of the Government and of one or other of the Houses of Parliament: perforce a politician with a politician's subtle game to play. Into the well-known parliamentary racket we will enter no further than to give one example of political Interest working at the highest level. This one, as was usual in that rarefied atmosphere, concerns Appointment rather than Promotion, for we are now in the realms where the latter is automatic.

It is the story of how Sir Edward Pellew came by the East India Command in 1804, and it has a double edge to it. Pellew, a very senior Captain at the time, was also a member of parliament. In the last days of Addington's wobbling administration he spoke in the House—and spoke well, if not altogether sincerely—supporting the Prime Minister in a naval debate. Thus he earned the gratitude of Addington and his Naval Lord, St. Vincent. His rewards were his flag—though that was due anyway—the command of a ship for his son, aged 17, and the East India Command for himself. But Addington soon fell, and an alienated Pitt succeeded. The flag and his son's command could hardly be rescinded, but what of the East Indies? Everyone expected that it would instantly go elsewhere. It did not, however, and the reason is most illuminating. Pellew was not only a Naval officer: he was a Voice in the House, and he was a Vote. Pitt, as yet not firmly in the saddle again, feared the Voice and coveted the Vote. So a bargain was struck. Pellew was to keep his command but resign his seat: and he even undertook to give every help in his power to his successor—Pitt's nominee. The lesson is that, in this strange politico-naval lay-out, a seat in the House was a dual weapon. It could procure what its occupant wanted both by aiding one political party and by threatening the other.[1]

This is the kind of thing which was happening at the top, and with appointments. The same was happening all the way down, and with promotions as well. Dillon, an expert on all forms of Interest, has no hesitation in pronouncing that of Parliament to be by far the most effective. Again and again he declares categorically that no officer can hope to do really well if he lacks it. He was exaggerating, from his own bitter experience. There is little sign of any really great officer failing through lack of it: for who can doubt but that real merit did surmount the evil system? Had he, however, modified his assertion, making it apply to all officers of ordinary ability, he would have been far from wrong. Bitterly he deplored his father's death in 1806, and that only partly because he was really fond of him. For the elder Dillon, who was Under-Secretary at the Board of Agriculture and a popular man of winning manners, was well in with those who counted at the political hub of things, Civil Servants, Peers and Commoners alike. But son William, at sea from the age of 9, was not: and though his father's friends sometimes found time to befriend him too, it was not the same thing. He became a Commander before his father died and secured his post-

[1] *Edward Pellew*, by C. N. Parkinson (London, 1934), pp. 310 *et seq.*

commission all right—we shall shortly see how. But from the moment of his parent's death something obviously went wrong with his appointments. Again and again he had to kick his heels in idleness, waiting for a job even in wartime. And when appointments at last came his way they were mean, disgruntling ones—an old crank brig, several temporary commands—a Temporary Captain cut but a poor figure, not being 'the Owner'—and a troop ship, undermanned, undergunned and not for fighting. Only in 1814, when the wars were petering out, did he secure command of an operational frigate. In the Navy's doldrum-period after the wars the very best possible Interest was imperative, with so many post captains chasing so few posts, and his longest period of unemployment—nearly 16 years—was very largely (though not entirely) due to his having no 'parliamentary' backing. His most heartrending experience of this deficiency occurred in 1831, when he had been twelve years 'on the beach'. He was then actually appointed Captain of the *Dublin*, 50, by the Board in full session, and remained so 'during the space of two hours': at the end of which period the First Lord allowed himself to be persuaded (by an M.P. who was also a naval officer) to reverse his decision in favour of a certain Captain Lord James Townsend (junior to Dillon on the post-list) 'to whom he [the M.P.] owed his seat in Parliament'.[1]

Could we but know the details, we should probably find quite a complex tale attached to most promotions, and most appointments too; with much earnest thought and real hard work put into each by the officer and his friends: and each tale would vary from the next. The whole series would run from vain endeavours where nothing at all came of the effort up to well-nigh fabulous successes. There follow here a number of selected examples: no more is possible. First come a few successful ones.

The most notorious case on record, probably, is that of the Hon. John Rodney, indifferent son of a brilliant if somewhat venal father. Lord Rodney took the lad to sea when he was 14½. When he was 15¾ he made him a Lieutenant and, five weeks later, made him first a Commander and then a Post Captain—on the same day, 14th October, 1780. All these promotions were confirmed by the Admiralty, grateful to Rodney for having just won the Moonlight Battle and relieved Gibraltar. The youth, however, went no further. Once on the Captains' ladder he was in the 'automatic' area where no father, however fond or however

[1] N.R.S., Vol. XCVII, p. 486.

famous, could accelerate his promotion. He now had two misfortunes. His leg was broken and had to be amputated: then *he* was broken, by a Court Martial. He left the Navy and, though ultimately reinstated, was too late to be promoted to flag-rank. So, when he died in 1847, his record looked, and indeed was, unique. He had risen from Midshipman to Captain in a few weeks, but died, still a Captain, sixty-five years later. This curious career does indeed underline what Interest could achieve in the latter part of the eighteenth century and what lack of ability and post-war stagnation could do in the first half of the nineteenth.

The sensational part of young Rodney's story happened, it is true, before our wars began. But it can be matched, nearly though not quite, during the Revolutionary War. Charles Paget entered when 12. On 7th June, 1797, he was a Midshipman, aged 18. So at least he did his apprenticeship at sea. But then things began to move fast. A mere four months later, being then just 19, he was a Post Captain, having been both Lieutenant and Commander in between. The precise strings pulled are unknown. It must suffice to know that he was son of the Earl of Uxbridge and one of a very political family.

Some families, indeed, were notoriously expert at the game. The Parkers were one, and the leading expert among them was Sir Peter, who had not himself done too badly, spending, as we saw, the last twelve years of his life as Admiral of the Fleet. Sir John Laughton, unkindly though not altogether unwarrantably, questions his motives for performing even the one act for which he is remembered today—his patronage of the young Nelson.

'It has been suggested that he must have had remarkable insight into character to have discerned in the boy-lieutenant the future hero of the Nile and Trafalgar. But Parker was as unscrupulous as any of his contemporaries in the abuse of patronage, and merely saw in Nelson the nephew of the Comptroller of the Navy.'[1]

This seems quite possible. He was a lifelong manipulator. His two most outstanding performances were to get his nephew George made a Lieutenant when he was still 13, and to have his son Christopher made post when still 17. There is actually no record in the *Commissioned Sea Officers of the Royal Navy*[2] of Christopher's ever having been either a Lieutenant or a Commander and, if he was not, here is a feat of Interest

[1] D.N.B., under Parker, Sir Peter.
[2] Admiralty Compilation, 1954.

which easily transcends all others. For though it was not uncommon for one of fortune's favourites to pass straight from Lieutenant to Post Captain—that merely meant a lucky first appointment to a post-ship—there is no recorded case, to the author's knowledge, of anyone skipping the Lieutenant's grade. But no eighteenth-century lists are entirely complete. It is much more likely that he was a Lieutenant, if only for a short while. One result of Christopher Parker's early appearance at the foot of the Captain's list was that he became a Rear-Admiral at the record-early age of 34. Thereafter the ball was at his feet. He had only to go on surviving to become the youngest-ever Admiral of the Fleet. He rose to be a Vice-Admiral, but—and even the Parker Interest could not avail him here—he died in 1804, aged 43.

Another family famed for naval jobbery was the Cochrane clan. We have seen the great Dundonald's early irregularities. Here is another family tour-de-force, concerning, this time, Dundonald's cousin (also Thomas), son of that same Uncle Alexander who worked his nephew's book-service. This boy, born in February, 1789, went afloat with his father in 1796, aged 7 and—how did they manage it?—as a First Class Volunteer. In June, 1805, now 16, he was made Lieutenant: in January, 1806 (still 16) Commander, and in the following April (just 17) Post Captain. He was too young to reach the top of that list while the war made the ascent comparatively fast. But such was his flying start that (having avoided young Parker's mistake) he came out on top in 1865 as Admiral of the Fleet: and he was only 76.

These are extraordinary cases. In their own day even, public opinion gasped at them, though with envy, not censure. It is only posterity which has disapproved, condemning the basic dishonesty of so misusing patronage as well as calling attention to its evil results. Some of these fortunate youths were frankly unworthy of their fortune, others did but little to justify it in their later years. Yet it is not fair to cite only cases which had few if any redeeming features and to omit others where the results were more satisfactory, even though the methods employed would not pass muster today. Let us then examine once more the supreme case of Nelson, and look a little more closely at the story of his first three commissions.

While it may be admitted that, as far as deserts went, he deserved all the Interest that was expended upon him, it cannot be overlooked that that Interest was very considerable. And though we may hope—and believe—that his outstanding qualities would have sufficed to bring him through in the end to the highest posts of trust and responsibility, we must also admit that he reached those posts at the age he did only because he commanded Interest well above average. But again, everyone will admit that the undue Interest exerted on his behalf redounded, in his case, to the public good. This is not to maintain, of course, that the general principle of Interest was a good principle. It is merely to affirm that in *some* cases a bad general principle had good particular results.

The youth, we saw, went to sea with his uncle Suckling one year before he should have done: but this, for those days, was so moderate as hardly to deserve the term 'offence'. He did not break the 'six-year-service' rule for Lieutenants—when he gained his first commission he had done six and a quarter years (10th April, 1777). But he was breaking another—he was only 18. A sure sign that Interest was working hereabouts is that he received the commission the day after he had passed the Lieutenant's Exam. Less well-protected officers usually had to wait for months, even years, to elapse 'twixt Exam and Commission. Here the Interest was wholly his uncle's. Indeed, young Nelson was singularly lucky in more ways than one. The Suckling patronage was not particularly potent when the boy first went to sea, so that his training was not hurried nor scamped. His uncle was doing him a real service here. His pre-lieutenant time was carefully thought out and varied: it did give him a good grounding in his profession, and made a thorough seaman of him. Then, in April, 1775, when he was 16½, and approaching the stage where a little special Interest would be most acceptable, the potency of the Suckling Interest took a sharp upward tilt. His uncle was made Comptroller of the Navy. This made him head of the Navy Board and as such responsible for all the Navy's material. But it did more. The Comptrollership carried with it a vast, if somewhat indirect, Interest in promotions and appointments. Sir John Laughton, indeed, actually affirms that his 'interest was in some respects more powerful than that of even the First Lord'. This is certainly an exaggeration, at least as far as men (and not material) were concerned. Yet even with men it was very considerable. It was the same old story—the Comptroller had an immense amount to offer as a *quid pro quo* for those who obliged him.

His elevation had come just at the right moment for his nephew. Nor did it end with Nelson's first step. It procured Interest for the Lieutenant in other highly useful quarters—Sir Peter Parker's was one. So Nelson was able to make his next step quickly. In July, 1778, Sir Peter, according to the custom already described, took him into his flagship in the West Indies and (8th December) gave him the *Badger* brig, wherein the Admiralty confirmed him as Commander. The securing of Sir Peter's Interest was actually the last service which Suckling rendered to his nephew, as he died in the very month in which Sir Peter received Nelson into his flagship. This fact makes one wonder whether Laughton was being quite fair to the old Admiral: for certainly Nelson's third promotion, which was also directly due to Parker, cannot have stemmed from Sir Peter's hopes of a *quid pro quo* from a Comptroller now dead for nearly a year. Indeed, it seems pretty clear that this promotion to Post Captain (11th June, 1779) was, as far as Nelson was concerned, a real merit-promotion, even though it was secured by a notorious old jobber. For there can be no doubt that Sir Peter, like almost all his contemporaries, was already impressed by the young officer's personality and professional excellence. Nelson now stood in no further need of 'promotional' patronage. At 20½ he was a Post Captain on the bottom rung of the ladder. Interest (as well as ability) could still procure him appointments, and good ones; but nothing could shorten the near-eighteen years interval before he could become Rear-Admiral of the Blue (20th February, 1797), at the age, still young for those days, of 38½. Here we leave him, having already seen how far he ultimately went and why he went no further.

Let us see next how the Comptroller of the Navy could help someone even nearer to him than nephew—his own son. Sir Henry Martin, after being Commissioner of Portsmouth for ten years, became Comptroller in 1790. This being so, the profession of his son Thomas Byam was almost a foregone conclusion. Like Nelson, he too was good material, destined to be one of the war's great frigate captains and—but only promotionally speaking—to go far beyond that most famous man. In his memoirs he is perfectly open about the Interest which he received. He went to sea under Prince William Henry in 1786 when 13 (though he had earlier 'book-time'). He had no difficulty, naturally, over his Lieutenancy, which he obtained (over two years early) in 1790, just after his father became Comptroller. He was 17½, but he looked a good deal younger: and an admiral-friend of the family, Sir John Colpoys, used to make a good story out of that fact. When young Byam, *then* 15 (as Colpoys alleged), heard of his promotion, he went down to his fellow-midshipmen and, with a deep sigh, said, 'Well, my lads, I have got it at *last*!' His own account of his next step, in 1793, is frankness itself, yet revealing a pleasing sense of responsibility in a lad of 19:

'I . . . had the happiness to learn . . . from my father . . . that an arrangement was under consideration for promoting me to the rank of Commander, not on account of the capture of the *Enterprise*, or any other account than the good name, interest and services of my father. I can feel at this moment the delight with which I received the intelligence, and at the same time the consciousness I had of the obligation brought upon me by such early advancement to leave nothing undone in the discharge of my duty.'[1]

He certainly kept his resolution so that, as with Nelson, a bad general principle had good particular results. His promotion to Captain—in the same year—was at once a 'merit' one and an 'Admiral-on-the-spot' one, the admiral being Lord Hood. He was now 20. With this start he became Admiral of the Fleet in 1849.

Turning next to somewhat less-favoured officers, let us seek examples of 'hero-promotions' and 'promotions-without-appointment'. The two kinds often amounted to the same thing. A 'hero-promotion', for instance, might, as we have seen, leave the promoted officer shipless and unemployed. But sometimes they were different things. A 'hero-promoted' officer might obtain a command at once; or—and this was becoming ever commoner as the war grew older—a man might be promoted-without-appointment without having distinguished himself in any particular action. In fact—but finally, and well after our period—this 'promotion-without-appointment' grew so common that it became the norm, as it is today: and, ultimately, 'promotion', as such, ceased altogether to depend upon 'appointment' as such.

Let us re-examine the career of Provo Wallis in this light. He was in effect twice 'hero-promoted', once 'with appointment', once without it. His social Interest was never very good, his grandfather having been, probably, the Carpenter of Howe's flagship in North American waters. But his father's Interest (as chief Clerk to the Commission at Halifax) sufficed to procure him his first step in 1808. It would hardly have taken him further, but then came his stroke of luck already described, and he was hero-promoted to Commander in July, 1813. Returning home, he obtained a command at once, albeit not a very distinguished one—a 12-gun sloop. But the sloop was paid off in December, 1814, and Wallis, in common with all his brother-officers, found himself faced with the bleak post-war prospect of long queues for employment and

[1] N.R.S., Vol. XXIV, p. 173.

poor chances of promotion. But the 'hero' element in his case was particularly strong. 'The officer who brought in the *Chesapeake*' was still something of a marked man, and he was made post in 1819. This was also, really, a 'hero-promotion'—a second barrel as it were of the famous duel: but, this time, he got no ship. He had to wait five years for that and, when the commission was over, another ten for his next ship: after that, another four for the next, and after that again five more before receiving his flag. This, of course, was a typical post-war career for a Captain; indeed, if anything above average in total length of employment. The rest of his career we know already.

Now for Dillon's promotion-history. For all his preoccupation with Interest, he never states how he secured the confirmation of his Lieutenancy. He only supplies the negative information that the patron was not Lord Hawke. Yet the whole atmosphere of the Narrative hereabouts makes it clear that it was someone's doing—perhaps one of the forty stalwarts who were championing him three years later? We have seen too how, in that year (1800), he failed to secure his second step. How he finally did this is another story altogether and, in this examination of Interest and Promotion, a most unusual and important one.

Still a Lieutenant when the Napoleonic War began in 1803, he was soon appointed First Lieutenant of the frigate *Africaine*: but, sent ashore into Helvetsluys under a flag of truce, he was illegally detained by the French and sent to the prison for British officers at Verdun. The downright treachery of this affair made it a *cause célèbre* in its day, and the victim secured the sympathy of every Briton, including, it would seem, the Admiralty's. Anyway, when from captivity he began to set wheels in motion to get himself promoted, his efforts received encouragement in several important quarters. It was an unusual if not a unique case. In normal circumstances a man who was a prisoner would have lost his ship, or been an officer in a lost ship, and the universal rule in such cases was that he could only get another ship, or be promoted, after standing a court-martial; which, of course, was possible only after his release. In other words, by the rules, a prisoner could not be promoted. But, as Dillon was not slow to point out, this did not apply to him. True, he was a prisoner, but not having been concerned in the loss of any ship he was not due to be court-martialled. He was not, however, relying solely upon this indisputable fact, nor upon the sympathy which his hard case had aroused. He records at great length, and quite brazenly, how he assembled a new corpus of Interest. At the home end his devoted father, Sir John, did his bit; but, this time, the heavy artillery was to be brought to bear from the Verdun side, where there were several distinguished captives.

'I sketched out a statement of my services . . . Lord Melville was then head of the Admiralty. I referred his Lordship to my friend Lord Gambier. But previous to closing my despatch, I thought I should do right by showing it to my two influential friends Lord Yarmouth and Colonel Abercromby. The former promised to urge his father the Marquess of Hertford to assist me with his powerful interest. The latter expressed himself very warmly in my favour . . . "I think," said he, "I can settle that matter for you. My brother has married Lord Melville's daughter".'[1]

It was a fine, well-balanced team, well equipped in every part of the field—in goal, Sir John with his well-organized quasi-political friends (Parliamentary); at back, Admiral Lord Gambier (Admiral 'remote'); at half, Lord Yarmouth supported by the influential Marquess (V.I.P.), and, last but by no means least, at centre forward, Colonel Abercromby, himself no mean man (being the son of the great General Abercromby), but, more important still, brother-in-law of the First Lord's daughter (Admiralty—and personal at that!). Add to this a general predisposition to favour a much ill-used officer (playing on the home ground), and it is no surprise to learn that victory crowned the endeavour. His promotion to Commander was dated 8th April, 1805, and he still a prisoner at Verdun.

With such a galaxy of talent in the field it would normally be hard to say which player was mainly responsible for the winning goal. But, this time, Dillon lets out the secret. At first he thought it was Lord Yarmouth but discovered in the end that it was the man whom one ought to suspect first—Colonel Abercromby. After all, it was that gallant officer's brother's wife's father who was the referee.

Here then is a pure—and an early—example of 'promotion-without-appointment', any actual ship-command being, of course, out of the question. Yet the triumph had its bitterness. He secured his release two and a half years later, but on reaching home had to wait four months for a command, and then received about the worst one possible—a minute, worn-out brig called the *Childers*. Undaunted, however, he coaxed her to sea and immediately put up a magnificent fight against a Danish ship of far greater power. For this he was instantly awarded a 'hero-promo-

[1] N.R.S., Vol. XCVII, p. 45.

tion'. Here was something much more healthy and, incidentally, much more modern. There were no manoeuvrings, no elaborate team-buildings. He just sent in his report to the Admiralty—a singularly modest one—and found himself a Post Captain. Frustration was still his lot, as we have seen, for this too was 'promotion-without-appointment', unaccompanied by a command of any kind. Still, he was 'made': he could —and did—become a flag-officer in due time, though he never flew that flag at sea.

Both Wallis and Dillon, though not enjoying the meteoric rise of the best-patronized officers, yet commanded rather more than average Interest as well as a certain amount of promotion-luck. Let us next look at one distinctly worse-backed and less lucky, who still attained in the end to a Flag, though a 'retired' one. Bartholomew James came from a somewhat decayed merchant family in Falmouth and had but little Interest either social or naval. He first went to sea in a cutter in 1764 with no better patron than its commanding officer, a Lieutenant. It was a bad moment to join too, because a war was just over. As was only to be expected from so unpromising a start, he rose the hard way, though he was always 'quarter-deck' in the sense here used. He got what employment he could during the peace-period, and saw plenty of hard and exacting service during the American Independence War. He was obviously a tough man and had the makings in him of a good, if eccentric, officer. In the West Indies his Admiral was our old friend Sir Peter Parker, and he it was who secured him his Lieutenancy; on what grounds—other than a recommendation from a former Captain—it does not appear. He certainly deserved it, so that it must be considered as possible (*pace* Sir John Laughton) that that was why Sir Peter gave it to him. He can hardly have contemplated any personal advantage accruing to himself from favouring so patronless an officer. But he helped him no further.

Still without a patron, then, James had got no further when the war ended, and he passed the succeeding peace-period as best he could—which was not very well, because he was always in debt and often in a debtors' prison. He also eked out his time in the Merchant Service. But war came again in 1793 and his one real stroke of luck came his way. In 1794 he joined the squadron bound for the West Indies under Sir John Jervis, as a junior and very lowly Agent of Transports—not even 'Lieutenant of' one of H.M.'s fighting ships. But he did well in that capacity and, on a red-letter day for himself, caught Sir John's eye. By him he was appointed to lead a party of seamen landed on Martinique, and did even better. As a reward Sir John took him on board his flagship, the *Boyne*; which, as we saw, almost always spelt promotion. In the end, too, it did, for Jervis, unlike many others, used his patronage on deserving subjects, and was noted for being as good as his word. But still there was a longish wait, for James had been appointed Ninth Lieutenant. He accompanied Sir John home before his turn came—and was as usual imprisoned for debt. While he was in gaol, as though to add to his miseries, the *Boyne* went up in flames with all his personal possessions on board (see p. 353): and, what with one thing and another, it was not until December, 1795, that he was able to follow Jervis into his new flagship, the *Victory*, where he served as First Lieutenant for six months, almost always at sea. With such an appointment promotion was now certain. On 8th June, 1796, he was 'promoted into the *Mignonne*', though as a temporary Captain only as she was a 32-gun frigate and therefore a post-ship. But he was soon 'confirmed into the *Petrel* sloop', and so, at last, a Commander (19th October, 1796). He had surely earned it. He was 43 years old, and had been at sea (when not in gaol) for thirty-two of them: fifteen without a commission and seventeen as a Lieutenant.

Now we see the advantage of enjoying the Interest of a man like Jervis, who never lost sight of merit. He had still to earn his next step, but he was not forgotten. On 28th December, 1798, he was not only made Post, but appointed Captain of a magnificent third-rate, one of Nelson's Nile prizes renamed *Canopus*. All his promotions were obviously 'merit' ones: but even so—though that should have been cause enough—he owed all of them to strict, and probably healthy, 'Admiral-on-the-spot' Interest. He did not serve afloat during the Napoleonic War, but spent the whole of it in command of the Sea Fencibles of Cornwall. He had not received his flag when the war ended, but he had started up the Captains' ladder early enough to escape the worst of the post-war block on it, and was made a Rear-Admiral (but, not having served afloat in the second war, only on the Retired List) on 4th June, 1825. He died in 1828.

James's Journal[1] and portrait reveal a rather uncouth, but humorous and oddly attractive character; a real leader too when given the chance. His rise was painfully slow, but at least he rose. We must now follow the career of one who did not, though he had much better opportunities.

[1] N.R.S., Vol. VI.

James Anthony Gardner had good connections, both social and 'service', numbering among other patrons that same Sir Henry Martin, later Comptroller of the Navy, who did so well by his own son. Gardner seems to have been a good, steady officer, and as a writer he was far ahead of most contemporary naval autobiographers,[1] though that by itself would not get him anywhere in the Navy. Professionally, however, he was a near failure. The prime cause of his ill-success, probably, lay in his persistence throughout in picking and choosing his appointments. He had plenty of good ones offered to him, but consistently thought in terms of personal convenience rather than of the good of the Service. He was temperamental too and, faced with the ordeal of his Lieutenant's Exam, was in a sad state of nerves. He need have had no fear, however, for

'... one of the commissioners was an intimate friend of my father's, and Sir Samuel Marshall, the deputy-comptroller of the Navy, was a particular friend of Admiral Parry, my mother's uncle.'

The old story! He passed with flying colours, even though he gave the wrong answer to the only serious question asked. He was immediately made a Lieutenant in the *Victory*. But there his promotion stopped. This was in 1795, and when the wars ended twenty years later he was still a Lieutenant, and had been for eight years in command of the signal station at Fairlight, comfortably if quite ingloriously dug in. Ultimately, indeed, he received nominal promotion—to Retired Commander in 1830, after fifteen years during which he neither obtained nor sought employment. His contribution to naval literature was infinitely greater than his naval career.

Our last example deals with another memoir-writer, John Harvey Boteler, whose career seems little more distinguished than that of Gardner, but for the more creditable reason that he got caught in the post-war slump. He could truthfully open his Recollections[2] with the words 'I may almost say .... I was born a sailor'. Of his three names the key one is Harvey, his mother's maiden name. The Navy of the wars teemed with Harveys, many of whom had highly successful careers. This, of course, made his 'Captain's' and his 'Admiral's' (on the spot) Interest as good as anyone's. In his younger days he never had a moment's anxiety about appointments, nor about his first commission. He recalls

[1] N.R.S., Vol. XXXI.
[2] N.R.S., Vol. LXXXII.

his Lieutenant's Exam in his usual breezy way. One of his old Captains, named Williams,[1] a friend of two of his naval uncles, heard that the young man wanted to take the exam but had not obtained the necessary Admiralty order. This, however, did not prevent him from summoning Boteler to his ship and greeting him with the (under the circumstances) astonishing remark, 'Bless my soul! What a fine young man you are grown! Great mind not to pass you, not to come and see your old Captain! How's my old friend John Harvey, and Tom Harvey too?' Thus explicitly informed of his success before the ordeal started, young Boteler was 'examined'. The questions put to him are easily told. There were none. After a little more talk in the same vein, in which Boteler's present Captain—another member of the Harvey clique—bore quite fanciful testimony to the candidate's seamanship experience, '"Well, well", said Captain Williams, shaking me cordially by the hand, "a very creditable examination".' At this moment the third Captain, whose presence was statutory, put in an appearance, and, not being of the Harvey circle, wanted to ask a few questions, saying, 'You are perhaps not aware of the late letter from the Admiralty on the importance of strictness.' He was quite right, and Williams quite wrong. The year was 1815, when the Admiralty was trying hard to cut down new candidates and to see that only the really efficient ones passed. But this in no way shook the old warrior. He counter-attacked. 'Captain Henderson, you have absented yourself from the examination . . . I have a great mind to put you under arrest, Sir, for inattention': then to Boteler, '*That* is not the way to pass, to linger there when you are told you will do!' . . . 'So out I bolted like a hunted rat and had to send the sentry in for my hat and logs'—which latter, by the way, were not nearly written up to date.

Admiralty confirmation followed promptly, and so did appointment—Boteler had scarcely time to buy his uniform.

'By this time my uncle John Harvey was appointed C.-in-C. of the West Indies, his nephew John Harvey flag-lieutenant, my brother Henry First Lieutenant and I junior.'

Visiting the Admiralty for his commission, he saw Sir Joseph Yorke, the senior Naval Lord. This officer, it seems, was a Harvey fan too, for he deigned to be facetious. When the wrong Boteler commission was accidentally produced, and Boteler said, 'That's my brother Henry's,

[1] The same Robert Williams under whom Mangin served in the *Gloucester*. See pp. 123 and 238.

Sir Joseph,' the great man replied, 'What, Sir, Uncle and two nephews? Father, Son and Holy Ghost! It must not be!' But so it was. Moreover, for the sake of his irreverent *bon mot* he seriously understated the facts. In that flagship there were five of the Harvey clique—Admiral John and *four* nephews, because a yet younger Boteler also went as Midshipman.

But—it was 1815. The Harvey Interest could do wonders, and did. It provided almost continuous employment for the young Lieutenant for the next fifteen difficult years, a considerable feat when compared with the experience of the other officers just discussed. But it could not work miracles. When all promotion was almost at a standstill, it could not get him promoted. Nor could it get a ship for him to command, and he never commanded one. He was made a 'without-appointment' Commander in 1830, when he went, and remained, on half-pay (still so-called, though we should now call it Retirement): and, still in that twilight, he received another step—to Captain in 1856. That was all, though he survived to write his memoirs in 1883 when he was 87 years old.

Enough has now been recorded to justify our earlier verdict—that almost all promotions in that strange régime of Interest, and most appointments as well, had their own individual stories. On the whole, the phenomenon was weakening as the long war went on; but only on the whole. Interest was potent to the last. It was deeply woven into the very fabric of the Navy; how deeply, let us try to discover by examining the attitude towards it of one or two of the very greatest and best officers.

Authorities have differed as to whether Collingwood was a genius or not. But all have acclaimed him a more than ordinarily straight and upright man with a very high sense of honour and an outstanding love of the Service he adorned. Yet he could allow the following strange thing to happen. He tells the story himself, so that there can be no doubt about it.[1] In 1806 a certain Charles Haultain, then 18 years old, was promoted Lieutenant. This officer, if we may believe O'Byrne, had quite a distinguished career, and was promoted Commander in 1814 for very meritorious conduct in the Baltic. But when we read Collingwood we find a very different account of him. He was 'as dull a lad as I ever saw. . . . And now [a month after his promotion] Captain Lechmere tells me he is so entirely useless that he is afraid he must try him by a court-martial to get rid of him.'

[1] *Private Correspondence of Admiral Lord Collingwood*, N.R.S., Vol. XCVIII, p. 185 and *passim*.

Well, naturally, bad appointments must be expected from time to time, and Collingwood was of course quite right in the strictures which follow:

'It is this kind of person that causes all the accidents, the loss of ships, the dreadful expense of them, mutinies, insubordination and everything bad. They must produce a certificate that they are 21 years of age, which they generally write themselves, so that they begin with forgery, proceed with knavery and end with perjury. . . . If the safety of the Country is to depend on the Navy, it must be reformed and weeded, for a great deal of bad stuff has got into it, and hangs as a deadweight where all should be activity.'

Very good. But how did this particular piece of bad stuff get promoted at all? Collingwood was a very honest man, and he does not attempt concealment. He promoted him himself, and with his eyes open to his faults:

'Admiral Roddam recommended Mr. Haultain to me, a relation of Coll's wife: he is 18 years old and as dull a lad as ever I saw. My conscience reproved me when I promoted him, which I made two or three attempts to do before I could bring myself to it. Nothing but it's being Adml. R's request could have induced me.'

That is all: no defence, no excuses: no hint of remorse, after-guilt, or of having done the wrong thing. What in fact he is saying, with crystal clearness, is just this:—'I knew the young man was breaking the rules by forgery and perjury: I knew he was bad stuff: I knew that bad stuff was ruining the Service—*but* Admiral Roddam, an old friend and former patron of mine, asked me to promote him. So—naturally—I did. What else could I do?'

'Well, well,' the kind-hearted may say. 'So he found him out and, to protect his beloved Navy, got rid of him?' By no means. He, the C.-in-C., Mediterranean, continued—redoubled—his protection of the 'bad stuff'. Six months later he was writing,

'. . . pray tell Adml. Roddam that I am afraid I shall not be able to save Haultain from destruction: he has been twice in confinement, and I have been obliged to write and soothe his Captain to save him from a court-martial. I would remove him to another ship, but nobody will take him that can help it. His messmates do not associate with him.'

One possibility remains—that O'Byrne was right in his estimate of the man, and Collingwood wrong. Perhaps: but unfortunately that makes no difference. Collingwood thought he was bad stuff, yet still promoted and protected him. He, the upright Collingwood, the model C.-in-C., was prepared to sacrifice everything to the sacred claims of Interest—and clearly saw nothing wrong or unusual in it.

What then of Nelson himself? He surely will be found to be above this sort of thing? To imagine so is to mistake the whole set of the contemporary tide. With him, as with Collingwood, this was just a thing which was 'done'. There survives an entry in one of his notebooks written during his long Mediterranean vigil. It concerns Lieutenant Peter Parker, grandson and namesake of that old Admiral of the Fleet so often cited here. What the note says is simply this—just a trivial memo:—

'[Parker] to get both steps as fast as possible—his grandfather made me everything I am.'

As it happened, Lieutenant Peter was a very good lad and, having been 'made', proved a very good Captain. But Nelson also had his counterpart to unsatisfactory Mr. Haultain. His own stepson, Josiah Nisbet, was not Haultain's superior, even if his equal. For this young man Nelson obtained three steps—a lieutenancy when he was under 17, a Commandership at 17 and a Post-Captaincy at 18. And in connection with the first of these steps he wrote to his wife,

'I regret Josiah has not served his time. I have wrote to Maurice [his brother at the Navy Office] to see if he cannot get a little cheating for him. It might be done and would be invaluable. I am getting from Captain Stirling a certificate, and I wish one could be got from Captain Sotheby, for if they will cheat, I shall do the same for *Boreas*.'[1]

This, shorn of polite verbiage, means that, if Nelson could persuade a Clerk of the Navy Office and two post captains of the Royal Navy to issue fraudulent certificates of his stepson's service, he would do the same himself. Presumably the scheme worked, for Nisbet's commission was signed within a month.

Four weeks later he was engaged upon an even more doubtful manoeuvre. Trying to secure a lieutenancy for his protégé William Bolton—then a mere relation by marriage, but later his nephew-in-law —he calmly announced to his wife that:

[1] Nelson's Letters to his Wife, 3.3.1797. N.R.S., Vol. C, p. 319.

'I have sent to Maurice to take out so much of a Captain William Bolton's time: *that is all fair*.'[1]

Let there be no mistake. We thought Sir John Dillon more than ordinarily honest (p. 170) when he refused to succumb to the temptation —thrust upon him—of taking another William Dillon's time for his own son William. Surely we were right; for here is Nelson himself *initiating* that very fraud, tempting his civilian brother to perpetrate it—nay, taking it for granted that he will do so: declaring in the same breath—could anything make the moral situation clearer?—'*that is all fair*'. Again he was successful. Young Bolton's commission is dated 11/8/97.[2]

Such revelations must not be allowed to warp our sense of proportion. Pleasant though it would be to find that, in this respect, Nelson had risen above the dubious morality of his day, we are not condemning him out of hand when we find that he had not. Our object, rather, was to show that neither he nor Collingwood ever realized that there was a moral issue at all.

Yet fairness demands the mention of one great contemporary who made a serious effort to break away from the insidious convention of 'what's done'. Sir John Jervis, Earl St. Vincent, was a man who, even yet, has hardly received his due as one of the creators of the modern Navy. He was not innocent of using Interest; indeed, believed in it when employed sensibly and in moderation. But, as early as 1801, we find him girding at a system whereby 'the influential secured the plums of the Service for the inefficient and lazy',[3] and, knowing the impossibility of a clean sweep, actually suggesting a huge promotion to flag-rank in order to let through promising men like Troubridge, Saumarez and Pellew; for 'if the First Lord could clear off the rust and vermin senior to it, the fleet would greatly benefit by it'. In plain speaking and in calling a spade a spade, as in several other respects, he had much in common with his spiritual heir of a century later—'Jacky' Fisher.

As First Lord he made a gallant, and all-but-one-man, attack upon corruption in its many forms; and one facet of that lonely and unpopular campaign was his attempt to loosen the indiscriminate grip of the octopus Interest. He kept trying to curb the spate of recommendations

[1] Nelson to his wife, 2.4.1797. Ibid., p. 320. My italics.

[2] The other William Bolton, who unwittingly 'lent time' to his namesake, had been made a Lieutenant 28.10.1790, and a Commander 23.10.1795. At this moment he was still a Commander, but was made post 14.2.1801.

[3] St. Vincent to Keith, 4.9.1801.

for the promotion of new men until he could obtain justice for those already waiting for it. In fact he was a stout advocate of some form of Promotion by Seniority in the lower grades. Indeed he might almost be called the first to try to introduce that characteristically modern institution, the 'Promotion Zone', which is a judicious blend of Promotion by Seniority and Promotion by Merit. But for all the old man's forcefulness, he failed. He was too far ahead of his time. Interest had many years of life before it.

CHAPTER VII

THE SHIP HIERARCHY: THE CAPTAIN AND THE WARD-ROOM

SEVERAL writers have described in some detail the internal economy of a Nelsonic ship of war. The intention here is not to retread the same ground, but to attempt to set the inhabitants of such a ship in their true relation vis-à-vis one another. In doing so, however, it is impossible to avoid touching once more on both social and geographical aspects of ship-life. As we saw much earlier (p. 24), the main naval divisions, stated in purely 'social' terms, were simple—'Quarter-deck' and 'Lower Deck'. But the 'ship hierarchy' was not quite identical with the 'social hierarchy', for where the latter had only two divisions the former had three—'Commissioned Officers', 'Warrant Officers' and 'Men'. These three it would be well to sub-divide at once into

(a) *Commissioned Officers*, (1) The Captain, (2) The Lieutenants, (3) The embryo-Lieutenants, and (4) The Marine Officers.
(b) *Warrant Officers*, (1) 'of Ward-room Rank', and (2) 'not of Ward-room Rank'.
(c) *Men*, (1) Petty Officers, and (2) the rest of the Ship's Company.

But those very words 'Quarter-deck', 'Lower Deck' and 'Ward-room', which are the names of actual parts of a ship, serve to remind us that there is another division to be considered—that of Ship-geography. This is the one which we shall follow now: and, here again, we can return to a very simple formula—'Forward, Men: Aft, Officers'.

Had some gigantic sword descended from heaven and cut a ship-of-the-line vertically in two, the blow falling some yards aft of the main-mast, it would have come very near to severing the living quarters of the officers from those of the men. There would be only a few minor exceptions. The forward part of the Quarter-deck (essentially officer-ground) would be found in the men's part: a portion of the Lower Deck, aft of the cut and therefore in the officers' part, would be inhabited by the men; and, lower still on the Orlop Deck, the quarters of the Carpenter and the Boatswain, officers both, would be forward of the cut and in the men's section. Otherwise, it would everywhere mark the boundary. In the larger fore-part lay the messing and sleeping quarters of the seamen and marines, with the places where they stowed their modest gear; almost all the workshops of the ship; the galley, where their food was cooked; the sick-bay where they were accommodated in ill-health. In the smaller after-part lived all Commissioned officers, all Warrant Officers (save for the above exceptions) and all embryo officers.

It is in the last-named part that we will begin our investigation. We shall find that ship-geography follows fairly closely on 'social' prestige, but more closely still on 'naval' prestige. Certain quarters were obviously more desirable than others. Therefore the man who was both socially and navally the superior—the Captain—had the best quarters, and his social and naval runners-up, the Lieutenants, had the next best. But at this point naval considerations began to outweigh purely social ones, and some of the class 'warrant officer', though socially inferior to the embryo-lieutenants, were preferred to them because they were navally superior. Indeed, the worst off of all in the 'officer' or 'after' part of the ship were most of the potential commissioned officers. Let us see how it worked out in an ordinary 'seventy-four' two-decker.

A. THE CAPTAIN

'The Owner', of course, fared not only best but much best. His abode was at the after end of the Quarter-deck, under the Poop. Service requirements no less than social right demanded his presence there. He had but to pass through his door to be beside the ship's wheel, with the compass binnacle in front of it. From here the ship was normally conned and fought. His quarters, in comparison with everybody else's, were commodious. He had a 'dining-room' and a 'drawing-room', the latter right aft, giving on to a stern-gallery and two quarter-galleries: he also had one or more sleeping cabins. In a seventy-four, the rooms were of a reasonable size with ceilings higher than anywhere else in the ship. In a three-decker they were really commodious. In the smaller ships, naturally, they were progressively less imposing, though, still, relatively the best. Even in a tiny 24-gun frigate, we learn, he had 'a dining-room and drawing room—with two bedrooms, closets, etc., etc.'[1]

He needed the accommodation for his naval-social requirements, especially during the early war-days, when nearly every Captain 'kept a table'. His was normally a lonely life, for the eminence of his position on board had to be constantly emphasized by strict non-fraternization. He would dine once a week, or even twice, with his Lieutenants, but otherwise in his dining-cabin, alone unless he were entertaining. Convention, however, made this a frequent occurrence, for any officer who 'kept a table' had a long list to get through. When in port, and fairly often even at sea, he would dine his fellow-captains or civilian friends. Sometimes he would take such people to sea with him either as passengers, as private guests or as public ones. If they were private, he paid for their entertainment, if public he did not, at least if he could secure from his Admiral an 'order' to take them. Sometimes they were ladies, when he might have to give up all his quarters to them. If they were 'private' they would normally be his wife and daughters; but, here too, he would often 'oblige' by carrying the families of brother-officers. Dillon cites a rather comical case which occurred when he was in command of the frigate *Horatio*. Being about to return home from Madras, he undertook to take to England the family of Commissioner Peter Puget, an officer who had, or said he had, important friends with 'parliamentary' Interest, which he promised should be liberally employed in obtaining a new ship for Dillon. He soon found out that he had undertaken more than he bargained for:

'Mrs Puget was attached to a maiden lady of a certain age, Miss Jeffrys, and she could not embark without having her as a companion. This, I confess, startled me. However, after a few words of explanation, I placed my cabin at the Commissioner's disposal. By doing so, I had to receive his wife, two daughters, the maiden lady mentioned and a certain proportion of servants.'[2]

The venture proved expensive and unprofitable. At the Cape the party went ashore and lived (at Dillon's expense) for three weeks. On reaching home, in spite of his warning, Mrs. Puget was caught smuggling many dutiable articles, and got poor Dillon into a horrid scrape. She then

[1] Captain Drury in the *Squirrel*. Peter Cullen's Journal, N.R.S., Vol. XCI, p. 57.

[2] N.R.S., Vol. XCVII, p. 405 *et seq.*

asked him to arrange a farewell dinner to the officers, and left him to pay the bill. Finally, when he ventured to name the sum due to him, about £200, she gave him bills on the Navy Office worth £180 and post-dated three months. In return for all this, the 'powerful friends in Parliament' never materialized at all; and, though Authority ultimately refunded the money spent on the Puget ladies, it turned out that they did not consider Miss Jeffrys their affair at all; and for her he was not paid a penny.

Such people, however, were guests from outside. 'Keeping a table' demanded something more than this. It meant the regular entertaining of all his officers—the socially-privileged ones, that is. It was a heavy, never-ending commitment. The three Harvey admirals, when captains (we are told by their nephew Boteler),[1]

'kept the same table, always having there the First Lieutenant, the officer and the mid. of the forenoon watch and an idler (as the Master, Surgeon, Purser and Marine Officer were designated), the Chaplain generally, so that there were invariably six at table.'

Perhaps 'entertaining' is not an altogether happy word. Many Captains who followed the custom did so from a sense rather of duty than of pleasure. There was usually but little of a social occasion about it. We have already noted the atmosphere at Captain Duff's table (p. 72); and the Reverend Edward Mangin's observant eye, here as so often elsewhere, reinforces the evidence:

'. . . I dined, for the first time, with the Captain, and was very kindly welcomed: but I took notice that the Lieutenant of the Watch . . . scarcely spoke three words. Upon going on deck after dinner, I mentioned the circumstance to an officer, and expressed some regret, saying that I concluded such sullen taciturnity must have arisen from some disagreement between the commander and his Lieutenant: whereupon I was undeceived and told with a laugh by my instructor that the parties were on the best possible terms, but that it was not according to Naval etiquette to converse at the table of a Captain of a man-of-war.'[2]

This almost ritual 'keeping of a table' began to lapse before the wars ended. Dillon hints that the causes were economic—the introduction of the Income Tax in 1798 and the cutting-down of the captains' prize-money in 1808: though he himself, a diehard in all service matters, per-

[1] N.R.S., Vol. LXXXII, p. 155.
[2] N.R.S., Vol. XCI, p. 21.

sisted, even when, in 1810, he was advised by the Senior Naval Lord himself to give it up and mess with the Lieutenants: even in 1814, when a live nobleman, Lord George Stewart, told him how old-fashioned he was.

'"You are wrong," said his Lordship. "You must injure your finances by so doing. All of us have given up the entertaining of young men who do not care about us. It's a mistaken notion. I have long left off blowing out their stomachs. I dine by myself at considerably less expense, and feel happier."'[1]

But this, even from a lord, did not shake him into giving up 'what had been so long an established custom'.

There is often more behind established customs than meets the eye, however, and there were probably two very different ideas behind this one. There was first the obvious one—the Captain's desire to get to know his officers, upon terms of as much familiarity as the isolation of his position allowed: a desire to make them feel that he did not regard them merely as cogs in a wheel. This aspect was well voiced by Admiral George Berkeley, C.-in-C. at Lisbon in 1811, who, approving Dillon's wish to keep one place at his table free at all times for one of his own officers, remarked, 'If you consider your officers, you may rely on them feeling your attention, and you will not be a loser by so doing': which advice was more humane and more forward-looking than Lord George Stewart's. But there was another side to it all.

To keep a table, it would seem, was widely regarded as part of a ritual: part, one might say, of the Captain's 'royalty-mystique'. Thus it was quite commonly held that the great man's invitation to dine was no ordinary social gesture. It was a command: and the junior who refused it without adequate excuse was committing something very like a breach of discipline. Dillon has two examples, one as it were from the receiving end, the other from the issuing. When a First Lieutenant in the West Indies in 1796, he refused his Captain's invitation to dine, he at that time nursing a grievance against him. That Captain, though a good friend to Dillon, was admittedly a choleric man, suffering at the time, perhaps, from a West Indian liver. Sending for his First Lieutenant, he flatly accused him of *mutiny*,[2] and announced his intention of bringing him to a court-martial. He even produced precedents and printed regu-

[1] N.R.S., Vol. XCVII, p. 286.
[2] Op. cit., Vol. XCIII, p. 280.

lations, the latter of which Dillon thought bogus. The thing petered out and they made it up. But it is significant that, thereafter, Dillon never again refused an invitation. On the second occasion, eighteen years later,[1] he had the same experience, but the other way about. He invited a Lieutenant of Marines to dinner and the young man refused. Unlike his former Captain, Dillon did not bluster. Rather, he ignored the matter—and the Marine officer. But such was the 'Owner's' ascendancy on board his own ship that this was enough. The Lieutenant was discharged, at his own request, to another ship, and there the matter ended. Such small misunderstandings are unimportant in themselves, but they do serve to stress both the quasi-regal position of a warship's captain and the kind of mystique surrounding it.

Now let the great man, his meal over, his guests departed, step out of his cabin to stroll upon the Quarter-deck. This, as has been indicated, was the place *par excellence* where all the ship's élite strolled at such times as strolling was encouraged. Yet all were not equal there: far from it. As the Captain opens his door there may be strollers on the starboard side. But before he has got past the compass binnacle, lo and behold, that side is unpopulated from end to end, and remains so as long as he cares to use it. This custom, still with us, was old in Nelson's time. It was but another manifestation of his solitary grandeur. There were many others. None could address him, unless it were upon strict ship-business. Everyone removed his hat when in his presence as he would in Royalty's. There was no inconsiderable ceremony when he left the ship, and a rather more considerable one when he returned to it. 'Side-boys' were dressed up for the occasion; special side-ropes to the gangway were rigged. He expected some of his officers and almost all his midshipmen to welcome him, his Boatswain to 'pipe the side', his marine sentry, who always guarded his door, to present arms. On his part, the Captain saluted—that is, touched his hat or perhaps raised it a trifle. This, however, was not primarily to acknowledge the honours he received. It was a token of respect for the one thing present which was superior to himself—the ship he commanded.

B. THE WARD-ROOM

Now for the lower levels, both of decks and of officers. Immediately underneath the Captain's cabin, on the 'upper' or 'second' deck of a two-

[1] Op. cit., Vol. XCVII, p. 306.

decker 74, lay the Ward-room, the home of the Lieutenants. Had our ship been a three-decker—a first- or second-rate—this would not have been so, for there would have been one extra gun-deck and, most likely, one to be housed who was even more important than the Captain. The ship would be a flagship, and there would be a Flag-Officer on board. Then the Admiral's cabin would lie on the upper deck just below the Captain's, and it would be as spacious and roomy as the latter's though not perhaps quite so lofty. In such a ship we should have to go down one level more, to the Middle Deck, in order to reach the Ward-room, immediately beneath the Admiral's cabin.

This place, like the cabins of both Captain and Admiral, received its main illumination from the stern, and though it seldom had a stern-gallery it usually had quarter-galleries, often used as lavatories. It is better, perhaps, not to regard it as a room in itself, but as the aftermost part of the deck on which it lay, separated from the rest of it by a bulkhead which could be moved backwards or forwards as required. The whole space would be about 35 feet long by 18 wide. The 'dining-room' part of it was a long narrowish central space stretching fore and aft with, down each side, a row of small compartments which subtracted considerably from its width. Some of these tiny places were sometimes used for the officers' stores, but mostly as officers' cabins. Other cabins were situated a little further forward, outside the bulkhead of the mess-room. Some of these were made of light elm, some were frankly of canvas: but all, whatever the material, were readily removable when necessary. For, when the ship cleared for action, away they all went, to leave the whole deck ready for what were after all the most important things on board, the broadside guns. An officer might even have one to share his cabin with him but, as a rule, these temporary cubicles were placed so as to nestle up against the transoms between the guns.

Had the Ward-room been the residence of the Lieutenants alone, we have found room for all their cabins and to spare, because a '74' carried not more than six of them. But they were not the only residents—indeed, less than half the residents. In such a ship during our wars there were normally thirteen 'Ward-room Officers'—the six Lieutenants, the Captain of Marines, two Lieutenants of Marines, the Master, the Surgeon, the Purser and the Chaplain. These—with of course the Captain—constituted the ship's élite, and all had the essential social privilege of 'walking the Quarter-deck'. But here in fact is the main difference between the purely 'social' and the purely 'naval'. For though all enjoyed in common the ship-status of Ward-room and Quarter-deck, only nine of the thirteen were commissioned officers. The other four were Warrant Officers: but—socially—Warrant Officers of a superior stamp, after 1808 officially known as 'Warrant Officers of Ward-room Rank', but, well before that, unofficially accepted as such. Since we are here concerned with the ship hierarchy and its geographical distribution, we shall consider them here along with their messmates who all had commissions, the Lieutenants and the Marine officers. Let us first see if we can assign cabins to this 'baker's dozen' of the élite.

Here Mangin will greatly assist us again. For he tells us how almost all of them were disposed in the *Gloucester*, 74, in 1812. There were here, however, only five Lieutenants and therefore only twelve Ward-room Officers. Six had their cabins in or beside the Ward-room on the Main, Second or Upper Deck—it was called by any of these names. They were the lucky ones—the four most senior Lieutenants, the Captain of Marines, and the Master. The last-named, however, normally used this cabin only when in harbour. At sea he scarcely ever left his day-cabin, situated on the port side of the entrance to the Captain's quarters; and he usually slept there too. One level below, beneath the forward end of the Ward-room, there slept four more. They were on the Lower Deck, the seamen's special domain, but still on the 'officer' side of the vertical cut, nearly but not quite at the stern. They were the junior Lieutenant, the two subalterns of Marines and the Chaplain. Incidentally, here too slept the Captain's Clerk and the Pilot, but they were not Ward-room Officers.

There remain only the Surgeon and the Purser, both appointed by warrant, but 'Warrant Officers of Ward-room Rank'. Their cabins were down below the waterline on the Orlop, the lowest true deck in the ship: but still 'aft'—that is, approximately under the junior Lieutenant and the Chaplain. They were important officers, seldom if ever young men and the bearers of immense responsibilities. Why were they so poorly housed, down there where no fresh air ever entered from without? The answer is that it was mainly in those stygian regions that their most important duties lay. In the immediate neighbourhood of the Surgeon's cabin was the After Cockpit, to which we shall return shortly in order to visit its ordinary inhabitants. But its extraordinary inhabitants—those who found themselves there in battle—were the wounded and the dying: and there the Surgeon and his mates did what they could for them, the Chaplain, and sometimes the Purser, assisting where possible. The

After Cockpit, in action, was the Surgery in its full sense—the casualty-clearing station, the amputating-theatre: and the amputating-tables were often the chests of the normal occupants. The Purser dwelt thereabouts for quite other reasons. The ship's stores for which he was solely responsible all lay on the Orlop or under it in the Hold. Perhaps the thing is most realistically summed up by mentioning that he slept on top of the spirit room, so that any entry, illicit and nocturnal, into that chamber would have to be made, almost literally, over the Purser's body.

Mangin describes in detail his own cabin on the Lower Deck. He even illustrates it in colour-drawings. Its external dimensions were 8 ft. long and broad, and under 6 ft. high—a little canvas box tucked between 32-pounder guns. Inside it was much smaller—'not quite 5 ft. broad at one end and less than two at the other', because of projecting ship-timbers. It was thus 'in shape precisely and in size nearly, the same as a grand-pianoforte, for it should be observed that, when the cot was slung . . . the entire space was occupied.'[1] Of that cot, however, he speaks in the highest terms. 'If it were not for concomitant circumstances, a more luxurious bed cannot be conceived . . . snugness is consulted in its dimensions; and, by its swinging with the ship's motion, sleep is promoted.' The principal 'concomitant circumstance' was the disagreeable proximity, every night, of several hundred men who, with few washing facilities, had spent many days in unremitting and sweat-inducing toil—

'. . . and the ports being necessarily closed from evening to morning, the heat, in this cavern of only six feet high and so entirely filled with human bodies, was overpowering.'

Though scattered for sleep on three separate decks, the Ward-room Officers were united for their meals and other daytime recreations. The meals, served in the Ward-room, and especially the dinners, were decorous affairs. They sat down at their single long table, each with his own boy-servant standing behind him: and they ate well—not, mostly, off ship-rations but from the proceeds of their mess-subscriptions which they handed over to one of their number whom they appointed mess-caterer. In the *Gloucester* that important post was filled by the Captain of Marines, who reckoned that their dinner, wine, tea, sugar, etc. worked out at rather over £60 per annum. This Mangin thought excessive, not because of the food and its quality which was, all things considered,

[1] N.R.S., Vol. XCI, pp. 9–10.

good, but because of the drink—its quantity as well as its quality—which was bad. Most of them, he thought, were drinking indifferent port and sherry because they considered it was 'not done' to drink on the average less than half a pint a day. And indeed, when a Lieutenant's wages were only just over £100 a year, it does seem improvident to have spent more than half of it at the table. So he resisted vigorously when one Lieutenant (the only one with means of his own) suggested raising the ration to one pint. It could not be worthwhile, he argued, 'to expend at least £40 for the nauseous purpose of swilling six glasses of sloe-juice mixed with sugar-of-lead.' He won his point, having the impecunious majority with him.

Yet this wine-drinking was symptomatic of something not unpraiseworthy in the characters of Nelsonic officers. To drink wine was then one of the hallmarks of gentility, and they firmly believed in the gentility of their calling. Moreover they were quite determined, even in such dismal surroundings, to go through the motions of living like gentlemen. The surroundings and the wine might be bad, but the motive was by no means wholly so. It was not just the fruit of idle vanity. It stemmed from a proper pride in their profession which, in spite of all discouragement, most of them persisted in regarding as the best in the world. For just the same sort of reason, then, the Ward-room was not content with accepting the occasional hospitality of the Captain. It returned it regularly, though it would seem that the Commanding Officer's presence put a curb on natural exuberance, and such entertainments were not very much gayer than the Captain's own. But when its entertaining spread downwards, as it always did: when specially spruced-up Master's Mates and Midshipmen dined in the Ward-room, then it would appear that both hosts and guests enjoyed themselves.

The First Lieutenant presided, and already there existed, if perhaps in a stiffer form than it appears today, a recognized distinction between 'on duty' and 'off duty'. There were, a good deal more often than in our own day, oversteppings of this invisible line. Quarrels were more frequent, and duels were not unknown, though they were always settled ashore. Indeed, the 'service' and the 'social' relations of officers to each other might, and sometimes did, become dangerously intermingled. Dillon cites a case, when he was a First Lieutenant. He incurred the wrath of the Second Lieutenant over what he considered a strictly 'service' matter and, as a result, was insulted at the Ward-room table and challenged to a duel. He made a 'service' affair of it, and demanded a Court Martial on his junior. This was only averted by the latter publicly apologizing.[1] Evidently the dangers of this kind of thing were appreciated, for we find an enlightened Captain of 1807 giving his Ward-room officers the benefit of his experience in print, and advising them in so many words to eschew the discussion of all ship-service matters at their mess-table. By relegating such 'shop' to its proper place—the Quarter-deck—he declares that 'many disagreeable altercations will be avoided'.[2] Subsequent generations of officers have not been unmindful of this wise advice. Still, amid such confinements and discomforts, with so few alternative relaxations, and among a company of youngish men who habitually 'wore swords', such things were only to be expected. On the whole they could not be called a quarrelsome lot.

(a) *The Lieutenants*

Let us now examine our Ward-room Officers a little more closely, as they served in the *Gloucester*, Captain Robert Williams,[3] in 1812. The Lieutenants, numbered from First to Fifth, enjoyed that order of seniority in the Navy List. James Grierson, the First, had a commission dated 20th September, 1795: and he was what we should now call 'the Commander', responsible to the Captain for the running of the whole ship. The Second Lieutenant, Joseph Neill, was his deputy—approximately what we should call 'Number One'. The Fifth or Junior Lieutenant, William Weekes, whose commission was barely six months old, was by long-standing custom specifically charged with the exercise of the men in small arms. One of the other two—in our case John Baikie, the Third—was the Signal Lieutenant whose duties need no explanation. The Fourth, a young man named Hunter, had no specific task, though, like the others, he was a regular watch-keeper.

Mangin found them all (save at times the wine-loving Second) pleasant and co-operative people. But they were clearly neither distinguished nor well patronized, and therefore did not go far in the years to come. Grierson, a rather silent Scot, was at last made a Retired Commander after forty-three years as a Lieutenant. Neill, a not very likeable Londoner, was 'son of a man of large fortune but obscure family'. He lived to get into both Marshall and O'Byrne, but is silent, in both, on his

[1] N.R.S., Vol. XCIII, p. 435.

[2] *Observations and Instructions for Officers of the Royal Navy*, by A Captain of the Royal Navy, London, 1807, p. 7.

[3] See p. 222.

parentage, which was clearly 'business, commercial, etc.' He reached Commander's rank in 1815—possibly an in-lieu-of-pension promotion, as he was not employed again. Baikie, from the Orkneys, was a rather gross man, though a competent Signals officer. He was not promoted. Hunter was the son of a Margate doctor, a quiet, intelligent lad: but from another source altogether we know that he was not lacking in spirit. Like Dillon, he had been a prisoner at Verdun, but (unlike him) contrived a daring escape. Soon after reaching home he had been made Lieutenant, but had no further promotion. William Weekes, from the West Indies though of Scottish extraction, was young and raw, violent in his likes and dislikes: 'but his heart was . . . not bad', and 'his natural talents were considerable'. He was a 'College Volunteer', but fared badly in the post-war slump. Unpromoted, he was for fifteen years in the Coast Guard (1825–40) and then launched out as an East Indiaman captain.

(b) *The Marine Officers*

There were three of them—the Captain and his First and Second Lieutenants. They were 'quarter-deck' both navally and socially, and were always regarded, like their confrères of the Navy and the Army, as 'officers and gentlemen'. In the *Gloucester* they make a good showing. The Royal Marine Captain—for such was his proper title after 1802—was Thomas Inches, and he earned Mangin's highest praise as a brave, handsome, amusing and well-educated man. 'Indeed I may say that in quitting the Service, my chief subject of regret was losing the society of Captain Inches.' His senior subaltern was an interesting man too, a Highlander named Peter McIntyre: fluent in the Gaelic tongue, in highland lore and poetry; something of a historian and a first-class mimic. The junior, by way of contrast, was a young Englishman, Lewis Woore, 'well-bred, cold, discreet and perfectly unassuming: a talented flute-player, but overfond of cards and, unfortunately, an epileptic'.[1]

The officers of 'the Corps' kept up a very high average even though, as during most periods in their distinguished history, promotion in it was but a slow, uncertain business. Then as now, there was a strong hereditary element among both officers and men, which undoubtedly helped to account for their *esprit de corps*, already famous. It was not without reason, we may be sure, that Lord St. Vincent, a most exacting officer and not one to be over-liberal with praise, passed his famous eulogy upon them—

[1] N.R.S., Vol. XCI, p. 25.

'There never was any appeal made to them for honour, courage or loyalty that they did not more than realize my expectations. If ever the hour of real danger should come to England, the Marines will be found the country's sheet-anchor.'

But naturally they were not all paladins like Captain Inches. J. A. Gardner fills his *Recollections* with a running commentary on his shipmates. He is by no means always kind, but his Marine Officers, with very few exceptions, show up well. Still, all long chains are said to have weak links. One with whom he served was 'insane from grog', and two Second Lieutenants were, one 'half mad' and the other 'invalided for insanity'. All the rest approximated to Captain Inches.

(c) *The Warrant Officers of Ward-room Rank*

Four members remain—the Master, the Surgeon, the Purser and Mangin himself, the Chaplain. All four of them were 'Ward-room', all four navally speaking 'quarter-deck'. But they were not necessarily 'gentle' in the wider social sense. That depended upon their individual backgrounds. Even these four fall into two unequal groups: the Master, and the rest.

(1) *The Master*. Mr John Jones, Master of the *Gloucester*, was probably not 'gentle' in the social sense, though, in a personal sense, no epithet could suit him better. He was clearly one of 'nature's gentlemen'. He was from Gloucestershire, 'a kindly being whom everyone loves and no one envies . . . humble, modest, silent and sweet-tempered . . . a perfect seaman and indefatigable in doing his duty': a man who ruled by kindness, never swore nor used hard words yet always had prompt obedience. Mangin gives no further hint of his background, but surely we may see in him a good example of a good type—the seafaring man, from youth dedicated to his calling, which was the safe navigation of ships: not, probably, educated for anything else, for no doubt he had begun humbly enough, perhaps piloting in the Severn estuary or even just 'before the mast'. Yet his singleness of purpose and his saintly temper had served him well, because everybody knew that he could be trusted. He will go quietly on, no doubt, till old age claims him, and then—even then—he will go out unostentatiously on a superannuation pension, with half his full-time pay. Indeed, the main quality required of a Master was trustworthiness, for no one on board, perhaps, had so

many opportunities of drowning the whole Ship's Company. Another manifestation of that trust, in quite another form, was that to him were confided the keys of most of the important locks and doors in the ship, including even that of the Spirit Room: for though the Purser was responsible for distributing its contents, even he could not enter it at will. His position of trust is further emphasized by the fact that he was associated with the Captain and the First Lieutenant in that exclusive little body which had to sign all important documents—the Muster Books, Pay Books, Tickets, etc.—the only other signatory being the Warrant Officer whose department was concerned with any particular document. In fact, in 'ship' (though not in 'social') status, the Master was, at the lowest, the third most important person on board.

He was seldom 'officer-class', though a good many of his kind would have had a better start than Mr Jones (if we have diagnosed him aright). Ever since Pepys's day Christ's Hospital in Newgate Street had been providing a regular, if not large, stream of recruits for the navigation branch of the Navy. Readers of Leigh Hunt, himself a 'bluecoat' boy of our period, will recall in his *Autobiography* his account of the 'King's Boys', as they were called; and how, after 'the Grecians', they lorded it over their fellows. In Hunt's day this source was still supplying good naval material, and, educationally speaking, its products were superior. But Mr Jones hardly sounds like one of them.

Historically, these Masters were interesting naval figures. They had come down in the world since the old days when they commanded ships of their own. But they had not fallen very far. Now they were subservient to the 'military' head, the Captain, but to no other soul on board. The Lieutenants had no jurisdiction over them, and even the Captain had not untrammelled control. On all points of navigation the Master was still in a very privileged position; and 'the Owner', though he did occasionally interfere, did so at his own risk, knowing that their Lordships would begin with an initial prejudice against him if anything went wrong after he had interfered. The Master, it is true, was still appointed 'by warrant' and not 'by commission', but he was an altogether exceptional Warrant Officer. If pay be any evidence of relative importance—and it often is—then he was the second-most-important man aboard, for (in our period) he was receiving more than (in the biggest ships half as much again as) the Lieutenants. No one knows exactly when 'the Wardroom Mess' formed itself. It was almost certainly intended originally for the Lieutenants only: but the first newcomer to it had been the Master, and he became a member of it, probably, very soon after its inception. Nor was his inclusion ever questioned.

Naturally (as with Captain Inches) not all Masters were quite so acceptable to their messmates as Mr Jones of the *Gloucester*. All our naval memoir-writers include examples of the breed: and, full and by, they come out of the ordeal with colours flying. Dillon portrays one in the *Defence* in 1793—Mr William Webster, already fifteen years a Master and a character. They called him (behind his back) 'the black badger', because black was the colour of the coat he always wore. It should, of course, have been blue because, six years before, all Warrant Officers had been given their first official uniform, and it was of that colour. But perhaps he was still availing himself of the kindly loophole afforded by their Lordships, who had ordained that officers might wait to make a change into anything new 'until they have occasion to make up a new suit of cloaths'. As it fell out, however, the poor Black Badger never shed his now old-fashioned skin. He was wearing it when he fell in action on 1st June, 1794.

Gardner has thumbnail sketches of no less than thirteen Masters, and—a good testimonial to their average excellence—not one is really derogatory. They were 'brave and meritorious', 'quiet good man', 'worthy honest fellow'. The worst is 'an odd fish': another—an obvious character—'A very good man, and one that was better acquainted with rope-yarns and bilgewater than with Homer and Vergil. He said a man's ideas should go no further than the jibboom end'. Another was widely different—'A strange fellow; he could speak six or seven languages fluently and was well known in every part of the Mediterranean'. Here clearly is an exceptional type, as is Cullen's Mr Rutherford—Master, of all things, of a cutter—who was 'a gentleman of good family in Scotland, an expert seaman and a brave fellow'. But the clear impression that we glean of most of them is that they were a fine, salty body of men wedded to the sea: seldom 'gentle', but quietly competent and exceedingly good messmates.

(2) *The Civilian Officers*. The remaining members of the Ward-room represented three of the four 'civilian' branches of the Navy. The fourth was the Schoolmaster, but as he was not then a Warrant Officer, still less (like these three) a Warrant Officer of Ward-room Rank, we must leave his more detailed story till later. But, first, a general word about all of them. These 'civilian' officers stand in contradistinction to the 'military' or fighting officers—that is, all the groups so far discussed as well as the

other Warrant Officers whose turn is yet to come. The 'civilians' were officers of the Navy, members of a profession which existed to fight at sea: but they were not there, primarily, to fight.

A ship was a self-contained, indeed a self-centred, community like, say, a lonely village; and as such it had to have its 'services'. The villagers need their Doctor to cure their bodies if he can, their Parson to cure their souls, their Schoolmaster to teach their children; and, especially if they are isolated, their own Shopkeeper and general purveyor. It was exactly these functions which were being fulfilled on board ship by our four Civilian Officers. The Surgeon practised medicine and surgery: the Chaplain took religious services and looked (as well as he could) after the spiritual welfare of his flock—the Ship's Company. The Schoolmaster taught the boys (when he could catch them). The Purser looked after the day-to-day needs of his community—their food, drink clothes, etc. He was not then (as he later became) concerned with their pay: he was rather the general business-manager on board. He even kept a shop there—the only one, and so something of a monopoly-shop. All were busy men, but their prime business was not to fight, or even to sail the ship. Let us look at them one by one.

The Surgeon. Mr Hugh Walker, Surgeon of the *Gloucester*, was an Irishman, 'I think from the neighbourhood of Belfast'. He sounds, socially, a cut above the Master, being 'a very steady good man, usually in high spirits, alert, assiduous and exceedingly skilful and humane . . . a valuable officer'. But it must be reluctantly admitted that all Surgeons were not worthy of such high praise. In the nature of the case the leading lights of the medical profession might well fight shy of life afloat, with its discomforts, its limited prospects and pay and its very limited scope for the exercise of professional talents. A ship was obviously not a very promising 'practice'. Nor, until just before our period, had Authority taken any serious steps towards removing such discouragements, which alone could pave the way for higher medical standards, or for the entry of better-qualified men. So it befell that for long—indeed from the very inception of the organized Navy—the naval surgeon was something of a by-word for inefficiency. The thing was a matter of elementary economics and scarcely needs enlarging upon.

From about the middle of the eighteenth century, however, the medical side of naval life had begun to improve. Two or three really good men (whom we shall meet later) had appeared on the naval scene, raising the general standard of medicine and of medical men, and inducing the authorities to face up to their responsibilities. They had, for instance, at last shamed the Government into providing Surgeons with adequate instruments and medicine-chests, with passable sick-bays on board and naval hospitals ashore. They had succeeded in establishing a superior grade known as Physicians to oversee and co-ordinate the work of ordinary ship-surgeons. And the medical profession had on the whole responded. The doctors were no less patriotic than any other section of the people, and their sense of duty sent many of them afloat, even though their prospects there were still less attractive than on land.

So the Hugh Walkers were no longer rarities, though not yet, perhaps, quite the norm. There was still the temptation for a third-rate practitioner, short of patients at home, to imagine that he could conceal his more noticeable failings if he went to sea. In wartime he would have no difficulty in getting there, because the demand for Surgeons' Mates (after 1806 called Surgeons' Assistants) would be very high. The Navy could not do without its quota of such people, and those responsible for examining medical applicants—the purely civilian Company of Barber-Surgeons—could not be too eclectic when fleets were mobilizing. No doubt their problem, in its small way, was similar to Pitt's in 1795, when he was looking for seamen. It cannot be supposed that he liked some of his quota-men: but presumably he thought them better than none.

Gardner's Surgeons do not compare favourably with his Masters. He describes twenty-two, counting such Surgeons' Assistants as, he tells us, were promoted. He speaks well of about half of them—very well of three or four. He is neutral about three or four more, but disapproving of seven. He never takes exception to their professional abilities: probably he was in no position to assess them. His criticisms are personal. They range from 'not very orthodox', *via* 'fractious little fellow' and 'crabbed as the devil' (twice), to 'loved his glass of grog', 'drank like a fish' and 'mad with drink'.

The other autobiographers are not rich in Surgeons, though one of them, Peter Cullen, was one himself. He reveals himself as a very precise young Scot, a stickler for propriety and a rather colourless character. Once only does he let the old Adam protrude for a moment. This was in his Cockpit days when he was a Johnny Newcome of a Surgeon's Mate:

'Mr Cullen, as usual with all novitiates, had tricks and annoyances played upon him by the young mids: one in particular was very annoying, more than the others. One afternoon . . . this midshipman, very finely dressed for going to a ball, began his annoyances. Mr Cullen thought this a favourable opportunity of ridding himself of all these petty troubles, by attacking him with his professional weapons. So, mixing some sulphuric acid with water in a gallipot, threw it directly at him, aiming at his fine waistcoat, neatly frilled shirt and superfine cravat. . . . Mr Cullen gained credit by this act, and was not any more disturbed by the petty officers.'[1]

We may well believe him.

Dillon has two Surgeons—not war-importations but old-stagers—each with a most unlooked-for characteristic. One, Mr. James Malcolm of the *Defence* and of nineteen years' standing, 'who was the cause of introducing flannel for the use of seamen in the Navy . . . could not perform the operation of amputating a limb'—an unfortunate failing at all times, but especially after the battle of the First of June when he was faced with over sixty desperate cases all needing that very treatment. Fortunately for them, however, his one and only assistant, William Yowell, was not so afflicted and, working twenty-two hours out of twenty-four, had them all off. Incidentally, here was a serious lapse on someone's part. The 1790 Regulations ordain *three* assistant surgeons for a third-rate like the *Defence*. Dillon's other odd medical character, Thomas Grey, also could not operate—at least his intended victims did not encourage him to try. But this was for quite another reason—he was near-blind. Yet he was a cultivated, scholarly man and, we must suppose, a good physician, because, having wisely given up a service where surgery was at a premium, he put up his plate ashore, built a good practice and was ultimately knighted.

One sign of all-round improvement in naval medicine during our wars reveals itself in a new corporate spirit which was spreading through the branch. This took the form of a strong demand for a distinctive uniform. Hitherto, as ordinary Warrant Officers, they had worn that same plain blue uniform which poor Mr Webster never ordered. Now they clamoured for one of their own, and obtained it, with distinctive buttons, in 1805. They were the first Warrant Officers to succeed here, though they were quickly followed by other branches.

Though not many of them were 'gentle' in the stricter contemporary sense, the very worst of them were bound, by virtue of their training, to

[1] N.R.S., Vol. XCI, p. 56.

be men of a certain education, and the great majority were of at least 'respectable' birth. It is not surprising, then, that they had found their way into the Ward-room some time before our wars began, after, but probably not long after, the Masters.

The Purser. The word 'Purser' conjures up in the minds of those familiar with the Navy of Nelson's day Rowlandson's water-colour (opposite p. 257). It shows a paunchy, be-spectacled little man myopically scrutinizing an account-sheet. Two large jars flank him on his right, and on the left is a goodly quart-pot. It is fair caricature and it may well be from the life, thiugh it does not happen to illustrate Mangin's Purser, Mr Thomas Wilson, who, like several of his ward-room messmates, was

'a Scot; taciturn, cautious, calm and economical. He appeared to be—like Shakespeare's Cassius—"a great discerner" and "to look quite through the deeds of men"—he was moreover not a fat man, nor "one who sleeps by night," but tall, lean and anxious.'

These Pursers no doubt had their anxieties. They were business men: they had themselves and their families to think of, and—if the going was good—their fortunes to make. For, odd as it may seem, the State did not even yet pay them a full salary direct, as it did to the other officers and the men. To make up, they remunerated themselves in various ways, some sanctioned, some not. Besides, a Purser had some initial leeway to make up. He had to put down cash of his own before he secured his pursery. True, he no longer actually bought it as he had once done: but he had to find what might be called 'caution money'. The Government had to let him handle considerable sums in the course of day-to-day business and to give him quite considerable powers to run up bills in its name: and it wanted some surety against his defaulting on them. In 1808 such sureties, to be found by himself or his friends, were for a First Rate, £1,200; Second Rate, £1,000; Third, £800; Fourth and Fifth, £600; Sixth and below, £400. Thus the Purser was no man of straw: he was a capitalist, if only in a small way. He also had to have some education, to be able to cast his accounts, keep his books, know the current value of things; and—and this was perhaps the heart of the matter—to save on all stores and monies entrusted to him. For here lay most of his income—in the various commissions he was entitled to draw; in the various commissions he was not entitled to draw, but drew, and in the ordinary profits which accrued from his monopoly-shop on board. On the other hand, he was entrusted with no wages due to other people. We shall not properly appreciate his odd position, problems and all too frequent backslidings unless we realize that he was not a 'Paymaster' at all, but simply, as we have described him, the ship's factor or business man, and its privileged shop-keeper.

Let us look at a few of his legitimate perquisites. On all provisions issued by weight he had a commission of 12½ per cent—i.e., one-eighth. This did not mean, of course, that he was justified in his '14 for 16' swindle, which consisted in issuing short measure to the seaman (see p. 100). That was fraud: this was the legitimate allowance for 'ordinary wastage'—though it was not very difficult to turn the legitimate into the illegitimate, and escape detection. Next, he had a commission of 5 per cent on all slop-clothing which passed through his hands. Again, on tobacco (when it became a ration in 1808) he had 10 per cent. We can assess, roughly, his profits from this one comparatively small 'line'. Everyone on board was entitled to draw two pounds of tobacco per lunar month, and the price charged was 1/7 a pound. The Purser of a First Rate (complement about 800), therefore, might issue no less than 20,800 pounds a year. On this amount his 10 per cent commission would be £165. This is a maximum, however, assuming not only the biggest sort of ship but also that all her people drew their full ration. Still, it was not bad: from this one source alone he doubled his basic salary at the very least, and might even treble it. Yet it is doubtful whether he really liked the innovation, for hitherto he had been allowed to provide and sell the commodity himself. The Navy Board, it is true, had fixed the price, but in advance, so that the quality provided was his own business: nor, if his clients found his wares indifferent, could they transfer their custom to a rival firm. There was no rival firm. Then for coals, firewood, turnery-ware, candles and lanterns he was allowed a halfpenny per man for every day that the ship was in commission. Here of course his profits depended upon his own management—how much coal or how many lanterns he could contrive *not* to issue: or on whether he could come to an understanding with the Carpenter or the Boatswain about firewood—whether he could get hold of odd ends of timber, or even old yards and topmasts, which they had 'expended'. There was plenty of scope, especially when, or if, there was interdepartmental collusion. He also had a similar allowance on 'ordinary wastage' in casks, bags, jars and many other articles in everyday use. To crown all, could he but persuade the Victualling Board to pass his annual accounts, he could draw a yearly bonus, ranging from

£25 (in a First Rate) *via* £20 (in a '74') to £7 in the smallest ship, as a reward for not having been bowled out.

In the hard school of war, the Admiralty soon became very conscious that irregularities were rife—and not confined to Pursers only. It took steps, therefore, to stop some of the more glaring breaches of its Regulations. In the greatly enlarged edition of 1808 page after page of new safeguards are introduced, designed to circumvent frauds of all kinds. This reveals their prevalence: unfortunately, however, it does not prove that they were eliminated. They were not, though doubtless the guilty parties were induced to become more careful—and more subtle. The fact is, the remedy did not lie in a multitude of minor regulations. The whole set-up bordered on the ridiculous, and nothing but a radical change would cure it. Every facet of it provided a direct invitation to deceive: to steal, or at best to perpetrate an unending series of petty frauds. We will go into them no further. 'Pussers' Tricks' have too often been exposed. All that need be added by way of moral is that, if there ever existed a really honest Christian Purser—and doubtless there were a few—the burden of his daily prayer must surely have been 'lead us not into temptation, but deliver us from an impossible situation'. This absurd arrangement lasted throughout our wars. It was only in the 1840's that Pursers at last emerged as Paymasters, having themselves petitioned to be relieved of the stigma attaching to the old name, and being at length relieved of their great temptations (or most of them) by the award of fixed over-all salaries such as all other officers received. But in fairness to this hated and despised 'profession-within-the-profession' those temptations ought to be remembered. The period was not conspicuous for personal honesty in material things. Petty peculations were rife in most walks of life: but some had more opportunities than others. It is very doubtful whether 'the Purser' as a breed was markedly more dishonest than the general run of people. The difference, probably, between Purser and General Public was this: the others would if they could, but often could not, and so did not; the Purser would, could, and did.

The main sufferers from this sorry, all-pervading racket were not the authorities, nor even the Purser's fellow-officers. The men bore the brunt. For this reason the Pursers received comparatively tender handling from the contemporary writers, most of whom were officers, though Dillon does tell of how, when a lad of only 13, he was the victim of a typically mean 'pusser's trick'.[1] And Mangin can dismiss his Mr

[1] N.R.S., Vol. XCIII, pp. 111–12.

Wilson with no worse an epithet than 'economical'. But what precisely did that mean? Was that the word on the lips of his lower-deck neighbours further forrard? Probably not. Most likely they used a word at once less stately, more forceful, and perhaps not even in the reverend gentleman's dictionary.

The Pursers' backgrounds varied considerably. Some of them were certainly 'gentle'. It is by no means accidental that their surnames in the Navy Lists are quite often the same as the Captain's. For a pursery could be made into a very profitable line of business, and—in selected ships—was obtainable by Interest which was worked along lines very similar to those at the commissioned officer's disposal. Doubtless it appealed sometimes to well-connected young men who liked the idea of fairly easy money. But the majority was not of this type. The norm, rather, was the small business man of the shopkeeper class: men who entered as Clerks, and when their time came invested their modest capital in a pursery in much the same way as their brothers and cousins bought a confectionery business. Some of them certainly prospered. Leading from the market place to the churchyard at Kirkby Stephen in Westmorland is a handsome porch called 'the Cloisters', erected in 1810 by one John Waller, 'a Purser in His Majesty's Navy'. This gentleman's motives are unknown to me. Was his object plain piety? Was the porch a thankoffering for a pleasant and useful life? Or for a profitable one? Or was it, possibly, intended as some small douceur for St. Peter at Heaven's Gate—St. Peter who might possibly have heard of 'pusser's tricks' and so have conceived an unreasonable prejudice against the breed?

Gardner's list of Pursers is a comparatively thin one. Several of them seem to have made but little impression on him: though he gives a name, he makes no comment at all. Of the rest the good and the bad just about balance. Two or three are 'most worthy fellows': of another he 'wants words to express my gratitude and respect for his memory.' On another his verdict is 'generous and thoughtless': and this man must surely be classed among the 'favourables', possessing as he did two such very unpurserlike qualities. At the other end come 'Insane before he died', 'I believe broke: most strange and unaccountable', 'Many good qualities and many bad'; and—in two cases—'took care of his eights'.

The most remarkable Purser whom Gardner knew, and conversed with, was a record-holder of another kind. Patrick Gibson was born—and the fact seems reasonably well-authenticated—in 1720. He was a large, lively and vigorous Irishman from Tipperary, immensely strong and, when put out, immensely formidable. When Gardner met him in 1799 he had just given up the pursery of a line-ship, where he found the work a little irksome, and was then, in his 80th year, Purser of a frigate. He was still full of fun and anecdote, and he had plenty to talk about, having among other things actually carried the dying Wolfe off the Heights of Abraham in 1759. Many years later Gardner called on him. He was still incorrigibly cheerful—

'He had enjoyed an uninterrupted state of health for upwards of 90 years: . . . he had nothing to do with doctors' bottles with collars round their necks, and look, says he, if you can find any of that craft on my chimney-piece.'[1]

Three months later he died. He was 110.

The Chaplain. The last member of the *Gloucester's* Ward-room was the Chaplain, Edward Mangin. Naturally he gives no character-sketch of himself; but it is not hard to supply. He was no nonentity, but an author of sufficient note to earn his place in the Dictionary of National Biography. Of Huguenot origin and Irish birth, he was Prebendary of Rath in Killaloe for forty-nine years, though he seems to have resided permanently in Bath, save when he went travelling. He was long the acknowledged head of the literary life in that city, where he was much admired and respected. He was obviously a talented, broad-minded man, humane in the best sense: he would clearly be an asset to any Ward-room in any age. But he was not in any way a typical naval Chaplain. This cruise in the *Gloucester*, which lasted less than four months, was his sole excursion into the naval world and was undertaken partly because he was temporarily hard up, partly out of curiosity as to how other folk lived. It is this motive which gives his journal its unique value. It is that of an intelligent outside observer viewing naval life through fresh and unbiased eyes, and seeking to tell other outsiders what that life was like.

If Mangin, then, was not a 'typical' naval chaplain, who was? The answer is curious. It is exceedingly doubtful whether there was such a thing. In several respects these naval clergymen differed markedly from all other naval figures. First in their status. They were not commissioned officers, and though (since Pepys's day) they had been appointed to their posts by Warrant of the Admiralty, they were not really regarded as Warrant Officers either. Nor were they paid as such, receiving up till

[1] N.R.S., Vol. XXXI, p. 215.

1797 the pay of the lowest rating in the ship and, after that date, a pay lower than the lowest—though, as we shall see, they had their allowances. Yet they were not, and were never regarded as, 'Lower Deck', either by the officers or the seamen. That could hardly be because, in the nature of the case, they were educated men with university degrees. In earlier times a Chaplain's status on board had depended almost entirely upon the personal whim of the Captain who, having appointed him, might either make him welcome in his own cabin (and therefore everywhere else on board) or ignore him, when his position became anomalous and his existence probably unhappy. But those days were passed. Now, being appointed by warrant, he was no longer, officially, the Captain's choice, though unofficially he very often was. Mangin, however, was not. He had wanted to go to sea with Captain Jahleel Brenton, but in the end volunteered for general service. He was accordingly sent to the *Gloucester* after one interview with the senior naval chaplain, then known as the 'Chaplain-General', and another with an official of the Admiralty office, who handed him his warrant. That warrant, too, made his status on board more secure than when he had to rely entirely on the Captain's favour; and well before the last decade of the nineteenth century—probably indeed by the middle of it—he was accepted, though still unofficially, as a Ward-room Officer, to be accorded such recognition and respect as his character deserved.

There was another big difference between him and his fellow-civilian officers, the Surgeon and Purser. They were to be found, without fail, in every commissioned ship. By 1790 it was also laid down in the Admiralty Regulations that a Chaplain should be appointed to every commissioned ship of fifth-rate or higher. But it is quite certain that this rule was not observed: and the reason was because there were nothing like enough clergymen who were prepared to go to sea. It is hard to blame them. If Mangin does nothing else, he has no difficulty in showing that the Parson on board a contemporary warship was very much of a fish out of water. This was not because his flock was more than ordinarily irreligious. Probably the opposite was the case, especially among the officers. But however Christian they were in their ultimate convictions, the life they were compelled to lead, in its crudeness and even brutality, was evidently not conducive to practical day-to-day Christianity. In those older days when the Chaplain's position had been so uncertain in both status and pay, not only had all parsons been rarities afloat, but good ones were almost non-existent, for these discouragements had had to be added to the ordinary difficulties of their ministry on shipboard: and those who did volunteer had tended to be among the dregs of the profession. Things were better now, however, for at least the Chaplain was as comfortably lodged and as respectfully treated as he could expect: and—incidentally in the very year of Mangin's servitude—his pay and prospects were increased in a way that may almost be described as generous (see p. 299). Mangin, in fact, must have been one of the first clergymen to enter under the new scales of pay; and, if he were by any chance typical of the new entry, it would appear that the standard went up at once. Be that as it may, however, it is certain that the standard did rise as a result of this 'Chaplain's Charter' which, for the first time, made the office economically worth while. And he was gaining more even than that. Until quite recently, before he could be paid his derisory wages, he had had to procure from the Captain, the Senior Lieutenant and the Master certificates to witness that he had done his job properly. From this humiliation, however, he had been relieved in 1808.

Yet Naval Chaplains remained in short supply throughout the war, and after it. It is not easy to explain why, but one reason perhaps was the temporary nature of their service. There were too many who, like Mangin, went to sea for a single commission or for part of one: too many part-timers, too many, as it were, 'amateurs': too few whole-time 'professional naval' clergymen—men resolved to make the Navy their life-service and His Majesty's ships their parishes. See what a difference this makes. Even had there been—and there had not—as many men who had served as Chaplains as there were men who had served as Pursers or Surgeons, it would still take at least twenty Mangins to produce the continuous serving-time of one Mr Wilson or one Mr Walker.

Evidence of this constant shortage is not hard to find. It is often revealed by our contemporary writers' silences on the subject—by, for example, the oft-recurring reference to the Captain taking Sunday Service, which he only did when there was no Parson. Dillon is three years in the *Leopard* in the Mediterranean without one; all over the world for three years in the *Horatio* without one; to India and back in the *Phaeton* without one. In the fourteen ships in which Gardner served there were only four—one in a flagship, two in 74's, one in a 50, and none in any smaller ship. Watson actually volunteers the information that while he was in the *Fame* 'the Captain officiated as Chaplain, as we had not any on board'.[1] More striking still, in 1814, when there were 713 ships in commission, the Official Navy List—the first 'By Order' Admiralty one—shows only fifty-eight Chaplains all told, of whom only thirty-one were in ships. The favoured few were; flagships, one; 74's, twenty-three; frigates, four; Receiving Ships, two; Guardships, one. By then it is clearly laid down in Regulations that every ship in commission is to carry a Chaplain—yet only one in every twenty-three does so. It might be supposed that these thirty-one were the regular 'general service' whole-time corps of Chaplains always prepared to serve afloat, and that the frankly temporary people like Mangin were not considered permanent enough to count. But that this is not so is shown by the fact that the 1814 Navy List also gives the officer-complements in full of every commissioned ship: and, here too, the number of Chaplains adds up to only thirty-one.

Further, not all the fifty-eight Chaplains appearing in the 1814 list were whole-timers in a modern sense. One was certainly not—a well-known Oxford character named John B. Frowd. He was not afloat in 1814, but two years later went to sea again as Chaplain to Lord Exmouth, and was with him in the *Queen Charlotte* at Algiers. He was a Fellow of Corpus, and one of the institutions of the University during the earlier decades of the nineteenth century. He

'was a very little man, an irrepressible, unwearied chatterbox, with a droll interrogative face, a bald shining head, and a fleshy under-lip which he could push up nearly to his nose.'

During the bombardment, of course, the Chaplain's place was in the After Cockpit, helping the Surgeon with the wounded and administering consolation to the dying. But Dr Frowd had other ideas.

'As the action thickened, he was seized with a comical religious frenzy, dashing around the decks and diffusing spiritual exhortation amongst the half-stripped busy sailors, till the First Lieutenant ordered a hen-coop to be clapped over him, whence his little head, emerging, continued its devout cackle, quite regardless of the balls which flew past him.'[2]

Gardner is not helpful, with his meagre four parsons. He cannot remember the name of one of them, though he does recall that he 'had

[1] Watson, op. cit., p.89.

[2] *Reminiscences of Oxford*, by the Rev. W. Tuckwell, London, 1901.

no dislike to grog'. Of another there is no description at all. But the third is a 'very worthy gentleman' and the fourth is Alexander Scott, Nelson's chaplain at Trafalgar. Gardner merely states that he was a Doctor of Divinity; but he might have said a good deal more. He was a fine linguist and an intelligent man of the world, and he served Nelson faithfully and well as interpreter and private secretary, in addition to his Chaplain's duties. He retired from the sea after Nelson's death.

Dillon too is weak in parsons. There was one in the *Defence*, William Hawtayne, whom he admired very much when still a child: but he too must be regarded as a 'temporary', as he was afterwards Rector of Elstree for thirty-four years. Of another (whom he does not name) he tells a story which illustrates the day-to-day difficulties of naval chaplains, and the importance of tact. On one occasion the *Glory*, in which they were both serving, ran into, and all but succumbed to, a terrific gale. She was saved, but only, as Dillon himself admits, after a 'scene of confusion, noise and swearing which beggars all description'. At length, drenched and exhausted, the officers repaired to the Ward-room for what refreshment they could find, and one of the Lieutenants asked the Chaplain what he thought of it all. He replied, 'I saw nothing but Heaven inside of my cabin and nothing but Hell outside of it'. Maybe he meant well, but the Ward-room thought otherwise. They took grave offence, and he was rudely silenced. 'He knew nothing of a sea life, and, not choosing to make allowance for its dangers, became very unpopular.' The Chaplain of the *Gloucester* would surely have managed things better.

Finally, there is one Chaplain whom we see exclusively through Lower Deck eyes. The Reverend John Dunsterville is damned with very faint praise by Robert Hay, who was his servant in the *Culloden* in 1804. He performed his duties regularly, it is true, but perfunctorily and without inspiration—he brought two or three dozen sermons with him and never composed one. He was a small, plump, dark man with large lack-lustre eyes, cold and repellent to his inferiors, whom he neglected, and who despised him. But to the Admiral, with whom he messed, he was a different man; likewise to the commissioned officers, with whom he 'could drink a good glass' and by whom he was regarded as 'a facetious very good companion'.[1] No man, we are told, is a hero to his own valet. But here, we suspect, was one who was not of heroic mould at all.

He was clearly one of the temporary sort, because on reaching India he secured a land appointment there, and was no more seen. His place

[1] Hay, op. cit., p. 82.

was taken by Mr Edward Locker (see p. 307), who thereafter combined the roles of Admiral's Secretary and Chaplain, as Alexander Scott was even then doing in the *Victory*. There was this difference, however: Scott was in Holy Orders, Locker was not. Yet he evidently did the job incomparably better than his clerical predecessor, winning the confidence of the entire Ship's Company, officers and men alike. Here perhaps we see one way in which the chronic shortage of Naval Chaplains was circumvented. In the absence of a parson, any really good man who chanced to be on board might well feel it his duty to step into the breach. The *Culloden* was lucky in finding one who could fill it so well.

CHAPTER VIII

THE SHIP HIERARCHY: THE REST OF THE SHIP'S COMPANY

HAVING decided to divide our Ship's Company into two groups, and to give a chapter to each, where shall we put the dividing line? At first sight, perhaps, the most obvious place would have been between the Warrant Officers and the rest—that is, between those appointed by Admiralty and those appointed by the Captain. But here the Ship Hierarchy principle intervenes, suggesting quite another dividing-point—that between the 'ship's élite' and the rest: that is, a division having Captain and Ward-room on one side of it and everyone else on the other, even though some of those others were Admiralty-appointed Warrant Officers. This is the policy which has been followed here, and there is another reason for it. It anticipates History, because it was at this point that, ultimately, the naval-social line came to be drawn—that between 'commissioned' and 'warrant' rank.

As the nineteenth century progressed, the Warrant Officers of Ward-room Rank advanced in ship, in naval, and indeed in social prestige; and all of them came in the end to be appointed by commission. The Masters were commissioned officers before they disappeared, merged into the true 'executive' commissioned officers in the latter half of the century. The Pursers became the Paymaster Branch, the Surgeons the Medical Branch, the Chaplain the Chaplain's Branch—all commissioned officers. But the Warrant Officers not of Ward-room Rank had no such rise in prestige: they remained Warrant Officers. Other 'commissioned' branches appeared too—the Engineering Branch for instance, though this does not come into our story at all since it first appears only in the 1830's.

One other branch which is now 'commissioned', however, was already represented in the ship we are describing—the Instructor Branch. And its representative was a very humble figure aboard—the Schoolmaster, then not even a Warrant Officer. He represented the last of our four Civilian Officers mentioned above, and we shall so far interfere with our Ship-Hierarchy order as to describe him first. There is another reason too for promoting him thus prematurely above the non-ward-room Warrant Officers. His story is most easily told while that of the Chaplain is still fresh in mind because, in several ways soon to be revealed, the position of the two was analogous. So, retaining our previous classification, we will bring him in as the last of the four Civilian Officers.

The Schoolmaster. During our wars he was still an anomalous being, swallowed these last hundred years into the ship's economy but not even yet digested. He appeared first at the very end of the seventeenth century, almost as a piece of private enterprise on the part of a few conscientious captains who had a vague idea that their youngsters would be the better for a little schooling. So he was a 'petty', not a 'warrant' officer, none but the Captain having any hand in his appointment. But also he was not a 'common man'. What then, was his official rating—for like everyone else he had to have one? Oddly enough, he was rated 'Midshipman'—oddly because many of his pupils were Midshipmen too. That might prove awkward in a modern school or, for that matter, in the modern Navy: but it was not so in a Nelsonic ship where he was appointed by 'the Owner' and had the vast weight of his authority behind him. Yet even so, things were not always too easy. When the Schoolmaster of the *Alcide* once whipped young Dillon, then a Youngster of ten who probably deserved it, one of the Oldsters, a hefty Midshipman, warned him that if he did it again he (the Oldster) would whop the Schoolmaster. The latter did not touch Dillon again: but if he had, and the Oldster had been as good as his word, there would have been nothing like mutiny involved. There was no regulation about one Midshipman having a scrap with another one.[1] Still, our Schoolmaster was no ordinary Midshipman, and certainly not one of the Quarter-deck-bound kind. Very occasionally, indeed, he did reach the Quarter-deck himself; but only three cases are known to the author. Normally he just went on pursuing his nebulous way until he faded out—one, for instance, ended up in Greenwich Hospital as a Pensioner.

His position in the Navy of our wars was very like that of the Chaplain a century or even a century and a half before, when the parson him-

[1] N.R.S., Vol. XCIII, p. 26.

self had not been properly digested. He had no status other than the Captain's backing, not even that of the Chaplain. He was paid the same wage as the youngest Midshipman, though he enjoyed a 'bonus' of £20 a year and—at first by the Captain's arrangement, but after 1812 by Admiralty Order—his officer-pupils each had to provide £5 per annum to supplement his pay. So 1812 was for him, as for the Chaplain, something of a red-letter date. But, up till then, his remuneration was much too small to enable a Captain to procure a good man: and it would seem that he very seldom got one.

The specimens known to us seem divisible into two sharply defined classes. First, men, not entirely illiterate or devoid of ambition, who had already achieved petty-officer status, perhaps in the Master's branch or the Purser's. We must presuppose in them at least a modicum of education, or a Captain would hardly have chosen them: but they had no sort of training as teachers; still less were they men with university degrees. Rather, they were men already serving on the Lower Deck and, hitherto, borne for other purposes: men who regarded the post of Schoolmaster as a distinct step up, or as a rope wherewith to haul themselves even higher. One such was Mr Humphreys, Dillon's Schoolmaster in the *Alcide*. We have a very clear picture of him, though it is seen through a pupil's eyes. He was not entirely devoid of education for he had been at Christ's Hospital, having intended originally, it would seem, to rise in the Master's branch. But clearly his was an uncultivated mind, and though his influence was not bad, his outlook on life was crude. He strikes one, in fact, as rather a poor pretentious creature. Yet he must have been above the average of contemporary schoolmasters because he scored a success unusual in his kind—he became a Lieutenant, through his Captain's Interest. But he went no further, and was evidently not a very good Lieutenant. His cabin in the *Alcide* was where Mangin's was in the *Gloucester*, on the Lower Deck.

The second type was the broken-down scholar, all too often a drunkard: a man whose natural talents qualified him for something much better, but who had for one reason or another made a mess of his life ashore. Our writers produce more specimens of this sort than of the other. Yet it is doubtful whether they really predominated. Probably they got themselves noticed because they were more colourful. Boys are like that. They remember the quaint masters whom they ragged long after they have forgotten the colourless ones who kept them in order but had not the character to impress them.

They were usually mystery men, with life-stories which they never told. Such a one was Mr Hickey, Schoolmaster of the *Gloucester* when Mangin was on board. He was no old hand, for he had just joined from a Receiving Ship. All he would tell the Chaplain was that he was a London-born Irishman who had been for five years a teacher in Paris, and that, having contracted a debt for £40, he had taken the bounty. Mangin did not believe him. He suspected him of being much superior to this, though he found him 'in the dress and station of a common man'. He spoke French fluently and

'had the manners and address of a gentleman, was a good mathematician and arithmetician, wrote a beautiful hand, conversed with very happy choice of expression, quoted various authors, poets, philosophers and orators; criticised with judgment and novelty of feeling statuary, architecture and painting—and played the violin finely: he, besides, impressed everyone with respect by his air of genteel and humble melancholy.'[1]

It would be interesting to know his story. All that can be said is that the *Gloucester* was very fortunate in both Chaplain and Schoolmaster.

But Schoolmasters were rare—rarer even than Chaplains. In all his ships Gardner mentions only two, though with one—Thomas Pye—he was shipmates three times. His comment on him is cryptic—'A Purser: fit Pye fit man'. He means, probably, that he became a Purser later; but he may well have been a Purser's Clerk earlier—just marking time as a Schoolmaster until he found an opening in his real line of business. Gardner's other Schoolmaster was a naval institution in his day. Everyone knew poor Andrew McBride. Dillon served with him once, but it is Gardner who expatiates on him, and the tricks which all who knew him —and loved him—played upon him when he was drunk. This was his one failing, but it was a tragic one. He lasted for a surprisingly long time, mostly in ships on the West Indian station: but, falling a victim at last to the twin assaults of the bottle and Yellow Jack, he was buried at the Palisades in Jamaica (see p. 407). Gardner's epitaph is:

'He was one of the finest mathematicians in Europe: an excellent writer in prose and verse, an able disputant, and possessed of a mind remarkable for the strictest integrity. "Tread lightly on him ye men of genius, for he was your kinsman." '[2]

Boteler's Schoolmaster in the *Orontes* in 1813, though of coarser clay,

[1] N.R.S., Vol. XCI, p. 21.
[2] N.R.S., Vol. XXXI, p. 79.

had two of McBride's qualities—he was talented, and he drank too much. 'With very little trouble it floored him, and then—I don't much like to record it—we used to grease his head and flour it.' This was the one who ended up at Greenwich, where Boteler met him years afterwards, asked him to dine in his ship and inadvertently made him drunk again, so that he had to be 'wheeled in a barrow to the dock gates, put into a one-horse two-wheeled bus, the things plying between Deptford and Greenwich, and sent home'.[1]

The most unusual of these curious 'midshipmen', however, was the Schoolmaster who all but altered history. A few years before the war, Mr Mears was Schoolmaster of the *Pegasus*, a small frigate which would not normally carry such a person. But her Captain was Prince William Henry, later—but only because Mr Mears just failed to murder him—King William IV: and his Young Gentlemen were more than ordinarily select. Mears was a brilliant navigator and draughtsman, and, in addition to teaching the youngsters in the Prince's fore-cabin, he had free entry into it at all times as he was preparing a series of drawings for the Captain. Whether he was a drunkard is uncertain: but he was certainly a madman. He made two deliberate attempts upon the royal life. In the first he must have come within an ace of succeeding. Prince William awoke one evening from a nap in his cabin to find that the Schoolmaster 'had hold of my wrist with one hand and a penknife in the other'. On the Prince's saying, 'God, Mears! What are you about?' he muttered a futile explanation and withdrew. For some unaccountable reason nothing was done about it for the moment: but at about 1.30 next morning Mears reappeared on the Quarter-deck brandishing a large carving-knife. He charged the Captain's door with such force that, though it did not fly open, a panel was knocked in. But this time the danger was not so great. The ever-present sentry, a big but quick-thinking Marine named Vaughan, rushed at him and

'caught Mears under the chin with his powerful arm, throwing the little man to a distance of full five yards: whereupon the unfortunate maniac gave the most hideous screech that ever issued from the lungs of man'.[2]

After that they removed him first to Antigua, then to England.

Granted that they were not all Mearses, nor all McBrides, there is little doubt that, even when not maniacs or alcoholics, they were a pretty

[1] N.R.S., Vol. LXXXII, p. 96.
[2] Byam Martin, N.R.S., Vol. XXIV, p. 60.

poor lot. It was the old trouble. If one wants an article of reasonable quality, one must pay a reasonable price for it: and this the Admiralty would not do. There is little sign of improvement during our period, even after the change of 1812. In fact it was not till 1816 that the Schoolmaster's salary was raised above 'that of the youngest midshipman', and he was not made a Warrant Officer until 1836, though he was then given ward-room status too, and the title of 'Naval Instructor and Schoolmaster'. He was granted a proper salary only in 1840, when his bonus was abolished, and in 1842 he became plain 'Naval Instructor'. But he was again left behind when, in 1843, the other civilian officers began to be appointed by commission, and had to wait till 1861 before catching up with them again and becoming a fully-commissioned officer.

(d) *The Warrant Officers Not of Ward-room Rank*

We can now return to the strict Ship Hierarchy, and go in search of that hard core of the Warrant Officers—the age-old triumvirate of 'standing' officers to be found in every ship of war—the Gunner, the Boatswain and the Carpenter. There were other, and minor, Warrant Officers like the Sailmaker, the Ropemaker, the Armourer, the Caulker and the Cook, whose functions need no definition, and the Master-at-Arms, head of the Ship's police. These, say the Regulations of 1808, 'though appointed by warrant are to be considered as Petty Officers' in one important respect, the Captain can disrate them at will. So none of them had anything like the prestige of the Standing Officers, whose tenure was terminable only by the Admiralty. That word 'standing'—older than 'warrant'—describes one of their essential features. They were static; regarded almost as an integral part of the ship, like its 'standing rigging'. Captains and Lieutenants, appointed for one commission of the ship, came and went: the Standing Officers came, but did not go. Even when their ship was 'in ordinary' they were normally to be found residing on board complete with wife and family: and when they did move, it was almost always to a higher rate of ship, for that was their sole means of promotion. The Purser and the Master had once been Standing Officers too; but, though they still moved less frequently than the Commissioned Officers, they had lost a good deal of their original static quality. They had also, as we have seen, 'gone upstairs'—socially, navally and geographically—into the Ward-room. But the static Big Three had not. They had few ward-room qualities or even aspirations. They were, as they had always been, pure seamen.

(1) *The Gunner.* If we penetrate right aft on the Lower Deck of the *Gloucester*, past the Chaplain's little snuggery, we reach the Gun-room, under the Ward-room. Here our first Standing Officer, a local princeling, rules over his own little departmental clique or 'family' of mates and more or less permanent assistants. These quasi-independent coteries were common to all the Standing Officers. They had strong local loyalties of their own, which were at times something of a thorn in the flesh of inexperienced captains and lieutenants. But, unlike the Boatswain and the Carpenter, the Gunner looked after others besides his immediate 'family'. He was charged with the bodily welfare of the most junior of the embryo-officers—those youngest of Young Gentlemen who were called in the later days of the wars 'First Class Volunteers' and, in the earlier, 'Captains' Servants'—or by a large variety of other names (see p. 155).

How came they to live there? The simplest answer, perhaps, is that it was the natural place for them, all things considered. The more senior Midshipmen (or 'Oldsters', as opposed to these 'Youngsters') were—or considered themselves to be—young men; and some of them not so young either.[1] Their domicile in the After Cockpit, which we shall shortly visit, was notorious for noisy, riotous and not always pleasant orgies. Even to the hard-bitten eighteenth century it might seem no ideal nursery for well-brought-up children of, possibly, eight or nine years old but certainly not more than fourteen. Besides, the Oldsters themselves might feel uncomfortably restricted by the presence of such extreme youth. Also, though no one seems to have given much thought to hygiene, it may have occurred to someone that the Orlop deck, where the Cockpit lay, never had any natural light at all nor any air that could by any stretch of imagination be called fresh: whereas the Gunroom positively had windows which might, under favourable conditions, be opened. So, once it was conceded that the 'officers' nursery' must not be on the Orlop Deck, the Gunroom was clearly the best, if not the only, place for it. It was not quite Stygian, and it was 'aft'. Moreover the Gunner was almost always a steady sort of man, risen from the pick of the guns' crews and the Gunners' Mates: not 'gentle' of course, but who in that age wanted a 'gentle' nursemaid anyway? He sometimes, as we have seen, had the Schoolmaster to help him.

Gardner's Gunners confirm our good opinion of them. Of the four-

[1] Dillon usually calls them 'elderly mids'. See also pp. 267 and 301.

teen he served with, not one receives a really bad character. The worst is 'Crabbed': the next worst 'Fractious from long illness'—others besides Gunners are that. One is 'a very good man with a very bad wife'—but this is really one up for the Gunner. The rest emerge very well—'a very good warrant officer'; 'good sailor but used to damn his poor eyes so'—a venal offence, surely, in the eighteenth-century Navy: probably a pessimist, in sharp contrast to another who was 'one of the drollest fellows I ever met'. Again the emphasis throughout is on that blessed word 'respectable'. Two are 'very much respected', three more 'much respected —one of whom, inconsequentially enough, 'kept a stationer's shop at Plymouth Dock'.

No portrait of a contemporary Gunner, however, can touch the self-portrait of that worthy, amiable man so often quoted in these pages—William Richardson. Son of a merchant skipper from Shields, he rose the hard way: a merchant-service boy, apprentice, then mate: twice pressed, and for some years pure 'lower deck'. Yet not for very long, because, as his whole narrative reveals, here was a fine, honest, steady character, knowledgeable in almost all the branches of his profession, and so worthy of trust that, before long, he could hardly fail to attract the attention of his officers. For here at least the Lower Deck had a pull over the Quarter-deck. The officers wanted the best men as Petty and Warrant Officers, and therefore always chose the best. There was here but little outside Interest to distract the selector and to compel him to choose worse than he need have done. So Richardson became an Acting Gunner after only two years in the Navy, and a confirmed Gunner after four. Thereafter he continued as one for another twenty-two, when, to his great content, he was superannuated with a pension of £65 a year. Thenceforward, as it were, he 'lived happily ever after', at least, to the ripe old age of ninety-seven. He tells us—without undue self-pity, however—that he did not enjoy good appointments. Indeed, he spent the great bulk of his gunner-life in two ships, the *Tromp* and the *Caesar*. This failure to secure plum posts was due, he says, to his having but little Interest; and it is disquieting to learn that this particular poison worked even at Warrant Officer level. Yet this Interest was clearly less unhealthy than much of the Quarter-deck sort. All he really meant, probably, was that he did not happen to catch the eyes of influential Captains and Admirals. His long service in so few ships was, of course, typical of the 'standing' nature of his class.

He gives the impression that he never quarrelled with anyone, nor anyone with him. He criticized few people and few aspects of the Navy. He took what he found, and certainly made the best of it. Yet, even so, his book is a striking refutation of that school of thought which pretends that the whole Nelsonic Navy was run on brutality, terror and unhappiness.

(2) *The Boatswain.* To find our last two Standing Officers we have at last to cross our vertical dividing line into the men's domain. We have also to descend to the lantern-lit Orlop, and we shall find them both, well forward of the cut, each with his small 'family' and workshops. Socially they were much the same as the Gunner, certainly no higher, and like him bred-in-the-bone seamen nurtured 'before the mast'—especially the Boatswain, whose title was the oldest in the Navy, with a continuous salt-water history covering many centuries. Neither of them was highly renowned for scrupulous honesty where government stores were concerned, and here they stood some way below the Gunner. But again, as with the Purser, it was perhaps only a question of opportunity. Their stock-in-trade was very expendable—and convertible—consisting as it did of tar, rope, twine, wood of many sorts, nails, paint and other articles as useful off shipboard as on it. But the Gunner could not find so ready a market on shore for his broadside guns, his roundshot, rammers and sponges. They were not particularly useful to him in his own home, nor so easily removable from the ship. In fine, even if the Gunner had the will to purloin, he did not enjoy the opportunities of the other two.

The Boatswain in particular had the reputation of having both will and opportunity, and of not noticeably resisting the temptation. The eighteenth-century Navy even had a word for temptation not resisted. It was called 'cap-a-bar' (in the vernacular, 'Capperbar'), and it meant the misappropriation of government stores. The practice was not of course confined to Boatswains. Frederick Marryat has a glorious example in *The King's Own* of a certain *Captain* Capperbar—'who should have been brought up as a missionary, for he could convert anything': a fictional character naturally, exaggerated certainly, and probably always rare at Captain's level. But not at Boatswain's. Here Gardner helps us again: not so much with evidence concerning 'cap-a-bar', as those activities did not perhaps fall under his immediate eye; but as giving a general assessment of the breed. Their record, as he found them, was the worst of any. Of his examples, only one is 'much respected', though two are 'worthy'. Six are 'good seamen'—and doubtless most of them were, or had been, that. But two were 'broke by court-martial' (including one said to have been Paul Jones's boatswain). One was a 'snappish cur', and one (whose character for badness is nowhere exceeded by Gardner) was an 'infernal tyrant, sycophant, Hun, Goth and Vandal'. Four were alcoholics. And there was the famous Johnny Bone—a real character this time.

'He would stick at nothing. It is related that the late Lord Duncan, when he commanded the *Edgar*, once said to him, "Whatever you do, Mr Bone, I hope and trust you will not take the anchors from the bows." '[1]

Gardner's epitaph on Johnny is classic in its brevity:—

'Dead from drink. Cap-a-bar.'

Now had Gardner been 'lower deck', there would certainly have been more 'infernal tyrants' in his gallery; for the Boatswain was the hated man with the rattan cane and the pipes, whose combined efforts made the poor seamen jump to it at every hour of the day and, if necessary, of the night. He was also intimately associated in their minds with the 'cat', *via* his Mates, one of whose less pleasant duties was to inflict official corporal punishment. In fact, a gentle voice and a meek manner would have been as odd in a Boatswain as in an old-fashioned Sergeant-Major, and as unlikely to produce the maximum results. Still, there were a few such amiable people, and Robert Wilson knew one of them. He was a Mr Evans who, though he

'used a stick made of three canes marled together, which was called "the Three Sisters", . . . seldom ever used it of his own accord. He was not like the generality of Boatswains in the Service, who greatly pride themselves when they are cutting a caper over men . . . and who the moment they issue an order follow it with a stripe, when scarcely the sound of the order has vibrated in the men's ears. But Mr Evans was too quiet for our ship: therefore he was not long with us.'[2]

An unusual feature of this particular evidence is that the writer was not an officer but, at the time an ordinary seaman, rated signalman, whose office enabled him to see much that was going on, including the Boatswain's capers. He proceeds:

[1] N.R.S., Vol. XXXI, p. 70.
[2] N.R.S., Vol. XCI, p. 144.

'When Mr Stove joined us, and was heard blustering and swearing boatswain-like, "Ah!" says one of our officers, "that's him that will make our lads move."'

Incidentally it was a well-commanded friendly sort of ship. But Mr Evans was not quite unique: he can be matched by William Richardson's Mr Cooper:

'We subscribed two shillings apiece to buy Mr Cooper the Boatswain a silver call with chain and plate, with a suitable inscription on it for his kindness to the Ship's Company, and a silver pint-pot for his wife.'[1]

Richardson too was a seaman (newly pressed) at the time, as were all the other subscribers.

(3) *The Carpenter*. The Carpenter, on the other hand, could afford to be of the mild 'respected' type; and, if we may judge from Gardner, he usually was. His collective record is nearly as good as the Gunner's. 'Much respected', 'very much respected', 'highly respected', 'quiet good man, clever in profession', 'good man, no dandy', 'good man, good bread-and-butter carpenter', 'very worthy fellow', 'droll fellow', 'good timberhead of his own'. Just one, alas, was 'broken by court-martial'; and we may guess why—probably he overdid the 'cap-a-bar'. Yet the really expert scroungers were not the ship-carpenters but their brethren in the dockyards, the Shipwrights. In 1806 the Carpenter went ahead of his 'standing' colleagues in one not unimportant respect. In the three biggest rates of ship he was given more pay. The cause of this was probably economic. His labour was more skilled than theirs, at least than the Boatswain's. Clever turnery was probably in shorter supply than breezy bluster.

On no account must we underestimate the Standing Officers and their essential usefulness. Though the commissioned officers supplied most of the higher leadership, it was these humbler 'Warrants' who had to lick unpromising material into shape—and perhaps 'lick' is no inexpressive word. They had to forge a fine tough blade out of a mass of iron by no means free of impurities: and, by hardly ever failing, they constituted themselves the very backbone of the ships, and so of the Navy. They had always been there: they are still there. For the Branch Officers of yesterday and the Special Duties Officers of today are their direct descendants.

[1] Richardson, op. cit., p. 70.

(e) *The Midshipmen's Mess*

Recrossing the perpendicular dividing-line, we are back again in the After Cockpit, in a loaded ship rather below the water-level. This is what was usually known as 'the Midshipmen's Mess'. Its inhabitants formed a very mixed bag, and they would vary greatly in age. The most senior members were Master's Mates, who might be anything from fourteen—Dillon was one before he was fifteen—to forty or upwards, according to whether they were in the succession for Quarter-deck status, or merely ex-Lower Deck men who had risen to be the Master's assistants in the ordinary way. The most numerous of the occupants were the Midshipmen, whose age-range could be equally large, and for just the same reasons. But the proportion of 'Lower Deck' Midshipmen would be a good deal smaller than the proportion of 'Lower Deck' Master's Mates. By the date of our wars, most of the former were young fellows aspiring to commissions, and the forty-year-old Midshipman was becoming a rarity. By our time, in fact, both 'Midshipman' and 'Master's Mate' were fast becoming what they ultimately became—naval ranks pure and simple; the recognized steps in a Young Gentleman's passage from First Class Volunteer (or Captain's Servant) to Lieutenant. Still, it must be remembered that not all the After Cockpit's residents were Young Gentlemen yet: nor were they all considered as such.

So much for their wide social range. In the ship-hierarchy, however, they were officially much more uniform, and of much less account. They were all, as the correct Mr Cullen calls them, 'Petty Officers'—that is, that lowest grade of officer promotable (but also demotable) by the Captain. Not, of course, that he was in the least likely to demote Midshipman the Hon. X. Y., son of his own patron, Admiral Lord W. Z.—for reasons which need no enlargement here. But he had the right to do it, and, quite often, he did exercise his power on the less socially favoured.

We have not yet, however, met all the denizens of the After Cockpit. There might well be more Young Gentlemen there—those, that is, rated to any post other than one of the ordinary 'young gentleman' ratings—'Able Seaman' for instance. After all, when Nelson was 'rated Able' in the *Seahorse*, it would be unrealistic to suppose that he actually messed and slung his hammock with the men on the Lower Deck. Of course not: he was 'quarter-deck' and, for all his rating, lived with his social equals in the After Cockpit.

We have seen that there was no upper age-limit. The senior Master's

Mate might well be a shellback of the old sort who would never see forty again. But there was a lower limit. The youngest ought to have been at least thirteen. He would be a naval officer's son allowed to enter at eleven, and he should have spent two years under the Gunner's eye before becoming a Midshipman. And indeed, though these age-limits were among the deader of the dead-letters, perhaps we need not be too shocked by some of the things we read. Thus Mangin, discussing, quite dispassionately, some of the difficulties facing the Chaplain in the execution of his duties, mentions that 'there were multitudes of women in her [the *Gloucester*]; some quartered with the Midshipmen in the Cable-tier and Cockpit, the rest with the common men'. A picture squalid enough in any case, but only revolting if one is thinking in terms of curly-headed little Victorian 'middies' and twelve-year-old cadets. The reality was not quite so bad. A number of these women, no doubt, would be the Midshipmen's wives: and there is every reason to believe that the really young Youngsters always stayed upstairs with the Gunner. This was but commonsense. No one wanted them below—neither the Mates and 'Oldster' Midshipmen themselves, nor (more important still) the Captain whose protégés they were. Moreover, even when they grew old enough to sleep on the Orlop deck, they still remained juniors by Cockpit standards: and there existed in many ships the ceremony of 'the fork'. At the setting of the first watch, round about 8 p.m., the president of the mess drove a fork into the table or a bulkhead. This was the signal for all youngsters to clear out: to their hammocks if they liked, but anyway—*out*. To be allowed to remain 'after the fork' was something of a milestone in a youth's career. He felt he was getting somewhere.

There were other members, too, of this strangely assorted mess—the Schoolmaster, the Captain's Clerk, the Assistant Surgeons. Sometimes such betwixt-in-between people slung their hammocks one deck higher, as did the Schoolmaster in the *Alcide* and the Captain's Clerk in the *Gloucester*. But most of them messed with the Midshipmen and revelled with them o' nights: and, like Cullen, had to be prepared to look after themselves. For all our witnesses concur in the view that life in the After Cockpit was a crude sort of experience. How crude it was would depend upon circumstances. Much would hinge, naturally, upon the influence of the senior members, and that in its turn might well depend upon the relative strength of the two somewhat conflicting parties who inhabited the place. If a majority was 'gentle'—quarter-deck-bound youths—the atmosphere, though always apt to be rowdy, would be more civilized; less bearish than if a bevy of hard-bitten ex-seamen held sway. This again might well depend upon the kind of man the Captain was; for that dictated the kind of youngsters he liked to collect around him. Here we may take evidence again from the class-conscious Dillon. Thus in the *Alcide*, which had for captain the young, dashing, but for all that, conscientious, Sir Andrew Douglas,

'It was a truly pleasing circumstance to me to find that most of these young gentlemen were highly connected. The names of some of them will satisfy you, such as Byng, Herbert, Digby, Pigot and Ayscough.'[1]

Again, on joining the *Hébé*, commanded by that fine officer Sir Alexander Hood, he was immensely gratified with his company—'four fine young men'—which included two future Admirals of the Fleet and Nelson's own Captain Hardy, all then Oldsters. But then we learn what a change of Captains might do. In the *Defence* he was very comfortable under Captain Gambier, an ambitious man who always knew on which side his bread was buttered. But Gambier left, taking with him, as was his right, several of the best—and best-connected—Officers and Midshipmen. Then Captain Thomas Wells arrived, very junior and evidently a mover in much humbler circles. His new First Lieutenant

'had a provincial twang in his speech which occasionally made one smile. Some of the Mids did not cut much of a figure as gentlemen. They were rough seamen "from before the mast" as the naval saying goes. Altogether our change did not appear to advantage.'

He thereupon got his father to pull a string or two, and soon left the ship to rejoin Gambier. But the fates pursued him. Gambier became a Lord of the Admiralty and was succeeded by Sir John Orde who 'brought with him his followers from the *Venerable*, 74. Several of the Mids were from the Merchant Service. They did not cut a good figure as gentlemen.' This time, feeling it unwise to try and engineer another move, young Dillon had to take other steps. With the remainder of his own cronies, he changed over 'from the Larboard to the Starboard Berth, leaving the other to be occupied by Sir John's friends whose society did not suit us'. Once there, his party gave the newcomers a very cold shoulder. Class-consciousness being what it then was, this was probably a common enough solution of that particular social problem.

[1] N.R.S., Vol. XCIII, p. 21.

(f) *The Men*

Our investigation aft of the vertical cut is now complete. It remains to climb up one level to the Lower Deck again, and turn our faces forward. Here we shall find none but marines and seamen, with such petty officers as have been promoted by the Captain from among them, but who have not attained to the dignity even of the After Cockpit. There were dozens of these Petty Officers, but they were, socially, little above 'common men', and, navally, merely regarded as the most trustworthy specimens of that breed. Among them were the Mates of all the departmental officers other than the Master's, the Quartermasters, (who often had the 'privilege' of sleeping among the cables on the Orlop), the Ship's Corporals, the Yeomen, of the sheets and of the powder room, the Steward, the Trumpeter and (though once a full Warrant Officer) the Cook, who was a pensioner seldom in possession at once of both arms, both legs and both eyes. These men had their messes on the Lower Deck, and slept either there or in the cable-tiers below, their superior standing securing for them the more favoured corners.

This Lower Deck, stretching forward from the mizzen mast to where the barrier which enclosed the Manger ran athwartships near the bows, has often been described at length, with its notorious discomforts, its stench, its all-but constant gloom, its perennial dampness. The sorry catalogue of them will not be repeated here. We will merely examine some of the Lower Deck's functions, as they affected the men who had to make the best of it. It was, all in all, the most important part of the ship, not only because of the multitude which lived there, but also because it housed the main battery of the ship—the 32-pounder guns. These, then (with the wherewithal to fire them), and the men (with the simplest of living-necessaries) were inextricably involved with one another in this far-from-large space. Add for good measure the huge rope cables which, entering at the hawseholes in the bows, passed right down the centre of the deck to nearly the mainmast before disappearing into the cable-tiers below. With so much on hand, there might have been chaos on the Lower Deck. But there never was. In all well-regulated ships, by day and between mealtimes, there were the guns and their impedimenta, with two long gangways, empty of all gear, running from end to end of the deck. All had to be ready for instant action. Yet, also, the bare furnishings for a series of primitive dining-rooms were always there. When hands were piped to dinner, down came a host of legless tables, hooked till then to the beams above. Each accommodated, tucked as cosily as possible between the guns, a 'mess', normally of eight men: and, quite often, canvas screens could be fixed up—entirely temporary of course—between mess and mess, in order to ensure a little privacy. As regards these messes, custom and the decision of authority, wise for once, had sought to secure a modicum of personal happiness for the otherwise neglected men. Samuel Leech thus describes the arrangement in the *Macedonian* in 1811:

'These [the individual messes] eat and drink together, and are, as it were, so many families.The mess to which I was introduced was composed of your genuine weatherbeaten old tars. But for one of its members it would have suited me very well: this one, a real gruff old "bull-dog" named Hudson, took into his head to hate me at first sight. He treated me with so much abuse and unkindness that my mess mates soon advised me to change my mess, a privilege which is wisely allowed, and which tends very much to the good fellowship of a ship's crew: for if there are disagreeable men among them, they can in this way be got rid of. It is no infrequent case to find a few, who have been spurned from all the messes in the ship, obliged to mess by themselves.'[1]

According to Ebenezer Collins, 'late of the Brazilian Navy under Lord Cochrane', who contributed notes to Leech's 1844 edition, the Navy had a name for these lower-deck pariah-dogs. They were called 'galley-rangers', and they were generally gluttons.

But now night has come, and the aspect of the Lower Deck is changed again. It has become a nearly solid lump of humanity, slung in hammocks from the beams. The standard width allowed per man was 14 in. This seems impossible, because the standard man would be more than 14 in. wide. But in fact they hardly ever had to pack so close. Experience had long since found an expedient. The starboard and larboard watches into which the Ship's Company was divided worked alternate shifts, and so were not below together. If, then, the men of one watch alternated with men of the other, each person could spread over 28 in. This, though not exactly luxurious, at least made the thing a possibility. Some Captains—like the author of Observations and Instructions quoted on page 238—used a three-watch system. Our informant does not say, however, how he disposed his men for sleeping. Nor does he say where he put the Marines, though, by 1807, the practice had become almost universal of causing them to mess and sling their hammocks aftermost

[1] Leech, op. cit., p.13.

TABLE VI

'FOR WATCHING THE SHIP'S COMPANY OF EVERY RATE'

(Abbreviated from *Observations and Instructions for Officers*, p. 55)

RATES	1st	2nd	3rd (medium)	4th	5th (large '32' frigate)	6th (medium)	Sloops
Number of Guns	100	90	74	50	32	24	18
Full Complement	839	738	590	349	254	175	121
Forecastle-men	60	51	45	30	18	13	9
Fore-top-men	63	50	45	30	21	16	9
Main-top-men	69	54	51	36	24	18	12
Mizen-top-men	27	18	18	12	9(?)	—	—
After-guard	94	80	60	30	36	25	12
Waisters	171	151	115	39	22	14	6
Quarter-masters	13	13	9	7	5	4	3
Quarter-gunners	30	30	19	13	9	7	5
Carpenter's Crew	13	11	8	6	5	4	2
Boatswain's Mates and Yeomen of the Sheets	8	8	6	4	3	2	1
Total Number Watched	548	466	376	207	152	103	59
Number of Officers, Marines, Servants, Idlers, and Widows' Men...	291	272	214	142	102	72	62

of all Lower Deck inhabitants—that is, between the seamen and the officers. It is not very clear how old this custom was, but that it was not universal before 1800 seems evident from the fact that, in this year, Lord St. Vincent succinctly ordered that they should 'be berthed close aft to the gun-room netting, without any seamen mixed with them'—the latter, it must be presumed, lest evil communications should corrupt good manners.[1] It was doubtless the many mutinies of the late 'nineties which standardized this arrangement. St. Vincent, as we have seen, was a great believer in the Marines; and it was he who had secured from the King their epithet of 'Royal'.

A few Captains even tried a four- (or quarter-) watch system, which, Watson tells us, was very popular with the men because 'at sea, we often could lie in our hammocks all night'.[2]

This relegation of the people into separate watches was not the only way in which the Ship's Company was broken up into smaller units. They were also sorted into 'divisions', a fairly recent innovation but an altogether admirable one which has lasted to this day. Each division was a cross-section of the whole crew, with its own Lieutenant specifically charged to look after it. Under that Lieutenant, a division was often allotted some special duty inside or outside the ship—to navigate a prize to port, assist another ship in distress, do a job in a dockyard, board an enemy. Unquestionably this Divisional System led to a much better cared-for crew, and its greater efficiency.

Every man, then, was in a division: but not everyone was in a watch. Our 1807 Captain shows a 'Table for Watching the Ship's Company in every Rate', which gives such a good picture of how a contemporary crew was disposed for everyday work that it is reproduced, in abbreviated form, in Table VI. It will be noticed that, in first-rates, a bare two-thirds of the total complement were 'watched', while in sloops less than one-half was. Those not so detailed were the officers, marines, servants (real ones), boys, widows' men and idlers. The first four of these categories are self-explanatory: with widows' men we are already acquainted (see p. 139). The name 'idler' was often given, in ordinary ship-parlance, to anyone who did not have to turn out when a watch was called: and we have found even officers so named (cf. p. 231). But the true 'idlers' were of altogether lower status: some of them very low indeed. We must not be tempted, of course, to take the name literally:

[1] *Britain's Sea-Soldiers*, by Col. C. Field, 1924, Vol. I, p. 204.
[2] Watson, op. cit., p. 70.

in that sense idleness was unknown on board, and quite impossible. The 'Captain of the Royal Navy' gives a list of them (p. 54). They were (the figures in brackets after each name indicating the number allowed in a first-rate):

Master-at-Arms (1), Ship's Corporal (3), Armourer (1), his Mates (3), Sailmaker and Mates (4), Holders (6),[1] Cooper (2), Boatswain's, Gunner's and Carpenter's Yeomen (1 each), Lady of the Gunroom (1),[2] Captain Sweeper (1), Sentinel at the Sick Berth and Loblolly-boy (3),[3] Admiral's Servant (3), Admiral's Cook (2), Butcher (2), First Captain's Servant (1), Second Captain's Servant (1), Ward-room Servant (3), Ward-room Cook (2), Hairdresser (2), Ship's Barber (2), Painter (1), Poulterer (1), Tailor (2), Purser's Steward and Assistant (3), Captain of the Head and Mate (2)[4], Ship's Cook (3), Fifer (1), Caulker (2), Writer to the First Lieutenant (1). Total, 62.

It is not pleasant to linger over horrors. Yet we are out to delineate life on the Lower Deck during our period, and must not altogether evade our duty. What, then, was the state of the Lower Deck on, say, the first dirty night when a newly commissioned ship was beating down-Channel into a stiff wind and a heavy sea—rolling, pitching, lurching, wallowing, shuddering? Not by any means all the Able and Ordinary seamen were good sailors, and it may be presumed that most landmen, Quota-men, etc., were bad ones. No one had found his sea-legs—some (and Nelson among them) never did. Let imagination hover for an instant over that tightly-wedged wad of retching men who could not even swing in their hammocks. Or again, let it envisage a very common occurrence on some stations—a widespread outbreak of bowel-trouble among the seamen whose only 'accommodation' was the wind-buffeted,

[1] 'The people employed in stowing the Hold.' Falconer.

[2] 'A steady seaman always stationed at the entrance of the Gunroom to prevent improper intruders.' Dillon.

[3] 'The man who attends the Surgeon and his Mates to . . . perform any service in their attendance on them (the sick).' Falconer.

[4] 'The Head' (in Falconer's delicate phraseology) is 'that part on each side of the stem which is appropriated to the private use of sailors'. The men had no conveniences in-board. Their seniors and the sick, however, had their 'round-houses'—'two convenient places near the head of the ship the one on the larboard side being appropriated to the private use of the Mates, Midshipmen and Warrant Officers; and the other on the starboard side to the use of those in the sick-bay' (Falconer). For the accommodation of the Ward-room officers, see p. 234.

wave-washed bows far overhead. Let us at least think, without attempting to put our thoughts into words, what *happened*. Having done that, perhaps we shall have some inkling of what Dr. Johnson meant when he delivered himself of his famous dictum about a ship being worse than a gaol: and, at the same time, we should the more honour the memory of those who stuck it out through the years.

But now the night is over. The next metamorphosis is due. There is not a moment lost: there cannot be, and Leech tells us why. In every aspect of ship life

'. . . each task has its man, and each man his place. A ship contains a set of *human* machinery in which every man is a wheel, a band or a crank, all moving with wonderful regularity and precision to the *will* of its machinist—the all-powerful Captain.'[1]

He gives several pictures of the machine at work, ending with one which shows the transformation of the 'dormitory' into the 'gun-deck'.

The Boatswain's sharp shrill whistle is heard, then his hoarse rough cry of 'All hands ahoy!' followed by 'Up all hammocks ahoy!' The Boatswain's Mates take up the cry and hurry below, each armed with a rope's end. The least delay on the part of a sleepy seaman is now extremely painful.

'With a rapidity which would surprise a landsman, the crew dress themselves, lash their hammocks and carry them on deck, where they are stowed for the day.[2] There is system even in this arrangement: every hammock has its appropriate place. Below, the beams are all marked, each hammock is marked with a corresponding number, and in the darkest night a seaman will go unhesitatingly to his own hammock. They are also kept exceedingly clean. Every man is provided with two, so that while he is scrubbing and cleaning one he may have another to use. Nothing but such precautions could enable so many men to live in so small a space.'

His editor (Collins) here adds a note:

'When Lord Cochrane commanded the *Jessamine* in the West Indies every hammock was passed through a hoop previous to being stowed

[1] Leech, op. cit., p. 14.

[2] In the hammock-cloths or nettings stretched along the bulwarks of Quarter-deck and Waist.

away; and woe betide the luckless wight to whom that hammock belonged that would not pass through the circumscribed space.'

He might have added that here was a fine example of ship-hygiene, based no doubt on the experience of centuries rather than on conscious medical forethought. The standards of hammock cleanliness were doubly high. The articles were not only constantly washed: they were also constantly aired! Probably, too, they were constantly damp—and rheumatic complaints of various kinds were always rife in ships—but one cannot hope for everything.

In an efficient ship with a hard-driving First Lieutenant, a hardbitten Boatswain and his hard-hitting mates, the transition from a sleeping ship to a fully operational one had to be seen to be believed. Dillon, when he was 'working up' a crew, contrived after a little practice to cut the operation down from thirty minutes to four and a half. Having once done this, he had a five-minute glass prepared which began to register on the first note of the Boatswain's call. When it ran out a bell was struck, and any man whose hammock was not up, correctly folded and stowed, found himself on the defaulters' list.[1] Here with a vengeance is Leech's human machine and its omnipotent machinist.

Oddly enough, the men did not seem to resent this kind of hustling *per se*. All depended upon the way in which it was done, and the personality of the man who did it. The whole system was such that the men expected to be driven, and seldom respected, or even seemed to want, any real laxity. Here is the testimony of a real old shellback, who spent his whole service life on the Lower Deck:

'. . . . I would always choose a ship in which every duty was attended to strictly, in preference to one in which a man did almost as he liked. Indeed, I've frequently heard old seamen say (when two ships were in commission and both wanting hands), "I'll go with Captain——: he's a taut one, but he is Captain of his own ship." '[2]

In fact, the seamen remained throughout our period the same strange, unpredictable, slightly uncouth collection of people they had always been, most unlike their land-contemporaries. Many of the latter, it is true, were now drafted into the fleet, but not in numbers which could materially alter the mixture, so that, on the whole, the new took on the colour of the old rather than *vice versa*.

[1] N.R.S., Vol. XCVII, p. 296.
[2] Béchervaise, *Farewell*, p. 56.

So much for life on ordinary days. But the great days for which all warships existed were, of course, those on which an enemy was sighted. For this climax the ship and her people had been training all the time. There must be no confusion then. Everyone must know exactly where to go and what to do. Our 1807 Captain records how, in his ship, he disposed all his men, by name and number, to Quarters: that is, Action-Stations. His list is too long and complex to reproduce here, but he has a smaller table which shows exactly where all the officers were to be found in a first-rate when, every trace of peaceful occupation having been bundled overboard or below, the long gun-decks lay clear from bow to stern, lest anything should impede the great ship's fire-power. Here is a summary of it. The figures in brackets at the end of each row indicate the number of men (over and above officers) at each action-station.

POOP. Captain of Marines and his 3 Lieutenants. (12 Marines).
FORECASTLE. 9th Lieutenant, Boatswain, 1 Mate, 1 Midshipman. (20).
QUARTER-DECK. Captain, 1st Lieutenant, Master, 2 Midshipmen. (55).
MAIN DECK. 4th and 8th Lieutenants, 1 Mate, 4 Midshipmen. (150).
MIDDLE DECK. 3rd and 7th Lieutenants, 1 Mate, 5 Midshipmen. (180).
LOWER DECK. 2nd and 6th Lieutenants, 2 Mates, 6 Midshipmen. (225).
AFTER COCKPIT. Surgeon, his Mates, and Chaplain. (4).
STORE-ROOMS. No officer. (4).
MAGAZINES. Gunner. (23).
LIGHT-ROOM. Master-at-Arms, Ship's Cook. (1).
SIGNALS PARTY. 5th Lieutenant, 1 Mate, 3 Midshipmen. (6).
'TO TAKE MINUTES'. 1 Clerk. (0).
'AIDES DE CAMP'. (attending on Captain and 1st Lieutenant), 3 Midshipmen. (0)
'HANDING OF POWDER'. Purser. (42).
FORE, MAIN AND MIZZEN TOPS. No officer. (7).

The Marines, we saw, were not 'watched': but of course they were 'quartered'. There were 120 of them, and they are all included in the above figures. Our 1807 Captain's Quarter-bill shows how they were disposed. They were not, as is sometimes assumed, all drawn up on deck with their small-arms: that would have overcrowded it seriously. In fact there were no small-arms men on the Quarter-deck, nor on the Forecastle, and only twelve, with all their officers, on the Poop. The rest were distributed in ones, twos and occasionally threes, among all the guns' crews, acting usually as powder-men. The guns' crews varied in strength—there were ten for the Main Deck 18-pounders, twelve for the Middle Deck 24-pounders and fourteen for the Lower Deck's 32-pounders—and each crew worked two guns, one on the starboard side, the other opposite to it on the larboard side. It was seldom necessary to man both at once, and one particularly competent man, called the First Captain, had immediate command of the team and of the gun in use: but there was also a Second Captain who looked after the other gun when both came into action together. On Main and Middle Decks a Mate or a Midshipman had charge of six guns each—three on each broadside—but on the Lower Deck they were responsible for only four each. The two Lieutenants on each gun-deck supervised half the guns each.

They were all in it now, every man and boy of them; and in a ship which, though huge to them, would appear but small to us, their numbers were surprisingly large. The full complement of a First-rate was—One Captain, twenty-four Officers (Commissioned and Warrant), thirty-one potential Officers (Mates, Midshipmen and Clerk), forty Boys (1st, 2nd and 3rd classes), eight Widows' Men (or sixteen, according to the size of the Navy), and 736 'Men Quartered'. Total, 840.

Of the many generalizations on the character of our seamen which survive, the one which still penetrates most deeply is a passage from old Richard Braithwaite's *Whimzies*:

'The breadth of an inch-board is betwixt him and drowning, yet hee swears and drinks as deeply as if hee were a fathom from it. His familiarity with death and danger hath armed him with a kind of dissolute security against any encounter.'

These words were written in 1631, so that they may be suspected of being dated: but, if so, in minor ways only. After all, the general conditions of life afloat had not materially changed since Braithwaite's day. Our seaman was a little less uncouth, a little less isolated and, after 1797, a shade more sophisticated. But when in danger he still alternated oath and prayer with marvellous impartiality, like the men who so shocked Dillon's Chaplain in the *Glory*: and he was still essentially a fatalist at heart, like the seaman who contrived to shock even the liberal Mangin. This man had fallen overboard and—but only after a desperate struggle—had sunk for the third time when a skilful rescuer followed him down with a boathook and caught him by the collar. After several hours of unconsciousness he recovered. Next day he was on duty, behaving exactly as though nothing had happened. Mangin, who saw the whole thing and doubtless talked to him afterwards, has this comment:

'. . . it was perfectly impossible to discover that he was in the smallest degree perplexed by the prospect of death, or exhilarated by his preservation.'[1]

Another contemporary, named William Robinson, writing under the pseudonym of Jack Nastyface, tells how two of his friends passed their time during that harrowing period when our ships were bearing down upon the Combined Fleet at Trafalgar. All who had anything to do were busily doing it. Nelson, all orders given, was on his knees. But these men, perforce idle at their guns,

'were making a sort of mutual verbal will, such as, if one of Johnny Crapaud's shots knocks my head off, you will take all my effects; and if you're killed and I'm not, why, I'll have yours!'[2]

There was, however, one very marked characteristic of the Nelsonic seaman that it were shame to omit. This was his essential loyalty: personal loyalty to his own mates always, and (if they deserved it) to his officers. Endless illustrations are forthcoming: but let us close with just two, both from Richardson: one concerning his equals, one his superiors. In his first naval ship, when he was still a newly-pressed rating, an excitable Welshman, in a drunken frolic ashore in Bombay, smashed a valuable bowl. He was cast into prison and could be released only if the exorbitant price put on the bowl was raised. No one on the Lower Deck had much cash—Richardson had just sold his watch to defray his share of his mess. None the less—in Richardson's matter-of-fact prose—'Therefore the Ship's Company subscribed 800 rupees (a great sum for the value of the bowl) and paid the owner for it.' That 'therefore' is surely a most revealing word.

The other passage concerns a 'happy ship'. What a wise man he was! Twice he paraphrases Collingwood's equally cogent dictum—'when a mutiny takes place on board a ship, it must be the fault of the Captain or officers'. And here is the reverse of the same medal:

'So I left the "happy *Prompte*", a ship where there was none of your browbeating allowed, nor that austere authority where two men durst hardly to be seen speaking together (as I have seen since in the Service). The

[1] N.R.S., Vol. XCI, p. 27.
[2] *Nautical Economy, or Forecastle Recollections*, 1836.

Prompte's crew was like a family united, and would, both officers and men, risk their lives to assist each other. This I know well, having belonged to her more than five years in continual active service and on many trying occasions too.'

'Risk their lives'; 'Officers *and* Men'; 'having *belonged* to her'!

(g) *The Women*

We have now been in all the inhabited parts of the ship, visiting everyone, from the lordly, lonely Captain in his spacious suite aft to the Common People herded far below on the steamy, reeking Lower Deck. But have we made the acquaintance of everyone? Well, perhaps not quite: for when we visited the men they may not have let us catch a glimpse of *their* guests, especially if the ship were at sea when we called. These were the Women, who maybe were not there at all. Yet maybe they were.

This raises a big if not very edifying subject. When Mangin complained of the embarrassment which the women's presence occasioned him, there was nothing that he could do about it. These female invasions were perfectly legal so long as the ship was in port. Sometimes too they were allowed to remain, with the Captain's sanction, between home-port and home-port: but not when the ship was at sea and 'operational'—that is, cruising for an enemy.

In port the problem was evidently a thorny one for all Captains. They tackled it each according to his temperament and character. A few took the high moral line. James Gambier, for example, that noted evangelical, made himself extremely unpopular in 1793 when, on taking command of the *Defence*, he insisted that all the women on board should show their marriage lines.

'Those that had any produced them: those that had not contrived to manufacture a few. This measure created a very unpleasant feeling among the tars.'[1]

And well it might, for such concern over his men's morals was most unusual in a contemporary Captain. Much commoner was the line taken by Captain Prince William Henry, whose orders for the *Andromeda* survive:

'*Order the* 8*th*, requesting and directing the First Lieutenant . . . to see all

[1] N.R.S., Vol. XCIII, p. 96.

strangers out of H.M. ship under my command at gunfire, is by no means meant to restrain the officers and men from having either black or white women on board through the night, so long as the discipline is unhurt by the indulgence.'[1]

Moreover, the Prince was quite as strict a disciplinarian as Gambier, though in a very different way. His order continues:

'The First Lieutenant is to pay the strictest attention that, upon the likelihood of H.M. ship under my command proceeding to sea, every woman is sent ashore, *unless he has received instructions in that behalf from the Captain.*'[1]

The italics are the author's, not the Prince's. The words make one think. It is unusual to provide for exceptions which never arise. It would indeed be instructive to know when, and for whom, His Royal Highness made exceptions which permitted a direct breach of his Royal Father's regulations.

A last example. Captain Richard Keats was a more intelligent man than either Gambier or Prince William: probably, too, a much better Captain. He seems to have made a virtue of necessity, and tried to extract at least something out of a radically evil system. In effect, he made a woman, as it were, a reward for a good seaman: and, per contra, if the seaman were a bad seaman, he stopped his woman, in much the same was as a modern Captain would stop a defaulter's leave. In his orders, he allowed women on board, in port, 'in proportion to the merits of the men who require them'. But he was nothing if not thorough. He believed in obedience to his own orders. So he furnished his Master-at-Arms with a printed form, to be filled up and presented every morning to himself. Its headings were—1. 'Woman's Name': 2. 'With whom': 3. 'Married or Single': 4. 'When received on board': 5. 'Conduct'.[2]

The whole question presents great difficulties. That the women were a very considerable menace, to discipline no less than to morals, is clear enough: for, apart altogether from the latter, many of them were notorious smugglers of liquor—and that into a place where drunkenness (as opposed to licentiousness) was a naval crime of a serious order, punishable with the cat. Yet it is hard to believe that the Gambier approach was the correct one. For all Leech's analogy, the men were not machines, and Gambierism did not work: it was defeated by petty

[1] N.R.S., Vol. XXIV, Appendix A., p. 347.
[2] *Mariner's Mirror*, Vol. VII, p. 317.

frauds. It was obviously aiming at a moral standard altogether too high for the people with whom it dealt. A really disgruntled crew was dangerous, because the line between obedience and mutiny was by no means impassable. David Hannay told a humorous story—a story only, he was careful to explain—which he had from his sailor father. It concerned a Gambier-like Captain of 1840 who refused to allow women on board at any time. His crew mutinied. The Captain made his report to the Admiral, a veteran of the wars, whose language when he read it was too blue to print. But what he *did* was to make the signal 'Send 200 women from the —— to the ——.' And the mutiny ended.[1]

The real trouble, of course, is crystal clear. It lay far deeper—in the whole illogical system of indiscriminate pressing, with its corollary of not allowing the men shore-leave when in port.[2]

So much, then, for the women aboard ships in harbour. But this is not all. They certainly went to sea too: not in anything like the same numbers, but still they went, clean contrary to regulation. The actual stowing away must have been quite easy. In the confusion of clearing ship before getting under way, it cannot have been hard to secrete a wife or light-o'-love from the eye of the preoccupied First Lieutenant. How often this happened it is impossible to say, but odd instances of women aboard turn up so regularly, and often so unexpectedly, that the thing cannot have been a rarity. Sometimes they were unexpectedly useful too. When Dillon's frigate, the *Horatio*, was once cruising operationally, she ran on to a needle-rock off Guernsey. She floated off and, leaking furiously, headed for home. Thereupon several women, hitherto unmentioned, appeared from nowhere, and they 'rendered essential service in thrumming the sail' which was lowered over the hole in the ship's bottom. But the sequel was tragic, as we shall hear later.

Other examples may be cited, though undoubtedly many are lost beyond recall. One good reason for this is that that normal source of

[1] *Mariner's Mirror*, Vol. IV, p. 181.

[2] A worse, but probably inevitable, result of thus forcing upon the men such unnatural abstinence was a considerable crop of homosexual offences. The Courts Martial of the period include a good many cases of sodomy on the Lower Deck, in spite of the ferocious punishment of death inflicted upon those found guilty. The memoir-writers hardly ever mention the subject, but Dillon records one case (II. 124) and probably another (II. 307). Both culprits were convicted and executed. About officers, they are even more reticent: indeed, all but mute. Yet again Dillon has one instance of a friendship which can hardly have been other than homosexual, though there is no evidence that it was anything but innocent. (*Narrative*, MS. Vol. I, p. 293.)

information, the Muster Book, is always silent here. The female was not 'rated', therefore her name is not 'on the books'. Yet some individual cases are authentic enough. There was certainly a woman in the *Defiance* at Trafalgar. Her name was Jane Townshend and, forty-two years later, she proved her claim to the General Service Medal. Further, Queen Victoria herself said that she should have it, though the Admiralty got out of giving it to her on grounds of dangerous precedent—it would, they alleged, 'leave the Army exposed to *innumerable* applications'.[1] Likewise, there were certainly two women present at the battle of the Nile—Ann Hopping and Mary Ann Riley—whose claims were not denied, but refused for the same reason. Now only those still living in 1847 could claim the medal, and many years—no less than forty-nine in the case of the Nile—had elapsed. If then there were still three certainties alive, it would be reasonable to assume that there were more, even if we had not John Nicol's word for it that there were several more. At the Nile, his action-station was the powder-magazine of the *Goliath*, under the Gunner.

'Any information we got was from the boys and the women who carried the powder. The women behaved as well as the men . . . I was much indebted to the Gunner's wife who gave her husband and me a drink of wine every now and then. . . . Some of the women were wounded, and one woman belonging to Leith died of her wounds. One woman bore a son in the heat of action: she belonged to Edinburgh.'[2]

There is another circumstance that has sometimes puzzled people. Daniel Maclise, in his well-known picture 'The Battle of Trafalgar', showed a group of personable women tending the wounded on the *Victory's* Quarter-deck. The painting is not contemporary, dating only from 1863, and it is to be feared that these ministering angels are the fruits of the artist's imagination: not because they are shown as being in the ship at the time—the fact that their names are not in the Muster Book proves nothing. What, however does seem fairly certain is that, if there, they would not have been on the Quarter-deck, but down in the bowels of the ship, on the Orlop, or, like Nicol's women, carrying powder to the gun-decks.

So far the problem has been considered mainly as it affected the men. Little has been told of the officers, save that the Captains sometimes

[1] W. B. Rowbotham, *Mariner's Mirror*, Vol. XXIII, p. 366.
[2] John Nicol, pp. 193–4.

took their wives and daughters with them, or brother-officers' families 'to oblige', or 'public' guests paid for by the State. All such cases were regarded as quite respectable and scarcely worthy of comment. Yet there is no reason to suppose that officers were exempt from the *general* regulation forbidding the carriage of females in operational ships. But, again, this does not mean that they always obeyed it. They certainly did not. Even ladies (as opposed to 'females') turn up in most unlooked-for places. One such odd case was the presence of Mrs. Fremantle at Nelson's assault on Teneriffe in 1797. This expedition, one would have thought, was as 'operational' as it could be: yet there was 'Betsy' on board her husband's operational frigate *Seahorse*, not only tolerated by the officer commanding the expedition but, being a great favourite of his, openly welcomed.

This, however, though odd to our way of thinking, was yet quite respectable. At least the lady was a wife and a bride. But other 'ladies' sometimes found aboard were distinctly less so. The crop of them is small but not at all creditable to those concerned. All, of course, would depend (as usual) upon the attitude of the Captain. If he winked at any irregularity—well, as far as his ship was concerned, it became regular. This presumably happened in the *Pickle* in 1808, where a Lieutenant had a female with him in the Mediterranean. Collingwood, the Commander-in-Chief, heard of it and curtly ordered her home—she to pay her passage—delivering himself of a scornful 'I never knew a woman brought to sea in a ship that some mischief did not befall the vessel'.[1] But he seems to have taken no step to discipline either the Lieutenant or his Captain. If the Captain himself was the delinquent, there was presumably no more to be said. Dillon mentions a case in 1809. He too was scornful of a Captain who had with him in the *Camilla* 'a kept mistress, a companion that did not do much honour to his station'.[2] But there is no record of anyone in authority intervening. Nor, as far as we know, was official displeasure ever conveyed to Captain Richard Bennet of the *Fame*. Watson, as a raw Lower-deck volunteer of 16, had him as his first captain in 1808, and thought very highly of him, both as officer and individual. So did the whole Ship's Company: yet

'nearly all the time he was with us there was a Miss Jen—gs on board as his mistress, and had left England with him. She was a lovely-looking

[1] N.R.S., Vol. XCVIII, p. 251.
[2] N.R.S., Vol. XCVII, p. 140.

woman and modest in a great degree, compared with the majority who ploughed the seas on the same footing.'[1]

And this was not all. On arriving at Minorca, she was sent home, and instantly replaced by a fascinating Spanish brunette with black, brilliant eyes: who, by all accounts, conformed much more nearly to the norm of sea-ploughing ladies, for she also had affairs with handsome midshipmen, and even practised her charms—unsuccessfully, he says—on young Watson himself.

In non-operational ships too all depended upon the Captain's attitude. Here extraordinary things could happen. Wives could be allowed openly and wholesale, and even at sea. Dillon had his wife and step-daughter with him in the troop-ship *Leopard* for a long time—his step-daughter till he got her married off to one of his Lieutenants, his wife for longer still. Moreover, not only did the wives of commissioned officers go, but those of warrant officers too, and even of men: and not only wives but whole families, and for long cruises. Richardson quotes an instance which seems to beat all records. When Gunner of the two-decker *Tromp*, he went in her to the West Indies in 1800. She was a properly commissioned ship of the Royal Navy, though not strictly operational as she was carrying stores for our forces out there. His wife decided to accompany him, which was not so strange, as the ship, when laid up, was her natural home (see p. 261). He demurred at first, not because of any irregularity in taking her, but because of the known unhealthiness of their destination—Martinique. However,

'after some entreaty I gave my consent, especially as the Captain's, the Master's, the Purser's and the Boatswain's wives were going with them: the Sergeant of Marines and six other men's wives had leave to go'.[2]

For good measure, it transpired later that the Boatswain had embarked his whole family, while the Captain's lady soon augmented the Ship's Company by 'being delivered of a fine boy'. It is only fair to the gallant Captain's memory, however, to record that this exceedingly young Young Gentleman's name does not appear on the books: nor, like the infant Walker, did he draw a Volunteer Bounty (see p. 168). As for the wives, for them, poor souls, Collingwood's gloomy views about women in ships proved only too right. They ran into a yellow fever epidemic, and very few returned.

[1] Watson, op. cit., p. 71.
[2] Richardson, op. cit., pp. 169, 170.

There is another category altogether of 'women-on-board'. A few—but probably a very few—actually masqueraded as men and did seamen's work. The most famous case, a little before our wars, was that of the doughty Hannah Snell, who served for at least five years as soldier, marine and seaman, and at Pondicherry was wounded, it is said, in twelve places (from one of which, if she would avoid discovery, she had to remove the bullet herself). She was never detected: when her ship came home she revealed her sex and received an annuity. But she came somewhat earlier—she died just as our wars started. During this period, probably, the majority of such heroines as have been recorded owed much to the sea-novelists and balladmongers. There is indeed a very romantic theme to be extracted from the faithful Susan who

Put on a jolly sailor's dress
And daubed her hands with tar
To cross the raging sea
On board a man o' war,

into which, naturally, her William had been pressed. Yet there are some real cases. The Annual Register of 1807 (p. 496) records one which came out during a court martial on a certain Lieutenant Berry:

'One of the witnesses in this awful and horrible trial was a little female tar, Elizabeth Bowden, who has been on board the *Hazard* these eight months. She appeared in court in a long jacket and blue trousers.'

She masqueraded, presumably, as a Boy. But there was certainly one who did not, and who must hold an easy record for length of deception. 'William Brown' was proved in 1815 to have served in the *Queen Charlotte* for eleven years. 'He' was a Negress and, by all accounts, a very prime seaman, successfully filling for many years the rating of Captain of the Main Top, a post given only to the most skilled and agile members of the crew.[1]

There is one more odd case, unique so far as the present author knows, of a woman being deliberately rated A.B. upon the order of no less a person than the Senior Naval Lord—that same Sir George Cockburn who was once one of Dillon's 'four fine young men' (see p. 269). Boteler tells the story.[2] On a visit to the Admiralty he was instructed by Sir George 'to engage a respectable woman . . . and that she was to be rated

[1] *Dictionary of National Biography*, under Snell, Hannah.
[2] N.R.S., Vol. LXXXII, p. 95.

on the Ship's Books as Able Seaman'. To be sure, there was nothing here to offend against morality—she was to act as lady's maid to some princesses who were about to embark: and Boteler simply trotted off to Greenwich and bespoke a pensioner's wife. Perhaps it was only a late survival of that same process which, at a higher level, once made Mr. Secretary Pepys a Captain in the Royal Navy for a single day.

CHAPTER IX

INDUCEMENTS: PAY AND COMPENSATION

****

A. INTRODUCTORY—CHOICE OF PROFESSION

THE object of this chapter and the next is to examine the material inducements which sent officers and men into the Royal Navy during our wars, and which kept them there. But it would be very wrong to suppose that material things were the only inducements, or even the main ones. No sane man does, or ever did, join the armed forces of the Crown for the sole purpose of profit-making. The principal motives which do—and did—actuate them may perhaps be classified under Predilection, Patriotism, Ambition and Personal Profit: and probably the last-named is, all in all, the least influential. Yet it must engage most of our attention because it is by so much the most definite, the most ponderable. But the first three, imponderable as they are, must not be wholly neglected.

First, then, Predilection, by which is meant a marked preference for one sort of career as opposed to other sorts, conceived early and thereafter not relinquished. How imponderable that is! Much too much so to make any profound discussion or analysis of it suitable in a work like this. It is rather a matter for the psychologist. Why does a young person set his heart and mind upon following any particular career? The reasons are extremely complex: but they are there, and we must accept them.

Sometimes indeed the urge is so strong as to amount to a 'call', as is usually the case with men taking Holy Orders, and often with those dedicating themselves to the teaching profession or to the various forms of art, science and research. There were—and are—people thus 'dedicated' to the Navy in all periods. Of those whose evidence we have taken in this book, Nelson at once springs to mind as one: a man who, from the age of 11 or so, never dreamt of being other than he was—a sailor. Cochrane was another, for years mutely opposing his father's intention to send him into the Army. John Nicol, on his lowlier plane, was a third. Dillon was not dedicated at first, entering the Service mainly because his father thought it would be a good thing: but he very soon came to live for nothing else. Poor little Leech was the other way about, dedicated at first but later changing his mind. With Boteler 'the Navy' was always a foregone conclusion.

But the best example of an authentic 'call' is, perhaps, Byam Martin's. In his case the predilection may well have been born in him as a naval officer's son, and this, very likely, is quite an adequate explanation why many of that breed followed their fathers' profession. But young Byam's call was something stronger altogether. When quite an old man he recorded it at length, with the thrill of it yet fresh upon him. He was seven years old, and was being taken to Portsmouth for the first time. The beach at Gosport was his road to Damascus, for there it was that he suddenly saw—a first-rate. It was the old *Royal George*, doomed in the very next year to her tragic end.

'I was so rooted to the spot, so perfectly motionless . . . so absorbed in wonder that I should have been there the whole day if they had not sent one of the boat's crew to fetch me down. . . . Ye Gods! What a sight—what a sensation! I feel it now as I write and if I live to the age of Methuselah it will remain unimpaired. It is impossible to forget the breathless astonishment and delight with which my eyes were fixed upon this ship. Nothing so exquisitely touching has ever occurred to me since to produce the same frantic joy. I remember old John Allen [then his father's coxswain] said, "I see, sir, you are already determined to be a sailor." He never spoke a truer word, for the first comment of my mind fixed in an instant, and for ever, that determination.'[1]

This is no doubt an extreme case of conversion: yet who can deny that Predilection, in a hundred milder forms, played its part, and a major part, in sending hundreds of future officers to sea; and hundreds of men too who, when their time came, joined as enthusiastic volunteers and, as such, remained for their active lives ardent naval men?

Next, Patriotism, surely as imponderable as Predilection: and to dissect it, as a motive, is again the task for psychologists, and philosophers too, rather than historians. It must suffice here to declare that the senti-

[1] N.R.S., Vol. XXIV, p. 4.

ment was strong, real and widespread in the Britain which was called upon to face the French Revolution and its many implications; and that, probably, the motive of patriotism was present, in greater or lesser degree, in very nearly all who joined the Navy during the wars: admittedly apt to be microscopic in the breasts of many of the Quota-men, and not exactly enormous among some of the pressed men: but even at these lowest levels not absent, and by no means negligible. How else could these crews, so largely composed of unwilling recruits, have displayed, time and again, their wonderful fighting qualities? Even after making all allowances for the excitement of battle and the disciplined morale of the Lower Deck, we cannot write off as non-existent the presence of some further psychological urge, if only it were that they 'knew what they fought for, and loved what they knew'. We expect our higher officers, our St. Vincents, Nelsons and Collingwoods, from time to time to give expression on paper to their patriotism: and they do. But, in less clear-cut forms, we get such expressions all the way down, even in the few spontaneous letters that survive from seamen actually serving. Here is one, from the (remaining) hand of a cheerful lad, a common seaman of the *Royal Sovereign*:

'But to tell you the truth of it, when the game [Trafalgar] began, I wished myself at Warnborough with my plough again: but when they had given us one duster and I found myself snug and tight, I bid Fear kiss my bottom and set to in good earnest, and thought no more of being killed than if I were at Murrell Green Fair. . . . How my three fingers got knocked overboard I don't know, but off they are, and I never missed 'em till I wanted 'em. You see by my writing it was my left hand, so I can write to you and fight for my King yet. . . .'[1]

So we will take Patriotism for granted too, allowing it as a motive which actuated all native British seamen, however different in degree.

Last of these imponderables comes Ambition: and again no analysis has been attempted here. Though it has not the selfless property of Patriotism, it is—or most people think so—no crime: at most a very human frailty. Nelson, we know, suffered from 'that last infirmity of noble mind'. He never disguised the fact that

> . . . if it be a sin to covet honour
> I am the most offending soul alive.

[1] Quoted by W. H. Long in *Naval Yarns* (London, 1899), p. 233.

And can it be doubted that all his fellow-admirals had much the same urge: almost all his officers too, and most of his men? Who can doubt, even, that this motive, in some form or other, sent many a volunteer to sea, whether 'quarter-deck' or 'lower deck'?

There were, of course, several distinct sorts of ambition; that like Nelson's and of so many more, whose urge identified itself with patriotism, and other kinds which sought quite other and less worthy things—despotic power, for instance, as wielded by the captains, or social position and prestige. This 'social' ambition in fact, was perhaps the commonest sort, especially lower down the naval scale. Many of those who were socially inferior were anxious to attain the cachet which would make them 'Officers and Gentlemen'. Indeed, the motive worked all the way down, from the Admiral thirsting for the glory of leading a British fleet into action to the landman hoping to be 'rated Able' for the extra shillings and minor privileges which would thereby accrue. So, while admitting many kinds and many degrees of Ambition, we must also admit its all-but universal presence.

Yet, unlike Predilection and Patriotism, Ambition—at least successful Ambition—had its economic as well as its social side. The others carried their own rewards: Predilection brought the fulfilment of a happy life, Patriotism the saving of the well-loved Country and the sense of duty done. Ambition, however, especially if successful, had its more visible rewards, and they were far from inconsiderable: among the upper ranks in terms of glory, popular applause and 'having a Gazette of one's own'; lower down, in being 'made post' and having a ship of one's own, right down to the receipt of the coveted commission, warrant or rating, whichever it might be. There were more mundane rewards too, particularly for the higher officers—for flag-officers knighthoods, baronetcies, peerages (for the really top ones grants of money and land): for successful captains, gazettes, better commands, 'Their Lordships' thanks', awards from the Patriotic Committee of Lloyds or from the larger cities. Even straight monetary awards were considerable, running into thousands for successful admirals, and into hundreds for praiseworthy captains. Great Britain—and this holds for Government and Public alike—was lavish in her gratitude to the Service which she rightly regarded as her saviour, even though she consistently fell into the common contemporary error of giving to 'him that hath' and forgetting 'him that hath not'.

It was in this spirit that Sir John Jervis, for his victory off Cape St.

Vincent, was created an Earl: Parliament voted him £3,000 a year, and the Corporation of London presented him with a magnificent sword:

'The shell of your sword will have two views of the action enamelled.... The hilt will have your ship with her name encircled with diamonds, the City Arms and your own, all enamelled, and executed I hope, to your taste.'[1]

The Second-in-Command was made a Baron, the other two flag-officers Baronets, Commodore Nelson a Knight of the Bath. They also received valuable boxes from the City. The Captains all had swords and medals. It was the same after most of the great actions. For Camperdown Duncan also had £3,000 a year, and was made a Viscount: innumerable pieces of gold plate were showered upon him, each valued at £300 or more: the Freedoms of at least fourteen cities and towns were conferred upon him in boxes of various shapes and values. For the Nile, Nelson received a Barony (no more because he was not a Commander-in-Chief); a pension of £2,000 a year; £10,000 from the East India Company; a diamond box worth £2,500 from the Czar; from the Sultan the famous (and recently stolen) Chelengk, a diamond spray valued at £2,000; and of course, among other tokens of great price, a coffin made from the *Orient's* mainmast, the gift of his own Captain Hallowell. For Copenhagen he had a Viscountcy only (again not being a C.-in-C.); but at Trafalgar he earned for his parson brother an Earldom, a pension of £5,000 to go with it in perpetuity (which, quite recently, turned out to mean rather less than 150 years), and a gift of £90,000 for the purchase of an estate. For his share, Collingwood received a Barony and a pension of £2,000.

The scale began to drop rapidly as soon as flag-rank was left behind. but officers who had single-ship actions to their credit still did not do badly. Dillon, for his action against the Dane, was made Post, thanked by the Admiralty and awarded £250 by the Patriotic Committee, of which 100 guineas went towards a sword. *The Naval Chronicle* published his despatch in full, and the historian James gave him 2½ pages of his monumental history. It was a gallant affair, but by no means unique; there were a hundred like it, equally lavishly rewarded. Lieutenants received promotion—occasionally double promotion like Quilliam after Trafalgar, and John Philips of the *Ardent* after Camperdown. Master's Mates and Midshipmen often had promotion too and, occasionally,

[1] W. V. Anson's *Life of St. Vincent*, p. 177.

17. The Ward-room. (The episode depicted is purely fictional.) *From a plate in Mitford's 'Johnny Newcome'*

18. The Purser, circ. 1799. *From a water-colour by Thomas Rowlandson in the National Mari*
Museum

19. (I) *Left:* Mr Cresse, boatswain of the *Venerable*. (Bottom left, his silver 'call'.) (II) *Above:* His mate, Robert Williams. *From water-colour drawings by P. J. Loutherbourg in the British Museum*

20. The *Vanguard* quarter-deck after the Nile. Right: the wounded Nelson leans on his Captain's shoulder; behind, his other officers; extreme right, his Marine Captain; right centre, two of his midshipmen (one clearly a very 'early entry'); above, the hammock-nettings. *From an aquatint by Clark after Atkinson in the National Maritime Museum*

21. Saturday night at sea. (Two 'messes' unite for their weekly jollification.)
From an etching by Cruikshank in the National Maritime Museum

22. Gun-crew in action. (The gun is a quarterdeck 12-pounder. *Left:* a woman tries to dr casualty from under the gun.) *From a mezzotint by Ward after T. Stothard in the National Mari Museum*

Sailors in port. *From a mezzotint by Ward after T. Stothard in the National Maritime Museum*

24. Failure: A Mid on half-pay. *From an aquatint, engraved by C. Hunt, in the National Maritime Museum.* (See page 314)

. Success: Captain Peter Rainier (Junior). 'Thirteen months ago a Mid.' Note single epaulette
ı right shoulder, indicating a Captain of under three years. *From an oil painting by T. Hickey
the National Maritime Museum*

26. Sailors carousing. (Note, left foreground, the frying pan and watches.)

From an oil painting by J. C. Ibbetson in the National Maritime Museum

27. The end of the *Boyne*. ('An opaque cloud like a round cap.' See p. 354.) *From an aquatint by Edy after Waller in the National Maritime Museum*

28. The loss of the *St George* and *Defence*. (Top left, the *Cressy*.) *From a line engraving by G. Thomson in the National Maritime Museum*

29. (I) Winners in the Prize Lottery: Sir Hyde Parker (The Younger). *From a pastel by Sir T. Lawrence in the National Maritime Museum*

(II) George Elphinstone, Viscount Keith. *From an oil painting by Anderson in the National Maritime Museum*

30. (I) Great Frigate Captains: Edward Pellew, Viscount Exmouth. *From an*

(II) Thomas Cochrane, Earl Dundonald. *From a mezzotint by*

31. (I) Sir Gilbert Blane. *From an unfinished portrait by Sir M. A. Shee in the possession of the Royal College of Physicians*

(II) Dr. Thomas Trotter. *From a stipple engraving by Orme in the National Maritime Museum*

32. The Royal Hospital, Greenwich. *From a drawing by W. P. Kay*

Masters (as James Bowen after the First of June). But thereafter this kind of material reward tailed off to nothing.

All such prizes were inducement to the ambitious man, but in the nature of things they were too irregular and uncertain to be counted upon. Let us turn now to what may be regarded as the steady inducement of 'Profit' which, Predilection, Patriotism and Ambition apart, might tempt a man to the sea-service, and keep him there: to the material rewards for service which might be expected to accrue in the ordinary run of things. Here we find ourselves in a much less philosophic atmosphere: indeed we have bumped rather firmly down to earth itself, for what we are now to examine is nothing but that most mundane of all things—money.

There were three main monetary inducements of this kind—one which would certainly materialize, one which probably would, and one which would if our officer ever reached to the command of a ship. The first was his basic pay which every man received, and—after 1794—every boy. Tied closely in with this were certain established allowances: which, however, existed only for flag-officers, commissioned officers and most, but not all, warrant officers. Next came Prize-Money and—what was not quite the same thing—'Prize Bounty' or 'Head-Money'. The third was 'Freight-Money'. Prize and Freight, however, have a chapter to themselves—as inducements they are well worth it. The rest of this chapter concentrates upon naval Pay and Allowances.

B. PAY AND ALLOWANCES

(a) *Pay*

The scales of pay in force when the Revolutionary War broke out were those listed in the Regulations of 1790. In 1794, as we have seen, there were changes in connection with the young Volunteers and Boys. There were also revised scales for most of the men in 1797, wrung from the Government by the mutinies: and, for the officers, a few minor adjustments. In 1806, however, there appeared what was virtually a new scale altogether which lasted, again with minor adjustments, until the wars ended. In Table VII, therefore, we take our stand at two points, one in 1793, as the wars began, and the other in 1815, when they ended.

The first thing to notice—for it is unfamiliar to the modern eye—is the fact that 'rank' by itself does not entitle an officer to any standard rate of pay. 'Post' is quite as important; often more so. Indeed, in most

TABLE VII

A. WAGES, VARYING ACCORDING TO RATE OF SHIP*

Per Lunar Month

RANK OR RATING	In 1793			In 1815		
	No. in Ship	1st-Rate	6th-Rate and under	No. in Ship	1st-Rate	6th-Rate and under
Captain	1	£28-0-0	£8-8-0	1	£32-4-0	£16-16-0
Master	1	£9-2-0	£4-0-0	1	£12-12-0	£7-7-0[1]
Carpenter	1	£4-0-0	£2-0-0	1	£5-16-0	£3-1-0
Boatswain, Gunner, Purser	1 each	£4-0-0	£2-0-0	1 each	£4-16-0	£3-1-0
Master's Mate	6 to 2	£3-6-0	£2-2-0	6 to 2	£3-16-6	£2-12-6
Midshipman	24 to 4	£2-5-0	£1-10-0	24 to 4	£2-15-6	£2-0-6
Captain's Clerk	1	£2-5-0	£1-10-0	1	£4-7-0	£2-18-6
Schoolmaster	1[2]	£1-17-6[3]	£1-10-0	1	£2-15-6[4]	£2-0-6
Master-at-Arms	1	£2-5-0	£1-10-0	1	£2-15-6	£2-0-6
Armourer	1	£1-5-0	£1-5-0	1	£2-15-6	£2-0-6
Carpenter's Mate	2 to 1	£2-0-0	£1-10-0	2 to 1	£2-10-6	£2-0-6
Caulker, Ropemaker	1 each	Not given		1 each	£2-10-6	£2-0-6
Quartermaster	8 to 2	£1-15-0	£1-6-0	8 to 2	£2-5-6	£1-16-6
Boatswain's and Gunner's Mate	4 to 1 each	£1-15-0	£1-6-0	4 to 1 each	£2-5-6	£1-16-6
Yeoman of Powder Room, Corporal ...	2 to 1 each	£1-15-0	£1-6-0	2 to 1 each	£2-5-6	£1-16-6

Sailmaker	1	£1-15-0	£1-10-0	1	£2-5-6	£2-0-6
Armourer's Mate	—	Not given		2 to 1	£2-5-6	£1-16-6
Caulker's Mate	—	Not given		1	£2-6-6[5]	—
Yeoman of Sheets	4 to 1	£1-12-0	£1-6-0	4 to 1	£2-2-6	£1-16-6
Coxswain	1	£1-12-0	£1-6-0	1	£2-2-6	£1-16-6
Quartermaster's Mate	6 to 2	£1-10-0	£1-5-0	6 to 2	£2-0-6	£1-15-6
Trumpeter	1	£1-10-0	£1-4-0	1	£2-0-6	£1-14-6
Captains of Forecastle, Fore Top, Main Top, Afterguard and Mast	—	As Able Seaman		—	£2-0-6	£1-15-6
Quarter Gunner	1 to every 4 guns	£1-6-0	£1-5-0	25 to 5	£1-16-6	£1-15-6
Carpenter's Crew	12 to 4	£1-6-0	£1-5-0	12 to 4	£1-16-6	£1-15-6
Gunsmith, Steward	1[6]	£1-5-0	£1-0-8	1[6]	£1-15-6	£1-9-6
Cook	1	£1-5-0	£1-4-0	1	£1-15-6	£1-14-6

* Simplified to show only the maximum and minimum wages of the officers concerned—that is, their pay in '1st-Rates' and in '6th-Rates and under'. An unabbreviated Table would have four more columns between '1st-Rate' and '6th-Rate', showing the progressively decreasing wages in 2nd, 3rd, 4th and 5th Rates.

Notes

[1] If of sloops, brigs and cutters, £6-6-0.

[2] In 1793, none in 1st- and 6th-Rates.

[3] *Plus* £20 annual bonus, *plus* (unofficially) £5 per head of pupils.

[4] *Plus* £20 annual bonus, *plus* (officially) £5 per head of pupils.

[5] Allowed in first four Rates only.

[6] Gunsmiths in first two Rates only in 1793: in first three only in 1815.

cases, the rating of the ship (and therefore the importance of the appointment) affects an officer's pay more than his rank does. For instance, there is a much greater difference between the pay of the Captain of a Sixth-rate and that of a First-rate than there is between a Sixth-rate's Captain's remuneration and that of a Lieutenant. In 1793 the respective differences are: between the Captains nearly £20 per month; between the most junior Captain and the best-paid Lieutenant only £1 8*s*. a month. This may cause surprise until we recall two things.

First, the whole Service had originally been built up on a basis of 'Post' and not of 'Rank'. On this basis the ship was regarded as the important thing: the man, save as he formed part of the ship and its complement, was nothing—unless, for instance, he was actually *the* Captain *of* a named ship, he was not a Captain at all. Thus regarded, the size of the ship was the all-important thing; and its size was most easily measurable by noting its hitting-power in war—the number of guns it carried and the number of men it took to work them. In the old days, then, the Captain's importance (and therefore his pay) varied with the number of men and guns in a ship. And it was this method of measurement—and of pay—which had survived, roughly, into the period of our wars. How this worked out in 1793 the following figures show:

	Captain's Pay	*Guns*	*Men*
First-rate	£28	100	840
Sixth-rate	£8 8 0	28	200

The proportions are not of course exact, but they are near enough to explain what at first sight looks so anomalous. Such extreme contrasts, it will be noticed, have largely disappeared by 1815, though the First-rate Captain still receives almost twice as much as the Sixth-rate one.

The other thing which helps to explain these great differences in basic pay is that, theoretically, an officer commanding a higher rate of ship was a captain senior to one commanding a lower rate. It is true that Theory had not much chance against Interest here, but this is how things stood officially. Indeed, during most of our period there was a line drawn between senior and junior captains which was so marked as to make it appear, almost, that there were two distinct ranks of Captain. By the Admiralty Order-in-Council of 1/6/1795 the two sorts were actually put into different uniforms. It was then that epaulettes were introduced for Commanders-and-above. But not all received the full ration of the coveted 'bullion', which all wanted. A Commander was confined to the rather lopsided wear of one epaulette, on the left shoulder; and the Captain of under three years' seniority was condemned to a similar lopsidedness, his 'bullion' to be on his right shoulder. It is when we come to the three-year-and-upward Captain that we find the real line drawn. He, in common with all flag-officers, may wear two. A senior Captain, therefore, could actually be distinguished from a junior one as he walked along the street—more readily than a junior Captain could be distinguished from a Commander. This strange regulation, however, did not quite survive our period because, by another Order-in-Council of 23/3/1812, all Captains and all Commanders were allowed to wear both, the Lieutenants being now admitted to the honour—but on the right shoulder only. They had to wait till 1840 before they secured the second: and then the Mates (late Master's Mates and soon to be Sub-Lieutenants) inherited the lopsidedness.

The Navy, therefore, escaped having two distinct ranks of Captain; but while this phase lasted it was a close thing, the distinction between 'over-threes' and 'under-threes' being, in other ways as well, quite as marked as that between 'under-threes' and commanders. Nor perhaps will it have escaped the reader's notice that the word 'Commander' does not appear in the Table at all, not even in the 1815 column. This, of course, is because both scales are still, primarily, matters of 'Post' and not of 'Rank' at all, as has just been explained. We may also remind ourselves again that every officer who commanded a ship was a 'Captain', in the old 'post' sense; and that his second-in-command was not a Commander, either by Post or Rank. He was a First Lieutenant by Post and a plain Lieutenant by Rank. Thus Dillon in his affair with the Dane was 'Captain of the (non-post) brig *Childers*', but by rank a Commander: and he was rewarded by being made a (ranking) Captain. And Quilliam, next in command of the *Victory* under Captain Hardy, was only promoted Commander (and, in his case, Captain as well) after the battle as a reward. So these pay-scales, though they cover the pay to which Captains of ships (i.e. posts) are entitled, also cover the pay (though they do not say so) of Commanders: and no one, even nowadays, would expect Captains and Commanders to have the same pay-scales. In fact, the only thing that brings a Commander into these scales at all is the inclusion of the two words under the heading 'Sixth-Rate'. They are 'and under', and they cover all Commanders, since under-sixth-rates were the only ships that they could command.

Little if any of the above applies to the Lieutenants, who received, with minor exceptions, the same pay in whatever rate they served. In 1793 the first two rates, whether flagships or not, carried a rather higher pay: in 1815 only flagships did so, irrespective of rate, a flagship Lieutenant being by then, as we have seen, a sort of embryo Commander. But the rest had a flat rate throughout, and there was no reason for favouring those serving in larger ships. Their cases differed markedly from that of the Captain. He, being the only one in any ship, had greater labour and responsibility the larger that ship was. But the number of Lieutenants rose progressively with the ship's size, so that a Lieutenant in a high rate had no more guns and men to look after than had one in a low rate. In fact, the proportion was much the same throughout—roughly eight Lieutenants to 800 men in a big ship and two to 200 in a small one. Indeed, the smaller rates probably gave the harder work: there was more watch-keeping to do because there were fewer to share it.

Warrant Officers' pay, on the other hand, was in this respect like the Captain's. There was never more than one Master, one Gunner or one Boatswain in any ship, however large, so that their responsibilities, like his, increased with its size. But their pay-ranges were much narrower than his.

The basic pay of Flag-Officers obeyed that unwritten law which obtained in almost all walks of life in contemporary Britain—'Unto him that hath shall be given'. Indeed the gulf between the highest and the lowest pay in a fleet-flagship of 1793 almost takes one's breath away. The Admiral and Commander-in-Chief had £140 per lunar month (or £1,820 per annum). The boy-servants had nothing. The difference is almost equally staggering if we regard the 'servants' (as they did) as apprentices, unworthy of any pay while 'articled'. The Admiral received, roughly, 150 times as much as an Ordinary Seaman: and this is in basic pay alone. The gulf is far wider when all sources of profit are taken into account.

We must bear those other sources in mind, too, when comparing the 1793 figures with those of 1815. There appears to be no difference in the flag-officers' pay at all, save that one, the Vice-Admiral, seems to have a little less in 1815, for some reason unknown to me. In actual fact they were better off, as we shall soon discover, but their relative rise was not so great, perhaps, as we might have suspected.

The Navy's basic pay-scales are too complex to set out in one table, and here, taking our cue from the Admiralty Regulations, we have divided them up into four. The first, dealing with Flag-Officers only, is simple enough to incorporate in the text because, like the Lieutenants', it is a flat rate.

Per Lunar Month	1793	1815
Ad. of the Fleet and C.-in-C. ...	£140	£140
Admiral	£98	£98
Vice-Admiral	£74 10 0 ...	£70
Rear-Admiral	£49	£49

The second and third tables include all ship-ranks and ratings, from Captain to Boy. One—Table VII A—covers those whose wages vary according to the rating of the ship they serve in. The other—Table VII B—shows those whose wages do not so vary. We find all the important people of the ship-hierarchy in Table VII A, save only the Lieutenants who, as we have seen, were almost all on a flat rate, and the Second Master, who appears only in the bigger ships anyway. The remaining people in Table VII B are Petty Officers or lower.

Our last pay-scale is that of the Medical Officers, here (as in the Admiralty Regulations) collected into a separate table—VIII. We will return to them presently.

An examination of Tables VII A and VII B will show what progress, if any, officers and men were making during the war-years. The Captain's fortunes we have already sufficiently followed. The position of all the rest is improved, uniformly as a whole, though one or two categories do considerably better than others. We will look first at Table VII A.

The Carpenters (in bigger but not in smaller ships) go well ahead of their fellow-warrants the Boatswain, Gunner and Purser: but the figures for the last-named mean little because, as we have seen, they represent only a part of his total emoluments.

The Captain's Clerk comes in for a spectacular rise. This was not in 1806, when they were still receiving (as in 1793) the same pay as Midshipmen. Their rise came only shortly before 1815.

The tables clearly underline the mean position of the Schoolmaster, who in 1793 is well behind the Midshipman, and only his equal even in 1815. But he did have his £20 'bonus' and, from 1812, his (official) £5 tuition fees (see p. 258).

The Chaplain's pay has already been reviewed, but here we see it in black and white. His position in the 1793 column is indeed stark, receiving as he does the lowest pay of any man aboard. Actually, however, things were not quite so bad since he also received his traditional 'groat'

TABLE VII
B. WAGES, THE SAME IN ALL RATES
Per Lunar Month

Rank or Rating	In 1793		In 1815	
	No. in Ship	Wage	No. in Ship	Wage
Lieutenant (1st 2 rates)	6	£7 0 0	—	—
Lieutenant (of Flagships)	—	—	8 to 2	£9 2 0
Lieutenant (all others)	4 to 1	£5 12 0	8 to 2	£8 8 0
Second Master (1st 3 rates only)	1	£3 10 0	1	£5 5 0
Sailmaker's Mate	1	£1 8 0	1	£1 18 6
Sailmaker's Crew	2 to 1	£1 5 0	2 to 1	£1 15 6
Steward's Mate (1st 4 rates only)	1	£1 0 8	1	£1 5 2
Midshipman Ordinary	—	£1 4 0	—	£1 13 6
Cook's Mate	—	£1 4 0	—	£1 13 6
Coxswain's Mate	—	£1 4 0	—	£1 13 6
Yeoman of Boatswain's Storeroom	—	£1 4 0	—	£1 13 6
Swabber	—	£1 4 0	—	£1 13 6
Cooper	—	£1 4 0	—	£1 13 6
Able Seaman	—	£1 4 0	—	£1 13 6
Captain's Cook	—	£1 4 0	—	£1 13 6
Ordinary Trumpeter	—	£1 4 0	—	£1 13 6
Volunteer Per Order	—	Nil	—	£1 13 6
Ordinary Seaman	—	£0 19 0	—	£1 5 6
Shifter	—	£0 19 0	—	£1 5 6
Barber	—	£0 19 0	—	£1 5 6
Gunner's Taylor	—	£0 19 0	—	£1 5 6
Landman	Nil	—	—	£1 2 6
Chaplain	1	£0 19 0[1]	1	£11 10 9[2]
Boy (Volunteer) 1st Class	—	Nil	—	£0 13 10[3]
Boy (Volunteer) 2nd Class	—	Nil	—	£0 12 4[3]
Boy (Volunteer) 3rd Class	—	Nil	—	£0 10 9[3]

[1] Plus 'groats'.
[2] In lieu of wages *and* groats, but allowed, as well, the Schoolmaster's £20 bonus and £5 per head per annum of pupils, if acting as Schoolmaster.
[3] Approx. wages per year £9, £8 and £7 respectively.

—his fourpence a month for each man in the ship. In 1797 he went—apparently—even further downhill, for his basic pay remained at nineteen shillings when all the seamen's pay went up as a result of the mutinies. In 1812, however, he received belated recognition, though his 'groats' were at last abolished. He was now comparatively well-off, his basic pay (of £150 a year) being better than that of anyone else on board save the Captain, the Surgeon and the best-placed Masters. He could also, if he wished to act as Schoolmaster as well, earn in addition his £5 tuition-fees.

Last to be considered in this group are the Midshipmen: and they will provide a useful bridge across our line of demarcation—our passage from Table VII A to Table VII B. For, it will be noticed, the word 'Midshipman' appears in both tables: those in Table VII A styled plain 'Midshipman', those in Table VII B called 'Midshipman Ordinary'. We know by now who the former were—all (whether men or boys) 'appointed petty' by the Captain to fill one particular rating on board, that is, the *post* of Midshipman. The other group needs explanation. We are once more up against 'Post' and 'Rank', and the transition from a 'post' way of running the Navy to a 'rank' way. For Midshipmen Ordinary were lads—always lads—who held the rank of Midshipman but not the post: while the plain Midshipmen were people—boys or men—who held both the rank and the post. This, incidentally, explains why the latter had more pay—they did the work of the rating 'Midshipman', while the former did not.

The key word here is 'ordinary', and an explanation of it must take us back once more to Samuel Pepys. He, we noticed, invented the Volunteer-per-Order (see p. 143). But he also invented (lest his protégé should be squeezed out) the Midshipman-per-Order—the same lad one stage later in his naval career. We watched the Volunteer-per-Order turning into the College Volunteer in 1731, and found that he was still flourishing, albeit in a small way, during our wars. With him survived the Midshipman-per-Order too, but only because the successors of Mr. Pepys insisted that he should. Time had shortened his title from Midshipman-per-Order to Midshipman Ordinary, but there he was, still with the same essential quality of being appointed by the Admiralty. The Captains, as ever, appointed their own Midshipmen to the relevant posts in their ships, but the Admiralty had long had its own rules about its 'per-order' young gentlemen. One was that as soon as a Volunteer-per-Order (now College Volunteer) had served his statutory two years as such, he was to be made Midshipman-per-Order (now Midshipman Ordinary): and, this being an Admiralty Regulation, it was not within the Captain's power to alter or ignore it. In this respect, indeed, the lad was akin to the Captain himself, the Lieutenants and the Warrant Officers—he was an Admiralty appointee. Authority even safeguarded its—and his—position still further. From 1731, when the official Admiralty Regulations started, there was always inserted in them one quite definite clause—'None are to be rated Midshipmen Ordinary but such as have served Volunteers by Order': which clause remained in every subsequent edition to the end of the century and beyond. So not only is a Captain compelled to promote a College Volunteer as soon as his two-year period is up: he may not slip a protégé of his own into the position of Midshipman Ordinary either.

In the 1790 pay-scale (and therefore in our 1793 column) there is no mention at all of the Volunteer-per-Order. This is because he received no pay at that time, thereby conforming with all his messmates of a similar age and standing—the Captain's Servants, etc. Nor, of course, are any 'servants' mentioned, since they too received no wages before 1794. But after that date they all make their appearance—as Boys (Volunteer)—having become wage-earning in that year. They all appear in the 1815 column, but under their new names. The former *real* servant is now 'Boy (Volunteer) 3rd Class': the lad training for seaman, 'Boy (Volunteer) 2nd Class': the 'privileged' servant (usually, in the old days, 'Captain's), 'Boy (Volunteer) 1st Class'. Moreover, it must be observed that the Volunteer-per-Order is still distinguished from the Boy (Volunteer) First Class. He even receives higher wages. Where the latter gets a mere 13*s.* 10*d.* a month he has £1 13*s.* 6*d.*—the same as his own senior kith and kin the Midshipman Ordinary. The reason for this preferential treatment, probably, was that the Admiralty was, as usual, trying to boost its Naval Academy (which in the very year of the new pay-scales—1806—it was enlarging and renaming 'Royal Naval College, Portsmouth'). It was perhaps only natural that it should be predisposed towards what was after all its own entry—indeed its only entry.

It is not so easy to explain why Volunteers-per-Order and Midshipmen Ordinary were awarded identical pay. The only explanation that occurs to one is perhaps rather cynical. Though College Volunteers were, still, not supposed to go to sea as Midshipmen, O'Byrne reveals how very often they did so—making use, of course, of 'book-time'. Is it then possible that—in this particular case which touched them so nearly—Their Lordships, though unwilling to create ill-feeling by forbidding 'book-time' altogether, decided that a boy who obeyed their rules should not be handicapped vis-à-vis one who did not, and therefore decreed that both should receive the same pay?

It remains only to note the rise in pay of the seamen and lesser petty officers. It had last been raised under the Commonwealth, and, we may recall, it was around this very point that the 'Breeze at Spithead' blew most forcibly in 1797. The mutineers demanded equality with the soldiers and their shilling-a-day. The Able Seaman got it, and rather more: the Ordinary Seaman missed it, though not by much, as the pay-month was a twenty-eight-day one. The Landman—quite a new rating, not mentioned in the 1790 scale—had only 22*s.* 6*d.* Relatively, he deserved no more—hereabouts were to be found the poorer 'quota' types. But no willing young fellow, rated landman merely through inexperience, would have to wait long before being rated Ordinary.

The Surgeons require a Table to themselves (Table VIII), if only because it was during the period 1793–1815 that the medical problem was really taken in hand, and a scale of salaries introduced which, for the first time, began to attract competent people. The figures speak for themselves. Let us only note that, by 1815, a Senior Physician was nearly up to a Rear-Admiral in basic pay, and a Junior Physician above all but First-rate Captains. The ship Surgeons, who used to be rather worse off than Lieutenants, were now but little below Captains (though, as we shall see, they were much worse off in allowances), while their Assistants, who used to be only a little better off than Midshipmen, were now on a level with, or above, Lieutenants. In a country like ours which makes a habit of buying its experience, often at heavy cost, a long hard war was just the fillip, and probably the only one, to bring about these commonsense but overdue reforms.

A single glance at our pay-tables will surely reveal the fact that here lay no particular inducement to join the Navy. If every man had had a sporting chance of reaching flag-rank, no doubt it would have been different. Even in basic pay Admirals did not do too badly. Nor did senior Captains. But, below them, in view of the onerous responsibilities, the unhealthy conditions and the back-breaking labour of it all, the rewards offered were remarkably inadequate. This general conclusion is confirmed by hard facts. In the lower levels the basic pay was nearly the only monetary inducement, while the chances of rising to the higher levels were remote, and known to be so. The result was that, in these

TABLE VIII

MEDICAL OFFICERS' PAY, 1793 and 1815

Title	1793: Rate of Ship and No. Allowed in	1793: Pay Per Month	1815: Rate of Ship and No. Allowed in	1815: Pay Per Month
Physician, over 3 years	1 in 1st-rate and Hosp. Ship	£28 0 0	1 in 1st-rate and Hosp. Ship	£44 2 0
under 3 years	„ „ „		„ „ „	£29 8 0
Surgeon, over 20 years	1 in all ships	£5 0 0	1 in all ships	£25 4 0
over 10 years				£19 12 6
over 6 years				£15 8 0
under 6 years				£14 0 0
Dispenser (Hospital)	—	—	1	£14 0 0
Mate (after 1806, Assistant) First	1 in all ships	£2 10 0	1 in all ships	£9 2 0
Second	1 in first 5 rates	£2 0 0	1 in first 4 rates	
Third	1 in first 3 rates	£1 10 0	1 in 1st and 2nd rates	
Fourth	1 in 1st and 2nd rates	£1 10 0	None	—
Fifth	1 in 1st rate	£1 10 0	None	—
Assistant (unqualified) serving as 1st or 2nd	—	—	in any ship where serving	£7 0 0
serving as 3rd			„ „ „ „ „	£5 12 0

regions, Authority never induced enough men to come in willingly, and so had to compel them. Higher up the scale, however, in the regions where a man might hope to rise higher still, enough men were induced to serve without compulsion. There was never any conscription among the officer-class. But it was not the basic pay that induced them. A young gentleman was certainly not persuaded to go to sea for the glittering prize of a Lieutenancy, worth about £100 a year. We must look for other monetary inducements.

(b) *Allowances*

Here again—as through all this 'inducement' story, told and to be told—sounds the melancholy refrain 'Unto him that hath shall be given'. 'Allowances' were granted from the top downwards, as far as the senior Warrant Officers and—as exceptions—the Chaplain and the Cook. There they stopped practically dead.[1] By far the main one was that called 'Compensation', introduced in 1794 when the 'Servant' system was abolished. It was then, as we saw (p. 152), laid down that 'compensation' was to be paid 'in lieu of Servants': but, naturally, only to such officers as were previously entitled to any. The sum allowed 'in lieu' was 19*s.* per month per servant, that sum (in 1794) being the wage of the lowest-paid man in the ship. On working out the actual figures, we seem to be faced with two rather characteristic, if minor, meannesses on someone's part: for whereas in all other naval wage-calculations (of officers and men alike) 'a month' means twenty-eight days, where compensation is concerned it means a calendar month. This, it would seem, was because of an Act of 1792,[2] which laid it down that all months except pay-months were to be 'calendar'. Thus, though the Ordinary Seaman was even then drawing £12 7*s.* a year (i.e. 19*s.* × 13), the officer who was to

[1] There were two small exceptions:

a. For urgent work in dockyards, ships 'in ordinary', and ships commissioning, men lent from a commissioned ship received an allowance, per diem, of: Lieutenant, 2/6: Master's Mate or Midshipman, 1/0: Boatswain's Mate, 9d.: Seaman, 6d.

b. If a ship had to be careened outside a dockyard, there was allowed per diem:—

	Own Ship	*Another Ship*
To the Carpenter	2/–	3/–
His Mate, Shipwright, Caulker and Smith	1/6	2/–
Sailmaker	1/3	1/9

[2] 32 Geo. III. Cap 34: quoted in abstract in Adm. Regulations and Instructions, 1808, Appendix 24, Sect. 28.

be compensated drew only £11 8*s.* (i.e. 19*s.* × 12). Further, when in 1797 the 19*s.* man's wages rose to 25*s.* 6*d.* no corresponding rise was given to the officers. The rate-per-servant-per-annum (for all but Flag-Officers, as we shall see) remained throughout at £11 8*s.* We can but hope that the ingenious official who hit on this subtle distinction was suitably rewarded: for, in its cumulative effect, his forethought certainly saved the country a good round sum.

In its working, this 'compensation' was rather like a snowball—admittedly an unusual one, because its nature was to roll uphill. The lower strata in the Navy got nothing out of it at all. People like the Cook, the Chaplain, the Purser, the Surgeon, the Master and ordinary Lieutenants had been allowed one servant, and now drew compensation for one—£11 8*s.* per annum. The Boatswain, the Gunner and the Carpenter, and a Lieutenant in actual command of a small craft were allowed compensation for two servants. Incidentally the last-named was allowed compensation for a Steward as well, but no more basic pay than an ordinary Lieutenant; so that, in effect, he acquired a little 'command-money' in this way—38*s.* per month (calendar of course) for his two extra servants. It is not quite certain whether this £11 8*s* was a clear gain to the officers concerned, for of course they still went on employing servants in the old way (only they were now called 'Boys, 3rd Class'). But probably it was, because the new Third Class Boys now received wages of their own, derisory though they were: and one can hardly see them being allowed two wages, one from the Admiralty and one from the masters they served. The more generous officers, of course, sometimes supplemented their pay with additional pocket-money; but, from what Robert Hay has to tell us, it would seem that this was a kindness, not an obligation. First and last, he was 'shoe-boy'—the Lower Deck's scornful nickname for a servant—to four of the *Culloden*'s officers. From the first, a Lieutenant, he does not say what, if anything, he received: from the second, a Master's Mate,[1] he got nothing but kicks and a knotted rope's-end: from the third, the Chaplain, a little 'pocket money',

[1] Hay, op. cit., passim. A Master's Mate was not officially entitled to a servant of his own, nor to a cabin. Apparently he had both, but, probably, Hay unconsciously explains the reason for these indulgences when he reveals that the officer —Crease—had 'come on board under the Admiral's patronage and was going to India to meet preferment'. Young Robert (then aged 14) came to hate and fear him. He at last ventured to complain of his treatment to the Captain who, to his credit, took Hay's part and reprimanded Crease in public, depriving him of the privilege of having a servant on the grounds that he did not know how to treat one.

but only enough to make him consider his master rather mean. From the fourth—the Admiral's Secretary, Edward Hawke Locker, son of Nelson's old Captain—he had most generous treatment in cash, books and kindness of every sort. He makes it pretty clear, however, that none of them *owed* him wages, so that it is safe to assume that all officers entitled to Boys were £11 8*s*. per servant better off for the change.

But now our unnatural snowball, bounding uphill, seems to grow larger and larger. Every Captain, we recall, used to be entitled to four servants for every 100 of his Ship's Company. Thus our Sixth-rate Captain was entitled to compensation on eight servants because his crew numbered 200: that is, £11 8*s*. × 8, or £91 4*s*. per annum. So we go up till we reach our First-rate Captain, with some 800 souls in his charge. This gives him a right to thirty-two servants and, 'in lieu', £11 8*s*. for each of them—that is, £364 16*s*. It just about doubled the basic pay that he was then receiving, and he shot even further ahead of the Sixth-rate Captain, let alone the Lieutenants and other more junior officers. Yet this new compensation, which looks so considerable on paper, was largely illusory. Most of it he had enjoyed for centuries, though in another form. Before 1794 he had, as we have seen, been accustomed to pocket the wages of his Captain's Servants. All that had happened now was that the said wages had been assessed at 19*s*., called 'Compensation', and recognized as part of his official emoluments. Indeed, he only stood to make any real gain out of the change if he broke the Law, and entered his protégés under the names of other ratings. But this—as, most regretfully, we have had to record—he very often did. (See p. 155.)

Let us see what our officers' salaries looked like, per annum and in actual life. The rather complicated sums are done for us in Steel's *List of the Royal Navy* for November, 1814. It is a formidable affair, even though it covers only commissioned and warrant officers, and not all of them. Table IX, which shows a somewhat simplified version of it, gives a remarkable picture of the whole pay-structure at the end of our wars. *En passant*, too, it should be put on record that the figures are Steel's, and not those of the author, who lays no claim to financial expertise. Here (in the text) but one fragment is extracted, in order to prove the point already made of the pay-differences existing between Captain and Captain. Steel, of course, is out to be practical, and to help his officers to discover what they really have to spend. So he nowhere gives 'gross income'. He begins with what is left after the statutory naval deductions

TABLE IX

'TABLE OF THE NETT ANNUAL PAY, ETC.'

(*Slightly abbreviated from Steel's List of the Royal Navy for Nov.* 1814, *p.* 72)

'After the Deductions of Three Pence per Pound for the Widows' Fund, the Shilling per month to the Chest, and Sixpence per Month to the Royal Hospital at Greenwich, are abated:[1] the Income Tax[2] deducted from each, and the clear Pay then remaining to be received.'

Rank, etc., of the several Officers	Nett Annual Pay			Income Tax			Clear Annual Pay		
	£	s.	d.	£	s.	d.	£	s.	d.
Captain of 1st-Rate (Complement, 837)	802	0	2	80	4	0	721	16	2
down to									
Captain of 6th-Rate (Complement, 135)	284	7	9	28	8	9	255	19	0
Commander of Sloop, Bomb, etc. (Complement, 121)	272	19	7	27	5	11	245	13	4
down to									
Commander (Complement, 75 & under)	250	2	11	25	0	3	225	2	8
Lieutenant commanding Prison Ship	137	4	8	13	1	8	124	3	0
Lieutenant in Flagship	128	4	5	11	14	11	116	9	6
Lieutenant in other ships	112	4	2	10	7	8	100	15	0
Master of 1st-rate	172	12	8	17	5	3	155	7	5
down to									
Master of Sloop	91	10	0	6	4	6	85	5	6

Second Master, Gun Brigs, Cutters, etc.	78 17 5	4 6 7	74 10 10
Second Master, Line-of-Battleship	67 9 3	2 12 3	64 17 0
Surgeon (20 years and upwards)	322 8 9	32 4 10	290 3 11
down to			
Surgeon (under 6 years)	178 5 3	17 16 6	160 8 9
Assistant Surgeon (qualified)	117 13 0	10 13 0	107 10 0
Assistant Surgeon (not qualified)	90 5 6	6 0 9	84 4 9
Carpenter of 1st-rate	96 9 6	6 19 6	89 10 0
down to			
Carpenter of Sloop (Complement under 100)	48 13 6	Nil	48 13 6
Gunner, Boatswain, Purser of 1st-rate	83 12 0	5 0 6	77 11 6
down to			
Gunner, Boatswain, Purser of Sloop (Complement under 100)	48 13 6	Nil	48 13 6

[1] For details, see pp. 311-12.

[2] Two shillings in the pound on incomes of £150 and over, graded to *nil* for incomes under £50.

have been made; then assesses what Income Tax is due—that all too familiar state-levy introduced by Pitt in December 1798 (for 1799); and finally reaches the 'clear annual' figure. Consulting this last column, we learn that the First-rate Captain is receiving not far off three times as much as the Sixth-rate Captain; or, in terms of actual figures, £466 more. But the Junior Captain's lead over the Senior Commander (for here Commanders are actually mentioned by name) is a mere £10. None the less, we must not overlook the fact that some small progress towards equity has been taken since the 1790's: for the First-rate Captain's basic salary, which was then three and a half times as large as the Sixth-rate Captain's, is now only twice as large. Having lost on the roundabout of basic salary, however, he has got most of it back on the swings of Compensation, so that he still receives (nett) nearly thrice as much as his junior—£721 16*s.* 2*d.* to £255 19*s.*

Rising now to the flag-officers, we find that their compensation was similar in principle, but somewhat different in practice. Unlike the Captains, the Admirals did not have the right to servants at the rate of so many per ship's crew. They did not 'own' ships as the Captains did. They were more like distinguished guests—occupying the best suite. Yet—we may depend upon it—they were not left out when any benefit was going. Before 1794 they had three separate categories of dependants, the numbers in each depending upon the flag-officer's rank. The smallest of these categories consisted of real servants, and, in the change of 1794, these were omitted from the 'compensation' figures: but, being borne on the Ship's Books in the ordinary way, they were now for the first time given wages, as all other servants were: and—their masters being such important people—they were paid as Able Seamen; that is, on the 1790 scale, 24*s.* a week instead of 19*s.* The other two categories were both 'compensatable'. The first was still labelled 'Servant', but the people who composed it were to the Admiral just what the Captain's Servants were to the Captain—protégés and quarter-deck-bound. But there was this minor difference—they were 'supernumerary', not borne on the Ship's Books. For these the compensation was the same as that of the Captain's Servants—19*s.* The last category was the oldest, largest and best-known. Its members were called 'the Retinue'. They usually moved around with the Admiral and were thus, like the last-named group, 'supernumerary': but, like the true servants, they counted for compensation as 'Able', so that the Admiral drew 24*s.* a month for each of them.

This explanation is admittedly complicated; and it can only be defended on the ground that the rules themselves were complicated: so much so that the contemporary 'experts' who set out to explain them to naval officers sometimes went wrong themselves. But this is how it seems to have worked out:—[1]

Name	*Servants* (*Real*) at 24/– (no Comp.)	'*Servants*' (Comp. 19/–)	'*Retinue*' (Comp. 24/–)	*Total* for Comp.	*Comp.* per month	*Comp.* per annum
Admiral and C.-in-C.	12	16	34	50	£56	£672
Admiral	10	12	18	30	£33	£396
Vice-Adm.	7	10	10	20	£21½	£258
Rear-Adm.	5	10	5	15	£15½	£186

From this we see that 'he that hath' continues to receive. The Admiral and Commander-in-Chief adds to his basic pay of £1,820 a 'Compensation' of £672, giving him a total of £2,492. But we have not even yet enumerated all his receipts, because he—with all flag-officers actually holding independent commands—was entitled to an extra allowance of 'Table Money'. This allowance was £1 per diem, so long as his flag was flying. If, therefore, he could keep it so for a full year, he added £365, thereby reaching a gross total of £2,857—no mean salary for those days.

The other flag-officers did not fare nearly so well: indeed the Rear-Admiral and those temporarily acting as such did very little better than Captains of First-rates, because most of what they gained in basic salary they lost in their smaller compensation. The gross figures seem to be Rear-Admiral, £823, 1st-Rate Captain, £802.

But already Great Britain was reaching that familiar phase in her financial history where 'gross' income becomes somewhat unrealistic. In Table IX we saw the effect of Mr. Pitt's intervention with his Income Tax, and also that there were certain statutory levies which were purely naval. Pitt's tax was a graded one, payable by everyone in the country

[1] Compiled from several small tables in Falconer's *Marine Dictionary* (ed. Burney, 1815) pp. 336 and 100. These, however, contain certain contradictions. In one place, for instance, Burney finds the 'Compensation per annum' by multiplying by 13 (i.e., using the lunar month): but in another—rightly, and followed here,—he uses the calendar month (multiple, 12). He has also, apparently, deprived his Rear-Admiral of his 'retinue' of five which he enjoyed in pre-1794 'servant' days: again wrongly, I think, because the Rear-Admiral's total 'Compensation', as laid down in the operative Order-in-Council of 23/8/1806, does not work out right unless he is allowed them.

whose income was more than £60 per annum.[1] The naval levies, of course, concerned naval men only. These were, first, the sixpence per month payable by all seafarers, merchant seamen, Royal Navy and Marines, officers and men alike, towards the upkeep of the Royal Hospital at Greenwich. Next, there was one shilling per month to be paid by all Warrant Officers into the Chatham—after 1803 the Greenwich—Chest for the benefit of sick and hurt seamen; and, last, threepence per pound annually levied on all officers for the Officers' Widows' Fund.

Again an examination of Table IX seems to reveal no particular inducement to join the Navy, even when Compensation is added to Pay, unless, of course, a man could be reasonably sure of at least commanding a first-rate. Lower down, there is practically no improvement at all. Our Lieutenant, for instance, though he has gained a trifle on Compensation, has lost it on taxes. He is still at the £100 mark.

Indeed, that Pay and Allowances alone furnished no sort of inducement to join the Navy, even as an officer, is confirmed from a rather unexpected quarter. Nelson, though no doubt nothing would have kept him personally from a sea-life, had other views about other people. Before the 1793 war began, when he was undergoing his one long spell of half-pay, he opposed the scheme of entering his step-son Nisbet into the Navy on two grounds—that the Service was a worthwhile one only in wartime, and that a youngster with only his pay to keep him was ill-advised to take up a naval life. As it happened, however, both these objections were removed almost simultaneously. War-clouds gathered and he himself obtained a ship (thereby acquiring the means to take the boy to sea); and young Nisbet inherited some money from his great-uncle. Thereupon Nelson instantly withdrew his opposition. 'My objection to the Navy,' he wrote to Mrs. Nelson, 'now he will be certain of a small fortune is in some measure done away'[2]—and he proceeded forthwith to take him into the *Agamemnon*.

This is significant. No one could accuse Nelson himself of mercenary motives: his own reasons for having gone to sea, and persevered there, were certainly founded upon the higher motives of patriotism, predilection—and ambition. But when it came to the essentially practical business of advising his wife on a profession for her son, he realized, as probably everyone did, that on the score of pay and allowances

[1] Starting at 2d. in the pound on incomes of £60, and rising by minute steps on every extra £5 of income to 2/– in the pound on incomes of £200 and over.

[2] N.R.S., Vol. C, p. 73.

alone—and in peacetime an officer could hope for few if any other rewards—the Navy was a poor and chancy profession.

(c) *Half-Pay*

What, then, about the time when our officer, his naval life over, comes ashore for good? As the wars drew to a close, this question must have interested him almost painfully. Indeed, even before the end the average officer was nearly as much interested in his Half-Pay as in his Full Pay, because he spent an appreciable part of his time out of employment anyway. But in 1815 it became of paramount importance to him, because employment became quite a rare exception, and there was no Retired Pay at all. Towards the end, it is clear that both the officers and the authorities were thinking hard; and the latter eventually laid down what was evidently intended to be a peacetime scale on 1st July, 1814. It superseded the previous figures which dated from 1806.

It will be noticed that this term 'Half-Pay' was, all the way through the wars, an approximation only: and it must be admitted that, in every case, both before and after 1814, it exceeded a strict half of Full Pay, though sometimes not by much. The post-1814 figures, too, were better than those of pre-1814, often not by much, but sometimes appreciably. The scales for such as were entitled to it were, per diem:—

	Pre-1814[1]	*Post*-1814[2]
Admiral of the Fleet	£3 0 0	£3 3 0
Admiral	£2 0 0	£2 2 0
Vice-Admiral	£1 10 0	£1 12 0
Rear-Admiral	£1 2 6	£1 5 0
Captain	12/– to 7/–	14/9 to 10/6
Commander	6/6	10/6 to 8/6
Lieutenant	5/– to 4/–	7/– to 5/–
Master	6/– (+)[3]	7/– to 5/–
Surgeon	6/– (+)[3]	15/– to 5/–
Purser	nil	5/– to 3/–

Before 1814 these sums were paid half-yearly; after 1814, quarterly. The 'standing' Warrant Officers had no half-pay, but they did, as we saw, enjoy superannuation pensions.

It should be explained that, in the cases where half-pay varies from one figure to another, the deciding factor was (unlike with their pay) pure seniority. It would not have been possible to pay them according to

[1] Campbell's *Navy List*, Aug. 1809, p. 92.
[2] Falconer's *Marine Dictionary* (ed. Burney), 1815, p. 694.
[3] 'and upwards, according to the time of service.'

the rate of their ship since, by hypothesis, they had no ship. Thus the first 100 Post Captains on the list had the maximum, the next 150 an intermediate figure and the rest the minimum. Likewise Lieutenants: the first 300, the next 700 and the rest received respectively maximum, intermediate and minimum half-pay. The last-named category was by far the largest—in the neighbourhood of 3,000. It should be noted, however, that the post-1814 rates were being unusually kind to 'him that hath not'. Though a 3*s.* rise on the top man's £3 is nothing much, the rise of 1*s.* a day on a junior lieutenant's 4*s.* (and still more of 2*s.* on a 5*s.* payment) is really very considerable. The 'half-pay lieutenant' was to remain proverbially poor, and to eke out a rather shabby existence: but this timely rise did save him, as a rule, from sheer indigence. Even half-pay captains had to be careful, unless they enjoyed private means. For several years during his longest unemployed period (1819–35) Dillon had to divide his time fairly equally between staying with his wealthy friends in England and flitting about the Continent where the living was a good deal cheaper: and where, incidentally, he was able to meet many of his contemporaries who were doing precisely the same thing. He emerged at length from this demoralizing period; not, however, by getting a ship, but by 'taking unto myself a wife who had an independent fortune'. Thereafter, though he still goes abroad, he travels in his own carriage with his own horses, or 'takes a pleasant house for the winter'.

This is one of the seamier sides of the Great Slump, with its sad, shadowy figures striving to make do, and to preserve at least the outward show of gentility. Nor can it have been very good for their morale. It had always been something of a temptation for the Captains to await dead men's shoes with what patience they could muster. But now the infection spread: not only the long-expected flag but also the higher rates of half-pay hinged upon their seniors' demise. Moreover the Lieutenants, hitherto largely immune from such macabre temptations, now perforce joined the party. And as for those unfortunates who failed, as the wars ended, to secure even the lowest commission of Lieutenant—well, Hunt's famous engraving (facing p. 321) is comment enough: a grimly cynical caricature, of course, yet enshrining an even grimmer truth. For the point of it, now apt to be overlooked, is that the Midshipman had no half-pay at all.

Still, it may appear to the reader that the Government was being more than ordinarily generous to the half-pay lieutenants: and—on paper—it was. Up to the effective end of the war their *full* pay was only 6*s.* a day, and it is incontrovertible that even 5*s.* a day—their lowest half-pay rate under the 1814 scheme—is a very generous 'half' of 6*s.*: while the favoured few, the 7*s.* half-pay lieutenants, actually appear to be better off than when they were on full pay. This would have been so but for one thing. There was another source of remuneration altogether which might come the way of all Lieutenants while the wars lasted: might indeed come the way of all naval people. And, if it did come, it might appear in such abundance as to make such things as Pay and Allowances look puny by comparison. That source was Prize-Money, a wartime phenomenon, but almost negligible in peacetime. So, in effect, our officer, in gaining his shilling or two, was forfeiting his chance of a fortune: and the Government's apparent liberality may be regarded in some sort as a compensation to him for his lost chance.

CHAPTER X

INDUCEMENTS: PRIZE AND FREIGHT

(d) *Prize-Money*

THERE can be little doubt that here was the most important of all material inducements to a naval career.

The history of Prize-Money is old. It starts with primitive man, long before there was any such thing as an organized navy, international law or even national law: for it stems from plunder and the spoils of war: is, in fact, these things themselves, canalized by the Law, and used by the Law for a useful purpose—the encouragement of fighting men. Some canalization was clearly necessary if a free-for-all fight were not to develop after every capture. Hence the very early idea of dividing the value of a prize into share-units, and allotting so many to each category of person on board the captor-ship.

By the beginning of the eighteenth century the main legal principles underlying the taking and disposal of prizes had been settled and, though thereafter there were changes in detail, these general principles were still in force during our wars. One quite cardinal principle was, even by 1700, in the process of being established. In all earlier days the Crown had, of right, taken its percentage of prize-money, so had the Lord High Admiral, most of whose remuneration came, in fact, from this source. The rest went to the captors. But, by his Order-in-Council of 1661, Charles II had defined the shares of the Crown and of the Lord High Admiral very much in their favour. He had divided all 'Prize' into 'Droits of the Crown' and 'Droits of Admiralty', and then defined their limits. The latter consisted of enemy ships which came freely into British ports, to surrender or through stress of weather, and those wrecked upon our coasts by an 'act of God' but not by the action of

British ships. 'Droits of the Crown' covered all the rest—all taken on the high seas and sent into British ports under prize crews—and this, of course, was by far the larger category of the two. But Charles had never intended to keep all his share. He proposed to have the value of it assessed in the Admiralty Court, and to distribute half the proceeds to the actual captors. A Prize Act of William and Mary established this threefold division, the beneficiaries being the Crown, the Lord High Admiral (with a smallish share) and the captors.

By 1708, however, two important things had happened. First, the Crown had ceased (at the Revolution of 1688) to 'live of its own'. It was now in possession of a Civil List, granted to it by Parliament to cover its private expenses: and it no longer had to find the money for running the State. At the same time the incentive aspect of Prize-Money was becoming ever more important, since, already, volunteers were failing to appear in sufficient numbers. Also, as it happened, at much the same time the Lord High Admiral himself disappeared as a single individual, his 'office' being 'executed' by a number of Commissioners who, as servants of the State, were now paid State salaries. So the 'Droits of Admiralty' were no longer needed to remunerate these successors of the Lord High Admiral.[1]

The outcome of this combination of circumstances was the famous 'Cruizers Act' of 11th March, 1708. The Droits of Admiralty remained indeed, but much smaller even than before, the money derived therefrom going into the Consolidated Fund to meet part of the Commissioners' salaries. But the other two shares of the William and Mary Act, now very much swollen, were merged into one. This now enormous share, it was clearly stated, still belonged to the Crown. But that was a mere technicality. To enhance the attractions of the Service, all the proceeds of the Crown's share were normally handed over to the captors, who now, in effect, received all but the small remaining Droits of Admiralty. There were, it is true, certain minor exceptions when the Crown still took its share, and a big one too: and it was still occasionally doing so during our wars. One such occasion took place in December, 1804, when several very valuable Spanish treasure-frigates were captured, before formal declaration of war. Here three-quarters of the value were adjudged 'Droits of the Crown', and the captors had only one quarter.[2] But this was most unusual.

[1] *Prize Money*, P. K. Kemp, (Aldershot, 1946), pp. 11–14.
[2] Marshall, op. cit., II, p. 176.

This 'Cruizer and Convoys Act', to give it its full title, was one of the major naval enactments in our history, for it established the whole system of convoy-defence and trade-protection. Its 'prize-money' clauses (VI–XII) were secondary to the main object. Yet they at once became, and remained thereafter, the basis of all Prize Law. They not only gave practically all prize-money to the captors—'for the better and more effectual encouragement of the Sea Service'. They also laid down exactly when the process of prize-taking should begin and how it should be regulated thereafter. The starting-pistol, as it were, was a Royal Proclamation without which no move at all could be made. Next, the Act laid down the whole procedure of 'condemnation', the High Court of Admiralty being appointed the sole authority, before which every prize had to appear for adjudication. It also dictated rules to stop the 'breaking of bulk' of prize-cargoes, enforcing them with penalties which were often ferocious. And, lastly, it laid down exact regulations for dividing the proceeds among the various interested parties.

Such were still the main features of Prize Law in 1793 when our wars began: and, if we would assess the value of Prize-Money as a naval inducement, we must know just how our various officers and men came out of the distribution. The share-out in force in 1793 is given below but, exactly a century after the Cruizers Act—1808—a new distribution was decreed by the Government, so that the shares during the last seven years differed, in some cases considerably, from those of the first fifteen. Here are shown, slightly modified, the distributions before and after June 15, 1808.

Category	*Pre*-1808	*Post*-1808
a. The Captain (or Captains)...	$\frac{3}{8}$ share*	$\frac{2}{8}$ share†
b. Captains of Marines and Army, Sea Lieutenants, Master and Physician; equal shares in	$\frac{1}{8}$ share	$\frac{1}{8}$ share
c. Lieutenants of Marines and Army, Secretary of Admiral, Principal Warrant Officers, Master's Mates, Chaplain; equal shares in	$\frac{1}{8}$ share	$\frac{1}{8}$ share
d. Midshipmen, Inferior Warrant Officers, Principal Warrant Officer's Mates, Marine Sergeants; equal shares in	$\frac{1}{8}$ share	$\frac{4}{8}$ share
e. The rest: equal shares in	$\frac{2}{8}$ share	

* Flag Officers to have one of Captain's eighths.
† Flag Officers to have $\frac{1}{3}$ of Captain's share.

It is not hard to see why Lord Mulgrave, the First Lord who made the change, was not popular with the Captains and Admirals: for he was departing most reprehensibly from the good old rule of 'unto him that hath'.

Flag-Officers participated in the distribution of all prize-money earned by ships under their command. This does not sound particularly equitable; yet it was only what was to be expected—the Admirals always had the best of all worlds. Before 1808, we see, the 'flags' received one-eighth of the full value—that is, one of the Captain's three-eighths. But the Commander-in-Chief got his full eighth only if he had no junior flags under him. If he had one, he gave up one-third of his eighth to him: if he had more, he took one half, the other half being divided equally between the junior Flags. 'First' (i.e. Flag) Captains of Commanders-in-Chief and Commodores with Captains under them counted as Flag-Officers in this context as in that of pay. Here was a gold-mine indeed, earned moreover without much exertion and still less risk. In practice one of the well-known prize-money commands meant an almost automatic fortune. The men of the earlier wars popularly credited with exceptional luck—Anson and Saunders are names which spring to the mind—probably made something between a quarter and a half million pounds apiece during their careers.

In our wars, Sir Hyde Parker the Younger and Lord Keith were among the more fortunate beneficiaries. Dillon, who served in the West Indies with the former, says that he realized £200,000, inferring that he netted this sum on that station alone. Moreover, not content with this—and Dillon is our authority again, though the substance of his charges was the common talk of the day—he even resorted to something perilously like veiled piracy in order to swell his total. At all events, a Privateer fitted out by himself and commanded by a ruffianly person called Antoine made some very profitable voyages which overstepped the dividing-line between privateering and piracy. On one occasion he came on board Dillon's ship, the *Crescent*, to show his papers, and Dillon's Captain, seeing Parker's signature, let him proceed. But the inhabitants of Jamaica, when they found that they could get no redress from the Navy, fitted out a ship of their own which went forth and caught him. He was tried, sentenced to death, and was only spared the gallows because his wife poisoned him in prison. His body (says Dillon) was then laid across the threshold of the Admiral's official residence, the Pen; and —it must be emphasized that Dillon is still our authority, for the story is very scandalous—Parker is alleged to have offered £100,000 'to obstruct any law-proceedings brought against him'. If this be true, he succeeded. Such stories were, very likely, only the gossip of the day, directed against a never very popular officer. Yet it is probably true that Parker's acquisition of such easy wealth went to his head.

Lord Keith's prize-money, on the other hand, though to modern eyes not very well earned, was all gained in strict accordance with the law. What the grand total was does not appear, but various partial accounts of it remain among his papers.[1] In two of the three years of his Mediterranean command (November, 1799, to November, 1801) his agents show £45,704, while an earlier paper (dated May, 1800) shows that he already had £64,000 in his prize-account as a result of his lucky stroke at the Cape in 1796, and the still luckier stroke of his subordinate Rainier against the Dutch East Indies. Here is indeed a good illustration of the fantastic unreality of the business. Peter Rainier, then commanding in East Indian waters, decided entirely on his own to attack, among other places, the islands of Banda and Amboyna. He proceeded to capture them with ease in February, 1796. But, in the preceding August, Keith had been appointed C.-in-C. over the vast area of ocean from the Cape of Good Hope eastwards. It is true that he made one incursion into the Indian Ocean and was on Indian soil for some two months. But his movements bore no relation whatever to Rainier's, nor did he ever get within a thousand miles of him, or have any say, or hand, in Rainier's operations. Yet Rainier's share of the Banda and Amboyna prize-money was £14,150, and Keith's was £28,300. It was with these sums, so effortlessly won in 1796, that he bought himself his estates of Tulliallen and Kincardine. Or again, while as C.-in-C., Mediterranean, he lay off the coast of Italy, Sir John Duckworth, off Cadiz, snapped up some Spanish frigates carrying quicksilver. For this Keith pocketed £10,000. First and last, he must have been easily in the £200,000 group.

Other admirals in our wars who were fortune's favourites were this same Rainier (who, for all his 'disappointment' at Banda and Amboyna, is said to have made £300,000 during his career) and Edward Pellew, Viscount Exmouth, who is credited with the same round number.[2] Both figures may be slight exaggerations—popular rumour also is apt to fall into that same error of adding 'unto him that hath'. But they are certainly not wildly out. Nor should it be forgotten that £300,000 then was worth something like a million now.

In striking contrast Nelson fared far worse. He was not, to his lasting

[1] N.R.S., Vol. XC, p. 394, and Vol. XCVI, p. 218.
[2] *War in the Eastern Seas*, by C. N. Parkinson, p. 349.

credit be it said, the man to put prize-money before service, and he undoubtedly lost some certain chances of enriching himself, as when, in 1798, he refused to waste an hour in taking a Spanish merchant fleet which he sighted as he was searching for Brueys. We must not, however, make too much of a paragon even of Nelson. That his eye was not blind to the pleasantness of prize-money is clear from his many day-to-day references to it in his correspondence, and his well-known lawsuit with his old friend and patron St. Vincent. (Keith was a party in that dispute too, but lost it.) Collingwood was another who did not make a fortune from this source. Though C.-in-C., Mediterranean for four and a half years, he netted, he tells us,[1] no more than £28,000 during the period. But so complete was our mastery of the Mediterranean by then that there were very few enemy ships at sea to be captured.

Balancing the modest receipts of our Nelsons and Collingwoods against the fabulous fortunes of the Hyde Parkers, Keiths, Rainiers and Pellews, we may perhaps assess the average value of a good Commander-in-Chiefship at around £100,000. Nor, of course, was this all, because all Admirals had previously, for many years, been Captains. What, then, of a Captain's chances of a fortune?

In the first place, they were decidedly more chancy. Where an Admiral was almost certain of a fair fortune, a Captain had to enjoy luck in order to make it: and many never did. Yet—when Fortune did smile—the results could be spectacular. Again the instance usually cited as classical falls outside our period. When the Spanish frigate *Hermione*, loaded with treasure from the Indies, was taken off Barcelona in 1762, the two heaven-favoured captains responsible, Sawyer and Pownal, took just on £65,000 each.[2] Had there been only one British ship present, her commanding officer would have made £130,000 in a day. (Incidentally, that other protégé of fortune, Admiral Saunders, also had his £65,000.) But our wars furnished examples only a little less striking. On 27th January, 1807, the *Caroline* frigate took the Spanish register-ship *San Raphael*. Prize-luck, it would seem, ran in families; for her captain (who for the loss of seven wounded had some £52,000 prize-money) was Peter Rainier junior, nephew of the lucky admiral. He was then twenty-two years old, and had been a Midshipman only thirteen months before. (The Commander-in-Chief, Pellew, had £26,000.) Two

[1] Collingwood, op. cit., p. 306.

[2] Robert Beatson, *Naval and Military Memoirs of Great Britain*, Vol. III, p. 412.

other famous captures took place on consecutive days—17th and 18th October, 1799—when the Spanish frigates *Thetis* and *Santa Brigida*, loaded with specie, surrendered to the British frigates *Ethalion*, *Naiad*, *Alcmene* and *Triton*. Though so many had to share, each captain received £40,730 for his not very dangerous pains. It was over this affair that Nelson and St. Vincent went to law, with Keith as third party; and after a long-drawn-out case Nelson won. These endless disputes and lawsuits, arising especially from the claims of junior flag-officers, were one evil inherent in the system.

Another famous (the Spaniards said infamous) capture was that of four Spanish treasure-frigates on 5th October, 1804, made before war was declared. One of the enemy ships, the *Mercedes*, blew up, carrying with her upwards of 800,000 dollars as well as other valuables. The other three were worth a million pounds: but these, like the ships mentioned on page 317, were adjudged 'Droits of the Crown', and for the same reason. Thus our (relatively) unlucky frigates shared out only about a quarter of a million pounds. As one of the captains concerned—Graham Eden Hamond—happened to figure in both cases, he probably regarded himself as an injured party. But since his share, even as things went, must have been in the neighbourhood of £100,000, we need not waste much sympathy on him. A very tragic story went with the *Mercedes*. On board was a certain Spanish merchant, Captain Alvear, accompanied by his wife, five sons and four daughters, and his whole private fortune of £30,000, the fruits of his life's labours. Just before the catastrophe he and his eldest son had gone on board one of the other frigates. But all the rest of the family and all his fortune were lost. It is pleasant to be able to report that the British Government did its best for him. It could not restore his family, but it did refund his fortune.

In a letter to Lord Keith,[1] his Agent, Mr. John Jackson,[2] writes that 'the *Alcmene*'s Captain may be entitled to the $\frac{3}{8}$ and no flag-share'. This cryptic remark introduces us to another condition of prize-distribution. We saw how, prior to 1808, the Captain had a three-eighths' share, but had to give one of the eighths to the flag-officer or officers under whom he was serving. But what if he were not serving under one at all? Then he was lucky indeed; he was allowed to keep the whole three-eighths for

[1] N.R.S., Vol. XC, p. 396.

[2] These Agents, too, were 'interested parties', and usually contrived to pull a nice plum or two out of the prize-pudding; e.g. Pellew's Secretary, appointed Agent for the *San Raphael*, netted £10,000 from it. (Parkinson, op. cit., p. 347.)

himself. He was, as the phrase went, 'sailing under Admiralty Orders', and his prospects could hardly be brighter. Hence the pleasurable anticipation of all on board *H.M.S. Thetis*—quite a different ship from the Spanish treasure-ship—when she left England for St. Helena at the outbreak of the Revolutionary War with her Captain, Francis Hartwell, and (as a very diminutive Midshipman) William Dillon. For Hartwell, being a special friend of the then First Lord, the Earl of Chatham, was 'under Admiralty Orders', with no flag to demand a share of the pickings. Everything was in their favour, and not the least thing was that homeward-bound French shipping did not know that there was a war on. So, when two fat French East Indiamen blundered into the *Thetis*, they were snapped up without difficulty. Down they all got, from Captain to Landman, to congenial little sums in simple arithmetic. One—the *Mangoff George*—they reckoned would fetch £30,000: the other—*Le Trojan*—they assessed at four times that amount. In their valuations time proved that they were approximately right; but one eventuality they had overlooked. On a dark and dirty night, owing to the lubberliness of their Second Lieutenant, *Le Trojan* with its prize-crew of a handful of men and two 'elderly Mids' parted company with the *Thetis*, who never saw her again. She was recaptured by the enemy. On the whole they took their disappointment philosophically enough, even Captain Hartwell who, Dillon tells us, 'lost £40,000'. All he did, it seems, was to send for his Lieutenant, and 'very coolly addressing him, said, "I made you a Lieutenant to lose me a fortune!" ' He did, however, have the consolation of making 'something under £10,000' on the other prize, while a colleague (not, unfortunately, 'in company' with him) had £25,000 for another French East Indiaman. Young Dillon, who was only thirteen, was more disappointed than his Captain. He received 100 guineas as his prize-share in the *Mangoff George*, but would, he tells us (though he gives no explanatory figures), have made 'not less than £800' on the lost prize.[1]

With this we too may descend to the lower ranks. Dillon, just made a Midshipman, was in Category *d* on page 318, sharing his eighth with a not very numerous band of junior Warrant Officers, Mates and Sergeants. The Lieutenants, Master and Marine Captain would get a good deal more, because there were only five of them to share their eighth. Indeed at times this Lieutenant group did really well. They had £13,000 apiece from the fabulous *Hermione*, £5,091 from the (Spanish)

[1] N.R.S., Vol. XCIII, p. 90.

Thetis and *Santa Brigida*. In the last-named case the Warrant Officer group received £2,468 each, the Midshipmen £791: even the seamen each had £182, while in the 'best-ever' *Hermione* they had had £485. On a somewhat smaller scale is Richardson's lugubrious little plaint of how he and his fellow-warrant officers lost £600 apiece in the *Caesar*, because her Rear-Admiral released a valuable East Indiaman sailing under American colours in 1806. Immediately afterwards she was picked up by the *Arab* whose lucky officers collected the money when she was condemned.[1]

But surely the best-ever Lieutenant's haul must be that of Henry (later Admiral Sir Henry) Trollope who, in 1779, took two enemy prizes deeply laden with seasoned ship-timber, and had £30,000 for his pains.[2] Naturally, the circumstances were somewhat unusual. Though Trollope was then only a Lieutenant by rank, he was a Captain by post, having the command of the cutter *Kite*, carrying ten four-pounders. Thus (being 'under Admiralty Orders') he received three-eighths of the total prize-value. This was rather before our period, but Trollope was not. As Post Captain and Flag-Officer he served throughout the first of our wars and survived the second by twenty-four years.

All the cases cited, and many like them, were of course inducements, if only because they remained to be talked about for years afterwards in wardrooms and after-cockpits and on countless lower decks, whose occupants, knowing that they had happened to others, could wish themselves into imagining that they might happen to them. For so they might, and in terms of wages the possible figures were indeed fantastic. The *Ethalion* seamen, for instance, had earned sixteen years' wages in one afternoon. But a sense of proportion is important. So far we have dealt in exceptions, the highlights in the lives of the very fortunate few. Much more often the Lieutenants—and still more those in the categories below them—thought that they had done very well if their shares reached three figures. Dillon records that the biggest single prize-sum he ever received was £500, earned when he was still a Lieutenant. But he was never lucky in the Prize-lottery and, perhaps as a consequence, was apt to carp at the delays and extortions of the Prize Courts, especially at the exorbitant 'expenses' charged in them.

We may be sure that there were real grounds for complaint here. The whole system must have been a paradise for officialdom and unscrupu-

[1] Richardson, op. cit., p. 224.
[2] Ekins, *Naval Battles*, p. 235.

lous agents. Once (in 1808), when he had taken a small prize condemned at £400 and had received only £28 for it, he showed that the fees charged by the Proctor of the Admiralty Court came to more than that—£31 16*s.* 8*d.*—and, not unnaturally, wondered 'why the individual in the office should receive, though not exposed to any danger or responsibility, the same sum as the Captain'.[1] His irritation becomes even more pardonable when we learn that, in taking this insignificant prize, he had sustained several painful wounds from whose effects he never wholly recovered. Nor was his experience by any means an isolated, or even extreme, case. Here are two more, exposed in 1810.[2] When a small French prize was sold for £291 11*s.* 1*d.*, the total 'charges' came to £221 1*s.* 4*d.* And here is an even stranger balance-sheet:—

Neutral ship brought in by Admiralty Order-in-Council.

Proctor's Bill	£168 12 3
Part only of cargo condemned	£13 16 6
Captain's Share	*—£154 15 9 !*

This case was of course quite exceptional: but it does serve to remind us that every officer faced certain risks. If he picked a wrong one, and failed to get his capture condemned in a Prize Court, he was liable to be sued for damages by the owners. In this respect there was an analogy with impressment (see p. 107): but, here, the officer was more likely to receive justice, because the courts, though usually anti-press, were seldom anti-prize.

Probably the best close-up sketch of corrupt Prize Courts in action comes from the embittered pen of Lord Cochrane who, in 1811, paid a special private visit to Malta to try to discover what was happening to prize-money due to him for his highly successful operations in the *Speedy* and the *Impérieuse*. Among endless other scandals, he unearthed the fact that a certain Mr Jackson filled both the all-important Prize-Court offices of Proctor and Marshal. The resulting situation was pure Gilbert. Surely Sir William had Cochrane's *Autobiography* in his hand as he wrote *The Mikado*? Surely Pooh Bah's original name was Jackson?

'The consequence was that every prize placed in his pands as Proctor had to pass through his hands as Marshal, whilst as Proctor it was further in his power to consult himself as often as he pleased, and to any

[1] N.R.S., Vol. XCVII, p. 116.

[2] *An Appeal to His Majesty, both Houses of Parliament, etc.*, by a Friend of the Navy, 1810, p. 23.

extent he pleased. The amount of self-consultation may be imagined. Right profitably did Mr Proctor Jackson perform the duty of attending and consulting himself as Mr Marshal Jackson.'[1]

A specimen list of such charges follows, ending with a handsome fee payable to the Proctor for attesting the oath of the Marshal!

The Prize-Court authorities naturally did their very best to block Cochrane's inquiries. But he was a hard man to hoodwink. A 'Table of Fees' had, by law, to be hung up in the Admiralty Courtroom. It was not there, and no one would produce it. He thereupon entered the Court when it was not in Session and, after a long search, at length found it 'wafered up behind the door' in the Judge's water-closet. He instantly pocketed it and smuggled it out of the island.

Another thing which made the Admirals and Captains furious was the new Scale of 1808. It certainly was a little hard on Dillon in particular, as he had been 'made post' only two months before. Nor would one expect the Captains as a class to welcome it, since it deprived them of the better part of one of their eighths. Nor would the Admirals like it, since it reduced their share from one-eighth to one-twelfth. Yet, though Dillon waxes eloquent over the iniquity of the First Lord (Mulgrave), the reform, in twentieth-century eyes, may seem admirable as well as overdue. For the new division actually began, in a small way, to redress the balance between 'haves' and 'have nots'.

Mulgrave had done two things: first, reduced the Captain's share from three-eighths to two-eighths (if he were 'under Admiralty Orders'), and from one-quarter to one-sixth (if he were under a Flag). Second, he had amalgamated the former categories *d* and *e*, bringing their occupants into a single larger '*d* + *e*' category. It was enlarged, however, not only in the number of its share-holders but also in the size of its shares, which had actually risen steeply from one-quarter of the whole to one-half of it. Yet he did not unduly neglect the interests of the old Category *d*, because he now introduced a sliding scale of shares within his new '*d* + *e*' category; thus:

The New (1808) *Category* '*d* + *e*'	*Shares*
Midshipmen, etc. (late '*d*')	4½ each
Inferior Warrant Officers, Captains of Tops, etc.	3 each
Able and Ordinary Seamen	1½ each
Landmen and Servants	1 each
Volunteers per Order and Boys	½ each

[1] *Autobiography of a Seaman*, p. 374.

This new distribution saw the wars out: but the Captains fought back in 1816, and for a time recovered their lost eighth. Now that peace had come, however, the whole business of Prize-Money was obviously of less account, so that no one protested very strongly when, in 1834, the upper ranks sustained a heavy defeat. The Admiral's share was reduced to one-sixteenth, and the Captain's to one-sixth of the remaining fifteen-sixteenths. What was left when this too was deducted was then divided into shares, of which the Commander received fifty-five, and so on down the scale to Boy Second Class, with one share.

As the more senior officers began to lose their favoured position, a specious and unworthy argument sometimes hovered on their lips. What is the use, it ran, of letting the common men have the money? They only waste it, get themselves into trouble, and are temporarily lost to the Service. This was often true enough—superficially. The tar rolling ashore, his pockets bulging with unaccustomed cash, was a stock subject for the cartoonist and the humorist. The sailormen who bought gold watches and fried them, or made sandwiches out of banknotes and ate them may or may not have been facts. But they were symptomatic of true things: of men constantly repressed escaping for a glorious hour or two with money to burn, but with the prospect of further repression just ahead. That they wasted their gold, when they had it, on wine, women and song none will deny; nor that they found plenty of land-sharks, male and female, to help them. But where did the blame lie? On the Seaman, or on the System?

Yet, though the seamen's prize-money was all too often wasted, there were intelligent officers who knew how to use the lure of it for the purpose originally intended—to keep morale high. Robert Wilson gives one admirable example of how his humane and imaginative Captain, Patrick Campbell, used it to keep his men happy on long operational cruises.[1] He went to great pains with his Agent to see that a constant flow of prize-payments should reach his frigate: often small but none the less sweet:

'1807 *12th July*. Each single-share man received three dollars prize-money.

25th September. One and a quarter dollars served out as prize-money to each single-share man.

1808 *22nd January*. Ship's Company paid fourteen lechins, two dollars and sixteen pence single share. A lechin is worth about 12/-.

[1] N.R.S., Vol. XCI, pp. 185, 202, 215, 222, 240, etc.

> *29th March.* Three and a half dollars served out to each single-share man.
>
> *13th July.* Each man received as single share six lechins prize-money from the Agent and twelve dollars prize-money from Captain for prize-money on board.'

In this particular instance, not only was the psychology sound, but the actual sums distributed were far from trivial to men who even now earned only £14 to £16 per annum. The lechins of the January distribution alone were worth over 8 guineas, and the total handed out between July and July doubled the single-share man's income, trebled the two-share man's, and so on. But this rate was certainly exceptional, as the frigate was often capturing local settees and trabacaloes at the rate of several a day. After the last-named distribution the men were allowed shore-leave at Malta (whence desertion was not easy), and enjoyed a glorious beano—'kicked up', says Wilson, 'what sailors call "Bob's-a-dying".' The various frolics which he describes were no doubt exceedingly childish and wasteful, but not unhumorous, nor vicious: and the Captain—wise man—looked on and laughed at some of the funnier extravagances. There can be no doubt that he commanded a happy ship, and that, though he was a fine all-round officer,[1] his intelligent use of Prize-Money had much to do with it.

Nor was it only the good officer who sometimes used the prize system intelligently. Occasionally—very occasionally, it is to be feared—the good seaman did so too. Were he lucky enough to make a good haul of prize-money—and strong-minded enough not to fritter it away—he could buy his discharge. Hay records two cases of its being done—one by a bosom friend of his named Robert White, who was a seaman in the *Valiant* in 1810 when she took the *Confiance* carrying a cargo worth £150,000: the other by a certain Richardson who in 1811 bought himself out for £80.[2]

The Privateer. Just as the frigate which went 'cruising' after enemy trade was much more popular with the prize-hunter, officer or man, than the line-ship which sought, mainly, the line-ships of the enemy, so the private ship of war was more popular, and often more profitable, even than the cruiser. For every ship of His Majesty's, even the smallest,

[1] Who can help admiring Captain Campbell? If any money was found in a captured trabacalo which the *padrone* claimed as his personal property, it was returned to him. (Wilson, p. 198.)

[2] Hay, op. cit., pp. 192 and 242.

had to spend a good deal of its time in non-prize-taking activities—reconnaissance, trade-protection, message-bearing, etc. But the Privateer could, and usually did, order his proceedings solely to secure prizes: and undoubtedly some fortunes were made that way, particularly at the start of wars and in out-of-the-way corners of the world. Yet his halcyon days were over. The big prizes such as Drake won in his time were not for him. Many small ones were the best that he could reasonably hope for. But representing as it did all that remained of the corsair tradition, privateering remained surprisingly popular. During the whole course of hostilities, indeed, the 'letters of marque' granted totalled four thousand.[1]

A privateer's life was no bed of roses. He was not usually very popular with anyone, especially the Admiralty, which considered him—as indeed he was—a formidable rival in the never-flagging hunt for men:[2] and it took the pick of his people whenever it could (see p. 112).

He had to be very careful too, in the excitement of the game, not to overstep the line between Privateering and Piracy, as our amiable friend Antoine did, when even his admiral-patron could not save him. Or again, he might make the mistake which Bartholomew James made in April, 1793. Though a Lieutenant of some fourteen years' standing, he was then (as was usual in peacetime) out of employment, and earning his living in the Merchant Service. In financial straits as usual, he conceived the idea of fitting out a 40-ton shallop as a privateer in the West Indies. He did not possess the *sine quâ non* of all privateers—that Letter of Marque wherein his Sovereign authorized him to wage private war upon the enemies of his country: but he thought that, if he could secure the permission of the local Commodore to 'wear a pennant'—that is, show national colours—all would be well. This leave he obtained, and off he went with fifteen tough men. The war had just begun, and there were still many potential prizes innocently sailing the seas. He was most successful. He soon had several captives in tow, and with them put into Kingston, Jamaica. He managed to satisfy the Commodore and his principal underling (who was none other than 'Breadfruit' Bligh of the *Bounty*): or rather, perhaps—as the sequel seems to show—he thought he had:

'. . . having bought most of the seamen's shares for forty dollars a man, so that I was sole owner and commander of the *Marlborough*' [or, as the

[1] Admiralty Registry of Issues, P.R.O. Adm. 7/325, 649.

[2] Between 1803 and 1806, 47,000 men were engaged in privateering (Barrow's *Life of Anson*, p. 467).

fancy took him, the *Little Maria*] 'the whole of the prize-money might truly be said to be mine, and which, on my coming into port, was valued, and would have sold, for £2,500. But at length they were claimed by the "Droits of Admiralty", and, to the shame and eternal disgrace of the authors of it, were condemned to them, leaving me saddled with my expenses, and a heavy loss by my purchase of the prize-money.'[1]

Unfortunately for poor James, the 'authors' whom he mentions were perfectly within their rights. All prizes taken by a ship having neither a commission nor a letter of marque were legally 'Droits of Admiralty'. Moreover, 'Breadfruit' Bligh would seem to have had the last laugh, because the Law also ordained that such captures were to be the prizes of the first Royal Navy ship that fell in with them.[2] We now begin to understand, perhaps, why Bligh (and probably the Commodore) were so obliging as to let him in! On the other hand, though his prize-money was legally denied him, James was not playing the pirate, because all his victims had been enemy ships. Later he went on another cruise, not realizing the futility of it. He was not nearly so successful this time. Yet he just succeeded in covering the expenses of the new cruise, and that by a method which carries us straight back through the centuries to Hawkins and Drake. He contrived to capture a number of Negroes, male and female, and, bringing them back to Jamaica, sold them privately to a Jew for £25 a head. He then joined a convoy bound for home, but, anchoring in the Downs, had the whole of his crew pressed.

It would be cruel to leave this tough, humorous officer without recording that, in the end, he did make prizes pay. After half a lifetime in debt, and sometimes in gaol, owing to the failure of a swindling broker, he ultimately obtained the command of a small, undergunned brig called *El Corso*, stationed in the Mediterranean. Here, in eighteen months, and without the capture of any really spectacular prizes, he made enough money not only to pay off all his debts but also to leave him with £25,000 on which to set up on shore.

(e) *Prize Bounty*

It may have occurred to the reader that this whole business of 'Prize', as an inducement to make men serve in the Navy, had in itself some dangerous implications. Since chasing after enemy merchantmen was, or

[1] N.R.S., Vol. VI, p. 217.
[2] Wilson, op. cit., N.R.S., Vol. XCI, p. 231.

might be, so very profitable, was it not conceivable that Captains, and good ones too, might sometimes be tempted to make this their primary occupation? Yet, clearly, the principal target of a warship in wartime should be the warships of the enemy. The Captain of a capital ship, it is true, though he might be tempted, would have but few opportunities of succumbing. But the 'cruiser' captain was not only tempted: he was apt to fall, since he cruised for the most part alone, or in company with other captains beset with the same temptations. After all, who was to know if, from time to time, he put profit before patriotism, chasing enemy trade when he should have been protecting ours, or scamping a financially unprofitable reconnaissance for the personal solace of a fat prize? Nor would his subordinates be in the least likely to give him away—their interests coincided too closely with his own. Such possibilities, it is obvious, must have occurred to responsible Authority almost from the first. And indeed Parliament, quite early on, had deliberately created a counter-inducement to keep—or to help to keep—its captains up to the mark. This counter-inducement was called 'Prize Bounty', or —even in our wars an official term, still often used—'Head-Money'.

This Bounty was paid only upon ships of war destroyed or captured. It had nothing to do with merchant ships. The first authority to inaugurate it was the Commonwealth Government, who decided to assess the 'prize' value of an enemy ship destroyed by counting the guns she carried and multiplying that figure by ten pounds sterling, the answer obtained being the amount to be paid to the victorious ship. This, however, was soon found to be too small an 'inducement'—a whole Ship's Company, for instance, would receive only £740 for sinking a '74'. So the Bounty was changed into a payment of five pounds per head of the crew of the lost enemy ship—hence the term 'Head-Money'. This was better. A '74' would now yield about £3,000.

It still compared most unfavourably, however, with the sums obtainable from captured merchantmen, even quite ordinary ones. For this, as far as sinking was concerned, there was no obvious remedy. Hence the strange paradox that to sink an enemy warship was the least personally profitable thing that a Captain could do to it. Indeed, this constituted one reason, no doubt, why the Admiralty was usually so free with its 'hero-promotions' which, though they did not put much immediate cash into their recipients' pockets, yet held out good financial prospects for the future. If, on the other hand, our Captain could capture his warship—and that was much the commoner occurrence in wooden-ship days—he would do better (financially) for himself: for, in addition to drawing Head-Money, he could offer the ship to his Government, not as a gift but as a purchase. The Government would usually buy it: at a fair price too, for skimping here would (or might) actively discourage the capture of enemy ships. Moreover, during the whole of the eighteenth century—humiliating though it be to have to admit it—the ships of our two commonest enemies, France and Spain, were so superior to our own that the Admiralty usually wanted them, and wanted them badly. Even so, however, nothing that anyone could do could make a warship the equal of a merchant ship in average cash-value; since cargo, the really valuable prize-asset, was not normally carried in warships. There are, therefore, no big figures to be recorded under 'Prize Bounty'. Even Trafalgar, the most shattering victory of the period, in ship losses as in other respects, brought little in cash, even to the top few. But then only four prizes survived to reach Gibraltar. Collingwood thought, rather doubtingly, that he might get £1,500. For the First of June, where all the prizes but one came home, the Captains received £1,400.[1]

The trouble in our wars, however, was not that Head-Money was too small. It was that Prize-Money was, or might be, too large. As Nelson knew only too well, 'lack of frigates' was the constant lament of Commanders-in-Chief. It would be cynical to assert that herein lay the secret of the constant shortage, but it would be unrealistic to pretend that it had nothing to do with it. Why else did the Admirals in command always have to complain that their frigates, sent to reconnoitre this place or that, invariably exceeded the time allowed for the operation? There were certainly some Captains who never put Prize before Duty, but it is much to be feared that, at some time or another, most of them succumbed to the lure: for not all our officers were dedicated men like Nelson.

We shall never be able to assess in figures the inducement-value of Prize: we shall never know with any exactitude, for instance, how many 'common people' fell to the bait of Prize-Money posters or the golden promises of recruiting Lieutenants. But we do know that, down there, it was not potent enough, because there were never enough volunteers. Higher up, however, there was never any shortage of officers: in fact, there was the reverse, a glut. And Prize was a factor in this—undoubtedly a very important one. Its call must have rung in the ear of anyone who had a reasonable chance of rising. Even for a Lieutenant,

[1] N.R.S., Vol. XCVIII, pp. 65 and 170.

though the chances of his making a fortune himself were far from good, the good chances, and the large fortunes, were well within his range if he had any ambition. He had only to achieve 'post' status. Nor need he quite despair, even if he missed promotion. He could still keep his fingers crossed and dream of the *Hermione* and her captors the *Active* and —apt name—the *Favourite*, whose Lieutenants had received in prize-money what, otherwise, they would have taken 130 years to earn. Or—more astonishing still—he could draw comfort from the contemplation of young Trollope, who in a happy hour had earned 300 years'-worth of pay—such as would only have been his had he continuously served as Lieutenant not only King George III, but both his Hanoverian predecessors, the whole Stuart Dynasty, the whole Tudor Dynasty and every sovereign of the House of York!

(f) *Freight-Money*

There remains one other considerable monetary inducement: which, however, frankly ignored all the lower folk and concerned itself only with Admirals and Captains. This was Freight-Money, a constant source of income to those whom it touched; sometimes overlooked but, as we shall see, often very considerable: often greater than Pay and Allowances; sometimes, even, greater than Prize itself.

Its story, like that of Prize, goes back long before Royal Navy days, to a time when all ships were 'private', though some of them were owned by the Crown and some by the merchants. In those far-off days, of course, all ships carried what seemed good to their owners, whether King or merchant: but the King's, being as a rule strong and well-found, often carried not only Crown goods but—for a consideration—other people's as well. Moreover, through long years of habit, the Captains of King's Ships had come to regard this carriage of non-naval cargoes as a proper and legitimate perquisite of their own. So another vested interest was born which clung on, as such interests will, even when the Crown gave way to the State, and King's Ships became State Ships. For a time, indeed, the naval captains continued not only to carry 'freight', but actually and actively to *trade*, regarding such commerce, even, as one of their most important duties, as it was certainly one of their most lucrative perquisites. Such things reached rather scandalous proportions in Charles II's time, and Mr Secretary Pepys set his face against them. In his view they detracted from the Navy's efficiency. He was, of course, quite right, and his efforts to stop the practice were partially successful. He killed the tendency of the Captains to turn H.M. Ships into merchantmen. So warship trading died out; and naval officers no longer bought, carried and sold their own merchandise. But the carriage of non-war material in warships—that is, 'Freight'—he could not abolish. It remained throughout the eighteenth century, and well into the nineteenth, as one of the two big subsidiary sources of a Captain's remuneration—the other, of course, being Prize.

Though Freight still flourished when our wars broke out (and indeed when they stopped), it had been narrowed down almost entirely to the carriage of one particular type of goods—precious metals, or, to use the technical term, 'Treasure': and this remained a very profitable vested interest, affecting far too many powerful and influential parties. One such, inevitably, was the Flag-Officer, who never let himself be left out of any distribution that was going. So he had established his right to a share, just as he had done in the matter of Prize. By the end of the eighteenth century custom had crystallized his share at one-third of the total payable by the owner. This time, be it observed, it really was a third of the whole sum paid: and the Captain had the other two-thirds—no one else participated at all. But, again as with Prize, the Commander-in-Chief shared with his subordinate flags, custom dictating a division identical with that which obtained in Prize-law.

The word 'custom', however, must be stressed, because the curious thing about Freight—and where it did differ essentially from Prize—was that the rights of all parties, Captains and Admirals alike, were based not upon Law, but upon Ancient Usage. No Cruizers Act, or its equivalent, governed it, and no official rates were laid down. All was decided by Custom or, failing that, by resort to the Law Courts. Unfortunately, but surely not surprisingly, disputes were all too frequent. There was no more fruitful source of naval litigation: which is, no doubt, one reason why the Government at last began to interfere.

But there was another reason. There had always been two separate sorts of Treasure—'Public', or State-owned bullion, and 'Private', or the property of individual citizens or corporations. For a long time, little or no distinction was made between them. But with the coming of these our major wars, distinctions began to develop. In the first case, with the ever-growing elaboration of the economies of States, the carriage of bullion and specie became more and more imperative, and therefore more and more common: and, naturally enough, the governments concerned wanted to have their Treasure conveyed by the safest possible means, which was (above all in wartime) in the armed ships of their navies. But, this being so, it was inevitable that, sooner or later, a Government would notice that it was not only paying for its own ships, but also paying extra for using them for one of its own purposes: and it would—ultimately—jib at such an uneconomic arrangement.

The case of the private treasure-owner was clearly rather different, and less likely to become acute so soon. In view of the century-old French policy of *Guerre de Course*—attack upon our trade—and the still-worldwide prevalence of piracy, he too found it desirable to have his treasure conveyed by the safest possible means, the warship. But in his case—unlike the other—he would expect, and be expected, to pay extra for the additional protection offered. So the real crux here was not the fact of freight-money itself, but the question of who was to receive it.

Not unexpectedly, then, the first move came on the 'Public Treasure' side. It was made in Britain in 1801, when all allowance for its carriage was stopped. As an instance of what tricks fortune may play, that same Captain Hamond, who had a grievance against the 'Droits of the Crown' in the matter of Prize (p. 322), brought home to England in his frigate, the *Lively*, a matter of five million dollars'-worth of species and bullion captured at various times from the Spaniards. It was considered the largest amount of Treasure ever embarked in one ship. And Hamond's freight-money was—*nil*. Again he was aggrieved, this time perhaps with better cause. The date was 1805. Four years earlier, or—as we are now to see—two years later, his reward would have run comfortably into five figures.[1] For, here as elsewhere, the Vested Interest—the age-old usage of a freight-percentage finding its way into a Captain's pocket—remained uncomfortably strong. As with Prize, the senior officers had come to regard it as an established part of their remuneration, and not only said so—loudly—but also set in motion the whole vast machinery of Interest. This, in 1807, proved powerful enough to force a partial repeal of the 1801 Order, and a 'gratuity' of one-half of one per cent was allowed for the carriage of all Public Treasure. Here, however, two things must be observed. First, though the 'gratuity' was insignificant, the recipients had gained valuable ground. For the first time Authority had acknowledged, on paper, the existence of a Captain's 'right' to receive some reward for carrying Public Treasure: and, second, no one had so much as questioned his right to freight-money on Private Treasure.

[1] Marshall, op. cit., II, p. 177.

Nothing, however, was settled. All the old and prolific grounds for dispute remained, whether between owner and captain, captain and admiral, or senior and junior flag-officers. Indeed, so many cases came up before the courts that at length, almost in self-defence, both the Court of Common Pleas and the King's Bench decided that flag-officers had no legal rights at all, even by 'custom', to any share in either the 'Public Treasure and Gratuity' or the 'Private Treasure Freights' (*Montague v. Janverin*, 1811).

There followed an even more drastic decision by the Court of Common Pleas—that, in law, no captain had any such rights either, not even in 'private' freights: for it could not be legal to use a King's Ship for any private purpose (*Brisbane v. Dacres*, 1813). The Court's decision was transparently right in logic, in law, and even in equity. But it takes much more than that to kill a Vested Interest; and these decisions did not kill this one because they still left open an immense practical loophole. Freight-money might have no standing in Law; but no one questioned the Admiralty's power to make its own regulations on the subject, which, though not upheld by the law of the land, could yet govern the relations between the Admiralty and its own officers. The long and short of it was that, in fact, everything went on very much as before. Those privileged to do so went on drawing their payment (thinly disguised as a 'gratuity') for Public Treasure carried, while, for Private Treasure, they continued to squabble with each other, and to make the best terms they could with the merchants.

It is just as the wars ended—two years after the law courts had apparently sentenced the whole thing to death—that Dillon presents us with by far the best surviving picture of what was really happening. His frigate, the *Horatio*, had recently been ordered to China. News of the battle of Waterloo had just reached him, and he was walking down a Portsmouth street when he was accosted, rather conspiratorially, by the principal East India Company agent of that town. He was dragged into a quiet corner of a bookshop and offered, then and there, '£2,000 for any quantity of money that may be sent on board your ship, on freight to India'. It sounded good. £2,000 for all but nothing! Yet Dillon hesitated, feeling that there was a catch somewhere: and so there was. At first he temporized, asking what the reason was for all this secrecy, and why the Company did not send the money out in one of its own ships. To this the agent replied that they were in a hurry to get it safely out east, and so wanted to use a fast frigate. Besides, he added smoothly, 'the

East India Company was desirous, on an occasion like this, to contribute its mite to the benefit of the Navy'. Unconvinced, Dillon returned to the attack, mentioning that his frigate was very roomy, and asking how much treasure the Company proposed to put into her. Thus directly challenged, the agent replied (or so it appears but we have to do the sum for ourselves) that they intended to send two hundred thousand pounds' worth. Dillon now did a hurried calculation and discovered that he was being offered 1 per cent freight-money. So he began to bargain, astutely as he thought. 'A due allowance ought to be made', he said, 'for the safety and the speed with which the money would be conveyed.' Besides, 1 per cent was not enough. It was 'not the usual freight in wartime on board of a King's ship', but that two-and-a-half per cent at least was what he understood 'to be the general rule going to India'. Note his language: not 'the legal freight-percentage'—not even 'the Admiralty rates'—but 'the usual', and 'what he understood to be the general rule'. No doubt he would have been more specific if possible. But he could not be, and he knew it. So, unluckily for him, did the agent, who instantly proceeded to call his little bluff. 'I shall give you a couple of hours to think of my proposal, but . . . recollect that there are, at this moment, 19 fine frigates lying at Spithead, and any one of their Captains would be too happy to have such an offer made to him.' Dillon tried another kick or two. He would not yield to a suggestion which appeared to him unfair: he could not dream of undercutting the market for the other captains, as he would be doing if he accepted a miserable one per cent: they would never forgive him. But he was well and truly squeezed, and they both knew it. So, with the best grace he could muster, and still 'vowing he would ne'er consent—consented'.[1]

He netted his £2,000 and, later, a good many thousands more: for once in the East, he was in the area where freights were most easily obtained. We next find him carrying considerable sums between Manila and Macao, where the risks from local pirates were real enough. Later still, on a second trip to the East, he carried out 1,200,000 dollars for the East India Company and other Calcutta merchants: and, owing to the friendly Interest of the Governor General, Lord Hastings ('who was an old friend of my Father'), he carried a million more from Calcutta to Madras. For the second series alone he received £5,000, which was a good deal more than he ever won from prize-money. He was acting within his rights all the time too. He was doing nothing irregular,

[1] N.R.S., Vol. XCVII, p. 333 *et seq.*

though, as he had feared, he was distinctly unpopular with other Captains for undercutting them, being told to his face that he 'had sacrificed the interests of the Navy by yielding to their terms', and that 'my naval friends were highly displeased at the agreement I had made'. Nor did he attempt concealment from his C.-in-C. at Portsmouth, who congratulated him on his fortune even though, it would seem, that sporting flag-officer took no pickings himself. The *Horatio* was sailing 'under Admiralty orders'.

The story of Freight-Money has now been brought down to the close of our wars, but its subsequent history is not altogether irrelevant, and too interesting to be ignored. It began with an unlooked-for turn. Only four years later the Law appears to have surrendered unconditionally to the Vested Interest. The Act of 1819 (59 Geo. III cap 25) authorized the Crown to take over the whole matter and to fix, by proclamation, the rates for the conveyance of treasure, both public and private, in H.M. ships of war, in both war and peace. It also laid down the proportion which was to go to various recipients. So—for the first time—the officers found that they had Statute Law behind them. The Order-in-Council of 12th July, 1819, implementing the Act, reads like this:—

Length of Carriage	*'Public'*	*'Private'*	
		Peace	*War*
Under 600 leagues	¾%	1½%	2%
Over 600 leagues	1%	2%	2½%
Beyond Capes of Good Hope and Horn	1%	2½%	3%

In this country, when Custom crystallizes into Law, the latter almost always reflects the actual usage at the moment of the change. So, in the absence of evidence to the contrary, it is fair to suppose that these were, approximately, the accepted rates of the late war-years. Dillon strongly corroborates this view, albeit unconsciously. Though a poor business man, he was a very honest one, so that when he told the agent that '2½ per cent at least' was 'the general rule', he was probably right: and his word is borne out by the above table. One per cent for 'private freight' was certainly a 'squeeze' according to that, and according to his brother officers as well. On the other hand, his own demand for 2½ per cent was just about right since, with Waterloo safely won, the Company might make something of a case for peacetime rates.

The Act also clarified the share-out, and altered it too. One-fourth was to go to the Admiral (or Admirals), one-half to the Captain, and—a complete departure this—the remaining fourth to Greenwich Hospital.

This new assignment may possibly explain Parliament's apparent surrender to the Vested Interest. The Hospital was crammed, its funds under great strain. A larger income seemed imperative, and here was a way of securing it without any new drain upon the Exchequer. But this is mere guess-work.

Freight had still nearly a century to run. There were several modifications, in 1831 and again in 1881; both in a downward direction, doubtless because the far-flung shield of Pax Britannica was making the risks fewer. By 1881, though 'public' rates remained as before, 'private' ones had fallen to a flat 1 per cent irrespective of distance.

But clearly the whole system was doomed: and the end came, quite suddenly, just after the outbreak of the 1914–18 War. On 26th October, 1914, a laconic Order-in-Council simply cancelled all previous orders, thus terminating the whole thing. By then the official view clearly was that all payment for carrying public goods in public ships and all private perquisites for naval officers were alike anachronisms.

Freight, then, in our wars was certainly an inducement, not only to Captains and Admirals but also to all those who aspired so to become. It also sweetened eastern commands, not otherwise particularly popular. For there, in the remoter pirate-infested waters, lay the best chance not only of public freight brought from Europe, but also of much private freight-carrying for local merchants, who could not drive hard bargains with the comparatively few naval ships in the area, and so had to pay at the higher percentage-rates. Anyway, we find Pellew complaining at one point that the reduction in percentages had lowered his income by a steady £2,000 a year.[1] There would seem, too, to be possibilities in the Mediterranean for Commanders-in-Chief who knew how to collect their dues. There survives an extraordinary item in the accounts of Messrs. Brown and Jackson, Agents to Lord Keith,[2] which shows that this source of income might be anything but despicable:—

Freight Money Sterling

1803, Jan. 31—1804, Dec. 31 . . . . £46,076 . 14 . 2

It is odd how, time and again, the same names crop up, whether the story is of Prize or of Freight. But the latter is the harder to piece together, because of the long-continued absence of official rates; for that led to merchants and officers coming to their own private arrangements

[1] *Parkinson*, op. cit., p. 349.
[2] N.R.S., Vol. XCVI, p. 218.

on the details of which, perhaps, neither party would be inclined to expatiate. There are even sundry hints, too, in Dillon and elsewhere,[1] of bargains struck over the carriage of illicit currency and other goods in H.M. ships, especially in the Far East. But here the story tends to leave Freight and enter the realm of Smuggling, which cannot properly be brought under the head of *official* inducements!

And how did this matter of Freight affect the lower grades of the Naval Hierarchy? Occasionally, no doubt, a more than usually generous Captain made some slight gesture in their favour; and, on one occasion at least, Dillon tells us that the East India Company 'authorized the officers of my ship to draw for £300, to lay in some stock for their mess'.[2] But he hastens to add that this was an act of grace, and not of custom, for he goes on, 'That was a generous act which was much appreciated by them'. The sad fact is that no one below the grade of Captain had any interest at all in Freight.

Insofar, then, as love of money lured men into the Navy of our period, dare we essay an 'order of attraction'? Can we report the result of the Inducement Stakes? It was probably this:

1. '*Prize*'; 2. '*Freight*'. Also ran: 3. *Pay;* 4. *Allowances.*

[1] N.R.S., Vol. XCVII, pp. 363 *et seq.*
[2] Ibid., p. 340.

PART FOUR: THE PRICE OF ADMIRALTY

ACTION, ACCIDENT AND DISEASE

'If blood be the price of admiralty
Lord God, we ha' paid in full!'

Rudyard Kipling, 'The Song of the Dead'

CHAPTER XI

THE COST IN SHIPS: BRITISH AND FOREIGN

THE beautiful Naval Prayer asks God to be pleased to receive into His Almighty and most gracious protection the persons of His sailormen servants and the fleet in which they serve: and to preserve them from 'the dangers of the sea' and from 'the violence of the enemy'. Had the prayer belonged to this century, the author, very likely, would have put these hazards the other way about. For a man usually puts first what he regards as most important, in his prayers as in his other activities. But of course the writer did not belong to this century. It is not even certain who he was—perhaps Robert Sanderson (1587–1661), Bishop of Lincoln, is as good a guess as any. Be that as it may, the prayer certainly existed in mid-seventeenth century, since it appears in the Prayer Book of 1661.

Now it takes no profound research to show that, in this country and in any century but the present one, 'the dangers of the sea' were Peril Number One and 'the violence of the enemy' quite secondary to it. This may not hold in all countries, because a good many of them have had no naval enemies, having no navy; while others, even when they embarked upon a naval war, did not really use the seas a great deal, so that its dangers did not have quite the same opportunity of catching them as did the violence of the enemy. Let us take as an example the French, in their long series of wars against the British, and especially in the last two of them which concern us here.

When their ships or squadrons put to sea, they might, of course, run into a gale, to drive them upon a lee shore: but, since it was seldom if ever part of their central war-policy to have their main fleets out upon the seas at all times and in all weathers, they had it very much in their power to stay in port if the weather looked to be coming up dirty, and not to emerge until it looked more settled. On the other hand, though they had, on coming out, a very good chance of not meeting with a dangerous sea, they had, as things were, an infinitely poorer chance of escaping a very violent enemy, who in fact actually made a point of lying just off their harbours if he possibly could, with the expressed intention of being desperately violent with them when they emerged. This happened to be the settled naval policy of this particular enemy—the British. So, certainly, a majority of the ills which French ships sustained came from the Enemy, not the Sea.

With the British it was quite the other way about. Their very decided strategy was to command and control the seas, and to deny them altogether to their enemies. But this could not possibly be done unless they were prepared to be out themselves, all over the place, and on foul days as well as fair ones. Under such conditions the sea was always about them, kind at times, at times—the reverse, while the enemy, more often than not, was snugly berthed in port. Thus the sea had far more chances of hitting the British than the enemy had: and, in the event, the blows she struck were much harder and a great deal more deadly.

But, it may be said, the policy of Britain in her twentieth-century wars had not altered very much. She still liked to hold the seas for her own use and to deny them to her foes. Why then have things changed now? Why—now—is the violence of the enemy a greater peril than the danger of the sea?

There are two simple reasons. First, the enemy is a good deal more violent than he used to be. Napoleon had no mines, torpedoes, submarines or aircraft. All these are weapons peculiarly suitable for launching by a country whose normal habitat is a defended harbour against an enemy who normally cruises in open waters: for all have the peculiar advantages of invisibility or high speed, or both—that is, the ingredient of 'surprise'. Indeed, these weapons have long since had the effect of pushing the British away from their enemy's front doorstep, so that (in the twentieth-century wars) he could emerge—especially if he did so under water or high in the heavens—without the near-certainty of a violent clash almost before his coastline was under the horizon astern. More, he could even resume the offensive, or something very like it: for he could go and stalk his enemy all over the seas, with an excellent chance of finding him too, since he was still almost certain to be cruising upon them, and not enclosed in his own harbours. Yes:

without any doubt the enemy is much more violent now than he used to be.

On the other hand, the seas are much less dangerous than they were; for many obvious reasons such as better charting of them, and much better methods and instruments of navigation: but most obviously of all because the ship is no longer so utterly at the mercy of the wind. No longer is a lee-shore the sailor's nightmare: no longer will a sudden squall carry away a goodly proportion of his total motive-power in the twinkling of an eye. The seas can still be dangerous, but they are infinitely less so than they were in the age of sail.

That 'dangers of the sea' were Enemy Number One during our wars can readily be shown by figures: figures, too, which are in their way very striking and worthy of more detailed consideration.

A. THE DANGERS OF THE SEA

Imagine yourself in a small boat at Spithead. It is getting dark, but not too dark for you to be aware, ahead of you, of a very large fleet lying there, unsubstantial, even ghostly. Approach—in spirit: there is no other approach. The flagship, it would seem, is a great three-decker first-rate of 100 guns, and she is supported by three more three-deckers only less vast, of 98 guns each. Then there is a fine 80-gun two-decker, no less than seventeen '74's', the ordinary stalwarts of the Line, and six '64's', the smallest ships to find a place therein. It is a powerful fleet by any standard, containing twenty-eight of the line, one more than Nelson had at Trafalgar. But this is a much stronger fleet than his, for it contains, also, five of those indeterminates, the '50's', and—and here, if you have any knowledge of 'Nelsonian' fleets, you will rub your knuckles in your eyes and look again. For, stretching far into the shadows lies a long, long line of frigates. Keep your head and your courage, and count them if you can, remembering that Nelson had four on his last and greatest day. Here there are sixty-eight, the largest of 44 guns, the smallest of twenty-eight. So you will find, all told, yet not going lower than 28-gun frigates (the smallest ships to which we gave that name), 101 ships of the Royal Navy. There is also a host of smaller craft which you cannot hope to number: but if you could you would count no less than 243 of these little ships, carrying anything from twenty-two to a mere four guns apiece. There lies in the darkness, in fact, a mighty fleet of 344 sail.

At first there is not a light to be seen. They look grey, thin, even transparent. But suddenly there is light and to spare. Ten of them are on fire from truck to keel! The first-rate is one of them: one of the '98's' is another, so is the '80': four are '74's', one a '64'; the other two are frigates. There is nothing to be done but to watch appalled. At first the only sound is the hiss of the flames; but suddenly, with an ear-splitting roar a '64' blows up, followed by a frigate. The light dazzles. You close your eyes an instant, reopen them and—the whole anchorage is clear of ships, clean empty. All are gone, back whence they came, which is to the bottom of half the seas of the world, or to wild and barren lee-shores where once the wind howled and the breakers leapt.

You pull for home, sobered and thoughtful. You have guessed? The ships of that great Navy were every one of them casualties of the last two French Wars: all British; all smashed or gutted beyond redemption; all dead and gone, but not one of them owing to the violence of the enemy. Those whom you watched going up in fragments or in flames finished their lives just so, entirely without the enemy's assistance. The rest had found the dangers of the sea too much for them. All told, 254 had been wrecked, 75 had foundered and 15 burned or blown up: great and small, 344 ships.

B. THE VIOLENCE OF THE ENEMY

Like as not, you did not notice as you came in, your mind still brooding over that vanished host, a very small fleet—no more than a detached squadron by comparison—which seemed to be beating out to St. Helens, bound for foreign ports. It consisted of one sail of the line (a '74'), one 54-gun ship and eight frigates. It is perhaps a pity that you missed it, for that little squadron represented the sum-total of the violence of our enemies upon us during the whole twenty-two years of fighting.

Here a word of explanation is necessary. If we follow the lists of our ships taken by our enemies, as given in the contemporary Navy Lists and in the detailed appendices of William James's *Naval History*, we shall find larger figures. For example, five '74's' are named as being captured, not one; one '54', one '50', and seventeen—not eight—frigates. And this enlarged list is accurate too. Yet ours is the more realistic set of figures because, of those five captured '74's', we actually retook three, while one more cannot fairly be counted as a 'loss'. It was the *Censeur*, a French ship which we captured but which the enemy re-took as she was on her way home unrepaired after the fight in which they lost her. So she never graced a British fleet, and therefore should not be counted at all, either as a loss or as a gain. So only one '74' was fairly and squarely lost to the enemy, and not retaken—the *Hannibal*, which went ashore under the Spanish guns of Algeciras in July, 1801, and had to surrender. Likewise, of James's seventeen frigates nine were later recaptured to serve once more under the British flag: so was James's 50-gun ship. Thus fourteen of his twenty-four 'captured' ships returned to their original owners, leaving only our ten ships—one '74', one '54' and eight frigates—as permanent prizes of the enemy and as permanent losses to us. Indeed, we might have gone even further and claimed that, since four of these 'lost' eight frigates were ships which we had previously captured from the enemy, our net frigate-loss was only four. But let them stand as losses since, undeniably, we won them, used them and then lost them again in fair fight. Let the single 54-gun ship stand too, for, though we later destroyed her, we never retook her.

Next, what of our violence *as* an enemy? To set against our loss of ten ships at the hands of our foes, what was their loss at ours? Truly the tale is very different. Spithead itself would hardly contain that fleet. For—again going no lower than 28-gun ships—we should find in it no less than 139 sail-of-the-line, headed by nine three-decker first rates carrying between 120 and 100 guns each. There would be nineteen 80-gun ships, the paladins among two-deckers, and eighty-seven '74's'—far more than ever assembled together in one place. The remaining twenty-four 'line' ships would be '64's'. Then—below the line—there would be nine '50's', ships not much favoured abroad. As for the frigates, there would be 229 of them, with the emphasis at the heavy end—44- and 40-gunned ships, which most of the continental nations favoured.

In Table X an attempt is made to record these and various other figures, still stopping short at 28-gun frigates. The decision to go no lower is partly dictated by the respective policies of the combatants. In publishing her losses at sea, Britain was singularly objective, and usually accurate. She was certainly thorough, going down to the smallest of craft, of four guns or so. Our enemies, particularly the French, were much less objective, especially under Napoleon, who had many of the propaganda tricks of the modern dictator. It would still have been possible, however, to record such enemy losses in light craft as we knew of, but for one thing. Our own authorities seem to have viewed with disdain anything smaller than a small frigate, and therefore failed to record such losses when they belonged to the enemy. The result is that, though we

TABLE X SHIP-LOSSES, 1793–1815

(Including only ships of 28-guns and upwards)

		BRITISH					ENEMY		
1 'Line' or 'Below Line'	2 Guns in Ship	3 Wrecked	4 Foundered	5 Burnt and/or Blown up	6 Total Accidental Losses	7 Losses by Enemy Action	8 Losses by British Action	9 Accidental Losses	10 Added to Royal Navy
'Line'	100 and over	—	—	1	1	—	9	12	83
	98	2	—	1	3	—	—		
	80	—	—	1	1	—	19		
	74	11	2	4	17	1	87		
	64	4	1	1	6	—	24		
Total 'Line' ships		**17**	**3**	**8**	**28**	**1**	**139**	**12**	**83**
'Below Line' (Frigates)	50	4	1	—	5	1	9	12	162
	44–40	4	—	1	5	—	94		
	38–36	36	2	—	38	6	80		
	32	16	1	1	18	2	37		
	28	7	—	—	7	—	18		
Total 'Below-Line' ships		**67**	**4**	**2**	**73**	**9**	**238**	**12**	**162**
GRAND TOTAL		**84**	**7**	**10**	**101**	**10**	**377**	**24**	**245**

know our own losses down to four-gun ships, we do not know those of our enemies below 28-gun frigates. If, then, our aim is comparison, we must stop at 28-gun frigates on both sides.

A series of such comparisons is now possible. First, let us see how far the figures in the Table bear out our contention that, where 'dangers of the sea' were Enemy Number One to Britain, with 'violence of the enemy' a very bad second, the exact reverse was true in the enemy's camp. Columns 6 and 7 show that for every one British ship taken or destroyed by an enemy, ten were lost by accident. Columns 8 and 9 show that for every one ship our enemies lost by accident they lost sixteen in action with us. Next, notice Column 10, and set it against Column 8. Here we shall obtain a rough measure of the physical damage that we did to the enemy's ships. Of the 377 which they lost, 245 were drafted into the Royal Navy. We did this, naturally, when we thought it worthwhile, and not otherwise. So the difference between 377 and 245—that is, 132—represents, roughly, the enemy ships actually destroyed or so badly knocked about as to be not worth repairing for our service. Then set Column 10 against Column 7. It is rather remarkable. While the Royal Navy was losing ten ships to the enemy, it was actually acquiring 245 from the enemy: not, of course, 245 new ones, but that number of serviceable secondhand ships. It sounds very profitable. Even when the content of Column 6 is added to that of Column 7, showing that we lost, from all causes, 111 ships of 28-guns and upwards, our balance-sheet still looks quite satisfactory. For while we were losing those 111 ships we were adding more than twice as many—245. Yet no war really pays. Ships were always wearing out, especially the British ones which were in such constant use throughout this long conflict. In spite of our reinforcing ourselves by the addition of 245 enemy ships, we were in fact building new ones of our own throughout, steadily and at times feverishly.

Let us next consider Columns 7 and 8, which invite a straight comparison between British and Enemy losses in action. We really deprived our foes of 377 ships of 28-guns and upwards while they deprived us of a mere ten. But one or two things should not be forgotten. First, though all these 377 ships were taken or destroyed by the Royal Navy—or, in a few cases, destroyed by their owners to avoid certain capture—they were not all, of course, the property of any one nation. At one time or another in the long wars, Britain was up against practically every European state, not to mention the U.S.A.; and scarcely any maritime country failed to make its contribution to the funereal list, though the main sufferers were France and Spain, followed by Holland and Denmark, more often than not mere catspaws of Napoleon's ambition. Next, no meticulous accuracy is claimed for the figures which, like most figures of this kind, are open to argument in detail. For instance if a ship is badly knocked about in a fight but escapes, only to meet shipwreck before she reaches safety, is this a case of 'violence of the enemy' or of 'danger of the sea'? It may be one or the other, it may be both: and different narrators of the same episode may take different views. In compiling these tables, then, the author seeks to avoid entanglement in minutiae of this kind. Indeed, it is not this sort of accuracy that he seeks. The true proportions may be a little greater or a little less than this 377 to 10. All he is concerned to show is that the violence of Britain's enemies was a pale thing when set against her own violence.

C. ACCIDENTAL CAUSES

(a) *Foundering*

The next to engage our attention are the British accidental losses, to be found in the earlier columns of the Table. We start with those in Column 4—'Foundered'.

Seven ships, ranging from '74's' to a 32-gun frigate, perished in this way—just went down, without striking rock or shoal or being the target of any foe. The test of gun-numbers is perhaps rather crude, but, if applied here, it shows that the ten ships lost through enemy action carried 414 guns while the foundered ships carried nearly as many —372. So the sea alone, unaided either by the land or by the enemy, was nearly as deadly to us as the enemy's efforts. Yet, all things considered, it is probably the smallness of this 'foundered' list which should impress us. During these two hard, world-wide wars, the Royal Navy was often at its wits' end to fulfil its myriad commitments, so that every available ship had to be pressed into service. All too often, a ship in crying need of a major refit could not be spared, but had to make do for another cruise or two. The wonder is that so few as seven failed to float. But these were '28-and-over' ships. The smaller ones, perhaps naturally, were not so lucky. No less than sixty-eight of them foundered.

Probing yet deeper into these disasters, we can usually—wise after the event—wag our heads and say, 'Well: how could a battered old lady like that do anything but refuse to float in dirty weather?' There are, it will be noticed, two '74's' in the list; and neither, though for different reasons, could be classified as 'A1 at Lloyds'. The *Brave*, which went down off the Western Isles on passage home from Jamaica in April, 1806, had been at Trafalgar the previous autumn—in the Franco-Spanish line. She was then an 80-gun ship called *Le Formidable*, carrying the flag of Rear-Admiral Dumanoir commanding the enemy van. She had escaped from the battle rather, but not desperately, damaged, only to fall in with the British squadron under Sir Richard Strachan a fortnight later. She was captured along with three other survivors from Trafalgar: but, this time, she was grievously knocked about, badly hurt in hull and masts and losing 200 men in killed and wounded. She was hurriedly patched up, her gun-carrying capacity being in the process reduced to 74—a sure sign that all was not considered well with her—and sent off to the West Indies, where ships were urgently needed. In one way she was lucky. When her end came all but three of her crew escaped with their lives.

No such fortune attended the other '74', the *Blenheim*, which vanished without trace in a cyclone off Madagascar on, or near, 1st February, 1807. All her people were lost, including the gallant and gifted Sir Thomas Troubridge, once the dear friend, and even near-rival, of Nelson himself. In April, 1805, he went out as C.-in-C. of the East Indian station. The ship given him was the elderly *Blenheim*, which apparently everyone knew to be worn out. She had been launched in 1761 as a three-decker of 90 guns, and she too, like the *Brave*, had suffered the cutting-down process; only more radically, because she had had one gun-deck completely removed in reducing her to a nominal '74'. She made the outward journey without mishap, thanks largely, one suspects, to the Admiral's superb seamanship and genius for getting the best out of his men. Then she went aground in the Straits of Malacca, sustaining so much damage that most of her officers declared her quite unseaworthy. But now orders came for Troubridge to return to the Cape, and—brave to a fault but, this time, overconfident—he insisted upon leaving India at once. The *Java* frigate (32), an old worn-out Dutch prize, accompanied him together with the *Harrier*, a very small 16-gun brig. Only the *Harrier* made the Cape, and no certain trace of the others was ever found.

The only other 'line' ship lost in this way was the '64' *York*, not, this time, a very old ship. She was spoken in the North Sea on Boxing day, 1803, and—sailed out of man's ken.

(b) *Fire*

Decrepit ships were the sea's natural prey. Fire was not so particular. It devoured all, old and young alike, once it could fasten its talons into them. Indeed Fire, with its inevitable comrade Explosion, was certainly the most dreaded of all menaces hanging over the sailing warship. Yet, as the Table shows, it was by no means the commonest of the 'accidental' destroyers: for a wooden ship, crammed full as it was with inflammables and explosives, was so obviously at its mercy that extraordinary precautions were usually taken to prevent it. Indeed, most captains—and all good ones—conducted regular routine fire-drills. Yet it is human to err, and men—even seamen—did let down their guard sometimes with ghastly results. After all, it needed only one little act of carelessness, laziness, or even lack of foresight, on the part of anyone from the Captain to the most irresponsible boy, and the terror was let loose. Not only was the hull itself far more combustible than an iron or steel one, but also the fire-fighting apparatus known and available would bring a smile of pity to the lips of the modern fireman. It should be added, however, that a distinct advance in this direction was made in the first decade of the nineteenth century when John Jekyll, Lieutenant, R.N., produced the first (and by no means ineffective) marine fire-engine.[1]

The factors of size, strength and seaworthiness were of no particular avail against this enemy. Indeed, Column 5 in the Table shows an undue proportion of good fine ships. The fleet lost by fire is a much more formidable one than the fleet lost in action; for, though numerically equal to it, it carried not far off twice as many guns—714 against 414—with a much bigger proportion of heavier ones. Against the one '74' in the latter list, there are here two great three-deckers—flagships both—one '80', three '74's' and a '64': no less than eight of the ten are 'line' ships. This was not mere chance. There was far more to burn in the bigger ships, and many more spots, between-deck, far harder to get at in a hurry. Indeed, the smaller the number of decks the better the seamen's chance of mastering the peril before it devoured them. Further striking proof of this lies in the fact that the number of 'under-28's' so destroyed was only four.

Detailed stories of all these tragedies are hardly worth the telling. There is a horrid sameness about them. Once the flames had really got hold it was just a question of clearing out quickly: and this applied not

[1] *Marshall*, VI, p. 65.

only to the Ship's Company, but to all other ships in the vicinity. For there was a climax to these disasters which might come sooner or might come later, but which, inevitably, would come. The flames would reach the magazines, forward and aft in the hold under the Orlop deck, and the whole would go up with an infernal roar. Let four examples suffice. In the first the climax came soon—in fact with no warning at all. In the others it came later, yet no less certainly.

The 22nd September, 1796, saw the *Amphion* frigate, Captain Israel Pellew, completing repairs in Plymouth harbour. She lay near the jetty and, as usual on such occasions, was lashed to a sheer-hulk. On her other side, quite close, lay the port Receiving-ship *Yarmouth*. Suddenly—and no one ever discovered why—the *Amphion* blew up. Nowadays, no doubt, sabotage would be suspected; and, just possibly, it should not be excluded in this case, for we know now—though few did then—that there was widespread disaffection on many a Lower Deck, destined to culminate a mere six months later in the Spithead and Nore mutinies. Yet the timing of the tragedy seems to put sabotage out of the question. As ill-luck would have it, she was due to sail next day, and two happy parties were in progress on board. In the Captain's cabin Pellew and his First Lieutenant were entertaining the captain of a '64' then in port. The first shock, with little if any effort on their part, shot both the hosts through the stern windows, and they were saved. Their guest was not. Below-deck the tragedy was much more heartrending. About 100 relatives of the men, including many women and children, were there to say goodbye. For some 300 of the 312 on board it was their last farewell, particularly harrowing to the town and neighbourhood in that almost all the sufferers were Plymouth people. The few who survived were those who happened to be on deck or aloft at the time. The casualties in the sheer-hulk and the Receiving-ship were fortunately much lighter.

On 1st May, 1795, the 98-gun three-decker *Boyne*, flagship of Sir John Jervis, lay at her moorings at Spithead. It was a perfect day, and danger was far from men's thoughts. But it was there. At 11 a.m. flames suddenly burst through the poop, coming, apparently, from the Admiral's cabin. In the matter of minutes the whole ship was ablaze from stem to stern. With commendable promptness and discipline the boats of the whole fleet turned out to assist her, and all but eleven of her people were saved. Then all hastened away, as did the other ships that lay anywhere near her. For now there occurred another unpleasant yet inevitable concomitant to fire. The *Boyne*'s guns were all loaded, and went off, first in ones and twos, then in a ragged broadside, causing many hits and some fatal casualties on ships, roundshot reaching even to the shore at Stokes Bay. After a while her cables burnt through, and she drifted east, to ground near Southsea Castle. Captain Brenton was watching, and he has left a graphic account of what happened when the end came. It might almost pass for the description of an atomic 'mushroom'.

'The afternoon was perfectly calm and the sky clear: the flames which darted from her in a perpendicular column of great height were terminated by an opaque cloud like a round cap, while the air was filled with fragments of the wreck in every direction, and the stump of the foremast was seen far above the smoke descending into the water.'[1]

His theory was that the flue of the Ward-room stove became overheated. Another widely-held theory, more picturesque if less probable, was that charred paper from the cartridges used by Marines exercising on the Poop flew in at the quarter-gallery window of the Admiral's cabin and ignited his papers. Nothing was certain, save that Britain had lost one of her finest ships.

An even larger and more famous ship was to meet a similar fate. The *Queen Charlotte*, a first-rate three-decker of 100 guns, had carried Lord Howe to victory on the Glorious First of June. Now, on the 17th March, 1800, she was flagship to Lord Keith, C.-in-C., Mediterranean, and was cruising under easy sail not many miles off Leghorn. Keith himself was ashore, but all his possessions and documents were aboard. There are odd and not altogether creditable features in the story which follows. It was discovered that the Half-deck was alight—well alight. The ship's carpenter, Mr Baird (who comes as well as anybody out of the affair), heard the news at 6.20 a.m. and hurried on to the Forecastle. But by then the whole ship aft of the mainmast was ablaze: even the sails were alight. The cause of the fire, he said later, was some straw carelessly thrown on to the tubs containing the lighted match used for signal guns. But why—apart from this initial carelessness—why was the fire allowed to fasten its fatal grip upon a ship on a full war-footing, in daylight and at sea? For it was in no inaccessible place: it might have been much worse. The Half-deck, the after part of the Upper or Main Deck, was situated relatively high up the great ship, immediately under the Quarter-deck and all but open to the air entering at the waist. There were

[1] *Brenton*, Vol. I, p. 228. See illustration between pages 384–5.

actually four levels below it—the Middle Deck, the Lower Deck, the Orlop and the Hold—and a blaze on any of these would have been a great deal more dangerous, since it would have been harder to reach and much nearer to the magazines. Mr Baird, together with Lieutenant Dundas who joined him on the Forecastle, now made a desperate but very sensible effort to prevent the flames from spreading downwards. They closed the hatches leading below, plugged the scuppers, opened the Lower Deck gunports and turned on the cocks; at the same time setting the pumps going so that the ship should not fill and sink. The two, with such company as could bear the heat, worked on the Lower Deck until the Middle-deck guns began to fall through on to them. They undoubtedly postponed the final catastrophe of explosion by several hours. In fact, it was only at 11 a.m.—some five hours after the fire had started—that the flames penetrated to the waterlogged lower regions and reached the after-magazine. There was thus, one would have supposed, ample time for the crew to escape. But no: 106 were saved, 673 lost.

It is hard to say why. It was certainly not due to any lack of gallantry in the Captain and First Lieutenant, both of whom remained in her to the last, perishing when she exploded: though it is possible that they were less efficient than brave. One reason is clear enough, though it does not explain all. Boats, any number of them, hurried to the scene and had plenty of time to take off survivors. But, as with the *Boyne*, the *Queen Charlotte*'s guns were all fully-shotted and were going off dangerously by ones and twos: moreover, though those on board might know that the great explosion had been postponed, those in the boats very likely did not—and were correspondingly shy. In a word, the boats hung back far more than they should. Lord Keith himself admitted it, though he did mention the circumstance, comforting to British pride, that they were almost all 'country' boats, manned by the local Italians. This was our greatest single ship-loss of the war, for the *Queen Charlotte* was the second biggest ship of the Royal Navy.

The last victim of fire to be noticed here was the 74-gun *Ajax*, burnt as she lay with Sir John Duckworth's squadron in 1807, about to go up the Dardanelles to Constantinople. This was in several ways the antithesis to the *Queen Charlotte* disaster. First, the original fire was located in an infinitely more dangerous position—in the After Cockpit, immediately over the after magazine. The outcome was happier, largely because her Captain, Henry Blackwood—the same who had commanded

Nelson's frigates at Trafalgar—was a man of decision, enterprise and commonsense. He instantly realized that the case was hopeless. Nothing that anyone could do could extinguish a fire raging so far below, and so little above the explosives. He ordered the Ship's Company to jump for it, himself leaping, the last of all, from the spritsail yard. Actually, though he could not be expected to anticipate it, the fire behaved unpredictably, at first spreading upwards only; and he could have saved more lives had he postponed for a while his order to abandon ship: for by then but few boats had arrived and, odd as it may seem, very few seamen of that day could swim. But to criticize him is to be wise after the event. Delay might have led to a hundred-per-cent casualty list where, as it was, some 380 were saved and 250 lost. No certain cause of the mishap was discovered: but the theory of a contemporary chemist is interesting—that it was due to the spontaneous combustion of coal stored in the after Cockpit. If this be correct, it shows that not all conflagrations were due to carelessness or lack of foresight: for very likely no one on board had even heard of spontaneous combustion.

(c) *Shipwreck*

The figures in column 3 of the Table show our losses by shipwreck. They are much the biggest. There are listed eighty-four ships of twenty-eight guns and upwards which perished on coasts, isolated rocks and unknown or ill-charted shoals. These are essentially the Price of Admiralty. Their number is shocking, and constitutes, at first sight, an indictment of British seamanship. Yet further reflection should convince us that the figure, grievous as it was, was no more than might be expected. After all, the average is only about four per annum, and during the whole period an annual average of well over 200 ships of twenty-eight guns and upwards was constantly courting this kind of disaster in all oceans, seas and archipelagos of the world. They were mostly engaged in that most dangerous of all sailing-ship duties—watching off enemy shores, often for months and even years on end. That this particular hazard was the cause of most of the casualties an examination of the figures will reveal. The ships which specialized in this close watching were the smaller ones and, as usual, the smallest class of which we take cognizance here are the frigates. So, of the eighty-four lost, sixty-three were frigates, and four were of the next smallest category, the '50's'. Line-ships participated, of course, in the major blockades of the greater enemy ports, but did not normally lie so close in with the land:

nor did they ever hardly—like the frigates—engage in cutting-out operations in, or all but in, enemy harbours. So the number of wrecked '64's' and '74's', though considerable, is much smaller—only fifteen. The three largest groups, '80's', '98's' and '100's', figured in the big blockading fleets, but normally lay farther out, being as a rule less manageable than the smaller ships. Two were lost, but, as we shall see, in exceptional circumstances.

The following list distributes the losses geographically. It includes the 'foundered' since all these, like most of the 'wrecked', owed their fate to the action of the sea: but not the 'burnt', which did not.

R.N. SHIPS WRECKED AND FOUNDERED

Geographical Distribution

A. WEST COAST OF EUROPE	
West Coast of France	18
Coast of Holland	8
West Coast of Spain and Portugal	8
Baltic, Jutland and Northern North Sea	7
TOTAL, WEST COAST OF EUROPE	**41**
B. COASTS OF BRITAIN	11
TOTAL, HOME WATERS	**52**
C. FOREIGN STATIONS	
West Indies	15
Indian Ocean and East Indies	10
Mediterranean	6
Coasts of North America	5
West and South Coasts of Africa	2
China Seas	1
TOTAL, FOREIGN STATIONS	**39**
GRAND TOTAL	**91**

There is little here to surprise. Our principal enemy throughout was France, and her western seaboard was at once her longest stretch of coastline and the most essential one for us to watch. We did so, therefore, without remission and so suffered our heaviest wreck-losses there, where the prevalent winds are westerly and the French coast a lee shore. Holland was our enemy for most of the time, often involuntarily. Here the shallow and shoally water constituted a danger which not all survived. The Baltic is not strictly 'home' water, yet ships operating there were mostly based on home ports, and there were dangerous waters to be negotiated both in and out. This is why, in the above list, the Baltic is associated with Jutland and the northern reaches of the North Sea. The figures for the west coast of Spain and Portugal demand no particular comment. Nor do those for the coasts of Britain since, sooner or later, all our ships must have passed that way. Of the foreign stations it is not surprising to find the West Indies in the lead. We always had many ships, mostly small ones, in those complicated island-studded waters where hurricanes were prevalent and unpredictable. These factors operated too in the East Indies, where charts were poor and typhoons common. The Mediterranean casualty-list is short in the light of the number of our ships constantly cruising there. For this, no doubt, the more temperate weather was accountable.

So much, then, for '28-and-over'. Clearly the chances of being cast away were at their greatest, however, among those 'under-28-gun' craft not analysed here. For these were the ones which were for ever hovering in danger's way, close in on enemy coasts, just off (and even in) enemy estuaries, rivers and harbours. First and last, 170 of them were wrecked, their bones distributed the world over. This was a grievous toll: yet, in just one respect to be noted later, it had its brighter side. The loss of human life involved was not so heavy as it might have been since many of the crews could, and often did, contrive to be washed ashore; as prisoners, mercifully, not as corpses.

Of the two '98's' that were lost, the fate of one calls for little comment. The *Impregnable* took the ground off the Poles near Hayling Island, with such force that in a very short time there were seven feet of water in her hold and, though her masts were instantly cut away, she was quickly lost. The date was 18th October, 1799, so that it was not too dangerously late for a three-decker to be out. In fact her loss was probably due to what in the Navy was a rather rare cause—carelessness. She was homeward bound for Spithead, which lay only a few miles ahead, and was so anxious to cast anchor there by nightfall that her Master failed to take proper precautions.

The other '98' was the *St. George*, and her loss in December, 1811, formed part of the greatest shipwreck catastrophe of the wars. A unit of the Baltic Fleet, she sailed for home in November, very late in the year for such a ship to navigate such difficult waters. She had with her several '74's' and a huge convoy of 120 merchantmen. A violent storm caught her on the 9th November while still in the Baltic. Of the convoy, thirty perished, and the *St. George* drove ashore on the island of Zealand. By dint of tremendous exertions her people got her off, but only after she had lost her rudder and all three masts. She was towed safely to Gothenburg and fitted with a temporary rudder and jury masts.

Thence she sailed again in December with two '74's', the *Defence* and the *Cressy*, told off to stand by her. But her luck was dead out. She had barely rounded the Scaw of Jutland when, on Christmas Eve, she ran into more heavy weather which settled to west-north-west at hurricane force and drove her on to the coast. Nothing now could save her. She went aground and broke up, all but six of her company perishing. The dead included her Captain and her Admiral, for, like most three-deckers, she was a flagship.

This, however, was not the end of the tragedy. Her two escorting '74's' were in nearly the same danger. Yet, not being so much damaged previously, both had a fairer chance to escape. One—the *Cressy* (Captain Paten) took his chance, wore and hauled clear. The other—the *Defence*—did not. The Master told her Captain, Atkins, that his only hope was to follow the *Cressy*: that, since the *St. George* could not wear, nothing could be done for her, and that failure to wear would mean the certain destruction of the *Defence* too. But Captain Atkins merely asked whether the flagship had made his signal to part company, and, on being told that she had not, replied, 'Then I will not leave her.' He did not. The *Defence* took the ground quite close to the flagship and, like her, was broken in pieces. Only twelve of her crew survived, and Captain Atkins was not one of them. Here was a nice problem of conflicting loyalties, which was, indeed, discussed at the time in the House of Commons. Which Captain was right? Very wisely and generously the sense of the House was that both were. This century might take a different view—that a Captain's first duty is to save his ship if the alternative is her loss without any compensating advantage to his country. Yet who, even today, would deny the moral value of Captain Atkins's decision?

Another '74' of this same Baltic fleet failed to reach home. The *Hero*, starting only on 18th December, emerged safely into the North Sea but was smitten by the same hurricane when off Holland, driven on to the Haak Sand near the Texel and smashed to pieces with the loss of all her people. In these three calamities some 2,000 British seamen were drowned.

We of this century have so 'supped full with horrors' like the sudden end of our battle-cruisers at Jutland, or of the *Prince of Wales* and *Repulse* off Malaya—and still more, perhaps, the shocking civilian death-rolls in our bombed cities, or of Hiroshima and Nagasaki—that it is hard to realize the impact made upon this country by the news of that fatal Christmas Eve. For war was still—relatively—a game of long bowls, and 2,000 corpses at one blow was a staggering, unprecedented loss. A wave, not of pessimism, but of unrelieved gloom spread over the country: yet her people, especially her naval people, reacted as is their wont.

'These losses made a lamentable impression upon the whole nation. Mr Yorke, the First Lord, it is said, never recovered the shock occasioned by that disaster. All the Navy were called upon for a subscription to relieve the widows and relatives. At Portsmouth all the officers and seamen contributed two days' pay to their assistance.'[1]

The remaining nine '74's' were lost 'all in the day's work', as it were. All have their living individual stories, but only one will be recorded here. She was the *Berwick*, a ship with a sad but exciting history. Caught in a squall in a Corsican bay in 1795 while under refit, she rolled all three masts over the side. Hastily jury-rigged, she was—rashly—sent to make Leghorn all alone: but, encountering the French Mediterranean fleet of fifteen of the line, was easily taken. She now spent ten years under the tricolor. At Trafalgar, however, she was retaken, only —like all but four of our prizes—to be wrecked on the Spanish coast. Here, perhaps, is one of those doubtful cases mentioned above, and an odd one: for though she was unquestionably a victim to the 'dangers of the sea', she was also a victim, not indeed to the 'violence of the enemy', but to the violence of the Royal Navy. We cannot count her as a ship captured by the enemy and not recovered, for she was flying the white ensign as she died. She must logically be counted as a British '74' lost by shipwreck. Of the remaining eight, seven went to their doom in 'home waters'—two off the west coast of France, three in Spanish or Portuguese waters, one off the Texel and one off Yarmouth. One was lost in the Mediterranean.

[1] *Dillon*, N.R.S., Vol. XCVII, p. 192.

CHAPTER XII

THE COST IN LIVES: 'THE VIOLENCE OF THE ENEMY'

SO FAR it is the ships which have engaged our attention. What of their people?

Here the pattern of the ships is closely repeated. Again the dangers of the sea were much more costly to us than was the violence of the enemy. But the men did not get off so lightly as the ships; in every action, naturally, fatal casualties were incurred by winner and loser alike. For instance, at Trafalgar the enemy lost twenty ships and we lost none: yet the price in human life was obviously not 'x' Frenchmen and Spaniards and no Britons. Our casualties were indeed almost always smaller than theirs, but they were continuous and cumulative throughout the conflict.

No grand total of British lives lost in action during these wars is known: nor would it be easy, or even possible, to complete such a list now. Yet available figures will be quite sufficient to establish two facts —first, that our battle-casualties were small compared with those of our opponents; and, second, that they were small compared with those inflicted by causes other than the hand and wit of man. In this chapter the first of these claims is examined: in the next, the second.

A. THE MAJOR ACTIONS

(a) *British Killed and Wounded*

Table XI shows the losses through death and wounds sustained by the Royal Navy in the six great actions of the double war. It also shows an estimate—of which more anon—of our enemies' losses, including prisoners.

TABLE XI

BRITISH AND ENEMY CASUALTIES

In the Six Major Victories

Battle	British			Enemy (estimated)				
	Killed	Wounded	Total	Killed	Wounded	Total, K&W	Prisoners	Grand Total
a. First of June, 1794 (+ preceding days)	287	811	1098	1500	2000	3500	3500	7000
b. Cape St. Vincent, 1797	73	227	300	430	570	1000	3157	4157
c. Camperdown, 1797	203	622	825	540	620	1160	3775	4935
d. The Nile, 1798	218	677	895	1400	600	2000	3225	5225
e. Copenhagen, 1801	253	688	941	790	910	1700	2000	3700
f. Trafalgar, 1805	449	1241	1690	4408	2545	6953	7000	13,953
Totals	**1483**	**4266**	**5749**	**9068**	**7245**	**16,313**	**22,657**	**38,970**

Our first concern is with the British casualties. As to their reliability, it must be observed that they are based, in most cases, upon the official returns, and must therefore be treated with a certain respect. But we must be careful not to regard them as accurate in any modern sense of that word, because the whole business of statistics was not the exact science which it has since become; and it is clear that, even at the time, they were not accepted as mathematically accurate, as the following will show. Here are the figures of three authorities, contemporary or nearly so, for the battle of Copenhagen:—

	Killed	*Wounded*	*Total*
Brenton	234	644	878
O'Byrne	240	642	882
James	253	688	941

The 'official' casualty-lists were normally based upon the Admirals' returns made in their dispatches immediately after the battle. But these returns are usually restricted to two categories only—'Killed' and 'Wounded'. A very important difference between such lists and modern ones is, of course, that the former have no 'died of wounds', 'mortally wounded' or 'dangerously wounded' sub-divisions. What seems to have happened was that, if a man was mortally wounded, or so badly wounded that he died before the list was made up and forwarded home, he would appear among the 'killed'. But if he died later as a result of his wounds themselves, or of the various complications resulting from them and their treatment in an age which knew no antiseptics, then he was not counted among the 'killed'.

This system, actually in operation, can be viewed in the *Victory* after Trafalgar. Under 22nd October, her log gives a model casualty-list: indeed one might almost say a modern one because, most exceptionally, it records the wounded under the three separate categories of 'dangerously', 'badly' and 'slightly'. There they are, all listed by 'Name' and 'Quality', the 'killed' leading off with 'The Right Hon. Lord Viscount Nelson, K.B., Duke of Bronte, Commander-in-Chief', down through Secretary, Captain of Marines, Ninth Lieutenant R.N., Midshipman, Yeoman of Signals, A.B., Ordinary, Landman, Private of Marines, to 'Collin Turner, third class [Boy]'—fifty-four of them. Then come the 'Wounded', seventy-nine in all, headed by the twenty-five 'dangerously'. But of these—inevitably—some died: Henry Cramwell, Landman, for instance, on 26th October (and entered in the log under that day);

Joseph Gordon, Ordinary, on 27th October; Alexander Palmer, Midshipman, on 29th October; and William Smith (2), Ordinary, 'at Gibraltar'.

These are all, of course, entries in the *Victory*'s log, and they are no doubt strictly accurate. But another list was under preparation, probably in the *Britannia*, flagship of Lord Northesk, third-in-command. This was the official list in embryo, prepared for, and ultimately sent home by, Vice-Admiral Collingwood. And this list showed, when published, that the *Victory*'s casualties were, not 'fifty-four killed, seventy-nine wounded', but 'fifty-seven killed, seventy-five wounded': revealing that it reached its 'final' form on or after 29th October, when Landman Cramwell, Ordinary Seaman Gordon and Midshipman Palmer, having died, could bring the 'killed' up to fifty-seven. At this figure it has remained 'in the records' ever since. Ordinary Seaman Smith (2), though soon dead, remained (officially) 'dangerously wounded' since the list was completed before he died: as, we may be sure, did others of that category: and very likely others of the 'seriously wounded' class; perhaps some of the 'slightly wounded', and even possibly (as we shall see) some not in the list at all. Almost certainly the real death-roll in the *Victory* was higher than fifty-eight, probably a good deal higher. Again, with three of the original wounded now dead, the official 'wounded' figure should read seventy-six, not, as it does, seventy-five. But this is a trivial discrepancy: indeed, as we are now to see, a minute one.

For, in all 'official' lists, the accuracy of the 'wounded' figures is even more precarious. Not only were there no sub-divisions in the lists, but also there was no sort of uniformity as to what wounds qualified for inclusion. Much seems to have depended upon the whim of the individual Captain, and many complaints survive from men not named in lists who felt that such hurts as they had received ought to have been recorded. Dillon, for instance, very sore after the First of June from being bruised, cut by splinters and knocked senseless by the wind of a shot which sandwiched him between two dead seamen killed by it, was even sorer at finding his name omitted from the list. For this he does not blame his Captain so much as the Admiral, who expressly ordered that 'slight ones were not to be noticed'.[1] There were sometimes odd omissions in the lists too. James in his meticulous way calls attention to the 'wounded' list after the battle of the Nile, and points out that, instead of the 677 included, there should be 678—'owing to the exclusion of the Rear-

[1] N.R.S., Vol. XCIII, p. 144.

Admiral's name'. That Nelson was wounded is common knowledge—'a little above his right or darkened eye', and sufficiently seriously for him to imagine for a minute or two that the hurt was mortal. This 'error', of course, is trivial—Nelson himself ordered it—and James's correction savours of the pedantic: but in other passages he shows that such mistakes might lead to really misleading results, even in the 'killed' column. Discussing the British casualties at the battle of Cape St. Vincent, where the total 'killed and wounded' was officially given as 300, he remarks that

'the slightly wounded, or those deemed so at the date of the despatches, were not allowed to be included in the returns. One consequence of this was that amputations arising from mortifications and other unexpected changes were actually undergone by several who had not been returned as wounded. In comparing, therefore, the loss in this general action with that in any other, it will be fair to consider the total of killed and wounded to have amounted, not to 300 but at the least to 400 men.'[1]

He also declares that the 227 'wounded' 'comprised only the badly wounded; a great number of whom died'. Again, the true figures at Copenhagen, he asserts, were even more at variance with the official list. Having given the latter figures as 253 killed, he goes on,

'Thus say the official returns: but it would appear that these take no notice of the slightly wounded . . . . which, according to the testimony of officers in the fleet, would have swelled the wounded total to at least 950, and the total of killed and wounded to upwards of 1,200. More than half the wounded enumerated in the returns are also represented to have died of their wounds. If this be correct, the loss may be stated thus: killed, and mortally wounded, 350; recoverably and slightly wounded, 850.'[2]

Where there are conflicting versions of casualties—and that is almost always—our Table usually follows James, who seems to take the most pains and to adduce the best evidence for his figures. But, though far from sure that he is wrong, I have not followed him in accepting his rather vague additions here suggested. Enough, however, has been said to show that all casualty-figures of the period, even official ones, can only be regarded with suspicion.

[1] *James*, Vol. II, p. 43.
[2] *James*, Vol. III, p. 76.

Indeed, what it all amounts to is this. Our experience of modern war tells us that every government is tempted to write down its own people's losses, at least while the war still rages; and, probably, to exaggerate the enemy's. This, we know, is often done deliberately, but not always—as in the case of the first British estimates of German air-losses in the Battle of Britain. But here, on the whole, our record is good, and it is perhaps fair to claim for our authorities that they have normally pursued a relatively objective policy: they have usually tried to be more accurate than most. Probably, indeed (we being of that odd disposition which seems almost to relish being 'up against it', and to get really angry only when we feel that our rulers have deliberately pulled wool over our eyes), the said rulers usually realize that it pays them to be objective, as witness the strikingly different ways in which the British and German governments handled the news of Jutland. Yet 'literal' truth is not always 'real' truth; and, when reduced to figures, the two may make very different reading. Let us see, then, if we can read the psychology of a British government responsible for furnishing an 'official' casualty-list. It is faced with conflicting aims. 'We shall,' it says, 'keep the figures as low as possible. Yet it is neither our desire nor to our long-term advantage to falsify them.' So someone has an idea. 'Let us,' he says, 'publish the exact figures, perfectly accurate in their own way, which our C.-in-C. sends us immediately after the action (having, perhaps, warned him first not to include any of the more trivially wounded). What happens afterwards, inside the casualty-list as it were, is another matter. We need not publish that at all.'

It is greatly to be feared, however, that the Admiralty sometimes had rather less creditable motives for omitting the less seriously wounded and so keeping down the totals. There had long been growing up the rather mean habit of assessing the merit of any individual performance in terms of the casualties sustained in performing it. Several cases are on record of an officer's claim for promotion, either for himself or for his First Lieutenant, being turned down on the inhuman grounds that the casualty-list—the 'butcher's bill', as Brenton realistically if crudely calls it—was not long enough to warrant it. This was procrustean and stupid. Clearly the merit of an officer's performance did not depend upon the number of his own men that he contrived to get killed or maimed. But, since every medal has to have its reverse, it is true that a commanding officer would sometimes get his own back by inserting, in the casualty-list which he forwarded, the names of seamen whose hurts were extremely trifling. This was but natural, even inevitable; the Admiralty had asked for it. Yet sometimes the initiative really came from the officer's side, as one almost humorous incident will show. Captain Molloy, suspected of not fighting his hardest in the engagements culminating on the First of June, 1794, was refused the medal which most of the other captains received, and considered his honour impugned by certain remarks made in Lord Howe's despatch. He demanded a court martial and there, to show how deeply his ship had been involved, he actually produced thirty-four entirely new casualties, none of whom had found a place in his first, and so in the official, list. This evidence, however, though supported by his own Ship's Surgeon, failed to achieve the result which so original a gambit perhaps deserved. He was dismissed his ship and not employed again. Nor do our figures for the First of June include the thirty-four sufferers.

(b) *The Enemy's Losses*

All this *suppressio veri* may not be entirely honest: but at least it is well in advance of what some of our enemies were doing. Napoleon himself was a notorious offender. Indeed, long before the end, the accounts appearing in the official French *Moniteur* had become a by-word, derided on both sides of the Channel. Here the analogy between Napoleon and Hitler is close. It is the old story of the rival claims of 'trusting the people' and 'bolstering morale'. If, then, we have run into trouble in trying to assess the real British casualties in the six great battles, what pitfalls await us when we turn to the enemy's? They will be formidable indeed, and we may as well admit at once that accurate figures are impossible. Yet approximations may still be profitable, provided that we bear in mind how uncertain they are.

We shall again take the estimates of William James as the basis of our attempt. For all his faults he was an eminently reasonable man, not lacking balance and judgment, and not at all prone to wave his little Union Jack at the expense of every other national flag. As far as 'killed and wounded' are concerned, he works methodically through all the first five actions, considering, and invariably discarding, the higher claims of British origin. But at last he has to confess himself beaten, and jibs at even an estimate of the Franco-Spanish losses at Trafalgar. It is hard to blame him: for what is he to count—the casualties inflicted by the Royal Navy alone? Or should he try to add to them the vast but shadowy company of Frenchmen and Spaniards drowned when their shot-riddled craft drove ashore in the storm following the battle? Modern Frenchmen, however, have made a great effort to reach the truth, and Colonel Desbrières produced figures. A special commission visited Cadiz to do its research on the spot, but had to admit that its findings were only approximate. Still, they are unlikely to be bettered now. They are, for storm as well as battle, those given in Table XI.

Some explanation of how the 'Enemy Casualties' in that table are assessed is necessary because few of them, as they stand, are to be found in any book of reference. First, it must be noted that there is a column for 'Prisoners', which is absent on the British side of the account. These must be shown in any comparison of relative losses since, for helping his side to fight, a prisoner is of no more use than a dead man. Next, the presence of this Prisoner column is bound to have a tremendous impact upon the relative casualty-figures of the belligerents because it is entirely one-sided. Nearly all prisoners who were taken came from surrendered ships, and in the six great battles no British ship surrendered, while upwards of fifty enemy ships did. A few more captives might be picked up from enemy ships which sank: but again, of the few that did, none was British. It would not be quite true to assert that no Britons at all were captured. At Trafalgar, for example, several small prize-crews in surrendered enemy ships were forced by the gale into Cadiz or on to nearby shores. But their number is negligible because in the nature of the case prisoner-figures, when they occurred at all, were bound to be large. Any ship which hauled down her flag normally lost her whole complement, either killed or captured: that is, her 'casualties' and her 'complement' became identical terms. In this difficult task of estimating prisoners this fact has proved very useful: for if the initial complements of the prizes are known, and we can discover the number of killed, the difference between the two will be, roughly, the number of prisoners. Some of these prisoners, however, will be wounded too, so that we must be careful not to count them twice.

Our next difficulty is that many of the records give only 'killed and wounded', failing to differentiate between them. The point is largely academic in the case of surrendered ships, where every man, dead, wounded or unhurt alike, had ceased to be of service to his side. But in uncaptured ships there would be a great deal of difference, from the man-power angle, between a 'killed' man and a 'wounded' one. One ceased to be 'effective' for ever: the other might or might not become so again. How many of the wounded did return to fight again must be to a great extent guesswork. Here, for statistical purposes, it is assumed that, on each side, 50 per cent failed to come back. This is not unduly pessimistic because, as we saw when examining British casualties, a good many of these allegedly wounded people were really dead people, while the limited surgical and medical skills of the day made complete recovery rarer than it would be today.

The estimates of relative losses in the six big battles, under the heads of Killed, Wounded and Prisoners, are given in Table XI. They have been reached by following the lines just indicated. But the process was complex and laborious; and it cannot be described briefly since it involved, among other things, a detailed examination of each battle separately. To follow its intricacies here would unduly interrupt the thread of the narrative. The argument is therefore relegated to an Appendix (p. 429).

(c) *Comparisons*

The figures in this table show convincingly enough the relationship between our violence and the enemy's. To ignore for a moment that one-sided 'prisoner' column, their total of killed and wounded was nearly thrice ours—16,313 to 5,749—while their 'killed' figure was more than sixfold—9,068 to 1,483. How are such wide discrepancies to be explained? There are several reasons. One—but not the principal one—is that our gunnery (though not, probably, our artillery) was better than theirs, especially during the first war. The French revolutionary governments, inheriting a fine ready-made corps of professional seamen-gunners, had been stupid enough to abolish it, holding apparently that pure republican zeal could be an effective substitute for technical skill. And bitterly they paid for that folly.

There is another and more cogent reason, however. It is deep-rooted in the respective war-policies, strategies and fighting tactics of the rivals. It is even true to assert that the British were trying all they knew to kill and wound their opponents, while the French were not: not, it is to be feared, for humanitarian reasons, but because they thought—wrongly—that they had a better way of winning. Their main target was the mobility of their enemy. With this in mind they deliberately fired high, launching their broadsides on the upward roll of their ships and gundecks, hoping to hit masts, yards and sails. This fire-policy often crippled the British, preventing them from pressing home their attack: but obviously it was not very deadly to British crews. We, on the other hand, believed in exactly the opposite gun-tactics, firing on the downward roll, straight into the hulls of our enemies; smashing through sides and decks and causing the splinters to fly. Those splinters were the most effective man-maiming weapons then known. The solid roundshot itself was, of course, deadly enough if or when it hit a man: even the 'wind' of a near-miss is said to have been fatal sometimes.[1] But, since it did not burst, its lateral area of destruction was strictly limited. Not so the splinters, which it sent flying as it passed through the wooden walls—jagged razor-sharp javelins of oak, sometimes a few inches, sometimes several feet long, and weighing several pounds: having, in fact, much of the disruptive effect which we associate with modern shellfire. This very marked contrast in fire-tactics goes far to explain the great differences in casualties inflicted.

Here is another measure of those differences. The British percentage of 'killed-to-total' casualties was just over 25—approximately, three Britons were wounded for every one killed. But their enemies' percentage was 55½—for every four who were wounded, five were killed. They were actually more likely to be killed than wounded. This great contrast was partly due, of course, to the different gun-tactics just discussed. But the really formidable executioner of those days was not the gun at all. It was the elements—the dangers of the sea and of fire assailing the ships' companies already smitten by the violence of the enemy. We escaped all such major disasters. No ship of ours went down or was burnt in any of the great battles: we had no such wholesale tragedies as befell the *Vengeur* at the First of June, the *Orient* at the Nile, the *Achille*, the *Indomitable* and half a dozen others at Trafalgar.

A final balance-sheet, including prisoners, and assuming that half the wounded men on both sides returned to fight again, reads like this:

	British	*Enemy*
Killed	1483	9068
Wounded (50% of total) ...	2133	3622
Prisoners	0	22,657
TOTAL	**3616**	**35,347**

No claim to exactitude is made here. These figures may well be quite badly out. Yet the result, with all its imperfections, shows the enemy as losing in this famous sextet all but ten times as many effectives as we lost ourselves. Perhaps it was only eight times, perhaps only six. All that is

[1] Cp. *Dillon*, N.R.S., Vol. XCIII, pp. 131 and 139.

maintained here is that, beyond all doubt, the violence wrought by the enemy upon our people was a mild thing compared with our violence to his.

B. EIGHT MINOR ACTIONS

These will be divided under two heads—(a) Minor Full-fleet Actions, and (b) Squadronal Actions. There are four of each.

(a) *Minor Full-fleet Actions*

In all four of these the fighting was partial only: none was fought to a finish. In all of them the relative casualties tended to follow the same lines as those of the major actions, enemy losses heavily outweighing British losses. Two features, however, mark the essential difference between the greater and the less—the smallness of the casualty lists and the paucity of prizes. Let it not be imagined that the writer is falling into that very error for which, lately, he ventured to castigate our authorities. Casualties are no automatic measure of victory, nor, necessarily, are numbers of prizes. But, in these actions, the reason why the casualties were low and the prizes few was because of the holding-back—perhaps the over-prudence—of the British commander. All four might well have been major actions; and in all of them save, possibly, that off the Ile de Groix, a really enterprising leader could probably have brought on a *mêlée*, with its heavier tale of prizes and toll of losses. It is indeed a fairly safe bet that, had Nelson been in command at any of them, that one would have been 'major'.

In this country we are apt to regard such occasions as lost opportunities, and so they usually were. But in several of them, as things turned out, the failure was not of supreme importance because the great victory was postponed, not lost for ever. Thus, had Hotham's very tame affairs off Genoa and Hyères in 1795 been anything like so decisive as the battle of the Nile three years later, there would have been, in all probability, no battle of the Nile at all: for the bulk of the ships which Nelson captured or destroyed in 1798 would have fallen to Hotham in 1795. Likewise, had Calder smashed Villeneuve off Cape Ferrol in July, 1805, there might have been a battle of Trafalgar, but it could hardly have been an action of anything like the size and importance that it was.

Little space, therefore, will be allotted to them. The figures are shown in Table XII. It will be noticed that, even in these not particularly

TABLE XII

BRITISH AND ENEMY CASUALTIES IN FOUR MINOR FLEET ACTIONS

Battle	British			Enemy (estimated)				Remarks
	Killed	Wounded	Total	Ships lost	Killed and wounded	Prisoners	Total	
Off Genoa, March 1795	74	284	358	2	c.500	c.1800*	c.2300	*Many of the prisoners were soldiers.
Off Hyères, July 1795	11	27	38	1	c.500‡	c.300	c.800	‡Mostly killed, in captured prize which blew up.
Ile de Groix, June 1795	31	113	144	3	c.700	1340	c.2040	
Off Ferrol, July 1805	39	159	198	2	476†	c.1000	c.1476	†Killed, 149; wounded, 327
Totals	**155**	**583**	**738**	**8**	**c.2176**	**c.4440**	**c.6616**	

creditable affairs, the enemy's total loss is swollen by the existence of a 'prisoner' column, which again does not appear on our side. For in all of them we captured ships (though fewer than we might) and lost none. The final balance-sheet, compiled as before, reads:

	British	*Enemy*
Killed	155	689
Wounded (50% of total) ...	291	744
Prisoners	0	4440
Total	**446**	**5873**

In three of these four fights—as with all the next four—it has not been considered worth while to try to differentiate between the enemy's 'killed' and his 'wounded'—a feat which would be largely guesswork anyway. In the summary just given, the 'killed-to-wounded' proportion of the Ferrol fight (which is known) has been used in all the actions.

(b) *Squadronal Actions*

The four engagements now to be considered are of a very different nature. The first was a drawn fight in which, in material results anyway, we came off second-best: the second was an indisputable success for us: the third and fourth were annihilations of our enemies.

1. *Algeciras*, 6th July, 1801. Here Sir James Saumarez with six of the line engaged an inferior fleet of the enemy in confined waters and, save in one particular, inflicted upon the enemy losses considerably heavier than he received, and in about the usual proportions. That particular, however, swung the figures, for once, in favour of the enemy. For here, alone among all the actions described, we lost a ship—the *Hannibal*, '74' (see page 347). So here, just for once, we and not the enemy (who lost no ship) have a 'prisoner' column.

2. *Off Cadiz*, 9th July, 1801. Only three days later, however, Saumarez got his own back, and more. In a scattered, running fight off Cadiz, with five of the line he engaged a Franco-Spanish squadron of nine. He came away with one French prize and very light casualties. But what made the affair significant, and exceedingly costly to the enemy in human life, was the fact that two Spanish first-rates took fire and were destroyed with (in killed and prisoners) the loss of practically every soul on board.

3. *Off Cape Ortegal*, 3rd November, 1805. This was an aftermath of Trafalgar, a 'mopping-up' but very brilliant operation in which Sir Richard Strachan with five line-ships met, and captured entire, a

TABLE XIII

BRITISH AND ENEMY CASUALTIES IN FOUR SQUADRONAL ACTIONS

	British					Enemy			
	Line-ships lost	Killed	Wounded	Prisoners	Total	Line-ships lost	Killed and Wounded	Prisoners	Total
Algeciras, July, 1801	1	121	250	500	871	0	586	0	586
Off Cadiz, July, 1801	0	18	102	0	120	3	1946	830	2776
Cape Ortegal, Nov., 1805	0	24	111	0	135	4 (all)	733	2207	2940
San Domingo, Feb., 1806	0	74	264	0	338	5 (all)	1510	1530	3040
Totals	**1**	**237**	**727**	**500**	**1464**	**12**	**4775**	**4567**	**9342**

squadron of four French ships, the most considerable splinter of the defeated Franco-Spanish fleet.

4. *San Domingo*, 6th February, 1806. Here Sir John Duckworth with seven ships came up with one of the halves of the 'forlorn hope' French squadron which was trying, after the débâcle of Trafalgar, to protect French interests in the West Indies. Of the five French line-ships engaged, two (including the finest first-rate in their Navy, the *Imperial*) were driven ashore and destroyed: the other three were captured.

The figures for these four actions are set out in Table XIII. Again no attempt is made to differentiate enemy 'killed' and 'wounded'. In most cases such an exercise would be rather academic. Off Cadiz a vast preponderance of the 'killed and wounded' were killed, and most of the remainder captured. Off Cape Ortegal all who were not killed were made prisoners, whether wounded or not: and the same is nearly true of San Domingo, for, though some of the unwounded escaped to the shore, it is to be presumed that all, or most, of the wounded ones were captured. Evidently there is no striking variation here of the general trends. But it is noticeable how even one solitary ship's company, when lost entire, has affected the final proportions. But for this, they would again be all but ten to one.

C. SINGLE-SHIP ENGAGEMENTS

In the twenty-two years of almost continuous warfare the number of single-ship encounters ran into many hundreds: indeed, if partial engagements, chases and boat-actions be added, into thousands. Here no attempt will be made to reach aggregate figures of casualties. That would be too herculean a labour, and there could be no guarantee of even approximate accuracy. Only a few of the general trends will be investigated.

First comes the question of announcing casualties, and the policies of the belligerents in the matter. We know but little here, but may probably assume that the respective lines taken in the bigger clashes were followed, roughly, in the smaller ones too. But here, perhaps, the Captains might be more prone to take the same line as the Admiralty and, if anything, to minimize their losses. Undeniably, it would sound well to be able to announce that one had taken an enemy ship of, perhaps, the same force as one's own, and lost few if any men in doing so. The known strength of the foe would bear witness to the importance of the affair, while a short casualty-list would surely indicate a high state of training, morale and efficiency in one's Ship's Company. There is not much evidence either way. But of very small affairs—boat-actions and the like—one quite good example survives: and there we find the Captain quite definitely minimizing losses.

Our witness is George Watson. In a boat-action off Ancona in the Adriatic in 1812, one man was killed outright and five more, including the First Lieutenant, were wounded. In the dispatch of the Captain (Sir Charles Collier) the Lieutenant is described as 'Severely wounded—since dead': for the dispatch is dated 23rd September and he had died on the 22nd. Another casualty—a landman—is similarly described, he too having died before the 23rd. The other three, all wounded by a single round of canister shot discharged at six-feet range, are described as 'Slightly wounded'. One of them was shot right through the body, and of his subsequent fate we know nothing, save that (Watson says) he lived, though severely wounded. The other two were taken to Malta hospital, both hit in the upper thigh, whose bone was completely smashed. One died of his hurt some months later: the last (who was Watson) only barely survived, lingered on in various hospitals for two years and remained a cripple for life.[1] The Captain's motive for understating his casualties is not clear. Obviously he was not seeking kudos by presenting a heavy 'butcher's bill'. Rather, perhaps, he felt that he might be accused of risking too many lives on too trivial an affair.

Anyway, whatever the motive, the results look like this:

	Dispatch	*Fact*
Killed	1	1
Died of wounds	2	3
Severely wounded	0	2
Slightly wounded	3	0

There is a wide difference between the two, especially in computing the final loss to the Service. The dispatch gives—by implication—only three permanently lost where, in fact, the number was at least five, and probably six. It would be unwise, however, to try to draw any conclusion from an action, so insignificant to all but Watson and his friends, which is only one out of so many hundreds. Here, then, we must be content to take the figures as contemporary records give them to us.

Next, in these wars as in those of the twentieth century, the advantage

[1] *Watson*, op. cit., pp. 178 *et seq.*

of heavier metal was very important, though not nearly so decisive as it was to become. In fact, other advantages could outweigh it, provided that the difference was not too marked. As a rule the British possessed in their single-ship actions those same two advantages over the French which we have observed in the larger fights, and for the same reasons. They had no better guns, but they handled them better, both because on the whole they used them more, and because the French had been, from the start, handicapped by the folly of their governments (see p. 369). Again, the respective fire-policies of the combatants, also discussed, still normally prevailed in single-ship engagements. The French still sought to cripple the British motive power and sail away themselves: the British strove to smash the French crews and their morale, to induce in them the will to surrender.

The results, in so far as generalizations are profitable and permissible, were as follows. When the British ship had the advantage of broadside weight, she was practically certain to prevail, though not infrequently the Frenchman's fire-policy so far succeeded as to allow him to break off and escape. When broadsides were approximately equal, the British ship almost always prevailed (with the same proviso as before). When the French broadside was rather the larger, the British still prevailed rather more often than not. Only when the French broadside was markedly the heavier did the decision tend to go the other way; and even then not always. Casualties followed the same course—'killed and wounded' casualties, that is: naturally, if a whole ship were captured, her casualties became 100 per cent. All this holds true, in a rather more marked degree, in Anglo-Spanish single-ship clashes. For the Spaniard's seafighting expertise and technique were certainly not better than the Frenchman's, while his will-to-win, during most phases of the war, was nothing like so intense.

The Anglo-American War of 1812–15 was an affair entirely distinct from the main war hitherto discussed in these pages—our struggle against the French Revolution, Napoleon and his vassals on the continent of Europe. I even hesitated whether to enter upon it here. For this was not like the War of American Independence, in which the rebel States and the French were allied, and making common cause against us. America was never allied with Napoleon: was, indeed, once or twice in a state of quasi-war with him. Yet I decided to make a brief incursion into this regrettable, and in fact unnecessary, war, especially when dealing with casualties. For though the wars and the enemies were different ones, it was the Royal Navy which fought both, and suffered casualties from both: relatively, indeed, suffered more heavily from the Americans than from the others. This was because the very fighting conditions were so different. In the Continental War, the Royal Navy was pitted against continental methods: but in the war of 1812–15, it was opposed, basically, by British methods.

So, in the relatively few single-ship encounters which took place—there were no fleet or squadronal actions—our late generalizations on Anglo-French and Anglo-Spanish tactics do not hold at all. Here victory went, almost always, to the heavier broadside, as did the number of casualties. The main reason for this, of course, was that, when we fought the Americans, we enjoyed no monopoly in the advantages just enumerated. The American Navy, however much it might feel inclined to deny it, was in the story of naval evolution the younger sister of the Royal Navy, with the same kind of tradition, outlook and training. Thus the Americans did not, like the French, have the tradition of high-firing but, like us, fired low to smash timbers and limbs. They even had some advantage here: for their gunnery was as good as ours, and sometimes better, because they could afford to spend more rounds on practice than we could. Also the complements of their ships were normally greater than ours: they could afford the extra hands since they had no main fleet to man and, unlike ourselves, no other enemies who had to be faced and fought at the same time. Those men too were, by the admission of both sides, very largely British-trained, though that was the limit upon which they did agree. Indeed this manning question was at the root of the war itself. The United States declared that Great Britain had pressed American seamen wholesale into her service: they did not deny that it was there that they had learnt their job. The British, on the other hand, maintained that the men they pressed were not Americans at all, but British deserters—also, of course, trained to the British method. This was the heart of the dispute which resulted in a war between two peoples then so closely akin. Probably, as usual in such sad cases, there was some right on each side—and some wrong. Some of the seamen whom we took from American ships were certainly British subjects by birth, and not even naturalized Americans, while others, whom we pressed in our need for sheer numbers, were certainly in both respects American nationals. In the heat of the quarrel, both sides claimed to be 99 per cent right. Contemporary Americans claimed that every seaman in every

American ship was American. Contemporary Britons persisted in maintaining that, though practically all the officers and most of the Marines were American, almost all the petty officers and a large proportion of the seamen were British deserters decoyed by the lavish and unscrupulous promises of the Americans. Of course there is exaggeration here. The American crews were certainly not so British as all that.[1] Nor do the British writers who make such allegations deign to mention the real cause for so much of the desertion—the wretched conditions of employment, living and recruitment obtaining in the Royal Navy.

There is little to be gained now from a detailed reiteration of such charges and counter-charges. The fairest verdict, long since accepted by the most reputable authorities on both sides, is that success in Anglo-American single-ship encounters, both in victory and in casualties, normally went to the possessor of the heavier weight of fire, irrespective of nationality. Yet it should be added that, in the opening stages of the war anyway, the British presumed too much on their relatively easy European victories. They underestimated their antagonists. This was not surprising, but it was dangerous. To feel that one will win is good for morale: to assume that one *must* win is not. The British began like that, and it came as a shock, profoundly disturbing to high morale, to discover that, here, they had no monopoly of victory.

In the European conflict, on the other hand, we had secured that monopoly long before the war ended: and this fact was so essential an ingredient of our success against our continental foes that it must not be ignored. The reasons for it are historical, and in no way disparaging to gallant enemies: nor do they asperse the morale and courage of individuals. The personal bravery of Spanish officers was notorious: they were let down constantly by weaknesses on all levels, in material as well as in personnel. The French began under equally bad, if not worse, handicaps. The Revolution had swept away not only their naval gunners: not only, even, practically the whole cadre of former naval officers: worse—even the greater part of that particular grade of French society which had for ages been providing France with officers. Many ships were thus left to the tender mercies of a new set of *soi-disant* officers, whose only qualification, apparently, was the loudness with which they could voice their republican zeal, and whose tenure of office was, to say

[1] For an attempt to estimate the numbers of British and American seamen in American and British ships, see Appendix II, p. 434.

the least, precarious. Nelson, watching the French frigate *Impérieuse* in the neutral port of Leghorn in September, 1793, was able to produce this gem:

'I have just heard that last night the crew of my neighbour deposed their Captain, made the Lieutenant of Marines Captain of the ship, the Sergeant of Marines Lieutenant of Marines and their former Captain Sergeant of Marines.'[1]

To such utter disintegration of discipline—which, however, improved gradually—must be added a perennial shortage of equipment, dockyard facilities and stores, as well as a curious feeling of inferiority in the French navy as a whole vis-à-vis the French army—a feeling fostered, consciously or unconsciously, by their various governments, and most of all, perhaps, by that 'land animal' Napoleon. Lastly, such was the pattern of war imposed upon them from the first by the more offensive strategy of the British, that the unfortunate French officers found themselves confined to port for an overwhelming proportion of their time. Now no Captain, however brave and competent—even brilliant—has ever been able to work up his ship to real sea-going and fighting efficiency without taking her to sea. Nor, as every officer knows, is endless makeshift rehearsing in harbour worth a single hour of the real thing, either for his men or for himself. Fighting morale and fighting experience, at all levels, are essential if the best results are to be expected, and the French, officers and men alike, were lacking in both, even when not deprived of them altogether.

The British, on the other hand, had plenty of both. They had come to learn what they could do, and so knew that they could do it. Their ships were no better than their enemies'—indeed usually worse, though often better-found. But they possessed in their low-firing hard-hitting method of fighting a very material advantage: both in a military sense, in that it was the more paying method, and also in the sphere of morale. With the best will in the world an officer of the 'fire-high' school could hardly dissociate himself from the idea that he was concentrating upon getting away—to fight another day, no doubt, but still escaping: still strictly defensive. But the low-firer could feel—would know—that he was out to win then and there: that he was on the offensive all the time. One other very considerable advantage the British had, so obvious that it is

[1] Letters to his wife, N.R.S., Vol. C, p. 92.

in danger of being overlooked. Our men fired their guns in anger so much more often than their opponents had the chance of doing, that, beyond any doubt, they came to fire them considerably faster. Here is an invisible factor worth remembering: one, moreover, which makes it a little dangerous to reckon the relative force of two opponents in terms of numbers of guns and weight of shot only. If a ship with thirty guns can fire four broadsides while her opponent with forty guns fires only three, each side, in the same time, has fired 120 shots: and so the apparent advantage of the 40-gun ship has disappeared.

How far these advantages could take the British in practice a few examples will show. But, naturally, not quite all actions ran true to form, and we shall later describe two in which the results were, to say the least, surprising. Let us begin, however, with a case of comparative equality in size and armament.

The *Phoebe*, Captain Robert Barlow, was rated as a 36-gun frigate of 926 tons, but she carried, according to the fashion of the day, forty-four guns. Her broadside weighed 407 pounds and her complement was 239. On 19th February, 1801, she encountered near Gibraltar the *Africaine*, a frigate too, but of 1,059 tons, and, though classed in the French navy as a 40-gun ship, carrying forty-four guns also, with a broadside weight of 334 pounds. She made up for this slight inferiority—on paper—because she had on board 715 men. But the advantage was on paper only; for, though her actual crew numbered 315—seventy-six more than the *Phoebe*'s—she also carried 400 soldiers whose presence was the very reverse of an advantage. They could only have helped had Captain Barlow been foolish enough to allow himself to be boarded. He did no such thing. A fierce two-hour gun-duel developed: then the French ship, badly wounded aloft and with her hull shot to ribbons, surrendered. The British had one man killed, the French 200: the *Phoebe* had twelve wounded, the *Africaine* 144: and the remainder, 371 men, of course became prisoners. Total casualties, the *Phoebe* thirteen, the *Africaine* 715.

Small as the *Phoebe*'s losses were, they did not constitute a record. There were four frigate actions, fatal to the French ships, in which the British suffered no casualty at all. They are worth a brief examination because they illustrate several of our points very clearly.

In October, 1793, off Barfleur, the frigate *Crescent*, Captain James Saumarez, engaged the frigate *Réunion*. The British ship—a '36'—carried just that number of guns, but the Frenchman, also a nominal '36', carried forty. The weights of broadside, however, were all but identical

—the *Crescent*'s, 315, the *Réunion*'s, 310. As usual, the French crew was larger than the *Crescent*'s—300 to 257—and the ship itself a little larger —951 tons to 888. The fight lasted for over two hours, and the *Réunion* surrendered. She lost, according to Saumarez, 120 killed and wounded: according to another account, thirty-three killed and forty-eight dangerously wounded. The *Crescent*'s losses were no killed and no wounded by enemy action, though one seaman's leg was broken by the recoil of his own gun. The points to notice here, perhaps, are that the British captain was an outstanding seaman and leader, who fought his ship with extreme efficiency: and that the French officers and crew, though they fought long and gamely, were a very inexperienced body of men. Throughout, it seems, only one French shot penetrated the British hull, and that did but little damage. Still, even so, the discrepancy in casualties is sufficiently striking.

The other three no-casualty actions were all fought in 1796. The first was the *Revolutionnaire*, Captain Cole, against the *Unité*, Capitaine (afterwards Admiral) Linois. The latter lost his ship, nine men killed and eleven wounded in a short fight from which the British emerged scatheless. But, though on paper the combatants looked pretty equal, in fact the British frigate was so much the stronger that further details are unnecessary.

One week later, the *Indefatigable*, 44, Captain Sir Edward Pellew, took the *Virginie*, 40, Capitaine Jacques Bergeret, after a fight of one hour and three-quarters. The French lost fifteen killed and twenty-seven wounded, the British again none. But once more, in that important factor of broadside-weight, we had the advantage. Further, though Bergeret was an officer much above the average, Pellew was one of the outstanding small-ship men of the wars, a natural leader, a magnificent seaman and a profound believer in gunnery-practice. It was this officer who, early in the following year, performed a feat unprecedented in sailing-ship warfare. In this same *Indefatigable*, and aided by another frigate, the *Amazon*, he engaged off Brest a French ship of the line, the *Droits de l'Homme*, a '74' carrying eighty guns, and contrived to drive her ashore, where she was totally lost. So was the *Amazon*: but Pellew brilliantly saved his own frigate. Fortune certainly favoured him in some ways. Yet the feat remains unique; for so superior as fighting units were line-ships regarded that frigates usually gave them a wide berth. In this remarkable encounter the *Amazon* lost three killed and fifteen wounded, but of course the rest (most of whom escaped drowning) were made prisoners. The *Indefatigable* lost no killed and nineteen wounded, of whom twelve were not much more than bruised. The French '74', crowded with troops from the ill-fated Irish expedition, as well as with her own crew of some 700, lost 103 killed and 150 wounded, and many more drowned.

In the last of the no-casualty actions, that between the *Unicorn*, Captain Thomas Williams, and the *Tribune*, fought off the Scilly Islands on 8th June, 1796, the French frigate was in all but one respect the superior ship, having fourty-four guns to her opponent's thirty-eight, a crew more numerous by 100 men, and a tonnage 961 to 791. Her actual broadside, however, was a little lighter. Her casualties after a long running fight were thirty-seven killed and fourteen wounded. The fact that she contrived to miss every soul in the British ship does not reflect great credit on her gunnery. But it must not be supposed that all her shot missed the *Unicorn* altogether—the yards and sails were badly damaged: which, of course, were the main targets of the Frenchman's fire. But the whole episode does reveal rather starkly the essential barrenness of the French method, for they did not even realize their modest ambition of escaping. While this action was in progress, the *Unicorn*'s consort, the *Santa Margarita*, was engaged in a very similar duel with the *Tribune*'s—an ex-British frigate, once the *Thames*, now the *Tamise*. The result was the same. The *Tamise* was taken, losing thirty-two killed and nineteen wounded: only, in securing this result, the *Santa Margarita* had two killed and three wounded. From the British point of view this was the more brilliant affair of the two, for the *Tamise* was the superior ship in everything but sheer size. Even in weight of broadside she had the slight advantage of 279 pounds to 250. Both British captains were good officers, but the *Santa Margarita*'s was the better-known. He was that 'old academite' Byam Martin.

In all the duels so far described, though the results were very one-sided, the disparity between the combatants was not great. It certainly looks as though there were approximate material odds which the British were prepared to accept and at the same time to look for victory. Yet there must have been a line beyond which enemy material superiority would be more than a match for British method and morale, and our next example seems to reveal just about where that line was drawn. The action had taken place nearly three years before the one just described, and one of the duellists was the same—the *Thames*, then British, but destined after this action to fight a campaign or two under the tricolor as the *Tamise* before returning to the Royal Navy. Her adversary was the *Uranie*, and their relative strengths were as follows:

	Thames	*Uranie*
Guns	32	44
Broadside (pounds)	174	403
Crew	187	320
Size (tons)	656	1100

The action was very severe for nearly four hours, when the *Uranie* broke off the action. But the *Thames* was quite unable to follow. She had lost eleven killed and twenty-three wounded (two mortally), which was no considerable number seeing what odds she faced; but she had also lost, not indeed all her masts, but all practical manoeuvrability. Meanwhile the enemy lay two miles away, apparently repairing her rigging, stopping shot-holes and working her pumps. There the duel ended. The *Thames* made sail in the only direction she could—straight down-wind—expecting at any moment to be attacked again. The *Uranie*, however, made no attempt to follow. But the British frigate was out of luck. Having barely lost sight of her late opponent, she ran straight into a fresh French squadron of three large frigates and a brig. Escape was impossible, for she could not even change course; and so she surrendered. The *Uranie*'s casualties, regrettably, are not known but, if analogies are worth anything, they would be quite as heavy as ours: and though the damage to her sailing-power was probably less, it is safe to assume, from the evidence of her pumps being worked, that she was even more damaged in her hull. Nor is it known whether it was a case of 'could not' or 'would not' which prevented her following the *Thames* and reopening the action. It should be recorded, however, that the gallant Captain James Cotes and his officers were so surprised at her not doing so that—wrongly—they thought she had gone to the bottom. Still, it looks as though the limit had just been reached where method and morale could no longer prevail over material strength.

We end with two encounters which, from every angle, must be labelled exceptional, because in each the outcome was clean contrary to known and accepted form. The first provided the most astonishing British victory over odds of the whole war, if not of any war. But it was also a personal exploit, for none but a man of outstanding daring, resource and genius for fighting would even have attempted it. The affair was the capture of the Spanish ship *El Gamo* on 6th May, 1801, by the

British sloop *Speedy*, Commander Lord Thomas Cochrane. The disparity of force between the duellists can only be described as ludicrous. The *Speedy*, though dignified in the Navy List with the rating of 'Sloop', was really an old coasting-brig of 158 tons, armed with fourteen four-pounder guns. This was, of course, the merest caricature of an armament, and Cochrane, an officer who often revealed a marked streak of sardonic humour—but also a very big man, who presumably wore clothes with ample pockets—once put the ship's broadside into the said pockets and walked the Quarter-deck with it. At the time of his feat, he had fifty-four men and boys in the *Speedy*: but they had been with him for many months and shared with him a long series of brilliant, ingenious and remunerative captures averaging between three and four a week. These produced not only credit and prize-money, but also a tip-top morale whose only danger lay in over-confidence. Everyone on board was utterly certain that whatever the Captain attempted was bound to succeed. They were largely in the right too, because this extraordinary man was surely the greatest small-ship man of his age, and would have been one of our greatest sea-officers had it not been for that difficult, quarrelsome trait in his character which he could never quite overcome, and which later ruined him.

The Spaniards, grown weary of the depredations committed off their shores by the insignificant *Speedy*, fitted out a ship on purpose to catch her. To make assurance doubly sure, they selected one which, by any known method of calculation, must make the outcome certain, should the *Speedy* ever cross her path. She was *El Gamo*, a ship which the Spaniards called a 'xebec' but which, for all purposes of comparison, was a full-blown frigate, carrying twenty-two long 12-pounders, eight long 8-pounders and two 24-pound carronades—thirty-two guns, throwing a weight of 376 pounds. She had a complement of 319 men.

In the event, David and Goliath met twice. In April, 1801, Cochrane was decoyed within hailing distance of the Spaniard, which was carefully disguised. Realizing her power, he thought, very naturally, that *El Gamo* was not exactly in his class. He therefore escaped by a characteristic ruse. He hoisted Danish colours and, when a boat from the *Gamo* came alongside, one of his officers who could speak Danish and was wearing a Danish uniform informed the officer in charge that the *Speedy* was just out of a Barbary port where the plague was raging. Now the Spanish officer knew quite well that, if he came aboard to investigate, he and his whole ship would have to endure a long quarantine on reaching a Spanish port: and this (as Cochrane expected) proved too much for his sense of duty. The ships parted amicably, the *Speedy*'s nationality remaining undetected.

Most Ships' Companies would now have hurried away, fervently thanking Heaven for its mercies. Not so the *Speedy*'s, who were quite cross with Cochrane for so unusual an exhibition of prudence. He therefore promised that, should they meet the *Gamo* again, they should have their wish. That event happened on 6th May following. This time the *Speedy* made no attempt to hide her identity, or to escape. A plain gun-duel was quite out of the question. At any ordinary range *El Gamo* would soon have knocked the little brig to pieces, receiving the while no harm whatever. So Cochrane closed the range to practically *nil*. Then, when the enemy shaped to make the obvious riposte of boarding, the *Speedy* sheered off at the last moment. This happened several times, but in spite of all their skill in manoeuvre, her people could not entirely escape punishment. Cochrane concluded, therefore, that there was only one thing for it. He ran right alongside the enemy so that her guns could not be depressed sufficiently to touch him. Then, collecting some forty men—nearly the whole crew, for already eight of his original fifty-four were casualties—he boarded *El Gamo*, leaving behind his Surgeon at the wheel and five others, mostly boys. Yet this was to be no last desperate rush. His extraordinary mind was at its coolest on such occasions. He split his minute force in two. Himself, his First Lieutenant and most of the forty scaled the *Gamo*'s side and appeared on her deck, ten feet above his own. The rest, under his young brother, Archibald, a Midshipman as incorrigibly brave as himself, pausing only to blacken their faces with soot, scrambled up over the bows and on to the forecastle to take the defenders in the rear, yelling like the black devils for whom they hoped the superstitious Spaniards would take them. The Spaniards obliged. They began to flinch.

Yet they could hardly fail to see how very small the boarding-party was, and they soon showed signs of rallying. Then, quick as thought, Cochrane played another card. Very coolly he hailed the *Speedy* and in a loud voice ordered fifty more men to be sent across. The ruse succeeded. Before the flustered Spaniards could realize that there was no one to come, they wilted: and, when at the same instant they saw the Spanish colours come fluttering down—Cochrane had had time to see to that too—they surrendered. This mad adventure cost the British one killed and eleven wounded, of whom three only (including the First

Lieutenant) were badly hurt. This brought their total loss to three killed and seventeen wounded, while the *Gamo* lost fifteen men (including her Captain) killed and forty-one wounded. Her remaining people—304 of them, counting the wounded—gave the *Speedy* quite a problem. But it was not beyond her ingenious commander's powers: and all, along with both ships, made Port Mahon in safety.

Yet, that British victory was in no sense automatic; that it always depended upon a nice combination of leadership, morale and naval expertise; that, were any of these conspicuously lacking, things might go very differently, let one last example show.

The *Baionnaise*, Lieutenant-in-command Richer, was what we in England barely classed as a frigate—Brenton actually calls her 'a large corvette'—though she carried at the time thirty-two guns and eight swivels. The *Ambuscade*, Captain Henry Jenkins, was an undoubted frigate, normally of thirty-two guns but here carrying forty. Neither side is very helpful about the respective broadside-weights: the French because they conceived it to be in their interests to write down the armament of the *Baionnaise* and to exaggerate the *Ambuscade*'s, the British because they did not much like talking about it anyway. The figures, however (assuming that each was armed with guns of the usual patterns), were: the *Ambuscade*, 288 pounds, the *Baionnaise*, 150, *plus*—for what they were worth—her swivels. At least there can be no doubt that, in this most important respect, the British had a very considerable advantage. On the other hand, as was usually the case, they were considerably outnumbered; for the enemy had on board a crew of either 250 or 280—it is not clear which—and a party of front-line troops, thirty strong, thus bringing her strength to 280 or 310. But the *Ambuscade*, from whom her Second Lieutenant and thirty-two men were absent in prizes, had to fight the action with 190 men and boys, the 'boy' complement being larger than usual. This, however, was by no means the worst of it. That 190 was not at all good material: certainly much below the normal standard of frigate-crews. Worse still, her Captain was not much good either. The sequel showed that there was nothing wrong with his courage, but he was clearly a careless commanding officer, and lacking in the elements of leadership: for he had managed to divide his people into two hostile cliques, the smaller of which alone was really loyal to him.

The action was fought off Bordeaux on 14th December, 1798. Through negligence in the look-out, the British frigate was taken by surprise and never cleared properly for action. Otherwise, however, things began normally enough, with the French trying hard to get away and taking a heavy pounding in the hull. Then one misfortune after another befell the *Ambuscade*. A gun on the main deck burst, putting eleven men out of action. The heavily-punished Frenchman still made all sail to escape, but, seeing that the British still followed, if but slowly, and must ultimately catch up, Lieutenant Richer—with, it is said, the advice of the officer commanding the soldiers—determined to try to board. This was not the normal French way, and a well-regulated British ship could usually avoid such a threat without difficulty. But it was rather an obvious thing for any officer to do if he knew, as no doubt Richer did, that in man-power, and there alone, he had the advantage. Two things, of course, combined to make the situation exceptional: first, here was a French officer prepared to do the unusual thing and, second, here was a British captain whose skill was so subnormal that he could not—or at any rate did not—avoid being boarded.

The *Baionnaise*, then, was allowed to approach and, either by design or accident, practically to ram her opponent, sweeping away her Quarter-deck bulwarks, mizzen shrouds and mizzen-mast, and unshipping her wheel. Then she fell away under the *Ambuscade*'s stern so that the people in her bows and on her bowsprit commanded with their musketry the whole length of their enemy's deck. Captain Jenkins, his officers and his few raw Marines did not lack courage. They fought back. But the French did not board at once: they simply mowed down the opposition with their uninterrupted fire. The First Lieutenant fell, mortally wounded: Jenkins had his thigh shot away: the Lieutenant of Marines, hit in thigh and shoulder, was carried below. The Master, upon whom the command now devolved, appeared on deck and was instantly shot through the head. The Third Lieutenant, hitherto lying dangerously ill in his cot, then most gallantly struggled on deck, only to receive a head wound which laid him low. The Purser now took charge and, as he did so there was an explosion aft, and the Gunner arrived to tell him that the ship was on fire near the after-magazine. It was then that the larger—the anti-Jenkins—part of the crew concluded that they had had enough and bolted below. Thereupon the French, led by their thirty seasoned soldiers, found that they had the *Ambuscade*'s Quarter-deck almost to themselves. They soon had possession of the ship.

It would seem reasonable to suppose that the respective casualties were as exceptional as the result. But no. The prisoner-figure of the British was of course high, including all survivors. But the 'killed and wounded' figures ran oddly to pattern—the British, ten killed and thirty-six wounded: the French thirty killed and between sixty and seventy wounded: which is a very striking commentary on much that has already been written here. It is evident that, before Richer could make up his mind to play his strong suit, the British hull-hitting methods had again proved their superiority. The Frenchman was, most deservedly, given double promotion direct to Capitaine de Vaisseau. Jenkins, when exchanged, was acquitted by the court which tried him. James suggests that his pitiful physical condition induced leniency: but in truth the decision was only fair—if for that time enlightened. Jenkins was brave enough, but professionally incompetent: and the proper remedy for that was not to punish him, but to see that he was not again put into a position where his incompetence could endanger his country.

This duel, then, ran true to form in casualties. But in result it was most exceptional, and we have seen why. Jenkins and his team lacked certain vital qualities which most of their contemporaries possessed. What were they? If we would summarize the really basic reasons for the very clear predominance of the British at sea, we can hardly do better than quote our leading adversary. Napoleon Bonaparte saw fit, again and again, to be cruelly sarcastic about the performance of his naval servants. Yet it was he himself who put his finger, with his customary exaggeration perhaps, yet with his usual acumen, upon the heart of the whole matter—'*The moral is to the material as three to one.*'

CHAPTER XIII

THE COST IN LIVES: 'THE DANGERS OF THE SEA'

A. FROM FOUNDERING, WRECK, FIRE AND EXPLOSION

THE second part of our assertion remains to be proved—that the dangers of the sea, including the various hazards to which British seamen were liable, were more deadly than the violence of the enemy. It will not be difficult: indeed, it is already half done. The proposition, as it concerned ships of 28-guns and upwards, has already been demonstrated—Britain, it may be recalled, lost 101 of them to the elements and only ten to the enemy. Moreover, the number of lives forfeited when a ship was lost whole, as by foundering, wreck, fire or explosion, was almost bound to be greater—much greater—than the number she would lose even in the hottest action. A few specimen figures will easily prove this. The *Brunswick* in her furious encounter with the *Vengeur* on the 1st June, 1794, lost forty-five killed; the *Bellerophon* in her most unequal contest with the *Orient* at the Nile lost forty-nine: but the number which perished in the *St. George* on the Jutland coast was at least fifteen times as great as either. Indeed, for purposes of comparison, one must contrast the fatal casualties in any of the greater 'accidental disasters' with those, not of individual ships in action, but of whole fleets. Thus the tale of dead when the *Queen Charlotte* was burnt was half as large again as the whole 'killed' list at Trafalgar: when the *Blenheim* and the *Java* foundered, they took with them about as many Britons as perished in all the other five great battles; while the people drowned on one day in the *St. George*, *Defence* and *Hero* greatly exceeded all our men killed in the six major battles—indeed actually exceeded, by about 100, all our fatal casualties in all the fourteen fleet and squadronal actions analysed in our preceding chapter. So, in these six sea-disasters alone, Death claimed more than twice as many victims as were slain in the fourteen largest actions of the war. Nor must it be forgotten that there were ninety-five other '28-gun-and-upward' ships in this 'accidental' list; nor—for now we are considering *all* fatal casualties—must we overlook the 243 smaller ships which were also lost.

This, however, is not all—not nearly all. So far we have been considering only the casualties in ships wholly destroyed by such accidents as foundering, wreck, fire and explosion. But such a disaster was only one of several ways in which 'the danger of the sea' in its wider sense could bring death to seamen. Those other ways are now to be examined, and they are grouped here, for convenience, under three headings. We shall find that at least two of these were much more formidable enemies than were foundering, wreck, fire and explosion all rolled into one: one of them perhaps three times as deadly, one perhaps as much as five times. We shall discover, in fact, that our enemies were responsible, directly, for barely one in ten of our full death-roll.

B. FROM INDIVIDUAL ACCIDENT

The first hazard to be considered is what may be called 'Individual Accident'. Life in a sailing warship was not, from an actuarial point of view, a good risk: the seaman, by the very nature of his calling, was highly accident-prone. Aloft, he was constantly expected to perform feats which, on land, are normally left to steeple-jacks or circus performers; and even these, as a rule, perform in reasonable weather, and in a good light. The ground, moreover, though it may be far below them as they perform, is at least stable and horizontal. But the seaman was aloft at all hours, in full day, half day or in the blackest night; in all weathers too: and his platform or tower sidled, tipped and corkscrewed as he worked. Further, the more it gyrated the quicker, surer and livelier he had to be, since that spelt bad weather, when it behoved him to work faster. On deck or below deck, too, his floor was in similar motion, while his work consisted largely in handling—raising or lowering, hauling in or pushing out—heavy, awkward and often dangerous loads: usually in confined spaces too, where headroom was quite inadequate.

The risk of fatal accident was never far away. A boat in being lowered or hoisted turns upside down or hangs by a single fall, throwing its occupants into the sea. A gun fired in practice or anger bursts, or—quite a common occurrence—breaks loose in a gale, becoming a deadly and uncontrollable monster until some intrepid, indeed highly-trained and skilled, seaman can 'trip' it, throwing it on its side, when it ceases to be an immediate menace to both ship and crew. Knippers break, and the cable, a monstrous inanimate serpent, becomes suddenly alive and takes charge. On wet, slippery or icy yards a man's numbed fingers fail him for a second: he falls, sometimes into the belly of a sail—and that is perhaps the best place to fall into, because, with luck, he can be hauled out by his friends before being catapulted into the sea. More often he bounces off the sail or drops straight into the sea, and this is possibly second-best, though rather a poor second: for a ship under sail, innocent of engine-power, is not easily stopped and still less easily put about, so that he has almost always been left far behind before the ship can come round or even before a boat can be launched. Most surely fatal of all, however, was the lot of the seaman who fell directly on to the deck, perhaps 100 feet below, to be broken on the hard planks or on a carronade. Here indeed was a double menace since, if the deck were crowded, he had a very good chance of killing someone else as well, should he fall upon him. Or again, every time he trod the deck in heavy rolling weather, if he momentarily relaxed his vigilance, he might in an instant be swept off Quarter-deck or Forecastle with no chance whatever of rescue.

That such mishaps and others like them were constantly happening no one can doubt who has studied the contemporary logs and journals, the many sea-recollections, autobiographies and reminiscences which survive. The sudden cry of 'Man overboard!' sounds like a sombre refrain through all of them. Some of the unfortunates were rescued, if the sea was calm and the light good; officers and men alike almost always did their utmost to save their shipmate. But they failed much more often than they succeeded. Dillon records one harrowing and rather unusual case. When (on an occasion already mentioned in another connection)[1] the *Horatio* hit a rock off Guernsey, the crew got a sail over the hole, and were making their best speed for the Solent, all hands working desperately at the pumps, when

'. . . unfortunately, in getting that sail over, one of the best seamen of the ship, a Boatswain's Mate—Jackson—fell overboard. A boat was instantly lowered to pick him up, and I shortened sail . . .'

But, for once, the men were not so eager—

[1] See p. 282 and N.R.S., Vol. XCVII, pp. 329–30.

'The seamen, noticing this, addressed me with anxiety. "Only one man, sir. We are upwards of 300. Pray save us. We have no time to lose!" "Surely," said I, "you can afford a quarter of an hour to save the life of a good seaman?" But it was evident that the majority were against the delay. After several minutes' search in the boat, he could not be found: sail was again made and we resumed our course. His wife was on board, and in sad distress at her loss.'

She should not have been there, poor soul. But her presence doubtless added to the difficulty of the Captain's decision. Perhaps his compromise was as good as any. He satisfied his conscience by stopping and searching, but it is clear that the search was more perfunctory than usual.

Another experience which he relates had a happier ending—for the moment.[1] As his ship, the *Aimable*, was going rapidly through the water a prime seaman—a topman—fell from the fore topsail yard.

'In his fall the bellying out of the sail sent him over the bows, and the ship passed directly over him . . . . Luckily, there was a fishing line over the stern, with a bait for the bonetta. Before sail could be taken in to lower a boat, we heard a voice astern calling out most lustily, and there we beheld our shipmate with one arm above water. The ship having gone over him, he rose and caught hold of the line. It slipped through his hands till the hook went through the palm of one of them. By that means his life was saved.'

But perhaps a seaman's luck, like his rum, was rationed. He was killed very soon afterwards boarding a French privateer.

Some idea of the number of men who fell overboard may be gleaned from a rather negative piece of evidence. By the time that he was thirty years old, Captain Frederick Marryat had collected twenty-seven life-saving certificates.[2] This was no doubt exceptional—the sea-novelist was an incorrigibly intrepid officer. Even he did not always succeed, though, and once came within an ace of being drowned himself. So it may fairly safely be assumed that this one officer in his time saw something like half a hundred men go overboard.

But 'Man overboard' was only one of the many possible 'individual accidents'; and even if we could assess the numbers of them which were

[1] N.R.S., Vol. XCIII, pp. 284–5.
[2] C. C. Lloyd: *Captain Marryat*, p. 164.

immediately fatal, we still should not know how many seamen were permanently bruised and broken by them. An attempt will be made later to reach an approximate answer to the first of these questions. As to the second, the ways in which a man might maim himself for life were almost limitless; clearly too numerous even to catalogue. Here, then, the examination is confined to only three, and these, perhaps, ways not often considered. All three, it is true, might almost be considered as diseases, which important subject has yet to be considered. But, if they were, they were what must be called 'occupational disorders', arising from the nature of the seaman's duties and the conditions under which he worked.

C. OCCUPATIONAL DISORDERS

(a) *Rupture*

One of the commonest hazards which every seaman had to face was Rupture, due, mainly, to the constant strain which his work put upon the muscles of the stomach. Sir Gilbert Blane, by far the most prominent of the Navy's physicians around the turn of the eighteenth and nineteenth centuries, has left on record the principal duties which were responsible for the alarming incidence of this disability. The first he names is the constant lying-out on the yards, working the while with both hands. The next is the constant lowering and hoisting of heavy barrels, mainly water-casks: and there were others, like endless hauling upon ropes and heaving capstans. So much we could no doubt have guessed, had we ever thought about it, without having to wait for the Physician to inform us. But then he goes on to tell us something which, probably, we should not guess—that the authorities, well before the wars were over, had taken decided steps to do something about it.

It is often supposed—alas, with all too much truth—that the men's general health and comfort were but little attended to: and this, by modern standards, is certainly the case. Moreover, even here, one suspects, it was Economics rather than Humanity which jogged the Admiralty. As the war went on, the demand for seamen grew: but seamen—proper ones—became ever scarcer, and the Admiralty at length realized that it must preserve the effectiveness of those it had. It could not easily reduce the strain on a man's stomach in making and furling sail: only the introduction of power into ships could do that. But it could, and gradually did, reduce the second most fruitful source of rupture, the hoisting and lowering of water-butts.

In so doing—if a brief digression may be pardoned—it inaugurated a major reform in the Royal Navy. From about the turn of the century the practice started of scrapping wooden casks altogether, and using instead iron tanks, permanently stowed in the hold and used as part of the ship's ballast, which at the same time became pigs of iron carefully fitted into the space available. This great innovation had three separate advantages, all fostering the health of the crew. First it relieved the men of one of the chief causes of rupture. Second, it made, for the first time in history, for a clean hold. Till then, a ship's ballast, composed of gravel or shingle, had been one of the surest disease-beds on board. It was practically never shifted—save occasionally by accident, when it might well send the ship to the bottom. It was never, therefore, drained, and it could not be cleaned or purified: while what went into that ballast through the years may be guessed without being intimately described. On the other hand, the pigs of iron which now replaced it could be moved, and fairly regularly were; so that, gradually, the ship's standing and stinking cesspool—the 'bilge'—became a thing of the past. The third advantage was almost as great. It nearly solved the age-old problem of keeping water fresh and sweet at sea. Wooden casks, it had long been known, could not do this, and had been constant sources of stomach and bowel troubles as a result. But iron tanks kept the water drinkable (if not exactly fresh) for much longer periods. These tanks, like the pigs, could be moved for cleaning, but, when water was taken in, stayed where they were, and were replenished by means of a hose and forcing pump. They had won official recognition by 1815, and were established as compulsory fittings in all ships of war in that year.

Though one source of rupture was thus removed, the Admiralty could not protect the seamen in their other jobs: nor could the Physicians and Surgeons cure them when they ruptured themselves. It only remained, therefore, for the Admiralty to get as much work as possible out of ruptured seamen. This it did by making trusses into something like a standard issue, supplied to all ships. Blane gives the figures. During the years from 1808 to 1815 inclusive, the average annual issue of trusses to seamen was—Single Trusses, 2,873; Double Trusses, 743; 'bag' Trusses, 98: total, 3,714. This was the *annual* distribution, so that in those eight years a matter of 29,712 were distributed in all. It is not possible to deduce from this with any accuracy how many British seamen in 1815 wore trusses, and were therefore presumably ruptured. Yet certain figures emerge, and they are sufficiently eloquent. The seamen, as we know, once caught and sent aboard, did not change very much—nothing, in the ordinary way, but death, total disablement or a cessation of hostilities could release them, Again, was a ruptured man, when he was discharged, allowed to take his truss with him? From all we know it sounds somehow improbable. So it would seem fairly safe to assert that quite a big percentage of those 29,712 men were still serving, trusses, ruptures and all, when the wars ended: that, in fact, something between 15,000 and 20,000 British seamen were then in some degree ruptured: something like one in every nine, or even one in every seven. An occupational disorder indeed!

This is in some sort a digression, because a rupture is seldom fatal by itself, and those who died of it would have no appreciable effect on our figures. Indeed there is evidence, in lists by Blane and his famous predecessor Dr. James Lind, that rupture cases were very seldom admitted into the naval hospitals. The reason is plain enough. If a seaman's disability was so pronounced that he could not pull his weight, even when trussed, then he was good for nothing but discharge, and must look after himself ashore as best he could, unless he could find someone influential enough to get him into Greenwich Hospital, or secure an out-pension for him. It did not accord with the ideas of contemporary officialdom that he should be allowed to fill a bed in an ordinary naval hospital, which might otherwise send a cured seaman back to the fleet. It is perhaps this absence of rupture cases from the hospitals which has served to conceal how common the ailment was.

(b) *Lunacy*

The second occupational disorder to be noticed is Lunacy. It may seem strange to call it by that name, but there is a good reason—Sir Gilbert Blane himself said that it was. He pointed out in a most valuable paper[1] that where in the whole of Britain there was one madman (it was thought) for every 7,000 of the population, in the Royal Navy the proportion was one in under 1,000. That is, the incidence of insanity in the Navy was more than seven times that in civilian life. These are alarming figures, and Blane was unable to explain them to his satisfaction. He did, however, offer one solution, rather tentatively, and almost as though he did not really believe it himself. Nor perhaps would it carry much weight with modern psychiatrists. Naval madness, he ventured to suggest, was mostly due to head injuries, sustained (he added) mostly

[1] In *Medico-Chirurgical Transactions*, Vol. VI, 1815.

during intoxication. That head-bumping was not only possible but even easy is demonstrable to this day. There was little room between-decks. Even in that lovely ship, the *Victory*, which was roomier than most, all but the shortest of visitors soon become aware of singularly hard oak beams in the near neighbourhood of their heads. They find themselves crouching as they walk, and they firmly resolve, after only one or two contacts, to risk no more. So do naval men in low-decked modern craft. So did the officers and men in the old wooden ships. *But not when drunk*: for then habit and discretion alike are apt to desert a man.

Rather more surprising is his revelation that the Navy actually cared for its lunatics in wards of its own at the mental hospital in Hoxton, North-East London. He gives a table of numbers received there during the years 1809 to 1813 inclusive. Here are given the headings, the figures for the five years, and the totals:

Year	*Received*	*Discharged cured*	*Discharged to friends*	*Discharged to Bethlem*	*Died*	*Remaining*
1809	76	10	3	43	9	112
1810	81	15	1	38	20	118
1811	85	4	3	53	16	128
1812	90	10	0	39	18	144
1813	93	17	7	55	13	140
Totals	**425**	**56**	**14**	**228**	**76**	—

From this melancholy table certain conclusions may be drawn.

(1) The diagnosis and treatment of Lunacy being still in its infancy, we may suppose that all these cases were fairly advanced ones—what we might nowadays call 'certifiable'—though doubtless many more would now be 'discharged cured'.

(2) On the other hand, we must suppose that the 'received' numbers did not include all who would nowadays be admitted, or at any rate removed from their ships. Many borderline cases no doubt remained afloat: and indeed all our autobiographies contain instances of men still on active service—even officers, even Captains—who in our own day would assuredly be, at the very lowest, voluntary patients in one of our mental hospitals: and who, even then, should certainly not have been at large and at sea, and above all in positions of trust there. Would a modern Mr Mears, for instance, have escaped our psychiatrists?

(3) The incidence of insanity was slowly but surely increasing. This is seen both in the 'Received' column and in the 'Remaining' (where the last figure is smaller than the last but one only because more friends than

usual have been persuaded to take charge). But this, towards the end of a very long and trying war, is not altogether surprising.

(4) The number 'discharged cured' (and therefore presumably returned to sea) is so small as to make it seem hardly worth while to have run the wards for the mere economic reason of finding more seamen for the fleet. It almost looks as if there were here some glimmer of humanitarianism: Bethlem—or Bedlam—was then a deservedly dreaded place.

(5) The 'Died' column, though larger than the 'Cured', is still not very large—about 18 per cent—and therefore does not materially affect any of our 'mortality' figures.

(6) 'Discharged to Bethlem'—that is, presumably, considered incurable—is about 54 per cent, just thrice as large as the 'Died' and four times as large as the 'Cured'.

(7) The rest—140 at the end of 1813—are, one supposes, to have another chance. Blane breaks up this group into 'officers' and 'men'. There are fifteen of the former, and he records their ranks, though not their names: One Captain, four Lieutenants, three Lieutenants of Marines, one Surgeon, one Assistant Surgeon, two Carpenters, one Gunner, one Master's Mate (modern Sub-Lieutenant) and one Midshipman. Fifteen officers to 125 men means, approximately, one to eight; and the average proportion of officers to men throughout the Service was, very roughly, one to twenty. So it would seem that the incidence of insanity was a good deal greater among the officers than among the men: yet it is to be hoped, and indeed believed, that the incidence of oaken beams upon intoxicated heads was greater among the men than among the officers. This—for what it is worth—seems to confound Sir Gilbert's explanation of the major cause of insanity in the Navy. But the authorities may have persevered longer with the officers before consigning them to the living death of Bedlam.

(c) *Drunkenness*

It is regrettable that drunkenness must be included as the third 'occupational disorder' of the Navy. But it is unavoidable. It was beyond all doubt a direct result of the seaman's way of life. We have only to look back at his dreadful living conditions already described, and to realize that all seamen were entitled, if they wished, to drown their woes daily in excessive doses of alcohol, officially issued. It is indeed almost impossible to avoid the conclusion that the bad conditions and the potent spirit were direct links in one chain of cause and effect: that Authority was actually sanctioning over-drinking as a means of doping the men into enduring the conditions. It is a shocking thought. Such a remedy for such conditions argues an amorality in high places which it is hard to credit. Nor indeed is it necessary to believe that the remedy was being consciously applied: it was rather the result of an ageless policy of drift, and refusal to look facts in the face. Yet those facts were there, painfully obvious to any observer standing clear of the times. Again and again it is borne in upon us that many of the men regarded their rum-ration as an anodyne, an antidote against the poison of everyday life, a solace—the only permitted solace—against the drabness and squalor of all the rest of their existence. Authority would not—indeed thought it could not—change the squalor. It therefore continued to permit the solace. And no one dared—at any rate no one did—lay sacrilegious hands upon the seaman's daily half-pint until 1824.

The men on the spot, the admirals and the captains, saw the evil at first hand. Experience showed them that the rum-ration was a constant source of inefficiency in their fleets and even of danger to their ships, both from the violence of the enemy and from the dangers of the sea. For the enemy also knew our weakness, or thought he did. When Dillon was illegally detained at Helvoetsluys, one of his captors

'was quite certain that if he fell in with one of our ships of war on a Saturday night he would capture her, under the conviction that the whole crew, being in a perfect state of inebriety, would not be able to defend themselves'.[1]

This, of course, was grossly wishful thinking. But there is no smoke without fire. Thus, when the *Culloden* ran aground near Surabaya, Sir Edward Pellew wanted to lighten her by removing her heavier guns and, in an ill moment, seized some passing coasting-craft in which to put them. Unfortunately, they contained among their cargo many casks of rum, brandy and arrack, and, the word passing swiftly round, in a twinkling the greater part of the Ship's Company was blind-drunk. The ship was saved, partly by the exertions of the small sober minority, but mainly by the fact that, on this occasion, delay did not happen to be fatal.[2]

The Admirals, then, were constantly urging the Admiralty to reduce the spirit-ration. But they seldom if ever connected the disease with its

[1] N.R.S., Vol. XCVII, p. 25.
[2] Hay, op. cit., p.155.

real cause: they seldom urged, along with a reduction of ration, a radical amelioration of living conditions. One such representation among many must suffice here. The writer is Lord Keith, a man of wide and varied sea-experience, in whom the Admiralty reposed great and deserved confidence. He is addressing Their Lordships in 1812:[1]

'. . . It is observable and deeply to be lamented that almost every crime except theft originates in drunkenness, and that a large proportion of the men who are maimed and disabled are reduced to that situation by accidents that happen from the same abominable vice. It is an evil of great magnitude, and one which it will be impossible to prevent so long as the present excessive quantity of spirits is issued in the Royal Navy: for men seem to have no other idea of the use of spirits than as they afford them the means of running into excess and indulgence in intoxication. There is [as] great a difference between a Ship's Company in a morning and in the afternoon as there can possibly be: for although their spirits are mixed with four times the quantity of water, and issued at two separate periods of the day sufficiently distant from each other, yet not only young and raw lads from the country, but the more crafty and experienced who contrive to purchase or cheat their messmates are often so drunk as to be insensible of the most severe fractures by falls, or even of having fallen overboard when under the influence of drink.'

Here Keith comes very near to supporting Blane. For drunkenness such as he describes is indeed temporary insanity: and some of the results of it, especially head-injuries, may well have had more lasting effects than the drunkenness itself, inducing, as Blane thought, real and permanent insanity. But we must follow Keith to his conclusion:

'It is at all times a delicate point to interfere with what is called an allowance or right, and the present may not be the moment for reforming even so great an evil: but in the event of peace, I am satisfied that not a more essential service could be rendered to the nation than to reduce the quantity of spirits now used in the Navy.'

There is something almost pitiable about the end of this letter, so right in its facts, so mean, even cowardly, in its conclusions. 'It is wrong', he says in effect. 'But do not try to remedy it now, or you will have trouble. Wait till the seamen are no longer necessary to you: then you can safely do it.' No word about the real evil: no mention of the true

[1] N.R.S., Vol. XCVI, p. 320.

reason why the men 'ran into excess and indulged in the abominable vice of drunkenness'.

In any assessment, then, of individual accidents in ships, rum must figure, indeed must take a high place; not so much as a direct cause, but as a leading contributory one. And its regular and permitted over-consumption must rank as an important, and very terrible, Occupational Disorder.

Returning now to the fatal casualties among all these 'individual accidents', can we estimate them in terms of yearly loss in naval men? We can at least clear the way for an attempt by considering the size of the problem. In what follows, a specimen year is taken for examination —1810, five after Trafalgar, five before the end. It is not maintained that it is a 'typical' year, for obviously there can be no such thing. Yet it seems a fair year in several ways. On the one hand the Navy was still large, though past its largest. In 1809 it had reached its numerical peak in ship-numbers, and was now on the decline. On the other hand, it was not a particularly spectacular year. There were no large-scale founderings or fires, though there was one unfortunately expensive wreck, that of the *Minotaur*, '74', when 360 men were drowned. There was also a series of actions distinctly expensive in human life—the battle of Grand Port, leading up to our capture of the islands of Mauritius and Bourbon: but there was no large fleet-action.

In 1810 the number of R.N. ships in commission (i.e., more or less fully-manned) was 764 and, in addition, there were sixty-four hired ships, manned partly by R.N. ratings. This gives a total of 828 ships: but let us reduce it for statistical purposes to a round 800 ships, fully manned by naval people; for clearly some of those accidentally killed in the hired ships would be non-naval men. Here, of course, the figure of 800 includes the under-28-gun ships as well as the larger classes whose fortunes have hitherto been our chief concern. This has to be, as soon as human casualties come up for discussion, because accidents to individuals happened in all ships, great and small alike.

Would it be unrealistic to suppose that each of these 800 ships lost, on the average, some two men every year as a result of all these possible accidents to individuals? The figure would doubtless be too high for the smallest ships which carried only forty or fifty men; for that would mean an annual accident-rate of from 5 to 4 per cent. At the other end, however, two lost out of a complement of 800 or so would almost certainly be too low—one quarter of 1 per cent. Or there is another way of testing the rough accuracy of our figure. The number of seamen and marines voted for 1810 was 145,500, and our postulated casualty-figure of two-per-ship comes to 1,600: that is, something over 1 per cent of the whole body. From all we know, it is not extravagant to reckon that one man out of every hundred met every year with a fatal accident in, or overboard of, his ship.

Subsequent investigations will tend to confirm the general accuracy of this estimate, though neither here nor later is any exactness claimed, especially here, where the expedient of multiplying the total number of ships by two is inviting wide margins of error.

Yet another test—a much more down-to-earth one—will be applied later, when a final attempt is made to assess all the mortal dangers that faced a sailor of our wars. But first we must consider what was by far his deadliest enemy—Disease.

D. FROM DISEASE

That Disease should have killed off more naval men than any other cause will not surprise anyone who has studied the casualty-lists of any war up to 1900. This is as true of armies as it is of navies. It was notoriously true of the Crimean War, where the relevant ratio was, roughly, as three to one, and it remained so even up to the Second Boer War, when it was about two to one.[1] It is primarily a matter of mass-hygiene and (in the Navy, the only Service to be discussed here) of the peculiar conditions in which the seamen had to live. Their floating home was of necessity cramped, apt to be chronically damp and, for much of our period, unnecessarily filthy. Their diet was bad, their food and drink usually vile—sometimes unnecessarily but generally unavoidably, since the preservation of food and water was an almost unknown art. Here is no place for a detailed history of sea-diseases, nor for any profound discussion on how they might have been—but for a long time were not—faced and fought. Our chief concern is still to assess their lethal incidence.

It must be recorded first, however, that even before our wars began a certain amount of progress had been made in the fight against naval disease, and, even as they ran their course, more victories were on the way. None the less, Disease remained to the end much the most formidable of the seamen's enemies.

[1] *Journal of the Royal Statistical Society*, Vol. CV, Pt. I, p. 12.

(a) *Scurvy*

The ailment which, above all others, had long been the most serious scourge to all seafarers was the Scurvy. But the worst of its assaults were over before our last French Wars began. It was in fact largely overcome by then, though the story of man's triumph over it is not particularly creditable to anyone save a few Surgeons like James Lind, Gilbert Blane and Thomas Trotter. Its connection with a dearth of fresh vegetable foods had been known for ages before authority condescended to take note of the fact. Even the efficacy of citrus fruit-juice—of the lime, the lemon and the orange—had been proved, and the remedy used with remarkable effect by Richard Hawkins in the sixteenth century and by Sir James Lancaster in 1601: and these pioneers, in their turn, had probably learnt the secret from the even earlier Portuguese voyagers. Yet its ravages were allowed to continue practically unchecked for the better part of two centuries. Perhaps the worst, or at any rate the best-known, epidemic was that which raged in the little squadron of Commodore George Anson on his voyage round the world in 1740–44. In bald figures, of the 961 men and boys who left England in 1740, only 335 were still alive one year later. The rest—626 of them—had succumbed to scurvy.[1] It was this and other almost equally shocking epidemics which enabled that pioneer of naval medicine, James Lind, not so much to rediscover the remedy (which had been there all along in reasonably available form) as to begin the process of forcing its value upon the attention of those who mattered. This was in 1754, and even then another forty-two years were to elapse before, on Blane's insistence, a standard issue of citrus fruits to all ships became general. By then (1795) Blane had become a Commissioner of Sick and Wounded, and had put his case in these forceful words:

'Every fifty oranges and lemons might be considered as a hand to the fleet, inasmuch the health and perhaps the life of a man would thereby be saved.'[2]

Blane was not the man to pull his punches. In 1796, as he very well knew, the Admiralty was prepared to go to great lengths to secure every 'hand in the fleet' that it could: even to doing what it ought to have done a century or more earlier. Incidentally, this persistent man used this

[1] These figures are deduced by Surgeon Captain R. S. Allison in his *Sea Diseases*, p. 101.

[2] Ibid., p. 173.

man-power crisis to secure another considerable victory for medicine and commonsense. Until then, incredible as it may sound, Surgeons had been expected to find their own drugs: but now, at last, the principal ones were supplied free. But it was not till 1804 that all drugs were issued as a regular practice.

There is another thing that sounds hard to believe too. Though, throughout our wars, fresh foods and vegetables were given to the men where possible, this obvious precaution seems to have emanated from the individual Captains, Pursers and Surgeons, all of whom had a personal interest in keeping their people fit, and not from the authorities who ought to have had that same object at heart. As late as 1808 a revised 'scale of Provisions' appears in the Regulations, and it lasted out the war. It is shown here as Table XIV. It will be noticed that there is no provision in it for fresh greens. Part of the twentieth regulation which accompanies it, however, does mention 'greens and roots' but, as a government-ordained issue, only indirectly. It says that 'some of the eldest Pursers of the Royal Navy' have presented a memorial in which they state that it had been their constant practice to serve out greens and roots whenever they are provided with fresh meat: and it tells Captains and Pursers to 'comply with what is contained in the said memorial'. At

TABLE XIV

ALLOWANCE OF PROVISIONS

(*From Regulations and Instructions*, 1808)

There shall be allowed to every person serving in His Majesty's Ships, a daily proportion of Provisions, as expressed in the following Table:

Day	Bisket lbs.	Beer gals.	Beef lbs.	Pork lbs.	Pease pints	Oat-meal pints	Sugar ozs.	Butter ozs.	Cheeses ozs.
Sunday	1	1	–	1	½	–	–	–	–
Monday	1	1	–	–	–	½	2	2	4
Tuesday	1	1	2	–	–	–	–	–	–
Wednesday	1	1	–	–	½	½	2	2	4
Thursday	1	1	–	1	½	–	–	–	–
Friday	1	1	–	–	½	½	2	2	4
Saturday	1	1	2	–	–	–	–	–	–
Forming a weekly proportion to each man of	**7**	**7**	**4**	**2**	**2**	**1½**	**6**	**6**	**12**

together with an allowance of vinegar, not exceeding half a pint to each man per week.

least the authorities have the grace to admit that it was not their idea. Meanwhile, the diet as it stands sounds as scorbutic as ever. Indeed, it had not changed since the last issue of the Regulations in 1790, save that the oatmeal ration of three pints was now halved.

(b) *The Fevers*

None the less, by 1793 the worst horrors of scurvy no longer faced British seamen. Indeed, scurvy was no longer Enemy Number One. That was now fever. There were two distinct types of it which took their toll, one not easily remediable as medical knowledge then stood, the other susceptible of remedy and, as the wars went on, actually remedied, at least in part.

(1) *Yellow Fever*. The first group comprised the local and mainly hot-climate fevers, which were not specifically sea-diseases at all. The commonest were the Yellow Fever—Yellow Jack, Bronze John, Lind's 'Black Vomit'—and his 'malignant fever of the intermitting kind'—Malaria. These diseases had attacked our seamen ever since they first visited, or rather lingered in, the tropical regions, especially the West and East Indies, and they continued to do so long after our period; indeed through the first three quarters of the nineteenth century. Then at length, in the 'eighties and 'nineties, their virus nature and the carrying propensities of mosquitoes were discovered. So, here, little blame can be attached to anyone. Indeed, the 1808 Regulations contain an order which would seem to show that authority was doing its best. It having been observed that infection seized mostly upon seamen sent ashore, they were all to be dosed, both on leaving their ships and on returning, with '2 drachm of Bark in half a gill of sound wine'. This was Peruvian or Cinchona Bark, the basis of quinine. But whether the Captains on the spot obeyed this order regularly is open to the gravest doubt. Our memoir-writers remain suspiciously silent on the point.

At once the most deadly, the worst-feared and the most spectacular in its assault was Yellow Jack. The heaviest casualties from it occurred in the West Indies, primarily because we had more men to die there than elsewhere. The disease was always about but, though not contagious, it came on in waves, sometimes hitting ships, and even whole fleets, with hideous force. One such onslaught happened in 1794, when Sir John Jervis and Sir Charles Grey were attacking Martinique and other French islands. Bartholomew James, who was there, has left some account of it.

'In a few days after I arrived at St. Pierre [Martinique] I buried every man belonging to my boat twice, and nearly all of the third boat's crew, in fevers, and, shocking and serious to relate, the Master, Mate, and every man and boy belonging to the *Acorn* transport that I came from England in. . . . The constant affecting scenes of sudden death was [*sic*] in fact dreadful to behold, and nothing was scarcely to be met but funeral processions in this town of both officers and men.'[1]

The crowded transports were the worst hit:

'I was informed by Capt. Schank of the Royal Navy, the Agent of transports, that during the expedition 46 Masters of transports and 1,100 of their men died of yellow fever. On board the *Brodrick* transport the fever raged with such violence that the Mate, the sole survivor, was obliged to send his boat on shore to fetch off negroes to throw the dead overboard, and himself died soon after.'[2]

The warships lost only less heavily. They were 'so extremely distressed that many of them buried almost all their officers and seamen'.[3] This emergency gave James a chance, as such things usually did to those who survived. He was taken into Sir John's flagship as Ninth Lieutenant. This was his grand opportunity (see p. 220), and he rose, through deaths alone, from Ninth to Fourth between May and August. Then his macabre 'luck' deserted him, and he had to wait two more years for promotion. On returning to England, he showed due gratitude to Heaven:

'. . . out of about 10,000 soldiers and sailors which left Europe in the fleet from Spithead on November 27th, 1793, I was one of about 500 that ever lived to see again this happy shore.'[4]

Another West Indian epidemic is recorded by Gardner. He was then Fourth Lieutenant in the *Brunswick*, '74', but rose in the course of it to be First. His ship was at Port Royal, Jamaica, and she (with a complement about 640 strong)

'had 287 men on the sick list and buried a great many of them. . . A short time before our arrival the *Topaze*, 36, [complement about 250] on a

[1] N.R.S., Vol. VI, p. 241.
[2] Ibid., p. 242, quoted by James from Willyams, App., p. 61.
[3] Ibid., p. 242.
[4] Ibid., p. 269.

cruise buried all hands except 55: the Captain (Church) and all the officers died, and the ship was brought in by the Gunner.'[1]

He also relates how he dined in the *Elephant*, whose officers, thinking they were going home at once, offered to take his letters to England:

'Poor fellows, little did they think that instead of going home, their bones would be left at the Palissades. I am grieved to say that out of the whole mess only two or three returned.'[2]

These 'Palissades' had an odious reputation:

'From this spot [Port Royal] up to Rock Fort, whence we drew our supplies of water, there ran a long, narrow sandy beach called the Palissades, where we generally buried those who had died of the yellow fever.'[3]

Year after year thousands of bodies were fed into it, yet it was never full: its other inhabitants—huge overfed land-crabs—saw to that.

'The grave is dug no deeper than just to hold the body, the earth covering it only a few inches, and all is soon consumed by the land-crabs. The black fellows eat them. When I asked why they eat these loathsome creatures, their answer is, "Why, they eat me". '[4]

Another dreadful epidemic which overwhelmed the *Tromp* in 1800 is described by Richardson. This was the cruise in which the twelve wives accompanied their husbands (see p. 285). He records the deaths of two only of the devoted women—the Purser's and the Master's wives. But, by inference, all but two failed to return—his own wife, who was, however, at death's door for a long time, and the Captain's lady who, with her husband, left the ship at the height of the epidemic and went home in a transport. The people whom he records as dying were the First Lieutenant, the Purser and his Clerk, the Master and his successor, the Marine officer, the Boatswain (leaving his entire family stranded), the Assistant Surgeon (the Surgeon himself having hurried off to hospital and got himself invalided), the Master-at-Arms, the Armourer, the Gunner's Mate, the Captain's Steward, Cook and Tailor and 'nearly all

[1] N.R.S., Vol. XXXI, p. 230.
[2] Ibid., p. 232.
[3] *Dillon*, N.R.S., Vol. XCIII, p. 369.
[4] Nicol, op. cit., p.51.

our fine young Midshipmen who had come out for promotion'. These were mostly officers; of the crew he gives no details. But few can have survived, for he concludes his sad story with the words, 'Of those who left England in the ship, only my wife and I, with two others, returned in her'.[1]

Our last witness shall be Boteler, in 1815 Master's Mate of the *Antelope*, '50'. His figures are less fearful than the others, save in one respect. The ship lost one Lieutenant, one Captain of Marines, one Chaplain, one Gunner, one Carpenter, one Captain's Clerk and eleven Midshipmen. Here it was the officers, and especially the young ones, who provided most of the victims—seventeen officers, matched by only ten seamen. He makes another interesting observation, confirmed from other sources, if not by modern experience. If a man was afraid of catching the fever, he caught it: and if, having caught it, he was afraid of dying, he was almost certain to be dead in three days. They often knew beforehand who would succumb, he says, and he gives several examples.

'Mr. Brown the Chaplain came into the Ward-room, holding up his hands and shaking his head. He was attacked with fever, and instantly gave in. He was in the habit of asking if such a fruit was wholesome, and, if not, dash it away with repugnance: and so, poor fellow, at the end of three days he was dead. . . .

. . . Midshipman Littleworth became very ill and thought dying, when one of the Mids said to him, "Johnny, what do you in your hammock all this time? I'm keeping double watch." "Well," said Johnny, "how is Bannister and Mr. Sparks, the Carpenter and Gunner?" "Oh, getting round nicely." They were both dead. "Well, I won't stay here any longer," and he stirred himself up and recovered. But the Surgeon's practice was an awful one; excessive bleeding to the extent of 60 or 70 ounces.'[2]

One of the squadron, the *Epervier* brig, had three Pursers in four days. The second of them, on going aboard, had to step over his predecessor's coffin as he entered the ship, and was so shaken that he died in three days. A new seaman was taken into the brig at Trinidad, and was so frightened at what he saw that he bolted for the foretop and refused to come down till the ship reached Barbados. He was then induced to

[1] *Richardson*, op. cit., pp. 173 *et seq.*
[2] N.R.S., Vol. LXXXII, p. 59.

descend, but instantly sickened and died. When the brig reached Antigua a new remedy was tried. She was cleared of everything on board and sunk for a week. The *Tigre*, another of the squadron, was treated in the same way. This drastic cure, says Boteler, eradicated the fever.

Much the best example, however, of the deadly effect of fear, and how it was overcome by supreme moral heroism, occurred in 1830. This is well after our wars were over, but the hero was a war-veteran, and the story should not be forgotten. Robert McKinnel was a Surgeon of a ship cruising off the west coast of Africa. The Yellow Fever—as usual—broke out. He was a thoughtful, observant man, and soon realized that the seamen were giving way to panic, having convinced themselves that the disease was contagious and that they were doomed. McKinnel thought otherwise: but we must not fail to stress that word *thought*, since half a century was yet to go before anyone *knew*. Something, he felt, must be done, and done quickly, because he saw that the fear was every bit as fatal as the fever. He therefore filled a wineglass with the 'black vomit' of a patient in the throes of death, drank it jokingly and publicly on the Quarter-deck, and continued to walk nonchalantly thereon for two hours, lest anyone should suspect that he had taken anything to counteract the effect of his nauseous draught. He suffered no ill-effects. The only result, as he hoped, was that the men accepted the truth of what they had seen with their own eyes. They believed him, banished their fears and—largely—the fever.[1]

(2) *Typhus*. The other major fever which decimated the eighteenth-century Navy was what Dr. Thomas Trotter called 'Hospital, Gaol, Camp, Ship, Low, Slow, Nervous, Putrid and Petechial Fever'—Typhus. His many alternative names provide a valuable list of the causes of this very widespread evil. The common factor was the overcrowding in insanitary and filthy surroundings of filthy and insanitary human beings: in hospitals, jails, camps, ships—anywhere indeed where such people congregated. This had long been recognized. Gaol-fever was the most widely-known and feared variety; but the old wooden ship, in so many ways like a gaol—Dr. Johnson, indeed, affirmed that it was worse—provided a breeding-ground only less prolific. No comprehensive mortality-figures for this disease in the Navy are known to me, but it prob-

[1] *Allison*, op. cit., pp. 204–5. The case is recorded, he writes, by H. B. Padwick in the *Journal of the Royal Naval Medical Service*, Vol. VIII, 2.89, and is retold in the words of Surgeon McKechnie, McKinnel's colleague who witnessed the episode.

ably reached its peak in the late 1790's and thereafter gradually declined. The reason for this is that there were conflicting influences at work which tended in some sort to balance one another. By 1793 at least one valuable counter-measure had been taken, but certain new circumstances were about to arise which were bound to encourage the disease still further.

During the War of American Independence it had become so formidable a menace to Ships' Companies—and therefore, at second remove, to the State—that Authority had been forced to do something. The problem was closely bound up with that of Impressment. A ship once in commission and out upon the high seas was often free from it—or had had her epidemic and shaken clear of it. Her Company might not be considered cleanly by modern standards but, subjected as the men were to a tight naval discipline which enforced such cleanliness as was possible, they were certainly a great deal cleaner than those of their countrymen who inhabited the gaols, slums and even hospitals ashore. It was when these people were brought wholesale aboard by the press-gangs that the epidemics always broke out afresh. Hitherto, they had been shovelled indiscriminately into all the ships in commission or being commissioned: thrown in as they stood, in verminous rags perhaps, or even with the gaol-fever active upon them; and they often took their instant revenge by broadcasting typhus through the fleets.

The remedy, as Lind and Blane saw it, was, somehow or other, to segregate the new arrivals, for long enough at least to clean them up, disinfect them, burn their infested rags and reclothe them. Such was the emergency, created by the joint impact of War and Typhus, that for once the Admiralty had to range itself quickly behind the doctors; and it made a very important move in 1781. On the recommendation of Lind it instituted 'Receiving' or 'Slop' ships, into which all pressed men were to be sent in the first instance. Here they were thoroughly scrubbed, and issued with more or less standard clothes, or 'slops'[1] before being drafted off in batches to the ships of the fleet.

[1] These 'slops' were no new thing, 'slop-stores' having been first introduced into naval ships in 1623. Nor were they 'uniform'. But each 'slop' article naturally bore a strong family likeness to its neighbour, so that they do mark a stage in 'uniform' history. The Purser, who had charge of the slop-store, had no intention, of course, of acting as a 'bespoke tailor' to his humble clients—he dealt out what he thought best, not what they did. Hence a certain uniformity in all seamen's dress which has never since been entirely lost, though 'uniform' in our modern sense did not become compulsory for seamen until 1857.

Though this reform was far from eradicating the typhus, its effect upon the incidence of the disease was for a time very marked. Then, however, things took a decided turn for the worse. The net of the press-gang had swept pretty near to the bottom before the American Independence war was over; but in 1793 and subsequent years it sank right down and, as we have seen, was stirring up the very lowest layers of scum. Yet the conditions in the ships themselves remained as favourable to the disease as ever. There was still, for instance, the gross overcrowding of the Lower Deck, unavoidable since there still had to be enough hands to man both sails and guns. So, when typhus once more grew dangerous, the only remedy seemed to lie in improving the ordinary day-to-day conditions of Lower-Deck life: to convey more air between-decks in order to diminish as much as might be the constant humidity which pervaded the ships: to eradicate unnecessary disease-breeding smells and effluvia, and to maintain as high a standard as possible of personal cleanliness.

It was objectives like these which engaged the attention of Blane, Trotter and the leading naval Physicians: and, considering the difficulties to be overcome, we may label their efforts as wonderfully successful, though to the last complete prevention was quite beyond their powers. If they failed to banish typhus, at least they reduced it, the while making the seamen's lives a good deal more comfortable.

Several experiments were made with a view to securing and maintaining a supply of purer air. For some time, ships with thoughtful Captains —or Captains with thoughtful Surgeons—had had 'wind-sails' fitted. These were canvas screens, wider at their upper ends, which were always turned into the eye of the wind. When the breeze was good, but not otherwise, these undoubtedly had some effect in bringing fresh air into the lower regions of a ship, where it was so sorely needed. How sore that need was may be proved by a fact which had long been noted—that the sea-diseases almost always attacked big ships more fiercely than small ones. Indeed, when ship-complements were being worked out at the Admiralty, it was usual to allow surpluses according to the number of guns carried. Thus a surplus of one-tenth of the crew was borne as 'expendable' in a 20-gun ship: one-fourth in a '74', and as much as one-third in a first- or second-rate three-decker. This sounds an odd arrangement until it is recalled that, when the gun-ports were closed (as they were more often than not at sea), the only natural ventilation filtered down from the top—directly on to the men's living-quarters in sloop, brig or frigate, but only indirectly on to the Lower Deck of a '74', and less directly still on to that of a three-decker. It is true that the men's living-quarters in the larger ships had one other form of ventilation—through the hawse-holes in the bows. But this was one which the seamen could well have done without, since it admitted almost as much sea-water as sea-air. Worse still, of course, was the atmosphere on the Orlop deck where the air had yet one more level to negotiate and where there were no ports to aid its entry.

All sorts of suggestions and inventions, privately sponsored for the most part, were made during our period: but the great weakness of all of them was that their operation demanded manual labour, which was always in short supply. Moreover, to carry a special supplement of men merely to work these devices would hardly make sense: for though the air below might be a trifle the fresher for them, there would be so many more lungs to vitiate it. The furthest progress reached by 1815, then, was the introduction into all ships of more or less permanent metal air-funnels built at right angles to the decks, bringing a down-draught, if an insufficient one, to where ventilation was most required. They were the forerunners of the modern ventilators.

In addition to introducing fresh air, Blane sought diligently to abolish dampness, rightly realizing that men living for so long under conditions of such extreme humidity would have their powers of resistance to the fevers seriously sapped. And not only this. Next after the fevers in the mortality-lists—though a long way behind them—came bronchial and lung troubles, and various forms of rheumatism, all of which might well be attributed to this ever-present dampness. He could not cure such evils as condensation in the under-ventilated, overcrowded deck-spaces, nor the tendency of oak to sweat: nor could he keep the sea altogether out of the hawse-holes. But what he could he did. He introduced a series of portable fires to burn between-decks—not without opposition, for any form of fire on board was, as we have seen, one added hostage to fortune. He also introduced hot sand for the deck-scrubbing, and scraping with 'holy-stones' instead of the endless washing with water. It would be wrong to imagine that, by the time he had finished, Blane had made the warship snug, dry and comfortable for its inmates. This was plainly impossible. But he certainly left it less dripping wet, less chronically damp, less grossly incommodious than he found it.[1]

Last—though the proverb tells us it is first-but-one—comes personal

[1] A great deal less smelly too, owing to his assault upon the 'bilge' (see p. 395).

cleanliness. We have seen the Receiving-ships busily scrubbing their reluctant guests from clew to earing. But what happened once they were safe in the fleet? Certainly day-to-day conditions afloat were not such as to encourage elaborate personal hygiene—all water but sea-water was a very valuable 'store', and far from being 'on tap'. By modern standards the seaman of 1800 was doubtless dirty. But his officers saw to it that he was a good deal cleaner than most of his opposite numbers ashore, as well as a great deal smarter. Yet again Authority was hardly doing its best to help the officers. Since soap cost money, it was not provided: not, at least, until Sir Gilbert took up the cudgels. In 1795 he was urging a regular, and free, soap-issue to all hands. But this was rather too much for the eighteenth century, and it was not until 1810 that the Admiralty was prodded into conceding soap at all. Then it was issued, but only upon a man's request and with a deduction from his wages. Still, it was a beginning, and once more the man behind it was Blane.

In fine, this enlightened man may not have been a great doctor. But he was a most notable pioneer, a most persistent protagonist of naval hygiene. He was modest too in his claims. He did not suggest that he had solved the problems. He knew that much yet remained to do: and when the wars were over he set down the size of them in a surprisingly modern way, which reveals him as something of a pioneer in the science of Statistics as well. Among other things, he pointed out that, in 1815, the disease mortality-rate in the Royal Navy was still 1 in 30.25, and that, in spite of all that had been done, this was still grossly in excess of the national rate. Most naval seamen, he said, were between 20 and 40 years old, presumably fit men in a group with a high expectation of life. But the 20-to-40 national mortality-rate was only 1 in 80, while even the mortality-rate of enemy prisoners of war was only 1 in 55. His comparisons are to the point. Why should nearly two of our lustiest age-group perish for every one of our enemy prisoners? And why should a seaman's chance of death by disease be nearly thrice that of an ordinary Briton of comparable age? In short, he inferred, he had done his best, but there was no cause for complacency.

(3) *Smallpox.* But little space need be spared for the Smallpox, though on shore it was probably the most persistent eighteenth-century scourge. It was never a specifically naval disease. Epidemics naturally occurred from time to time in individual ships, and they were apt to be serious owing to the near-impossibility of isolation. On the other hand, the seamen, seldom allowed shore-leave, were the less likely to pick up infec-

tion from the land. Thus epidemics were rather less frequent than they were ashore, the infection usually being brought on board only in port, by the Jews, the bumboat women and others allowed to enter the ship. Already, too, Dr. Jenner's new vaccination was assaulting the disease. Here the medical protagonist in the Navy was not Blane, but that very practical, lovable and forceful figure, Dr. Thomas Trotter. He it was who, as Physician of the Channel Fleet, first introduced vaccination into the Navy on any appreciable scale. By 1798, under his orders, all his Surgeons were freely practising it though, here again, Authority plodded along far behind, and made vaccination compulsory only in 1858.

E. THE NAVAL HOSPITALS

To cope with all these wounds, accidents and diseases, a number of specifically naval hospitals had begun to appear soon after the middle of the eighteenth century, and some brief account of how they stood at the end of it seems necessary.

(a) *Greenwich*

To every seaman of Nelson's day the word 'hospital' meant, first and foremost, one thing—the Royal Hospital at Greenwich. It was at once the oldest, largest, grandest and best-loved of all such places; begun, to Queen Mary's memory and Wren's design, in 1696, and receiving its first inmates in 1705. It was not, of course a hospital at all, in the normal modern sense of the word. Rather, it was at once an enormous Almshouse and a Pension Scheme in its own right, primarily for old or disabled seamen but also for a number of officers.

During our wars its staff consisted of a 'military' branch—Governor (a famous Admiral), Lieutenant Governor, four Captains, eight Lieutenants and two Chaplains—and a 'civilian' branch—three Administrators, a Secretary, Steward, Cashier, Clerk of the Check, Architect and Clerk of the Works. On the medical side were a Physician, a Surgeon, a Dispenser (or Apothecary), up to six Assistants (according to numbers of Pensioners), and four Matrons, usually widows of commissioned officers. They all boarded and lodged in the Hospital.

As to the pensioners, no officers lived in, but a certain number drew out-pensions. In 1814, when the Hospital machinery was in full running order, ten Post Captains, fifteen Commanders and fifty Lieutenants were enjoying its benefits. Of the seamen, the numbers were very large, and growing throughout our period. Some lived in, some out. To allow for as many of the former as possible, one long range of the building—King Charles Quarter, West—was enlarged in 1811–14, after which the maximum number was fixed at 2,710. As for the out-pensions, these were derived from the Hospital's funds and from the famous Chatham Chest, established by John Hawkins but transferred to Greenwich in 1803, the two sources being amalgamated in 1814. Every man in the Royal Navy and the Royal Marines, save only Commissioned Officers, and Warrant Officers in receipt of Superannuation pensions, could claim either a place in the Hospital or an out-pension, and—theoretically—would get one if he was found to qualify under the rather intricate rules of the institution. His out-pension, if he secured one, was graded according to his rank or rating, his hurts or diseases contracted in the Navy, or the sheer length of his service. Could he but obtain a place in the Hospital itself, no distinctions were made, and his future was assured. '*Otia Tuta*' —'Safe Ease'—was the motto of the Hospital, and it was a most apt device.

Under such circumstances, the numbers who wanted Hospital places always exceeded the number of vacancies, so that recommendations from senior and influential officers were, as we have seen, essential in fact, though not in theory; and, once more, the typical eighteenth-century phenomenon of Interest was decisive.

The lucky ones who secured a place seem to have lived very contentedly and, for those days, well; receiving board and lodging quite free and one shilling a week in pocket-money. A 'Boatswain'—one in charge of each of the 'wards' in which they lived, and selected from their own number—received half a crown, and his two 'Boatswain's Mates' had one-and-six. They all wore a uniform—a blue tail coat and breeches, cocked hat and blue stockings, Boatswains and Mates being distinguished by broad and narrow gold lace on coat and hat. Nightgowns, neckerchiefs and bedding were also provided, as well as great coats for the frail and the elderly. Delinquents were distinguished by being put into yellow coats with red sleeves until they had worked their passage back to grace. There were periodic scandals about the finances of the establishment: and doubtless there was a good deal of quiet peculation in one way and another. Yet, all in all, the Pensioners were happy and carefree; which latter state most likely helps to account for their notorious longevity. In 1803, for instance, there were 96 who were over 80, 16 over 90 and one who was a centenarian. One batch of 100 averaged 82.5 years apiece and 25 years of service. Six of them had over 50 years' service.[1] After all, they were mostly the picked, brine-pickled survivors of a gruelling existence from which the weaklings had long since faded. In the quiet courts and colonnades of the Royal Hospital no enemy stalked them, no likelihood of fatal accident, no sudden onset of sea-disease, not even a nagging fear for tomorrow's daily bread: only Old Age.

The sums awarded to out-pensioners could not keep them in comparable comfort. Yet they had this advantage over the Pensioners—they could live with their wives and families, who were not allowed to reside in the Hospital. In the years immediately following the peace of 1815 there was naturally an enormous increase in the number of applicants, and unquestionably some, like poor old Nicol (see p. 92), were disappointed: how many it is no longer possible to tell. A careful study of Nicol's pathetic account of his failure, however, leads to the conclusion that the fault was at least partly his own. He was one of the feckless sort which takes little heed of tomorrow; and when he was fobbed off by an Admiralty clerk who told him that he had not applied in time, there was probably some truth in the excuse. He seems to have waited seven years before making any application, and when he came to London to do so, he found his old Captain just dead, everyone else he knew away on holiday, and himself and his services quite forgotten.

In the south-west corner of the Greenwich establishment was the Infirmary, which was the Pensioners' hospital in the modern sense, and, across the road to the south of it was their last resting-place, the Seamen's Cemetery. Throughout the whole of the eighteenth century, up to 1815 and well beyond, 'the Hospital' was regarded with affection by the seamen and pride by the whole nation: and indeed, for its day, it was a uniquely enlightened institution.

(b) *For the Sick and Wounded*

The oldest regular hospital of the modern sort was Haslar, projected in 1745, opened in 1754 and completed in 1762. It was closely followed by Plymouth Hospital, begun in 1758, receiving patients in 1760, and completed in 1762. Chatham's Hospital came into being at much the same time, but it does not appear to have been used for naval purposes during our wars. Instead, there was a smaller establishment at Deal. As time

[1] *Greenwich Palace* (R.N. College Guide, 1948 edition).

went on, another was opened at Paignton, then one at Yarmouth, while, in addition to these, there had sprung up by 1814 a series of Sick Quarters all round the coasts, each attended by a Surgeon—at Belfast, Dartmouth, Douglas, Dover, Dublin, Exmouth, Fowey, Greenock, Hull, Ilfracombe, Leith, Limerick, Lynn, Milford, Penzance, Poole, North Shields and Swansea. Overseas, the same kind of growth was taking place, and by 1814 either hospitals or sick-quarters existed at Antigua, Barbados, Bermuda, the Cape of Good Hope, Gibraltar, Halifax, Jamaica, Madras and Malta.

At first all of them were run by their medical staffs alone, the larger ones headed by a Physician and supported by a Surgeon, a number of Assistant Surgeons (according to size), a Dispenser, Matron, Chaplain and Steward. But very soon—in 1795—a change was made, and a 'military' branch, under a Post Captain and Lieutenants, was put in, as at Greenwich. There seem to have been two reasons for this. First, the old discipline was bad, and this led, among other undesirable things, to a great deal of desertion, comparatively easy during a patient's convalescence. In 1797, for instance—and that after the executive officers had taken charge—108 seamen 'ran' from Haslar alone.[1] But, once it had settled in, the new management, who knew all about desertion, made it nearly as difficult to run from a hospital as from a ship, whose general discipline they borrowed.

There was another reason for this tightening-up. Authority had come to the conclusion that the medical people themselves needed watching. They had always been entitled to indulge in private practice, on the understanding, of course, that the naval patients had first call on their services. It was discovered, however, that they were often ignoring the understanding, living outside the hospital premises and only attending for duty when there were no fees to be pocketed elsewhere. In 1795, then, the doctors' private practices were forbidden, and the Post Captain in charge was ordered to see the new rule enforced.

It is not easy to picture what life in these hospitals was like. The care, comfort and hygiene of patients would naturally shock medical opinion of today, but it must have been far above the standards prevailing outside. The most glaring contrast between then and now, probably, was in the nursing. There were women called nurses, but they bore no real relation to the modern ones. To call them ward-maids, or even charwomen, would be to insult two honourable callings. They had no sort of

[1] *Allison*, op. cit., p. 157.

training at all, and were paid about half a crown a week. There were some exceptions, of course, but the majority of them, being so grossly underpaid, were entirely uneducated and of the lowest class. They left a trail of trouble and mischief in their wake. They brought in drink for the patients and helped them to run: they stole the property of the dead and the dying, and were often not above wantonly soliciting the seamen. George Watson, who spent upwards of two years in the Malta and Plymouth establishments, has much to reveal of life there in the last days of the war.

'The nurses of the hospital [Plymouth] were chiefly of the frail sisterhood. . . . Being accustomed to the manners and associations of sailors, those ladies are exceedingly bold and audacious, and without concern make use of the most indecent observations and actions in their common conversation. I had a great deal to do to repulse the temptations I met with from these Syrens.'[1]

Yet, as ever, this cheerful and charitable young man looks for, and finds, whatever is good in his surroundings. He has nothing but praise for the Surgeon at Malta, a Mr Allen, and his Assistant, both of whom are careful, humane, skilful and intent upon their patient's comfort and cure. He even manages to find—at Malta—a passable nurse, or one who by contrast seems so.

'I made myself useful to the nurse by making clothes for her child, and even for herself after she had formed them. . . . She was a generous kind-hearted creature, and very fit to be a nurse to sailors as she was not over-burdened with delicacy, and, being of a pleasing disposition, she could accommodate herself to the healthy as well as the sick.'[2]

Life in the wards had this in common with that on the Lower Deck—it was tough, but it was colourful. Taking it all in all, he found it pleasant, even gay. He has several fantastic stories to tell. One is of a maniac Marine who chased a Negro patient round and round the ward with a surgical instrument, then dived under Watson's bed. He himself could not move at all, but all the patients who could totter leapt out of their cots and grappled the madman, sheer weight of numbers at last extracting him and lashing him securely in his own bed. Another episode had serious consequences to Watson. Two ward-mates, coming to his bed

[1] *Watson*, op. cit., pp. 201–2.
[2] Ibid., p. 187.

for a chat, 'got into controversy with each other and . . . growing warm upon it, they got to hard names, and then to blows: unluckily for them, and for me too, they each had but one arm and . . . having no arm at liberty to support them in their fall, they tumbled with all their weight upon my hapless thigh which at that time was beginning to unite, and disparted anew'.[1]

This resulted, he thought, in a permanent crookedness, and a further shortening, of his wounded limb. Incidentally both these noisy incidents ran their course without any member of the Staff being aware of them: and next morning his kind Surgeon was much mystified at his patient's relapse. But Watson did not enlighten him, as that might have got his 'armless champions' banished into the guardship.

After all allowance is made for Watson's constitutional optimism, the report of hospital life he leaves behind remains a good deal more favourable than might be expected of that hard age. At least he invariably meets with kindness and attention, and there is everywhere obvious a real desire that he should recover. At least the Hospital Ward compares favourably with the Lower Deck.

F. SUMMARY

We are now as near as we shall ever get to analysing such mortality-figures as we have, and recording in percentage form the various ways in which our seamen might leave the world. The year upon which such calculations are based is, as we saw, 1810. Once more it is Blane who gives us the wherewithal to start. In that year, he records, 5,183 seamen perished from all causes. That what follows is no exact computation must be apparent from the outset, because it is based upon another figure of Sir Gilbert's which is presumably a generalization—that one-half of the total should be regarded as the victims of disease: that is, say, 2,591, leaving the remaining 2,592 to perish from all other causes. Now James records that, in 1810, 281 men were killed in action and that another 530 died by the wreck and foundering of ships.[2] Two other causes of death remain. The first, a smallish one, is the category 'Died of Wounds' which, we may recall, was not normally added to 'killed in action' lists. Let us, rather arbitrarily, put it at 150—it is too small a

[1] *Watson*, op. cit., pp. 188–9.
[2] *William James*, op. cit., Vol. V., Appendix 16.

figure anyway to make an appreciable difference in percentages. So far, then, on our way towards our grand total of 5,183, we have accounted for 3,553—2,592 by disease, 281 killed in action, 530 by ship-accidents and 150 died of wounds. Subtract 3,553 from 5,183 and we get the number which must have perished from the only other lethal cause which remains—what we have here called 'individual accident'. The figure is 1,630. Earlier (p. 401) an attempt was made to reach the number of 'individual accidents' by a completely different (and admittedly much vaguer) route. That computation brought them to 1,600—sufficiently near to show that both our estimates are at least in the region of accuracy. But this later estimate is based upon figures which are, by a good deal, the more factual: so we will use them here.

FATAL CASUALTIES IN THE ROYAL NAVY IN 1810
IN NUMBERS AND PERCENTAGES

Cause of Death		*Number*		*Percentage*
By Disease		2592		50·0
By Individual Accident		1630		31·5
By Foundering, Wreck, Fire and Explosion		530		10·2
By the Enemy, killed in action ...	281	431 ...	5·4%	8·3
By the Enemy, died of wounds ...	150		2·9%	
All Causes		**5183**		**100**

It has been pointed out that there is no such thing as a 'typical' year. Every year, therefore, will have features which vary from the average of all the years. A feature of the 1810 list which we suspect of being such a variant is the percentage figure for deaths by foundering, etc.: not so much by comparison with total casualties as when compared with enemy-inflicted casualties. James shows that, in 1810, two ships foundered, twelve were wrecked and none lost by fire or explosion: fourteen ships. This is only a little below the yearly average: in the twenty-two years of war 344 were lost from such causes, giving an average annual loss of fifteen and a half. But in 1810, though one wreck caused, as we saw, a severe loss of lives, in no less than ten of the thirteen others the fatal casualties were very small indeed—to be exact, ten in the whole ten ships. They were a good deal more than usually lucky. On the other hand, though there was not much widespread fighting to swell the 'action' casualties, the series of confused encounters during our capture of the Mauritius group was unusually expensive in killed and died of wounds. One frigate alone, the *Nereide*, Captain Sir Nesbit Willoughby (not for nothing called 'the Immortal'), had casualty-figures which were probably a record for the whole war. She ran on to a shoal within point-blank range of many opponents, and only surrendered after having lost 92 killed and 137 wounded in that one engagement—229 out of a total crew of 281. It seems fair to suppose that, in most years, the gap between 'Foundered, etc.' and 'by the Enemy' would be distinctly wider: each, let us say, by 2 per cent. Then the percentages in the table would read, 'Foundering, etc.', 12.2 per cent and 'By the Enemy', 6.3 per cent: which seem more like the results to be expected from the figures quoted earlier in this book.[1]

This, however, is a descent into minutiae which it would be well not to labour, seeing how many of our figures are, at best, 'intelligent' surmises. But certain broad and significant conclusions can be drawn. Disease and Individual Accident obviously account for an overwhelming percentage of all fatal British casualties. Our calculations, for this one year, have made them 81.5 per cent. They may have been somewhat more or somewhat less, and this year may have differed somewhat from other years: no doubt it did. But clearly these two remain by a very wide margin the prime causes of fatal casualties. Next comes the third commonest cause of death—the ship-disasters of foundering, wreck, fire and explosion. These bring the percentage up to well over 90; even, perhaps, to 93½—all of them fatal casualties not inflicted upon us by human hands: all due to the dangers of the sea in the widest sense of those words, and not in any way to the violence of the enemy.

Or, if we decide to mistrust such figures, as founded upon too uncertain knowledge, we can at least revert to the sporting metaphor used at the end of Chapter X. This at least will be beyond contradiction:

Mortality Stakes

1. (by many lengths) *Disease.*
2. (a comfortable second) *Individual Accident.*
3. (a poor third) *Ship Accident.*

Also ran, *The Enemy.*

Yet all—the whole 100 per cent—occurred in ships: all occurred as a direct result of waging, and winning, the 'Great War' of 1793–1815. The sum amounts to the Price of Admiralty.

[1] For another estimate of the war-casualties, made a century ago, and based upon an entirely different method of approach, see Appendix III, p. 440.

EPILOGUE

EPILOGUE

WE HAVE now followed our naval forbears from the cradle to the grave. Let us see if we can give some final picture of a 'typical' pair of them—an Officer and a Man.

Our officer came from a gentle, though probably not a noble, home; and whatever his motives he came voluntarily. Our man came from a seafaring home, not gentle—indeed, rough, but of that peculiar kind of roughness which the sea had bred in his ancestors. He too may have come voluntarily, but probably did not.

They came on board, these two, the one an officer the other a 'common man', miles apart: and at that distance they remained throughout their careers. The officer probably became a Lieutenant or, with a little luck, a Commander: but—if he were typical—he went no further. Unless he did, he had a hard life, on not much more than £100 a year. So he certainly did not make his fortune. Yet he enjoyed, in his way, a happy life. He tried to live in the style of a gentleman, and usually succeeded. As a gentleman too he was regarded, and as a fighting man looked up to by his contemporaries. If, however, he was one of the lucky ones who rose to post rank, he made a fair competence: if one of the very lucky ones, he made a fortune. Whichever he was, when it came to action he fought hard and he fought skilfully, for he knew his job, and he had his heart in it. If his fortune were doubtful, his efficiency was never in question. On his own element he was the best fighting officer in Europe, if not the world.

Our man made no fortune, unless he were indeed one of Fortune's darlings. He lived incredibly hard in crowded, fetid surroundings, kept up to a high pitch of efficiency by the strictest of disciplines, yet not—our man is after all a typical man—*not* insensately flogged. He did not, probably, win a 'warrant', but was for long a trusted Petty Officer: a cheery, philosophic soul by nature, obstinately loyal to his shipmates, and prepared to follow his officer to the death, once he thought him worth following. When well led, he was the most formidable fighting man on earth.

When their time came, these ancestors of ours departed. If they had not lived to see the Peace, but had been part of the Price of Admiralty, they had probably died of disease—most likely of the Yellow Jack in the West or East Indies: but if not, then they had come to the end of their journey by reason of some day-to-day accident on board. Less likely still, they had been drowned when their ship foundered or went ashore. It was quite unlikely that the enemy killed them.

If, on the other hand, our officer survived, he went ashore on half pay: if one of the lucky ones, with a store of worldly goods sufficient to keep up appearances: if not lucky, to a dreary round of making-both-ends-meet, the proverbial Half-pay Lieutenant: not as a rule very happy, often perhaps rather soured; yet proud—proud of his Service, proud of being one of those who had helped England to save Europe.

Our man, if young enough, went on earning his bread from the sea, in the Merchant Service where he originally belonged: or, if too old for that, secured a very small pension or a snug berth in the great Hospital by the Thames, where he swapped yarns and baccy with his cronies until claimed by the crowded cemetery across the way. Life had not a great deal to give him; but he was not unhappy, because he never expected very much.

APPENDICES

APPENDIX I

(See page 369)

ENEMY CASUALTIES IN THE SIX MAJOR BATTLES

WE MUST study the evidence for each battle separately and on its merits.

(1) *The First of June*

The 'Total (killed and wounded)' shown in Table XI is 3,500. This is James's figure, and Brenton supports him. It is moderate—the French themselves admitted to 3,000 killed and mortally wounded alone. Yet there are reasons for suspecting that—for once—they were actually exaggerating the number of their dead. Unable to conceal the loss of their ships they may well have been forced back upon the propaganda line of 'Yes. We lost the ships, but only when almost all our republican heroes, preferring death to chains, had perished!' They also declared—surely part of the same propaganda pattern—that in the seven lost ships 1,010 were killed and a mere 580 wounded. This is a suspiciously high proportion of 'killed-to-total' casualties by the standards of sailing-ship warfare. It is 63½ per cent—higher than the percentage in any of the other actions save the Nile, which is a special case (see p. 431). It is even a shade higher than Trafalgar, which is hardly credible. In that fight many French and Spanish ships were cast away whole, losing almost all their people. But on the First of June only one ship, the *Vengeur*, went down and—*pace* the notorious lie of Barras—at least half her men were picked up by the British. So the French figure, though contemporary, is rejected here, and James's 3,500 accepted. Within that figure, the 'killed' are assessed at 1,500 and the 'wounded' at 2,000, giving a proportion of 43 per cent 'killed-to-total'. This approximates to the fairly well-substantiated returns for the battle of Camperdown.

As to prisoners, the initial complements of the seven lost ships numbered about 5,000—out of which, we recall, all who were not killed were captured: including (to scotch once for all the Barras myth) 380 of the *Vengeur*'s people. Yet this figure of 5,000 at once puts out of court all the more extravagant English claims. Our exhilaration over this early victory was excessive. Public and Press alike were in boasting mood—the *Annual Register* for 1795, for instance, claims by inference 7,000 prisoners. This is absurd: we took no prisoners from ships other than the seven. Thus even 5,000 is too high unless no one was killed in the seven ships; which is also absurd. So again we fall back on the more modest estimates of James and Brenton, who both go into the question quite deeply and—for once—agree. We adopt, then, their figure of 3,500.

(2) *Cape St. Vincent*

Our 'Total (killed and wounded)' figure is again James's—'little short of 1,000'. Other known figures go far towards confirming it. The casualties of the four captured ships survive—261 killed and 342 wounded: total, 603. Another 200 casualties in the great *Santissima Trinidad* are admitted by the Spaniards. This leaves under 200 for all the other ships, which is not excessive. Our 'killed' and 'wounded' figures have been reached by dividing the 1,000 in the same ratio as in the four lost ships. The 'killed-to-total' percentage is then 43, as on the First of June.

Our 'subtraction' method gives us 3,157 prisoners—that is, the residue of the four captured Ships' Companies after their killed and wounded have been subtracted. This cannot be far out: and James corroborates it when he reports that, some days later, 'about 3,000' Spanish prisoners were landed at Lagos—there was time for a hundred-odd of the mortally and seriously wounded ones to have died.

(3) *Camperdown*

The evidence is relatively good here: detailed too, for it distinguishes between 'killed' and 'wounded'. It is the contemporary Dutch figure—though the contemporary Dutch attitude towards publishing casualties is unknown to me. It is not, however, likely to be an exaggeration. The 'killed to total' percentage is a little higher than the preceding two: it is $46\frac{1}{2}$ per cent. But then Camperdown, in common with all Anglo-Dutch actions, was a very hard-fought affair.

As for prisoners, James records that the original complements of the Dutch captured ships totalled 4,575. Of the 1,160 'killed and wounded' most (but not all) were sustained in the much larger portion of their fleet which was captured. So we have supposed 360 of their killed and wounded to have come from untaken ships and the remaining 800 from taken ones. This 800 has then been subtracted from the known total complement, leaving a total of 3,775 prisoners.

(4) *The Nile*

There is much vagueness here. Nelson's despatch omitted all definite enemy losses, merely making an untidy claim for 'taken, drowned, burnt and missing, 5,225'. The complements of the nine captured ships, Brenton tells us, were 6,400, and he is obviously right, or nearly. Lastly, James plumps, rather undecidedly, for a 'killed and wounded' total of 2,000. The subtraction method seems to fail here. Even if all the casualties were in the captured nine (and most of them were, since the only two that escaped were but lightly engaged) the bag of prisoners should be at least 4,400. But this battle had one unusual feature: it was fought so near the shore that the enemy officers and men could swim for it to avoid capture. This some of them certainly did—practically the whole crew of the *Timoleon*, for instance, and an unknown number more. The best we can do about prisoners is far from good: it is simply to accept James's 2,000 casualties, and subtract them from Nelson's comprehensive 5,225, having accepted that also. This leaves us with 3,225 prisoners and that may well be all, the remaining thousand-odd of our subtraction being written off as 'escaped to land'. As for the sub-division of the 2,000 casualties, the Table, it will be observed, shows no less than 1,400 killed and only 600 wounded—at first sight a rather surprising allocation, with a much heavier 'killed per total' percentage than any—70 per cent. But there is a very good reason. The flagship *L'Orient* was a 120-gun ship whose complement in the French service would normally be upwards of 1,100. She was not, perhaps, quite fully manned, and she may have had a watering-party ashore: but she blew up during the action with the loss of all but seventy of the people on board. So, in this single fatal instant, *L'Orient* alone must have contributed nearly 1,000 souls to the 'killed' total as assessed here, leaving only 400-odd as the tally of the rest of the fleet. This can be no exaggeration: is probably indeed an underestimate, for the hulls of all our prizes were found to be shockingly cut up.

(5) *Copenhagen*

The conditions under which this action was fought, with Danish defenders passing to and from their immobile hulks lying aground along the shore, again make the computation of losses hard. The Danish Commodore assessed the killed and wounded as 'according to the lowest estimate between 1,600 and 1,800 men'. The British again fail us badly, giving only a combined total of 'about 6,000'. This seems a good deal too high. Indeed, James gives the total complement of all the Danish ships engaged as only 4,849, though he is uncertain whether soldiers are to be counted in it. There certainly were not a few who rowed out from the shore to reinforce the ships, so that it may not be wrong to raise to 6,000, or even rather more, the full number of the enemy engaged. But obviously they were not all killed, wounded or made prisoners: and, once again, the intrepid could, and certainly would, swim for it to avoid capture. Here 1,700, the average of Commodore Fischer's figures, is accepted for the killed and wounded; and that figure is sub-divided at the Camperdown rate. The prisoner-figure I have taken—arbitrarily—as a round 2,000. So we have claimed altogether only 3,700 in place of the swollen English claim: perhaps too few, but it is better to err on the side of moderation, if err we must.

(6) *Trafalgar*

For 'killed' and 'wounded' Colonel Desbrières' figures have been used (see p. 368). He apportions them as follows between the allies:

	Killed	*Wounded*	*Total*
French	3370	1160	4530
Spanish	1038	1385	2423
	4408	2545	6953

It would be presumptuous to challenge these figures: but it is permissible to wonder whether they are intended to include French army losses too. It is sometimes forgotten that Villeneuve had many troops on board. Collingwood said 4,000: and, according to an extant letter from a surviving military officer,[1] losses among them were fantastically heavy. In one ship—unnamed, but probably the *Indomitable*—'whose crew and troops totalled 1,400 men, not 150 escaped, and of 24 officers only two were saved from the wreck': while of two fine battalions (one of nearly double strength) or perhaps 3,000 men, only 756 survived.

[1] Reproduced in N.R.S., Vol. XCVII, pp. 59, 60.

These figures are only specimens, as it were, of what happened in several ships.

Desbrières does not help over prisoners: and Collingwood positively hinders, because on one occasion he claimed no less than 20,000. This must surely be wrong, even if he meant that number to represent all who had surrendered. For Collingwood did not even try to bring home all that he caught. He had the humanity to release the wounded Spanish seamen, knowing that, if he kept them, they would perish wholesale. He merely demanded from the local Spanish authority a general *parole d'honneur* that they would not serve against us until formally exchanged: and, in return, he secured the release of the few British prisoners from the prize-crews. But even if he were including all those whom he released, as well as the untold number who perished when their ships were lost in the gale, 20,000 is still much too large a figure. It is more than the original complement of all the captured ships. Here then we must subtract the known or estimated casualties of each ship, individually, from what we know (roughly) was the initial complement of each. This, a laborious process, yields a round figure of 7,000: and, however inaccurate it is, it must be a great deal nearer to the truth than is Collingwood's 20,000.

APPENDIX II

(See pages 378-9)

THE ANGLO-AMERICAN IMPRESSMENT CONTROVERSY

THIS rather confused dispute, the principal cause of the unhappy War of 1812–15, has cropped up several times in the preceding pages. As it nearly concerned some thousands at least of our seamen, it seems to invite some clarification.

Its most important historical features are the legal rights and wrongs of it, and the numbers involved in it. The second of these questions has not, I think, been impartially investigated by modern British writers: but in the U.S.A. the task has been attempted by James F. Zimmerman in his *Impressment of American Seamen*, New York, 1925. His work is eminently fair and objective, but even he is fain to admit that anything like accurate figures never were, and cannot now be, reached. The following remarks, especially those concerning numbers, owe much to his careful and valuable work.

A. THE LEGAL ASPECT

The heart of the controversy may be very simply stated. It stemmed from two radically opposing views on International Law.

(a) *The status of a Merchant Ship*. Great Britain held that a merchant ship was *not* part of a nation's sovereign territory. The U.S.A. held that it was. The British therefore held that it was not a violation of another nation's sovereignty to board its merchant ships, examine them and, if British seamen were found therein, to remove them. The U.S.A. held that such action *was* a violation. It admitted a right of search, in wartime, for contraband articles and 'persons in the military service of the enemy':

but nothing and no one else. Thus, though a serving Frenchman or Spaniard could be removed, no Briton could be; nor, of course, any American. Here was an insoluble divergence of view.

(b) *The Nature of Nationalization.* Great Britain held the doctrine of 'Indelible (or indefeasible) Allegiance'—that the native-born subject of a State cannot, without the consent of that State, change nationality at all, nor relinquish his obligation to his original State (e.g. escape his obligation to serve it afloat by taking out alien nationalization-papers). The U.S.A., on the other hand, held the doctrine of 'Voluntary Expatriation'—that, after proper qualifications had been fulfilled, and a person formally accepted by another State, that person changed his nationality entirely and permanently, thereafter holding no allegiance to any State save the new one which he had voluntarily joined. In the United States the requisite qualification of residence was first laid down in 1790 as two years. This was lengthened to fourteen years in 1798, but changed again in 1802 to five years: and at that it stood during the whole controversy.

It is hardly surprising to find Britain and America holding such different views on Nationality. We had been, if not Britons, at least Englishmen, Welshmen, Scots or Irishmen for many centuries; and everyone else, save only our sons and daughters overseas, had been 'foreigners'. The Americans had been American citizens for only a decade or two. Even when the war broke out in 1812, every American over 30 had been born a subject of King George, and so had already changed his nationality once in his lifetime. No wonder the United States saw no vital distinction between 'native-born' and 'naturalized'. Moreover, since America was a young country, occupying a large and sparsely populated sub-continent, she was not at all averse to increasing her numbers by immigration, and was therefore disposed to encourage it by granting her brand of nationality on easy terms.

Holding such views, then, the States did not feel it consonant with their new sovereign dignity to be obliged to issue certificates to every naturalized citizen, since they regarded such a person as no less American than the one who had become so at the Independence. They would not normally, therefore, furnish their nationals with such evidence. This was particularly unfortunate because Great Britain, believing as she did in 'indelible allegiance', regarded herself as entitled to impress any English-speaking person who did *not* produce such evidence. It is true that many American seamen had 'protections' of a sort. But they were not official governmental documents. They were either certificates issued by American consuls in Britain on their own responsibility, or affidavits procured by the seamen themselves. Zimmerman (p. 32) gives an example of the last-named:—

'I, Henry Lunt, do solemnly swear on the holy Evangelist of Allmighty God that I was born in Portsmouth in the County of Rockingham, State of New Hampshire, and have ever been a subject of said State.

Sworn before me,
Thomas Veale, J.P.'

But this sort of evidence was easily forged, and frequently was—often by a British seaman seeking to evade the Press. The result was that British captains regarded all American 'protections' with grave suspicion, and were apt to ignore them.

B. NUMBERS CONCERNED

Here there were two sharply-marked categories which yet, in the Anglo-American controversy though not in Law or Equity, tended to cancel each other out—Britons who, for any reason, were serving in American ships, and Americans (whether of Independence status or subsequently nationalized) who were pressed into the Royal Navy. The first category was almost certainly more numerous than the second. But there was this difference: the Britons were, practically all, there by choice; the Americans, mostly, by compulsion.

(a) *Britons in American Ships*. We must rid our minds of the notion that these men were necessarily 'deserters' in any narrow sense of that word, though certainly some—a large number—were. Before the countries went to war, any British merchant seaman was clearly entitled to sign on in an American merchant ship if he so desired. And many did, for the monetary inducement was very great. Wages in the American merchant marine were often 100 per cent higher than in the British service; and therefore, of course, a good deal more than twice as high as the Royal Navy's. Many, then, had joined from motives of fair profit only. But others, beyond the shadow of a doubt, had a less innocent reason—to save themselves from being pressed into the R.N. (We must not forget that Great Britain had been in an almost constant state of war for nearly twenty years before she went to war with the U.S.A.) Obviously the difficulty in distinguishing between these two sets of British subjects was, at the time, very great: and it is much greater now. But there was also a third category, and unquestionably a large one—British subjects already in the R.N. who deserted to American ships. These were in every sense deserters, and they were somewhat easier to spot: but not much (luckily for young Leech who was one of them), since they would always do everything in their power, if retaken, to conceal their identity.

Zimmerman frankly refuses to estimate the number of Britons thus lost to America. But he regards the figure as very large. He quotes a letter from Thomas Barclay to Lord Hugh Seymour in 1801 in which the American says he believes that 'where Britain had one American seaman, America had fifty British'. This is probably mere rhetoric, and Zimmerman rejects it, supported by the British minister at Washington who 'deplored it as unreasonably extreme'—though it was probably nearer the truth in 1801 than it would have been later when, as we shall see, the British had increased their Pressing activities. He also condemns contemporary British reports which claimed thirty or forty thousand. But he seems much more prepared to accept the British Admiralty's estimate of 20,000, made many years after war-fever had died down.[1]

(b) *Americans in British Ships*. Here again Zimmerman has to report the wildest divergences of figures. What Great Britain claimed was, not that there were *no* Americans in British ships, but that the comparatively few who were there had come from two sources:

(1) Volunteers: and there certainly were some—of long standing too (see p. 131)—though probably not very many: and

(2) Men pressed because they appeared to be British, and had no papers to prove that they were not some of that 20,000 who (we claimed) were serving in American ships. We admitted that we may have made mistakes here and there, since the possession of a common language sometimes made identification difficult.

Nor were we the only ones to affirm that the true figure of Americans impressed into our ships was a small one. The controversy overflowed into American home-politics too. The Federal opposition, which did not believe in the war, and wanted not only to stop it but also to discredit the Republican Government, sought to show that the Government's figures were gross exaggerations, the same men often 'being reckoned three or four times'. A report emanating from this camp in

[1] Report of Nationalisation Committee (1869), App. 35.

1813[1] contained the testimony of fifty-one shipowners. It showed thirty-five instances of British impressment, of whom only twelve were Americans: and, of these, nine had since been discharged and one had escaped! At the other end, contemporary estimates given in Congress, by newspapers and by public speakers, ranged from 10,000 to 50,000.

All these figures, of course, are profoundly suspect, being characteristic features of political or war-propaganda. The extremes (which thus appear as 50,000 and *two*!) are both ridiculous—the first because (as Zimmerman shows) there were never more than sixty or sixty-five thousand American seamen all told, and probably many less: the second because the British themselves owned to many more. But Zimmerman does make a gallant effort to reach the truth, and undoubtedly succeeds in getting a great deal nearer to it than this.

The U.S.A. accused Britain of illegal pressing from the very start of our French wars: so he divides his findings under two heads—the first war, 1793–1802, and the second, from 1803 down to 1812, when the Anglo-American War began. For the first of these he reaches relatively firm figures—2,410. For the second, he has much greater difficulty because, by then, passions on both sides were fully roused. The foundation of his calculations is the record of impressed Americans kept in the American Consulate in London. This shows the figure of 5,987: which when added to the first war-total, gives 8,397. This may be said to be his minimum estimate. He thinks, however, that another 1,594 names should be added to it. These are cases not reported in London, but direct to the American Secretary of State; and thus we reach an upper estimate of 9,991. This, he declares, 'could be justified by statistical count', which seems to imply that he considers it rather too high, probably because he suspects that some names in the London list are duplicated in that of the Secretary of State. But he also takes note of the fact that the figures in all the sources which he is using end on 1st January, 1812, and that there were certainly some more between January and June, when war was declared. It would seem fair, then—though Zimmerman does not do so—to set the probable but unknown over-estimate before January, 1812, against the small but certain figure of new seizures between January and June, and so to estimate, in round numbers, a total of not less than 8,400, and not more than 10,000.

These, however, are estimates of the total number of Americans

[1] Report of Committee of House of Representatives, Massachusetts, on Impressed Seamen, 1813.

impressed from first to last in the two wars. They certainly do not represent the number of Americans serving in the Royal Naval at any one time. To begin with, Zimmerman implies that all pressed during the first war were released at the end of it: and this is exceedingly likely since, in the Amiens interlude, the Navy was largely demobilized, and nearly 70 per cent of its men discharged (see graph, p. 119). Further, an American report made in March, 1814, lists 1,995 of those said to have been impressed between 1803 and 1812 as 'discharged' or 'ordered to be discharged'; while, since the war began, 680 had been 'discharged and detained as prisoners of war'. It is not clear whether these were some of the 1,995, or additional to them; but we can still get somewhere near the limit figures of Americans in the Royal Navy in March, 1812. By simple subtraction we find that there can hardly have been more than 5,600, and there may have been as few as 3,300 of the Americans originally impressed. But even these figures—the maximum and the minimum equally—must certainly be whittled down further, for they pre-suppose that all the men originally pressed and not released were still serving in the R.N. They make no allowance at all for desertions or casualties from battle, individual accident and disease. And what that number was, who shall say?

Nor can any figure be given—even Zimmerman does not attempt it—of the number of admitted British subjects taken from American ships.

APPENDIX III

(See page 421)

HODGE'S ESTIMATE OF BRITISH CASUALTIES IN THE WARS OF 1793-1815

SOME time after I had begun my investigations into the casualties of our wars—but also some time before they were completed—my attention was drawn to the work of the mid-eighteenth-century statistician William Barwick Hodge, whose paper on the subject in the Royal Statistical Society's Journal of September 1855 (Vol. XVIII, p. 201) is still, apparently, widely accepted by statisticians as the last word on the subject. Though there is much in it that I am disposed to question, I would certainly not deny that it contains a great deal of valuable and ingenious material, and much more statistical acumen than I am capable of. For its approach, as might be expected, is just that—statistical. But its principal weakness, in my view, lies in the fact that (on his own admission) the author was not very familiar with, and therefore inclined to pay insufficient attention to, the contemporary conditions of life afloat in the Royal Navy. His method, therefore, is very different from mine. So was the scope of his investigation, which is smaller. Thus, though he did make a somewhat generalized assessment of 'disease' figures, he confined himself mainly to the battle-casualties and those resulting from the loss of ships by wreck, fire, etc. Nor—and here is a very considerable difference between us—did he anywhere attempt to differentiate between Disease and what I have called 'Individual Accident'. Incidentally, he has nothing whatever to say about prisoners of war either.

I realized from the first, of course, that this paper was far too valuable to be ignored: but I decided at once, upon reading it, to continue my own investigations in my own way, which was so very different from his, and to reach such conclusions as I could quite independently of him; but, having completed them, to use his findings for purposes of comparison, where they would be, and indeed are, of immense value.

On one cardinal point we were agreed—that we were both working upon a problem which admits of nothing like an exact answer. Though he had the advantage of me in being a century nearer to the events discussed, he did not, I think, rely upon any sources or facts unknown to me. Indeed, like me, he trusted very largely to the admirable William James: in fact, accepted his evidence more literally and more frequently than I have been prepared to do. Nor did he venture far beyond James—for instance, he even followed him in leaving blank the enemy losses at Trafalgar, which I (having the great advantage of being able to consult Desbrières and the French Commission) was able to assess.

In spite, however, of all our differences in aim, scope and method, a comparison between his conclusions and mine seems to reveal a surprising measure of agreement.

His final figures, based upon a mean strength of 110,180 men per annum, are

CAUSE OF DEATH	
In Action	6663
Drowned or destroyed in ships accidentally wrecked or burnt ...	13,621
Died from disease or ordinary accident on board	72,102
TOTAL	92,386

These figures would have been rather, but not a great deal, smaller than mine, had I attempted at any time to arrive at a Grand Total. But I did not, preferring to concentrate upon a single year in which I felt myself to possess some really solid data. Purely for the purpose of further comparison, however, it would be interesting to turn my one-year figures into figures for the whole war. It is easily, though not necessarily accurately, done. He was working on the basis of a war which was actually 'declared' for just over twenty years—he rightly omits the Amiens peace-interlude. So I must multiply my findings by twenty. In doing so, of course, I am introducing an undesirable element of chance. In fact, I am supposing 1810 to have been in every respect a 'typical' year: which, as I have already stressed, I do not think it was—there was no such thing as a typical year in that sense. But at least I can take the opportunity of making that slight modification mentioned on page 421, in order to eliminate what I thought to be the principal 'exceptional' feature of 1810. So I shall transfer 2 per cent of my 'By the Enemy' casualties to the 'By Foundering, etc.' category. I shall also put both sets of figures into percentage form.

ESTIMATED FATAL CASUALTIES FOR THE 20 YEARS OF WAR

CAUSES OF DEATH	Totals		Percentages	
	Hodge	Self	Hodge	Self
Disease and Individual Accident	72,102	84,440	78·1	81·5
Foundering, Wreck, Fire, Explosion	13,621	12,680	14·7	12·2
The Enemy	6,663	6,540	7·2	6·3
Total	**92,386**	**103,660**	**100**	**100**

The biggest discrepancy between his findings and mine seems to be in 'Disease', reflected also in 'Total'. Here Hodge was criticized in his own day by naval officers whom he says he consulted. They declared that he had understated the mean number of men serving—110,180—and, as he was working his 'disease' figures in proportions, this would affect his findings both there and in his grand total. This certainly seems to be so, the underestimate being not far off 5 per cent. To correct this one would have to add nearly 5,000 to his 'disease' and 'total' figures, bringing them to about 77,000 and 97,000 respectively, and thus considerably lessening the gap between us.

Our assessments of the numbers who died by Enemy Action are remarkably close. This, we saw, was the part of the problem on which he concentrated most carefully—as in fact I did. But it was also—and clearly we both found it so—the least difficult part: for here there survives the best evidence that is available.

There is one further point. It must be recorded that Hodge's figures, as given here, are his 'gross' figures. They are not the ones which he finally adopted as the true statistical price of the war in terms of human life. The ones he decided upon were 'net'. His 'by the enemy' numbers are as here stated, but his 'wrecked' figures are deliberately reduced by about 10 per cent: for he considered that some at least of these dead men would have met with a comparable fate had they not been serving in the Navy, and in the war. A similar, but much larger, reduction appears in his 'disease' figures, on the ground that a very great number of such fatalities would have occurred anyway, war or no war. Of course they would—in twenty years! But there are several reasons why I am not tempted to follow him into speculative fields of that kind. First, I do not see how it is possible to make anything like the right reductions, even by the method he employs, which is very ingenious. Second, I think that his method has landed him into serious over-reduction—he actually whittled his gross 72,102 down to a net 44,662. But my third reason is much more important. Even had I been moderately sure of deducting the right number, I should not have dreamt of doing so, because it would have nullified my whole object, which was to try to assess the sum-total of British lives lost in the winning of our war: nothing else. Hodge's way of looking at it is doubtless right for the pure statistician, especially if he wants to assess scientifically the lethalness of one war as against that of another. But this is no concern of mine. Nor am I short of good company. Any government—at least any modern government—which tried to assess war-casualties along Hodge's line would not last a week. It would not deserve to. It is perfectly true, of course, that a service-man who died of some tropical fever in Burma in the 1940's *might* have died of tuberculosis had he stayed at home: or, for that matter might have fallen off a ladder or been run over by a bus. But the existence of such possibilities has not deprived him of his place on the national Roll of Honour, nor his family of their right to a war-pension.

Here again, then, I compare like with like. I met him just now by bringing my one-year figures up, to match his twenty-year set. I am justified now in setting his gross-casualty figures against my similar ones. And how surprisingly close they are, all things considered! At least we agree on all the main points—that the total price of victory was somewhere in the neighbourhood of 100,000 lives: that the bill for 'Disease and Accident' combined was some four times heavier than that for Wreck and the Enemy combined; and that, of the two last-named, the Ship-accident was just about twice as deadly as the Enemy.

A LIST OF CONTEMPORARY SOURCES QUOTED IN THE TEXT

A. *Not Printed*

Public Record Office, Adm. 7/867 Misc., *Progress of the Navy*, 1764–1806.

Public Record Office, Adm. 7/325,649, *Registry of Issues*.

National Maritime Museum, MS. 9281, Keith Papers, Adm. Letter 19/1/1813.

National Maritime Museum, 57/031, Marine Society Records.

Admiralty, Orders in Council, 9/7/1794.

Admiralty, Orders in Council, 1/6/1795.

Admiralty, Orders in Council, 19/1/1803.

Admiralty, Orders in Council, 5/12/1804.

Admiralty, Orders in Council, 15/8/1805.

Admiralty, Orders in Council, 23/8/1806.

Admiralty, Orders in Council, 23/3/1812.

Admiralty, Orders in Council, 12/7/1819.

Admiralty, *Commissioned Sea Officers of the Royal Navy*, 1660–1815.

Dillon, Sir William, *Narrative of my Professional Experiences*: MS.

Penrose, Charles, *Memoirs of James Trevenen*: MS.

B. *Printed*

I. OFFICIAL AND SEMI-OFFICIAL PUBLICATIONS

Admiralty Regulations and Instructions, 1790.

Admiralty Regulations and Instructions, 1808.

Annual Register, The, 1795.

Annual Register, The, 1807.

Campbell's Navy List, August, 1809.

Official Navy List, The, December, 1814.

Steel's Navy List, November, 1814.

Keats, Captain Richard, Orders of, Mariner's Mirror, Vol. VII, p. 317.

William Henry, Captain Prince, Orders of, Navy Records Society, Vol. XXIV. Appendix A. (ed. Vesey-Hamilton).

II. AUTOBIOGRAPHIES, MEMOIRS, LETTERS, ETC.

(a) 'QUARTER-DECK'

Barham, Lord, Letters of, (Vol. II), Navy Records Soc. XXXVIII (ed. Laughton).

Boteler, John, Recollections of, Navy Records Soc. LXXXII (ed. Bonner-Smith).

Collingwood, Lord, Private Correspondence of, Navy Records Soc. XCVIII (ed. Hughes).

Cullen, Peter (Surgeon), Journal of, Navy Records Soc. XCI (ed. Thursfield).

Dillon, Sir William, Narrative of, Vol. I, Navy Records Soc. XCIII (ed. Lewis).

Dillon, Sir William, Narrative of, Vol. II, Navy Records Soc. XCVII (ed. Lewis).

Dundonald, Earl, *Autobiography of a Seaman*, London, 1860–1.

Gardner, J. A., Recollections of, Navy Records Soc. XXXI (ed. Hamilton & Laughton).

James, Bartholomew, Journal of, Navy Records Soc. VI (ed. Laughton & Sulivan).

Keith, Lord, Papers of, Vol. II, Navy Records Soc. XC (ed. Lloyd).

Keith, Lord, Papers of, Vol. III, Navy Records Soc. XCVI (ed. Lloyd).

Mangin, Rev. Edward, Navy Records Soc. XCI (ed. Thursfield).

Martin, Sir T. Byam, Letters and Papers, Vol. I, Navy Records Soc. XXIV (ed. Vesey-Hamilton).

Nelson, Lord, Letters to his Wife, Navy Records Soc. C. (ed. Naish).

St. Vincent, Earl, Letters, Navy Records Soc. XCII (ed. Craig).

Walters, Samuel, Lieutenant, R.N., Liverpool, 1949, (ed. Parkinson).

(b) 'LOWER DECK'

Béchervaise, John, *Thirty-six Years of Seafaring Life*, Portsea, 1839.

Béchervaise, John, *Farewell*, Portsea, 1847.

Hay, Robert (Landsman), London, 1953, (ed. M. D. Hay).

Leech, Samuel, *Voice from the Middle Deck*, London, 1844.

Nicol, John, Life and Adventures of, Edinburgh, 1822, and London, 1937.

Pemberton, C. R., *Pel. Verjuice*, London, 1929.

Richardson, William, (Gunner) *A Mariner of England*, London, 1908.

Robinson, William ('Jack Nastyface'), *Nautical Economy, or Forecastle Recollections*, 1836.

Watson George, *Adventures of a Greenwich Pensioner*, Newcastle, 1827.

Wilson, Robert, Navy Records Soc. XCI (ed. Thursfield).

III. HISTORIES, BIOGRAPHIES, ARTICLES, PAMPHLETS, ETC.

Beatson, Robert, *Naval and Military Memoirs of Great Britain*, 1790.

Blane, Sir Gilbert, Contribution to *Medico-Chirurgical Transactions*, VI, 1815.

Brenton, Capt. Edward, *Naval History of Great Britain* (1837 edition), London.

Captain of the Royal Navy, 'Observations and Instructions for Officers of the Royal Navy', London, 1807.

Ekins, Sir Charles, *Naval Battles*, London, 1824.

Falconer, William, *Marine Dictionary* (Dr. William Burney's edition), London, 1815.

Friend of the Navy, *An Appeal to His Majesty, etc.* (pamphlet), 1810.

James, William, *Naval History of Great Britain* (1837 edition), London.

Marshall, John, *Royal Naval Biography*, London, 1823.

Naval Chronicle, The (in half-yearly vols.), 1799–1819.

Naval Yarns, (Collection by W. H. Long), London, 1899.

O'Byrne, William, *Naval Biographical Dictionary*, London, 1849.

O'Byrne, William, *Naval Biographical Dictionary* (2nd edition, to 'G. only), London, 1859.

Padwick, H. B., Article in *Journal of R.N. Medical Service*, VIII.2.89.

Patten, Admiral Philip, *Strictures on Naval Discipline* (Murray & Cochrane, Edinburgh) no date.

INDEX

INDEX TO SHIPS' NAMES

II. Foreign